THE
AMERICAN
GOLFER'S
GUIDE

BY HUBERT PEDROLI & MARY TIEGREEN
FOREWORD BY CURTIS STRANGE

Turner Publishing, Inc.

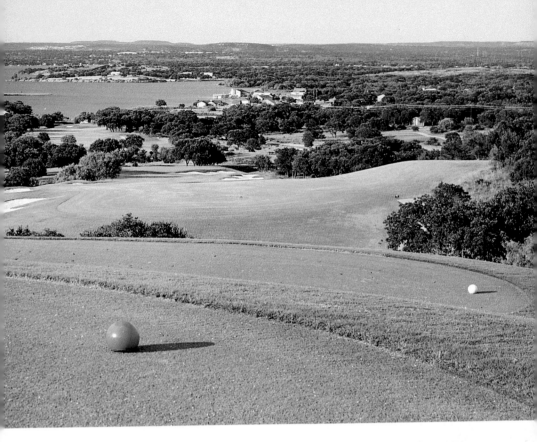

ABOVE: JACK NICKLAUS,
LEGENDARY PLAYER
AND CREATOR OF
GREAT COURSES YOU
CAN PLAY SUCH AS
GRAND CYPRESS IN
FLORIDA, BREKENRIDGE
IN COLORADO, AND
THE BEAR AT
GRAND TRAVERSE,
MICHIGAN (LEFT).

however, the fine technique of carefully harmonizing greens and fairways with less spectacular, but no less deserving natural landscapes is truly representative of the new age in golf architecture. Increasingly, the work of people like Rees Jones, Jay Morrish, Tom Weiskopf, Dan Maples and many other modern architects is being celebrated for the expertise and finesse they employ in protecting and enhancing nature's gifts to mankind: pristine forests, fragile marshlands, vast deserts and endless shorelines. This welcome trend forms a merging of art with social concerns that serves all of us, golfers and nongolfers alike. And, as courses become more and more aesthetically pleasing, we are drawn into the beauty of the surroundings, and we come to fully appreciate the part nature plays in our love of the game.

These are the glory days for golf course architects. Across the vast American continent, magnificent landscapes hold the promise of many future great layouts for us to play. These golf courses will help us stay in touch with our environment and keep us conscious of its priceless wonders.

ABOVE: ARNOLD PALMER HAS BUILT MORE THAN 200 GOLF COURSES AROUND THE WORLD. BUT HIS HEART REMAINS IN THE USA, AND ESPECIALLY AT HIS BEAUTIFUL BAY HILL CLUB IN FLORIDA (TOP). OPPOSITE: SINGLETREE (COLORADO), A JAY MORRISH/BOB CUPP DESIGN, ENHANCES THE SITE'S NATURAL BEAUTY.

CHAPTER ONE

HAWAII

Imagine this early morning round of golf: from behind a majestic volcano, the Sun King slowly rises to illuminate fairways still shining with the night's dew. The first tee is surrounded by bright red hibiscus and plumeria trees. Exotic birds sing to the new day. From the shore below, the deep blue Pacific Ocean sends warm breezes heavily scented with all the fragrances of Polynesia. This is no fantasy, and this is no ordinary place. This is Hawaii.

Golfers are especially well cared for in these islands of Paradise. Maui's status as the favorite Hawaiian golf destination, earned from the reputation of excellence of great courses such as Kapalua and Wailea, is being closely challenged by Kauai, "the Garden Island," and Hawaii, "the Big Island." Both offer new courses with superlative layouts in which greens and fairways are laid among ancient black lava flows, lush tropical vegetation, and spectacular ocean vistas. The contrasts in color are breathtaking.

On Kauai, Robert Trent Jones, Jr.'s, Prince Course at the Princeville Resort and Jack Nicklaus's Kiele Course at the Kauai Lagoons have opened to rave reviews. On the Big Island, it is Jay Morrish and Tom Weiskopf's new Kings' Course at Waikoloa that steals the show.

Island weather is perfect for golf year round, as ocean breezes cool off even the hottest sun. Sporadic tropical showers are only here to water the greens and paint marvelous rainbows in the sky. In this magical little corner of the world, playing golf is the experience of a lifetime. Go and enjoy it! Aloha!

PUBLISHED BY TURNER PUBLISHING, INC.
A Subsidiary of Turner Broadcasting Systems, Inc.
One CNN Center, Atlanta, Georgia 30348

First Edition
Library of Congress Catalog Card Number 91-66926

10 9 8 7 6 5 4 3 2
ISBN 1-878685-10-4

PRODUCED BY LITTLE LAKE PRODUCTIONS
133 West 19th Street, New York, New York 10011

PROJECT DIRECTOR	EDITOR	DESIGNER	ASSISTANT DESIGNER
Hubert Pedroli	Tim Gray	Mary Tiegreen	Dianna Russo

Distributed by Andrews & McMeel
4900 Main Street, Kansas City, Missouri 64112

CHAPTER OPENING PHOTOGRAPHS:
1   THE BLOOMINGDALE GOLFERS CLUB, FLORIDA
2-3   THE LINKS AT SPANISH BAY, CALIFORNIA
4-5   BOYNE HIGHLANDS RESORT, MICHIGAN
6-7   PORT ARMOR CLUB, GEORGIA
24-25   KAPALUA GOLF CLUB, HAWAII
36-37   PEBBLE BEACH GOLF LINKS, HOLE NO. 7, CALIFORNIA
68-69   SKYLAND COUNTRY CLUB, COLORADO
88-89   TROON NORTH, ARIZONA
114-115   GOLF CLUB OF ILLINOIS, ILLINOIS
148-149   THE SAGAMORE RESORT, NEW YORK
178-179   NAGS HEAD GOLF LINKS, NORTH CAROLINA
226-227   MARRIOTTS GRIFFIN GATE RESORT, KENTUCKY
244-245   PELICAN'S NEST GOLF CLUB, FLORIDA
278-279   RIDDELLS BAY GOLF COURSE, BERMUDA

COVER PHOTOGRAPH: THE SEDONA GOLF RESORT, ARIZONA

— CONTENTS —

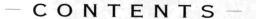

— A C K N O W L E D G M E N T S —

Our thanks go to Ted Turner and Turner Publishing Inc., especially to Michael Reagan, its President, who had enough faith in us to support our ambitious project, and to Michael Walsh, Design Director, who gave us the guidance needed for its completion. We worked hard so that their trust would be justly rewarded. Our appreciation also goes to Lena Tabori and Welcome Enterprises. She believed in us when The American Golfer's Guide existed only in our imaginations.

As could be expected in a project of this scope, the list of those who contributed their work and spirit is as long as the first hole at Spyglass Hill: Tim Gray, our demanding and tireless editor who took charge from the start and without whom this book would not have been possible. Thanks again, Tim. Dianna Russo, our perfectionist Quark expert who lovingly cared for the intricate layouts from the first to the last page; Robin Siegel, our researcher extraordinaire, and all around troubleshooter who never left a stone unturned or any head professional, golf or marketing director alone; Suzanne Lincoln, our editorial assistant from Indiana who came to New York in the interest of golf publishing, and who's welcome back anytime; Michael Lattner, our Macintosh specialist, Adobe Illustrator cartographer and gourmet chef; Jim Kingston, who took us to the forefront of electronic publishing technology and never ceases to amaze us with his magic; Patricia Corsiglia, our sensitive photo editor and official time manager; Mitch Nauffts and George Arthur for their life-saving editorial help with golf course descriptions; Mutsumi Hyuga and Scott Park for their precision work with maps; and, last but not least, Sara Weiner for her assistance in sorting, filing, and organizing gigabytes of data.

Our special thanks also go to Robert Griffin and the associates at Robert Griffin Inc., Toni Konstantopoulos and Lisa Tordo, for tolerating the frantic activities of Little Lake Productions with grace.

Naturally, we need to thank our many longtime and newly made golfing friends who contributed their knowledge and experience of golf and golf courses: especially Glen Artist Jr., Bill Bertha, David Chaffee, John Elliott, Bob and Tricia Irish, Kent Lamberty, Don Mills, Betsy Nieporte, Janet O'Meara, J.M. Painvain, Joe Puglia, Richard Whitney, and Cindy Wolfson; PGA Professionals Jack McGown, Joe Nieporte, and Bob Palmeri; Marsha McPeak at the National Golf Foundation and Tony Zirpoli at the USGA; and many more companions of the links.

Finally, perhaps our greatest appreciation goes to all the Head Professionals, golf pros and assistants, directors of golf, and marketing and public relations managers who patiently answered our questions and contributed many of our beautiful photographs. We hope our readers appreciate your efforts as much as we do.

Hubert Pedroli and Mary Tiegreen

— F O R E W O R D —

As a professional player, I have had the opportunity to travel over the five continents, and play some of the finest courses of Europe, Asia and Australia. Yet, in my opinion, no other country in the world can challenge the United States when it comes to the beauty, quality and diversity of its golf courses. Americans can justly be proud, considering the spectacular courses that exist throughout their land: high mountain golf in the Rockies, seaside links on the Carolina shores, or desert layouts amidst the rugged canyonlands of the Southwest.

American golfers are fortunate in another way: unlike many countries around the world, a remarkable number of the best golf courses in America are open for the public play.

If anyone needs convincing, a significant tribute to American public golf comes from the PGA Tour itself. In 1992 for example, over 20 regular Tour events will be hosted on public and resort courses. The Kingsmill Resort in Williamsburg, Virginia, which I've been associated with for many years, will return as the traditional site of the Anheuser-Busch Classic, as it has since 1981. Places like Doral, Torrey Pines and Bay Hill have also been on the Tour's roster for many years and are already quite familiar to the American public. Other, more recent additions to the Tour are Cog Hill, the famous public golf complex outside of Chicago, which will host of the Centel Western Open on its Dubsdread Course for the second year in a row, and Pinehurst #2, where The Tour Championship will be played in late October. These top-rated layouts have one thing in common: they are public and resort courses whose challenge and aesthetics rival the best private facilities in the country.

A book dedicated to the best American courses open to the public has been long overdue, and it's a great pleasure for me to finally see a guide where all the championship layouts mentioned above—and hundreds more top-quality public courses—are listed and described in detail.

The American Golfer's Guide delivers all the practical information required to locate and play the best layouts in the nation, together with a wealth of interesting facts about the courses, their architects and history, and a selection of truly inspiring photographs.

For someone who loves the game as much as I do, it is a complete, handy reference book. And for anyone who refuses to travel without his or her clubs, it's an essential vacation and business planning guide, a traveling companion that's as good as a trusted driver or putter.

So, get ready, pack *The American Golfer's Guide* in your bag, and go out to explore the great American golf courses of your dreams!

CURTIS STRANGE

— INTRODUCTION —

As the great game of golf grows in leaps and bounds, and hundreds of thousands of new players join the ranks of the sport's legions of enthusiasts, a book presenting and paying tribute to America's best courses open to the public was overdue. To help all golfers discover and appreciate these beautiful courses, we thought that a practical and inspiring guide would be quite useful. With this in mind, we designed *The American Golfer's Guide* to be the perfect companion to everyone's golfing adventures.

WHAT IS IN THE AMERICAN GOLFER'S GUIDE?

The American Golfer's Guide presents a selection of the best of over five hundred courses that the public can play. As one could guess, such a selection is not an easy task: there are more than 13,000 golf courses in the country, and even subtracting about 5,000 private clubs, the field of candidates is quite vast! In addition, close to 300 new courses are being built each year, many of them open to the public.

That last qualification, public accessibility, was one of the issues we had to resolve for the listing. While a large number of golfing facilities are open without restrictions, an increasing number fall somewhere between the completely public and completely private categories. To qualify for *The American Golfer's Guide,* we considered any course that can be played for a fee, as long as membership or a member's introduction is not required. Understandably, some semi-private clubs or so called "private resorts" do not wish to be represented as public or even open to the public. Yet, since the paying public supports the continuing operation of those courses, we felt it would be fair to consider them for this guide. In fairness to the resorts and club owners, operators, and members, however, we were careful to mention any limitations to public accessibility. *The American Golfer's Guide* indicates clearly such restrictions, if and when they apply.

The courses are listed in ten chapters, eight for the continental United States, and two covering Hawaii and the Caribbean Islands. We attempted to represent each region in a balanced way, even though some of the regions boast an overwhelming number of excellent courses compared to others. For equity, each state is represented by at least one or two entries, even those where quality public golf is limited. Luckily, a few areas in the country offer an abundance of first-class golf. *The American Golfer's Guide* introduces them under the heading "Great Golfing Destinations." Included are: The Monterey Peninsula, and Palm Springs in the West; the Phoenix-Scottsdale area in the Southwest; Northern Michigan in the Midwest; and Pinehurst, Myrtle Beach, and

Hilton Head Island in the Mid-Atlantic region. The guide gives the potential visitor a description of the destination and its landscapes, information on the climate, and an area map with the location of the best courses.

To present each entry in a practical, yet attractive fashion, essential information such as restrictions on public access, green fees, reservations, and ratings are contained in a small "information box." For each course, a short description follows, in which *The American Golfer's Guide* gives the reader a feel for the experience ahead, including the special challenges of the course, its architecture and surroundings. Whenever possible, we illustrated the entries with informative and inspiring photographs. Besides enhancing the descriptions, we hope that these images of rolling fairways and serene greens will allow you to fashion countless, imaginary shots and help you daydream your way through the cold winter days...

While playing, researching and comparing all of these courses, we also came to fully appreciate the diversity and dynamic nature of golf course design in America. To share some of our findings with the readers, we dedicated a short section of *The American Golfer's Guide* to golf architecture and the best known course architects. For assistance to those who have recently taken up the game, we also added a few short sections on understanding the USGA slope rating system, preventing slow play, and protecting yourself from the serious danger of lightning.

HOW WERE THE COURSES SELECTED?

The American Golfer's Guide is a book researched and written by golfers for golfers. None of the courses paid a fee of any kind to be included. Our selection came from personal experience in playing and visiting the courses, as well as the experience of many of our golfing friends across the country. We compared and supplemented our findings with extensive research in the national and regional press, and confirmed our facts and conclusions with the mailing of hundreds of questionaires to the golf courses themselves, followed by countless telephone calls.

Obviously, a selection of the best golf courses can only be a subjective matter. Of all considerations taken into account, quality of design and architecture was the single most important. For many of us, however, golf is also a great mental and physical escape from our daily environment. While we enjoy the challenge and the friendly competition, the sport also lets us appreciate the sights and sounds of nature like few others can. For that reason, *The American Golfer's Guide* attaches a significant amount of importance to the scenery and surroundings of a course. Difficulty, on the other hand, was not a factor. Though it is true that the best layouts are often the most demanding, modern golf architects have recognized the need to accommodate both men and women of all levels of experience, age and talent. As a result, a majority of the new courses presented in this book are built with a selection of four, and sometimes five tees on each individual hole. For its part, *The American Golfer's Guide* presents a selection wide enough to challenge all levels of expertise. When golf facilities or resorts offer several courses, the guide provides details for all the courses, not just the most difficult track. In fact, counting all multiple entries, *The American Golfer's Guide* presents a choice of more than 650 eighteen-hole layouts on which to test your skills.

Finally, a word about cost. The fees charged by the courses listed cover an entire range from inexpensive to very high. Since the guide focuses on the best courses, one would expect fees to be somewhat higher than average. Luckily, many of the entries listed are operated by cities and states, and their fees are very reasonable. In addition, daily-fee courses, an increasingly popular style of golf course operation, usually fall in the moderate price range. Needless to say, playing at the top resort and semi-private clubs can be rather expensive. Indeed, a round of golf at one of these manicured architectural gems should be appreciated and enjoyed the same way one savors dining in a fine restaurant or seeing a popular Broadway show. From that point of view, few will argue that the great American courses offer excellent value for the money. Nevertheless, *The American Golfer's Guide* recommends that you carefully consider different options available to reduce the cost of your golfing experience. Playing at the nation's great resorts, for instance, is usually significantly more affordable when arranged through special packages. In *The American Golfer's Guide,* each entry's "information box" indicates such opportunities for reduced fees.

As much as we tried to offer the best selection of courses, we were, in a few instances, unable to obtain some necessary details. A number of facilities declined to provide such information, for reasons ranging from concerns about their image of exclusivity, to explanations such as "too busy as it is." Others simply did not respond in spite of our repeated efforts, and some just replied too late. These courses are nevertheless part of the best layouts one can play in America, and you will find them listed at the end of each chapter, under the heading "Other Excellent Courses in the Region."

Now, before you pick up the phone and make reservations for your next tee-off time or vacation, please take a few minutes to read the next section. It explains how *The American Golfer's Guide* is organized, and it should make your playing and traveling companion even more informative, and more enjoyable to use.

H O W   T O   U S E   T H I S   B O O K

The American Golfer's Guide takes the player on a grand tour of America's best golf. The journey begins in Hawaii, continues eastward to the West Coast, then crosses the continent to conclude with the Caribbean Islands. Along the way, all fifty states are represented as well as the islands of the Caribbean and Bermuda.

The book is divided into ten regional chapters, with courses arranged by state within each region. A map at the beginning of the chapter has numbered flags corresponding to the courses contained in that chapter for general location. To find a specific course within the book, an alphabetical index is provided beginning on page 294. Following is a brief explanation of the information items listed for each entry in *The American Golfer's Guide*.

◆ PHONE NUMBERS:
This is the number for the pro-shop, starter, or resort operator.

◆ ACCOMMODATIONS:
These may be part of the golf resort complex or nearby but separate businesses. Whenever affiliated hotels were too numerous to list, we suggested that you call the course itself for further details.

◆ NUMBER OF HOLES:
All the courses in this book have either eighteen or twenty-seven holes. If a club or resort has more than one course, each one is listed separately. Occasionally, information on 9-hole courses may appear only in the descriptive material.

◆ PAR:
If par changes depending on the set of tees played, we indicated par from the middle tees. On courses with three 9-holes, par may differ depending on which combination is used and was therefore omitted.

◆ YARDAGE:
Three yardages are provided for each course: Championship (back tees or blue tees), Regular (men's, middle or white tees) and Ladies (forward or red tees). When courses have more than three sets of tees, the second yardage is taken from the average handicapper's tee (usually in the low 6000-yard range). For 27-hole courses, space limitations restricted us to indicating regular yardages only.

◆ USGA AND SLOPE:
We chose to take all ratings from the regular tees. Championship ratings are more impressive, but less useful for the average player. For 27-hole courses, ratings change depending on the combination played, and had to be omitted. On some new or redesigned layouts, ratings were not yet

available. For a short explanation of the USGA Slope rating system, please refer to page 260 of this guide

◆ STYLE:

This is intended to give the reader an indication of the course's architectural style, its dominant features or surroundings.

◆ ACCESS:

Remember: A course's access policy can change according to season or for any number of reasons. It's always wise to call for confirmation before planning to play.

> "NO RESTRICTIONS" indicates that there are no limitations for public play, other than availability of tee times.

> "HOTEL GUESTS ONLY" indicates that access to the course is reserved to the guests of the resort(s) or hotel(s) listed under "accommodations."

> "PRIORITY TO HOTEL GUESTS" indicates that play by nonguests is accepted, but usually limited to availability of tee-off times.

> "RESTRICTIONS ON TEE TIMES" indicates that the course keeps some tee-off times for members with reservation privileges.

◆ SEASON:

This indicates which months of the year the golf course is open.

◆ HIGH:

This refers to "high season," the time of the year when the course is busiest.

◆ GREEN FEES:

We have rated green fees according to $ symbols. Since fees tend to vary depending upon many factors (season, day of the week, etc.), our rating is based on the most expensive case—i.e. what a "walk-on" can expect to pay for an 18-hole round, on a weekend, in normal or high season. We have done so deliberately, in an effort to spare the reader any unpleasant surprises. In most instances, however, lower fees are available and are indicated under "reduced fees".

"Includes cart" indicates that the green fees quoted by the course include a power cart for one person. If the mention "includes cart" does not appear, and walking is not permitted, you should add the cost of a cart to estimate the actual price you are likely to pay. With a few exceptions, power cart fees range from $9 to $15 per person.

The fee ranges below are given as an indication only, as fees are always subject to change.

$............Inexpensive, typically $20 or under
$$...........Moderate, typically $21 to $40
$$$.........Expensive, typically $41 to $60
$$$$.......Very expensive, typically $61 to $80
$$$$$.....Luxury, over $80

◆ REDUCED FEES:
These abbreviations indicate when and how fees lower than indicated above are available. Reductions can be substantial. In Florida, the Southwest, and the California desert, for example, summer rates can be half of what they are in the winter. When you make reservations, always inquire about reduced fees. You could realize some significant savings.

WD.........Reduced fees during weekdays
HG..........Reduced fees for hotel/resort guests
LS...........Reduced fees during low season
TW..........Reduced fees for twilight play
PK..........Special golf packages available

◆ RESERVATIONS:
This indicates the standard reservation period available to the general public. Resort guests can usually reserve well ahead of nonguests. If you plan a resort vacation, always check when tee-off times can be booked. In a few cases, courses had reservation systems too varied to be included in a limited space. In such instances, we just mentioned "Recommended." You should still make a reservation to play, but you will need to call for specific rules. If a course does not accept reservations, and it is located in a densely populated area, you should have a local friend or acquaintance make the necessary arrangements, especially if you plan to play on a weekend.

◆ RANGE:
This indicates availability of a driving range at the course.

GOLF COURSE ARCHITECTURE

Looking at a golf course for the first time, the untrained eye may never suspect the hand of man in the seemingly natural arrangements of weaving fairways, contoured lakes, and neat putting surfaces. Most golfers know that, in reality, golf courses are the product of an architect's imagination and his ability to reshape the land with talent and skill.

In the past decade, it is Pete Dye's dramatic—and sometimes controversial—creations at the TPC at Sawgrass and PGA West that have truly crystallized the golfing public's interest in course architecture. They were innovative, bold, full of suspense, and a real headache for the pros. As course construction keeps flourishing across the country, there is a continuing interest from professional players and amateurs alike in comparing the merits of each new design. The specialized press carries articles on the subject, and everywhere, legions of armchair golf architects are busy working on the blueprints of their imaginary layouts. As a result, there is a better understanding of the basic virtues shared by successful designs, whether they be classics by Donald Ross and Robert Trent Jones, or the modern creations of Pete Dye, Jack Nicklaus, Tom Fazio and so many others.

Golf architects used to differentiate between three basic design styles: strategic, penal and heroic. A strategic layout aims at rewarding shot placement. Playing safe is always a possibility, but it leaves little chance for a good score. Doglegs curving around lakes make perfect strategic holes. One of the best examples of the strategic style is the Robert Trent Jones-designed double dogleg thirteenth at the Dorado Beach's East Course: both corners are protected by water and challenge a golfer's mind as much as his or her skills. In a

ABOVE: PETE DYE, SEEN HERE ON THE SITE OF THE KIAWAH ISLAND OCEAN COURSE WHICH HE DESIGNED.
OPPOSITE: AMELIA LINKS, ANOTHER DYE LAYOUT, WINDS THROUGH THE FLORIDA SWAMP AND MARSHLAND, INTEGRATING CHALLENGING HOLES IN THE NATURAL LANDSCAPE.

THE PETE DYE-
DESIGNED 17TH HOLE
AT PGA WEST'S TPC
STADIUM COURSE
IS APTLY NAMED
"ALCATRAZ."
UNIMPRESSED, DURING
THE 1987 SKINS GAME,
LEE TREVINO CON-
QUERED THE 166-YARD
PAR 3 WITH A SINGLE,
DECISIVE STROKE: HE
SIMPLY ACED IT.

penal design, on the other hand, the path of a hole leaves no room for error. A bad shot results in a lost ball or an unplayable lie. Prime examples of this concept are Pete Dye's fearsome No 17th island holes at both the TPC at Sawgrass and PGA West Stadium courses. Briefly summarized, the philosophy there is "Hit the green or reload." A third idea is for the architect to incorporate dramatic terrain features in the layout of a course. High cliffs make a beautiful setting for heroic golf, and Pebble Beach' s fantastic stretch of seaside holes from Nos. 6 to 10 is probably the most spectacular and heroic mile and a half in all of golf.

Nowadays, everyone realizes that good course design relies on a combination of these three philosophies: strategic holes to reward thinking and shotmaking, heroic holes for challenge and drama, penalizing holes to keep players on edge. Knowing where and when to follow each particular style is the architect's craft.

One of the pure joys of the game is learning to appreci-ate the talent and experience of the many designers who are doing so much fine work across this country. When you play a Jack Nicklaus course, notice the dra-

LINKS COURSES: AN OLD WORLD LEGACY

LEGENDS: HEATHLAND COURSE

Many of the golf courses listed in this guide call themselves links or links-style courses. The adjective became quite popular in the eighties, as U.S. architects rediscovered the unmistakable appeal and drama of the great layouts of Scotland and Ireland. To define a links course is to describe the land it is built on. True linksland exists only along seashores, where the forces of wind and ocean have combined for thousands of years to form acres of tumultuous sandy terrain. There, among the treeless expanses of grassy mounds and valleys, a golf course can be laid with little more help than the architect's imagination. Small greens fit naturally on the multitude of plateaus and depressions; knolls, grass hollows and sand pits create fearsome bunkers and natural obstacles. Between the tall, heather-covered dunes, emerald fairways flow like peaceful rivers. On the high ridges, tee-boxes buffeted by fierce ocean winds offer dramatic views of the nearby seas and the stormy terrain around.

While many courses in America incorporate typical links features, only a few come close to providing the feel of the real thing. Here are some of the places where you can get a chance to experience the thrill of the Old World's links.

LINKS COURSES YOU CAN PLAY IN AMERICA

◆ GRAND CYPRESS, NEW COURSE
Orlando, Florida,
(page 258)

◆ KIAWAH ISLAND, OCEAN COURSE
Kiawah Island, South Carolina,
(page 222)

◆ LEGENDS, MOORLAND COURSE
Myrtle Beach, South Carolina
(page 212)

◆ LEGENDS, HEATHLAND COURSE
Myrtle Beach, South Carolina
(page 212)

◆ THE LINKS AT SPANISH BAY
Monterey, California
(page 54)

◆ MONTAUK DOWNS STATE PARK
Montauk, Long Island, New York
(page 163)

◆ NAGS HEAD GOLF LINKS
Outer Banks, North Carolina
(page 191)

◆ NEW SEABURY RESORT
Cape Cod, Massachusetts
(page 167)

◆ WENTWORTH-BY-THE-SEA GOLF CLUB
Wentworth, New Hampshire
(page 172)

◆ WILD DUNES, LINKS COURSE
Isle of Palms, South Carolina
(page 224)

matic routings that he uses to fit the course to the landscape. Take time to study how Pete Dye, a master of psychology in this most mental of games, uses all the tricks in his bag to challenge a player's patience, not to mention his or her shotmaking abilities. When facing the work of a Robert Trent Jones Jr. or a Tom Fazio, appreciate the thinking that goes into their combinations of architectural styles.

Beyond the classic concepts, another dimension of course design is receiving more attention than ever before: the art of creating golf courses that live in harmony with nature. Thousands of urban golfers, starving for the greenery of bucolic landscapes and lush forests, demand courses where scenery is an integral part of the game. Naturally, special sites have always attracted prime golf courses and architects. The courses of California's Monterey Peninsula for example, or those built over the dramatic canyons and deserts of the Southwest continue the tradition of what could be called the "scenic school" of course design. Perhaps,

ABOVE: ROBERT TRENT JONES, ONE OF THE MOST PROLIFIC GOLF ARCHITECTS EVER, DESIGNED NOT ONE BUT THREE 18-HOLE LAYOUTS AT THE FAMOUS HORSESHOE BAY RESORT IN TEXAS (TOP).

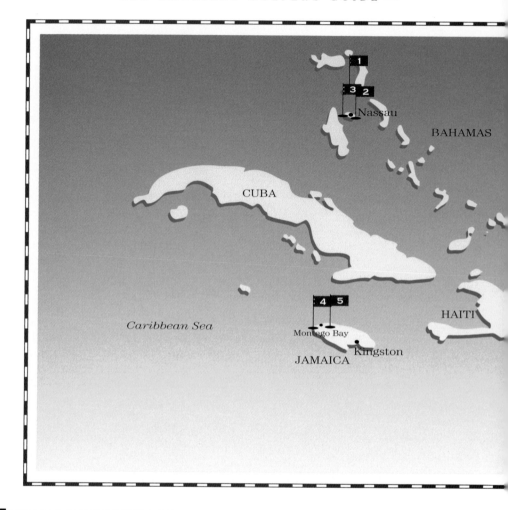

COTTON BAY CLUB

1

ROCK SOUND, ELEUTHERA, BAHAMAS (809)334-6101 *(12 mi. S of Rock Sound Airport)*
ACCOMMODATIONS: COTTON BAY CLUB RESORT (809)334-6101, (809)334-6156

COTTON BAY CLUB
18 holes   Par 72   7068/6594/5826 yds.
STYLE: Oceanside
ACCESS: Hotel guests only
SEASON: All year   HIGH: Feb.-Apr./Nov.
GREEN FEES: $$
REDUCED FEES: LS, PK
RESERVATIONS: Not needed
WALKING: Yes   RANGE: Yes

Opened since the early 1950s, Cotton Bay is considered one of Robert Trent Jones's best creations. Here, Jones created the challenge by designing outstanding greens (seeded with grainy and confusing Bermuda grass) and building no less than 129 bunkers! The par 4s, requiring long drives and accurate second shots are exceptional, but the most memorable hole is the No. 6, a 546-yard, par-5, dogleg, with the Atlantic Ocean encroaching onto the fairway. It demands two excellent first shots, then a delicate approach to a two-tiered green. For all its difficulty, the course remains a thing of beauty, overlooking the turquoise waters of Cotton Bay and the yacht basin.

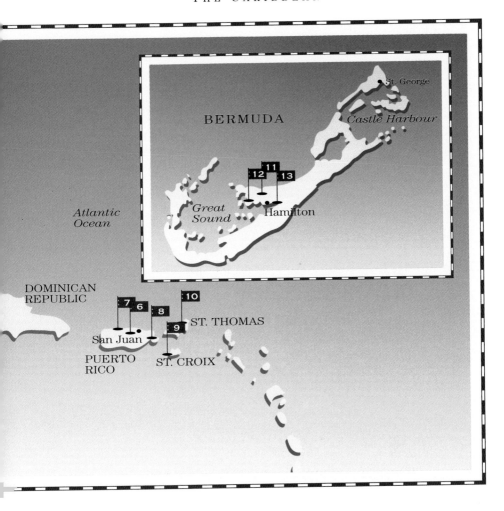

PARADISE ISLAND GOLF COURSE

2

PARADISE ISLAND, NASSAU, BAHAMAS (809)363-3925 *(2 mi. from Nassau)*
ACCOMMODATIONS: MERV GRIFFIN'S PARADISE ISLAND RESORT AND CASINO (809)363-3000

Paradise Island's course, designed by Dick Wilson, is a picturesque bird sanctuary that opened as a golf course in 1959. As might be expected in an area where shore birds congregate, there is a lot of water on this course. Thirteen holes have lateral water, and the ocean comes into play on three of them: No. 6, situated on a coral reef, No. 13, where the ocean is a backdrop for the green, and No. 14, surrounded by bunkers and guarded by the Atlantic on the left. This tropical course is further enhanced with bougainvillaea, hibiscus and oleanders, along with Australian pines and ficus trees. Paradise Island is the home of Merv Griffin's annual Star Sports Spectacular.

PARADISE ISLAND GOLF COURSE
18 holes   Par 72   6770/6419/5836 yds.
USGA: 71.3
STYLE: Tropical, lakes
ACCESS: No restrictions
SEASON: All year   HIGH: Jan.-Apr.
GREEN FEES: $$
REDUCED FEES: LS, PK
RESERVATIONS: 6 months
WALKING: At times   RANGE: Yes

DIVI BAHAMAS BEACH RESORT AND COUNTRY CLUB   `3`

P.O. BOX N-8191, NASSAU, NEW PROVIDENCE, BAHAMAS (800)367-3484
(SW shore of New Providence Island)
ACCOMMODATIONS: DIVI BAHAMAS BEACH RESORT (800)367-3484

DIVI BAHAMAS GOLF COURSE
18 holes   Par 72   6707/6300/5908 yds.
USGA: 71   SLOPE: 124
STYLE: Tree-lined fairways, lakes
ACCESS: No restrictions
SEASON: All year   HIGH: Jan.-Mar.
GREEN FEES: $$$
REDUCED FEES: HG, LS, TW
RESERVATIONS: 1 month
WALKING: No   RANGE: Yes

The Divi Bahamas Resort is located in a quiet, secluded part of New Providence, and its Joe Lee-designed championship layout is considered by many to be the best on the island. The course is built on rolling terrain, which is quite unusual for this area of the Bahamas. Another unique feature is a large "blue hole" of sea water that borders the fifteenth green. The fairways are bordered with lush palm trees, and each hole is named after a different Bahamian island. Large, contoured greens complete the challenge on this well-kept and interesting course.

TRYALL GOLF, TENNIS AND BEACH CLUB

4

SANDY BAY P.O., HANOVER, JAMAICA (809)952-5110, EXT. 202 *(15 mi. W of Montego Bay City)*

The classic Tryall course was opened in 1959 and has hosted a number of international events over the years. It's an extremely scenic layout of championship caliber. At around 6,400 yards from the championship tees, the track is short by modern standards. The front nine sticks close to the shore, while the back nine is carved up into the foothills. The par-5 No. 3 and par-4 No. 4 are ocean holes that can be especially challenging on windy days. When the wind doesn't blow, Tryall is there for the taking, but those days are few and far between.

TRYALL GOLF, TENNIS AND BEACH CLUB
18 holes   Par 71   6407/6104/5764 yds.
USGA: 70
STYLE: Rolling hills, woods
ACCESS: No restrictions
SEASON: All year   HIGH: Nov.-Apr.
GREEN FEES: $$$$$
REDUCED FEES: HG, LS
RESERVATIONS: 1 day
WALKING: Yes   RANGE: Yes

THE TRYALL GOLF COURSE

HALF MOON GOLF CLUB

5

P.O. BOX 80, MONTEGO BAY, JAMAICA (809)953-3105 *(7 mi. E of Montego Bay)*
ACCOMMODATIONS: HALF MOON GOLF TENNIS BEACH CLUB (809)953-2615

HALF MOON GOLF CLUB
18 holes Par 72 7115/6582/5990 yds.
STYLE: Tree-lined fairways
ACCESS: No restrictions
SEASON: All year HIGH: Dec.-Apr.
GREEN FEES: $$$$
REDUCED FEES: HG, LS
RESERVATIONS: Usually not needed
WALKING: Yes RANGE: Yes

Half Moon Golf Club, situated only two hundred yards from the sea, was designed by Robert Trent Jones and opened in 1961. The fairways are lined with thousands of mature palm trees intermingling with beautiful oleander, hibiscus, and bougainvillaea. The course's aesthetics are enhanced by five water hazards, which come into play on seven holes, and over a hundred bunkers of different shapes. The long par-5 No. 3 can be reached in two with well-struck shots, but it is heavily guarded by bunkers, requiring a decision to go for it or lay up to the right side of the green. Half Moon plays very long from all tee blocks. It regularly hosts international tournaments and is the site of the Jamaican Open.

PUERTO RICO

HYATT REGENCY CERROMAR BEACH

6

DORADO, PUERTO RICO 00646 (809)796-1234 *(45 mins. from San Juan Airport)*
ACCOMMODATIONS: HYATT DORADO AND CERROMAR BEACH (800)233-1234

HYATT REGENCY CERROMAR BEACH
ACCESS: Priority to hotel guests
SEASON: All year HIGH: Dec.-Apr.
GREEN FEES: $$$
REDUCED FEES: HG, PK
RESERVATIONS: Nonguests 1 day
WALKING: No RANGE: Yes
• **NORTH COURSE**
  18 holes Par 72 6841/6249/5547 yds.
  USGA: 71 SLOPE: 120
  STYLE: Tropical, oceanside
• **SOUTH COURSE**
  18 holes Par 72 7047/6298/5486 yds.
  USGA: 71 SLOPE: 121
  STYLE: Tropical, lakes

Robert Trent Jones, Sr., was not stingy with water on Cerromar Beach's two courses. On the North Course, the water challenge begins in earnest on the first hole, an "easy" 475-yard par 5 from the middle tee. Steering clear of the "wet stuff" is not so hard on that one, but staying dry on the third and fourth holes demands an already well-grooved swing. The course is routed through beautiful palm trees and dotted with many bunkers, some of them very large. It is a fun and enjoyable track every step of the way. Its ten par 4s, and four par 3s and 5s yield a respectable length, and it is not always easy to be long *and* straight. One of the most memorable moments comes at the 148 yard par-3 seventh. The hole faces the sea, and putting on the green overlooking beach and ocean is an enchanting experience. The South Course is seemingly more open, but water hazards loom on at least twelve holes. Palm trees and coconut groves provide an exotic look to this challenging course.

HYATT DORADO BEACH

7

DORADO, PUERTO RICO 00646 (809)796-1234 *(45 mins. from San Juan Airport)*
ACCOMMODATIONS: HYATT DORADO AND CERROMAR BEACH (800)233-1234

HYATT DORADO BEACH
ACCESS: Priority to hotel guests
SEASON: All year   HIGH: Dec.-Apr.
GREEN FEES: $$$$
REDUCED FEES: HG, PK
RESERVATIONS: Nonguests 1 day
WALKING: No   RANGE: Yes
• **EAST COURSE**
18 holes   Par 72   6985/6430/5805 yds.
USGA: 70.2
STYLE: Hills, oceanside
• **WEST COURSE**
18 holes   Par 72   6913/6431/5883 yds.
USGA: 70
STYLE: Tropical, lakes

The two courses at Dorado Beach were first built in the 1950s on Laurence Rockefeller's estate. They have seen several transformations and renovations since, but the maturity of the Robert Trent Jones, Sr., courses is evident from the size of beautiful trees that line the fairways.

The East Course displays the most character: on Nos. 2 through 6, the player first encounters a series of wooded hills more typical of New England than a tropical, beachside setting. After the turn, the course adopts a definite local style: No. 10, a 480-yard par 5, runs along the palm-tree-lined beach and can play into a severe shore wind. Water comes into play on six of the back nine, nowhere moreso than on the famous 540-yard, par-5, double-dogleg thirteenth. Players there face an interesting dilemma: drive over the dangerous water-protected corner and set up easy second and third shots, or play conservatively to the right and face an approach shot completely over water. The home-stretch, a series of four-hundred-yard par 4s, makes the clubhouse a very welcome sight indeed.

The West Course has a more consistent tropical appearance. The whole course is laid out among numerous— and treacherous—lakes and lagoons. Large palm trees sway in the wind, and the surf even comes up just behind the green at No. 13.

Dorado Beach is Jones at the top of his game—and golfers had better be at the top of theirs when they come here.

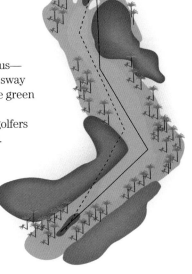

EAST COURSE: HOLE NO. 13
THIS HOLE COULD BE NICKNAMED DOUBLE TROUBLE. A SAFE DRIVE TO THE RIGHT WILL INEVITABLY LEAVE A THIRD SHOT OVER WATER. THE ALTERNATIVE STRATEGY FOLLOWS THE DOTTED LINE, BUT THAT TEE SHOT HAD BETTER BE A GOOD ONE!

PALMAS DEL MAR

8

BO. CANDELERO ABAJO, RT. 3, ROAD 906 KM 86.4, HUMACAO, PR 00661 (809)852-6000, EXT. 54
(30 mi. SE of San Juan)
ACCOMMODATIONS: PALMAS DEL MAR (809)852-6000

PALMAS DEL MAR
18 holes   Par 72   6690/6120/5424 yds.
USGA: 69.7   SLOPE: 121
STYLE: Hills, oceanside
ACCESS: Priority to hotel guests
SEASON: All year   HIGH: Nov.-Apr.
GREEN FEES: $$$$
REDUCED FEES: HG, LS, TW, PK
RESERVATIONS: Recommended
WALKING: No   RANGE: Yes

The Palmas del Mar course has been open since 1974. Gary Player designed the front nine to wind through a coconut grove and the back nine to travel around and over a considerable hill that offers spectacular views of the Caribbean. The course's challenge comes from its narrow, tree-lined fairways and small greens. In addition, no less than seventeen water hazards come into play on ten holes. No. 14, the par-4 signature hole, has an elevated tee from which one can admire the Caribbean Sea, Vieques Island, and the rain forest.

CARAMBOLA BEACH RESORT AND GOLF CLUB

ESTATE RIVER, ST. CROIX, U.S.V.I. 00851 (809)778-5638 *(10 mi. W of Christiansted)*
ACCOMMODATIONS: CARAMBOLA BEACH RESORT (809)778-3800

9

ST. CROIX

CARAMBOLA GOLF CLUB
18 holes   Par 72   6843/6228/5424 yds.
USGA: 69.8   SLOPE: 123
STYLE: Rolling hills, lakes
ACCESS: Priority to hotel guests
SEASON: All year   HIGH: Jan.-Mar.
GREEN FEES: $$$
REDUCED FEES: HG, LS, TW, PK
RESERVATIONS: Nonguests 1 day
WALKING: No   RANGE: Yes

Playing at Carambola's Robert Trent Jones-designed course is like playing in a botanical garden. Tucked in a valley surrounded by mountains, the course's rolling hills are covered with colorful tropical flora and mahogany trees. Bougainvillaea and hibiscus are a feast for the eyes every step of the way. The course also presents a strong golfing challenge: the front nine is characterized by short dogleg holes, but the back nine is long and demanding. Outstanding holes include No. 5, No. 14, and No. 17, all of which carry across water.

CARAMBOLA GOLF CLUB: HOLE NO. 18

MAHOGANY RUN GOLF COURSE

`10`

1 MAHOGANY RUN RD. N., ST. THOMAS, U.S.V.I. 00801 (809)775-5000, (800)253-7103 *(on St. Thomas)*

MAHOGANY RUN GOLF COURSE
18 holes   Par 70   6022/5609/4873 yds.
USGA: 68.9   SLOPE: 119
STYLE: Rolling hills, oceanside
ACCESS: No restrictions
SEASON: All year   HIGH: Jan.-Apr.
GREEN FEES: $$$
REDUCED FEES: LS, TW
RESERVATIONS: 2 days
WALKING: No   RANGE: Yes

Mahogany Run is a hilly, storied course that rises and drops along St. Thomas's coastline of cliffs and crashing blue seas. George and Tom Fazio designed this roller coaster experience, which opened in 1979. Much of the course runs through dense, lush rain forest, until it reaches Nos. 13, 14, and 15, which comprise the famous and intimidating "Devil's Triangle." Carved from the cliff's side at ocean's edge, the Triangle demands several carries over vertiginous drops, with the ocean roaring at the bottom. Tough, but fun and breathtaking—in short, an unforgettable experience.

MAHOGANY RUN: PUTTING GREEN

THE GALLERY AT MAHOGANY RUN'S HOLE NO. 14

B
E
R
M
U
D
A

BELMONT HOTEL AND GOLF CLUB 　11

P.O. BOX WK 251, WARWICK WK BX, BERMUDA (809)236-1301 *(4 mi. from Hamilton)*
ACCOMMODATIONS: BELMONT HOTEL AND GOLF CLUB (809)236-1301

BELMONT HOTEL AND GOLF CLUB
18 holes　Par 70　5777/5547/4890 yds.
USGA: 67.9　SLOPE: 126
STYLE: Rolling hills
ACCESS: Priority to hotel guests
SEASON: All year　HIGH: Nov.-Mar.
GREEN FEES: $$$
REDUCED FEES: HG, LS, TW, PK
RESERVATIONS: 1 day in high season
WALKING: Yes　RANGE: Yes

Less is sometimes more, and that's the case at the Belmont. The course plays under six thousand yards from every tee, but every one of those yards can break your heart. For openers, greens are elevated and small and fairways exceedingly narrow. The good news? You can leave your driver at the hotel, and a terrific combination of superb ocean views, gorgeous flowers, and exotic birds may make you think you're in a pleasure garden, not on a golf course. Architect Deveraux Emmet took special note of the surroundings when he designed the signature hole, No. 17. It's a 160-yard, par-3, which offers an especially picturesque view of Bermuda's Hamilton Harbour and the Great Sound.

PORT ROYAL GOLF COURSE 　12

P.O. BOX 189, SOUTHAMPTON, BERMUDA SNBX (809)234-0972 *(7 mi. from Hamilton)*

PORT ROYAL GOLF COURSE
18 holes　Par 71　6565/6057/5571 yds.
USGA: 69.7　SLOPE: 126
STYLE: Rolling hills, oceanside
ACCESS: No restrictions
SEASON: All year　HIGH: May-Nov.
GREEN FEES: $$
REDUCED FEES: TW
RESERVATIONS: 2 days
WALKING: At times　RANGE: Yes

When Robert Trent Jones set out to design this course for the Bermuda government, he didn't have a lot of land to work with, but he got full measure out of every square inch. The most memorable hole on the property is the 163-yard, par-3 seventeenth. It sits along a cliff, and while it might easily strike fear into a golfer's heart, it brings a smile to photographers who happen by: it is one of the most widely photographed holes in Bermuda—or the world, for that matter.

PORT ROYAL: HOLE NO. 17

CASTLE HARBOUR GOLF CLUB

13

TUCKERS TOWN, BERMUDA (809)293-2040 *(3 mi. E of Hamilton)*
ACCOMMODATIONS: MARRIOTT'S CASTLE HARBOUR RESORT (809)293-2040

CASTLE HARBOUR GOLF CLUB
18 holes   Par 71   6440/5990/4995 yds.
SLOPE: 123
STYLE: Steep hills, oceanside
ACCESS: Priority to hotel guests
SEASON: All year   HIGH: Spring and fall
GREEN FEES: $$$$
REDUCED FEES: LS, TW, PK
RESERVATIONS: Nonguests 1 day
WALKING: No   RANGE: No

Architect Charles Banks took full advantage of rolling terrain and stunning ocean views when he planned the layout at Castle Harbour. According to the scorecard, the course plays a mere 6,440 yards from the championship tee, but that is a deceptive figure. To start with, many shots are played uphill, but a more important factor is the wind. With healthy breezes blowing from the ocean, your approaches to the rather small and well-guarded greens must be played with great care and shotmaking finesse.

OTHER EXCELLENT COURSES IN BERMUDA AND THE CARIBBEAN

BAHAMAS
● BAHAMAS PRINCESS RESORT, Freeport (809)352-6721
● TREASURE CAY GOLF CLUB, Abaco (305)525-7711

BARBADOS
● SANDY LANE GOLF CLUB (809)432-1145

BERMUDA
▲ RIDDELL'S BAY GOLF AND COUNTRY CLUB (809)238-1060
● ST. GEORGE'S GOLF COURSE (809)297-8067

DOMINICAN REPUBLIC
● CASA DE CAMPO HOTEL AND COUNTRY CLUB (809)523-3333
■ PLAYA DORADO GOLF CLUB (809)586-4262

NEVIS
▲ GOLF COURSE AT FOUR SEASONS RESORT (809)469-1111

U.S. VIRGIN ISLANDS
● BUCCANEER BEACH HOTEL, St. Croix (809)773-2100

▲ RESTRICTIONS MAY APPLY   ■ HOTEL/RESORT GUESTS ONLY   ● OPEN WITHOUT RESTRICTIONS

PHOTOGRAPHY CREDITS

INDEX

COURSES ARE LISTED ALPHABETICALLY

LAKE RIDGE GOLF COURSE, NEVADA

TIDEWATER GOLF CLUB, SOUTH CAROLINA

PALMETTO DUNES RESORT, SOUTH CAROLINA

EAGLE RIDGE INN AND RESORT, ILLINOIS

PERSONAL GOLF RECORD

For those memorable days when your powerful drives split the fairways, your iron shots bore through the sky and your putts roll decisively towards the cup, here is a place to immortalize the special event. If you should need more entries, feel free to simply photocopy the pages provided here.

COURSE _____ DATE _____

LOCATION _____ TEE TIME _____

LENGTH _____ SLOPE _____ WEATHER _____

PLAYER _____ SCORE _____

PLAYER _____ SCORE _____

PLAYER _____ SCORE _____

PLAYER _____ SCORE _____

COMMENTS:

COURSE _____ DATE _____

LOCATION _____ TEE TIME _____

LENGTH _____ SLOPE _____ WEATHER _____

PLAYER _____ SCORE _____

PLAYER _____ SCORE _____

PLAYER _____ SCORE _____

PLAYER _____ SCORE _____

COMMENTS:

ABOVE: INNISBROOK RESORT AND GOLF CLUB, FLORIDA

COURSE _____ DATE _____

LOCATION _____ TEE TIME _____

LENGTH _____ SLOPE _____ WEATHER _____

PLAYER _____ SCORE _____

PLAYER _____ SCORE _____

PLAYER _____ SCORE _____

PLAYER _____ SCORE _____

COMMENTS:

COURSE _____ DATE _____

LOCATION _____ TEE TIME _____

LENGTH _____ SLOPE _____ WEATHER _____

PLAYER _____ SCORE _____

PLAYER _____ SCORE _____

PLAYER _____ SCORE _____

PLAYER _____ SCORE _____

COMMENTS:

COURSE _____ DATE _____

LOCATION _____ TEE TIME _____

LENGTH _____ SLOPE _____ WEATHER _____

PLAYER _____ SCORE _____

PLAYER _____ SCORE _____

PLAYER _____ SCORE _____

PLAYER _____ SCORE _____

COMMENTS:

COURSE _____ DATE _____

LOCATION _____ TEE TIME _____

LENGTH _____ SLOPE _____ WEATHER _____

PLAYER _____ SCORE _____

PLAYER _____ SCORE _____

PLAYER _____ SCORE _____

PLAYER _____ SCORE _____

COMMENTS:

COURSE _____ DATE _____

LOCATION _____ TEE TIME _____

LENGTH _____ SLOPE _____ WEATHER _____

PLAYER _____ SCORE _____

PLAYER _____ SCORE _____

PLAYER _____ SCORE _____

PLAYER _____ SCORE _____

COMMENTS:

COURSE _____ DATE _____

LOCATION _____ TEE TIME _____

LENGTH _____ SLOPE _____ WEATHER _____

PLAYER _____ SCORE _____

PLAYER _____ SCORE _____

PLAYER _____ SCORE _____

PLAYER _____ SCORE _____

COMMENTS:

HELP US CREATE A BETTER AMERICAN GOLFER'S GUIDE!

If, as a player, you discover a course you feel should be included in *The American Golfer's Guide,* or if, as a professional, you wish to have your course considered for future inclusion, please take a minute to fill out this short questionaire and mail a copy to: Little Lake Productions, PO Box 1106, Old Chelsea Station, New York, NY 10011. Thank you for your help.

Course Name: _____ No. of holes: _____

Address: _____

City: _____ State: _____ Zip: _____

Phone Number(s): _____

Public Accessibility (please check one):

❏ No restrictions to public play

❏ Some restrictions apply

❏ Resort Guests only

❏ Other (please specify): _____

Course Architect: _____

Approximate Green Fee in season: _____

Please explain briefly why this course should be included in the top courses open to

the public: _____

_____

_____

YOUR NAME:_____

IF A GOLF PROFESSIONAL, PLEASE INDICATE AFFILIATION: _____

PHONE NUMBER: _____ DATE: _____

SIGNATURE: _____

LITTLE LAKE PRODUCTIONS, PO BOX 1106, OLD CHELSEA STATION, NEW YORK, NY 10011

MARY TIEGREEN AND HUBERT PEDROLI AT
BODEGA HARBOR GOLF LINKS

ABOUT THE AUTHORS

Born and raised in France, Hubert Pedroli discovered the game of golf more than twenty years ago on the seaside links of Normandy. He brought his passion for the game with him when, in 1976, he moved to the United States to pursue a career in international currency trading. While living in Los Angeles and San Francisco, he spent his weekends playing golf along the California coast before becoming a resident of New York City in 1980. Combining extensive travel with his love of the game, he has enjoyed the diversity of golf courses not only throughout America, but around the world. Currently working for a major financial institution, Mr. Pedroli hopes one day to play a round of golf with Arnold Palmer. *"The American Golfer's Guide"* is Mr. Pedroli's first book for Turner Publishing.

Recipient of numerous national design awards, Mary Tiegreen has contributed to several books, most recent among them Turner Publishing's "MGM: When The Lion Roars" and "Kisses." Her participation in *"The American Golfer's Guide"* fulfills her genetic predisposition to the sport (Tiegreen women have been playing golf in America since 1900). Born in Chicago, she initiated her design career in London in 1976, before relocating to New York several years later as an art director. Currently a partner in Little Lake Productions, she looks forward to future golfing adventures and perfecting a sometimes unpredictable swing.

The American Golfer's Guide was created on the
Macintosh IIci and IIsi using Filemaker, Microsoft Word 4.0,
Quark XPress 3.0. Photoshop, & Adobe Illustrator 3.0.
The typefaces are ITC Century, Copperplate & Bauer Bodoni.
Color separations were made by Graphics International, Atlanta.
The book was printed and bound by R.R. Donnelly.

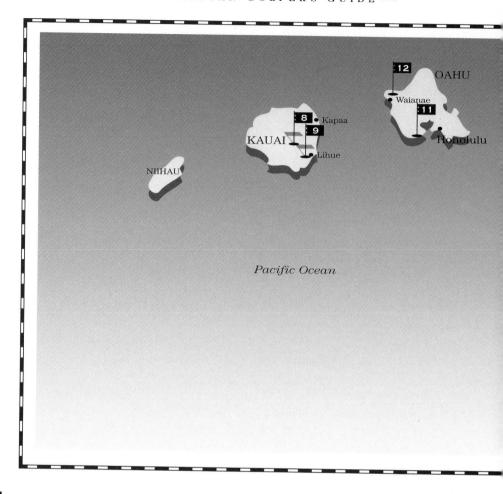

MAUNA LANI RESORT

P.O. BOX 4959, HAWAII KOHALA COAST, HI 96743 (808)885-6655 *(Kohala Coast)*
ACCOMMODATIONS: MAUNA LANI BAY HOTEL (808)885-6622, RITZ CARLTON MAUNA LANI (808)885-2000

FRANCIS H. I'I BROWN GOLF COURSE
ACCESS: Priority to hotel guests
SEASON: All year HIGH: Dec.-Mar.
GREEN FEES: $$$$$
REDUCED FEES: HG
RESERVATIONS: Nonguests 1 day
WALKING: No RANGE: Yes
• **NORTH COURSE**
  18 holes Par 72 6968/6335/5398 yds.
  STYLE: Oceanside
• **SOUTH COURSE**
  18 holes Par 72 7015/6370/5331 yds.
  STYLE: Oceanside

The Francis H. I'i Brown Course is the home of the Senior PGA Tour Skins Game. This award-collecting course was one of the first to use and display the Big Island's spectacular blend of lush green fairways, black lava flows, white sand beaches, and deep blue water bays. The famous course, considered by many to be one of the ten most beautiful in the world, has now been divided into two equally remarkable eighteen-hole courses, the North and the South. Each incorporates nine holes from the original classic, including the fearsome, oceanside, par-3 No. 6 and the one surrounded by a lava amphitheater, No. 17.

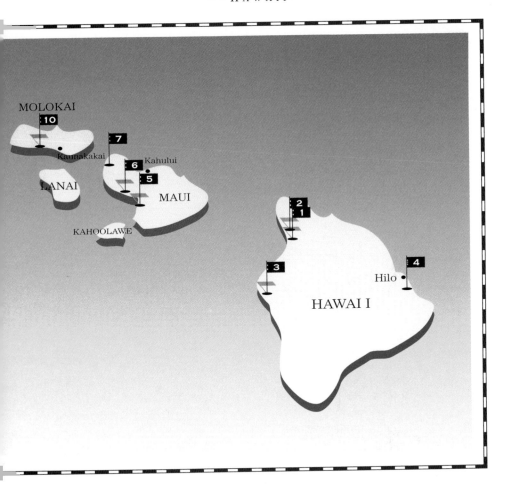

MAUNA KEA BEACH HOTEL

ONE MAUNA KEA BEACH DR., KOHALA COAST, HI 96743 (808)882-7222 *(Kohala Coast)*
ACCOMMODATIONS: MAUNA KEA BEACH HOTEL (808)882-7222

Designed by Robert Trent Jones, Sr., and open since 1964, this classic layout has been ranked among the top courses in Hawaii. The course features black lava outcrops, beautiful palm tree-lined fairways, and 120 sandtraps. The much photographed par-3 third requires a two-hundred-yard carry over the ocean, and the eleventh, another par 3, is usually buffeted by the Kona winds, which can seriously affect your score. You'll enjoy the challenge—as well as the breath-taking views—from this recipient of *Golf* magazine's coveted Gold Medal. Considered one of the world's toughest oceanside courses, it will soon be joined by a new Arnold Palmer-Ed Seay eighteen-hole layout.

MAUNA KEA GOLF COURSE
18 holes   Par 72   6737/6365/5277 yds.
USGA: 70.6   SLOPE: 126
STYLE: Oceanside
ACCESS: Restrictions on tee times
SEASON: All year   HIGH: Jan.-Apr.
GREEN FEES: $$$$$
REDUCED FEES: HG
RESERVATIONS: 1 day
WALKING: At times   RANGE: Yes

WAIKOLOA GOLF CLUB

HC02 BOX 5575, WAIKOLOA, HI 96743 (808)885-4647 *(25 mi. NW of Kailua-Kona)*
ACCOMMODATIONS: CALL GOLF CLUB FOR INFORMATION

Waikoloa's two courses are carved out of a five-thousand-year-old black lava flow on the slopes of the Mauna Kea volcano. The Beach Course, a 1981 Robert Trent Jones, Jr., classic, features generous landing areas and large, contoured greens. Magnificent views of the blue Pacific are available from every point, and several holes directly overlook the ocean. The Kings' Course, a Jay Morrish and Tom Weiskopf Scottish-style design (unique in Hawaii), was an instant success when it opened in 1990. It is simple and beautiful and requires all fourteen clubs to negotiate massive, treacherous bunkers and black lava outcrops. The Kings' was a runner-up in *Golf Digest*'s rating of the best new resort courses in 1990.

> **WAIKOLOA GOLF CLUB**
> ACCESS: Priority to hotel guests
> SEASON: All year HIGH: Dec.-Apr.
> GREEN FEES: $$$$$ (includes cart)
> REDUCED FEES: HG
> RESERVATIONS: 1 month with credit card
> WALKING: No RANGE: Yes
> • **BEACH COURSE**
>   18 holes Par 70 6507/5920/5039 yds.
>   STYLE: Oceanside
> • **KINGS' COURSE**
>   18 holes Par 72 6594/6010/5459 yds.
>   USGA: 68.2 SLOPE: 124
>   STYLE: Scottish links

BEACH COURSE: HOLES NO. 12 & 13
THE SPECTACULAR PAR-5 NO. 12 TUMBLES 500 YARDS DOWNHILL TOWARDS THE OCEAN. THE THIRD SHOT IS PLAYED TO A LARGE GREEN, SURROUNDED BY THE BLUE PACIFIC, SWAYING PALM TREES, AND LAVA ROCKS. THE PAR-3 THIRTEENTH TAKES THE PLAYERS BACK UP THE SLOPING FIELDS.

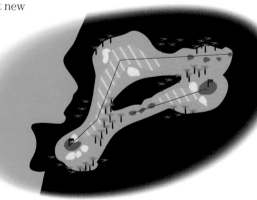

VOLCANO GOLF AND COUNTRY CLUB | **4**

P.O. BOX 46, HAWAII VOLCANO NATIONAL PK., HI 96718 (808)967-7331 *(30 mi. S of Hilo)*

This course's unique location—the slopes of Mauna Loa in Volcanoes National Park—provides dramatic mountain views. In addition, Volcano's four-thousand-foot elevation guarantees golfers ideal temperatures and crisp, clean air in a tropical setting. An annual rainfall of 130 inches provides a natural irrigation system resulting in the lush fairways and vegetation. The greens are generally small and fast, and the rough is unyielding. The 385-yard, par-4 No. 15 is a dogleg left with large ohia trees in the corner; long hitters will be tempted to cut this one, leaving them with a wedge shot to the green.

VOLCANO GOLF AND COUNTRY CLUB
18 holes   Par 72   6270/5965/5499 yds.
USGA: 68.6   SLOPE: 125
STYLE: Rolling hills
ACCESS: Restrictions on tee times
SEASON: All year   HIGH: Summer
GREEN FEES: $$ (includes cart)
RESERVATIONS: 6 days
WALKING: No   RANGE: Yes

M A U I

MAKENA GOLF COURSE | **5**

5415 MAKENA ALANUI, KIHEI, HI 96753 (808)879-3344 *(5 mi. S of Kihei)*
ACCOMMODATIONS: MAKENA RESORT, MAUI PRINCE HOTEL (808)874-1111

Makena's course is built on wooded hills in a secluded area of Maui. The Robert Trent Jones, Jr., design features narrow fairways and fast greens. No. 1 is easy and relaxing, but the challenge increases as you near the back nine. The par-3 fifteenth has a hundred-foot drop toward the Pacific, while the par-4 No. 16, a dogleg along the ocean, is played with a drive to an elevated landing area followed by an approach shot to a two-tiered green that slopes away from players. Manicured conditions and an abundance of exotic flowers will give you the feeling of playing in a botanical garden. An additional eighteen-hole course is set to open in late 1992.

MAKENA GOLF COURSE
18 holes   Par 72   6739/6210/5441 yds.
USGA: 69.4   SLOPE: 118
STYLE: Hills, oceanside
ACCESS: No restrictions
SEASON: All year   HIGH: Dec.-Apr.
GREEN FEES: $$$$ (includes cart)
REDUCED FEES: HG, TW, PK
RESERVATIONS: 3 days, longer if prepaid
WALKING: No   RANGE: Yes

WAILEA GOLF CLUB | **6**

120 KAUKAHI ST., MAUI WAILEA KIHEI, HI 96753 (808)879-2966 *(in Kihei)*
ACCOMMODATIONS: CALL GOLF CLUB FOR INFORMATION

WAILEA GOLF CLUB
ACCESS: No restrictions
SEASON: All year   HIGH: Jan.-Apr.
GREEN FEES: $$$$$ (includes cart)
REDUCED FEES: HG
RESERVATIONS: Nonguests 1 day
WALKING: No   RANGE: Yes
• **ORANGE COURSE**
  18 holes   Par 72   6810/6304/5644 yds.
  USGA: 69.1   SLOPE: 126.7
  STYLE: Hills
• **BLUE COURSE**
  18 holes   Par 72   6743/6152/5686 yds.
  USGA: 68.6   SLOPE: 112.1
  STYLE: Tropical

Wailea's Orange Course, a traditional Maui layout, is hilly and narrow. With old lava stone walls bordering or encroaching on fairways, it presents a tough challenge from the back tees. All tee shots must be strategically placed, and guidance from a local player can greatly help to avoid costly mistakes. Fortunately, there are always the sensational ocean views to help one forget the score. The easier Blue Course is enhanced with lush landscaping, including four lakes, and has a more open and tropical feel. A third eighteen-hole course, the Gold, designed by Robert Trent Jones, Jr., is planned for completion in 1994.

KAPALUA GOLF CLUB

300 KAPALUA DR., KAPALUA, MAUI, HI 96761 (808)669-8044 *(7 mi. N of Lahaina)*
ACCOMMODATIONS: KAPALUA BAY HOTEL AND VILLAS (800)367-8000

> **KAPALUA GOLF CLUB**
> ACCESS: Priority to hotel guests
> SEASON: All year
> GREEN FEES: $$$$
> REDUCED FEES: HG, TW, PK
> RESERVATIONS: Nonguests 2 days
> WALKING: No   RANGE: Yes
> • **BAY COURSE**
>   18 holes   Par 72   6600/6051/5124 yds.
>   USGA: 69.8   SLOPE: 131.3
>   STYLE: Hills, oceanside
> • **VILLAGE COURSE**
>   18 holes   Par 71   6632/6001/5134 yds.
>   USGA: 68.1   SLOPE: 132
>   STYLE: Hills
> • **PLANTATION COURSE**
>   18 holes   Par 73   7263/6547/5620 yds.
>   USGA: 71.3   SLOPE: 128
>   STYLE: Hills

The Ben Crenshaw-Bill Coore golf course design team has recently added new excitement to the well-established Kapalua Golf Club. Like the two classic Palmer-designed Bay and Village layouts, the new Plantation Course takes advantage of Kapalua's naturally dramatic setting. The track is routed over 240 acres of precipitous hills just north of the Village Course. Its wide and expansive fairways are surrounded by vast pineapple fields, at times interrupted by deep ravines. The 663-yard, par-5 eighteenth "home" hole illustrates the course's heroic but still playable proportions: playing downhill and downwind, the receptive green is quite reachable in regulation. The site offers the widest and most dramatic ocean vistas available from all of Maui.

The Bay Course, still Kapalua's most famous, has hosted the Isuzu Kapalua International Tournament for many years. Situated among sloping pineapple fields and tropical vegetation, the Bay is also renowned for its great ocean views. The par-4 fourth is a downhill dogleg that leads to a lava peninsula. No. 5 is a testy, 184-yard par 3 that requires a daring shot over the turquoise Oneloa Bay.

The Village Course at first takes the player uphill through fragrant eucalyptus and ironwood tree groves. The tee at No. 6 claims the course's best vantage point; from there, it's nine hundred feet downhill to the clubhouse!

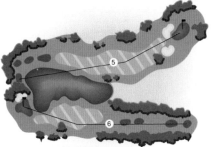

VILLAGE COURSE, HOLES NO. 5 AND 6
*THESE TWO PAR 4S ARE BOTH SITUATED
AT THE PROPERTY'S HIGHEST ELEVA-
TION. THE LAKE THAT SEPARATES
THEM COMES INTO PLAY ON THE DRIVE
AT NO. 5, AND ON THE APPROACH SHOT
AT NO. 6.*

PRINCEVILLE RESORT 8

PRINCE COURSE: 5-3900 KUHIO HWY. (808)826-3040, MAKAI COURSE: 4080 LEI O PAPA RD. (800)826-5000
PRINCEVILLE, KAUAI, HI 96722 *(30 mi. NW of Lihue)*
ACCOMMODATIONS: PRINCEVILLE HOTEL (808)826-9644

Makai's three nine-hole courses, opened for play in 1971, were the first solo design effort of Robert Trent Jones, Jr. In a record that speaks for itself, it has been rated by *Golf Digest* as one of America's one hundred greatest courses for sixteen consecutive years. Each one of the nines—the Ocean, the Lakes, and the Woods—has a distinct scenic flavor that is reflected in its name, and each takes advantage of the variations in the terrain alongside the spectacular Hanalei Bay.

> **PRINCEVILLE RESORT, KAUAI**
> ACCESS: Priority to hotel guests
> SEASON: All year HIGH: Dec.-Mar.
> GREEN FEES: $$$$$ (includes cart)
> REDUCED FEES: HG
> RESERVATIONS: 1 week
> WALKING: No RANGE: Yes
> • **PRINCE COURSE**
>   18 holes Par 72 7309/6521/5338 yds.
>   USGA: 71.7 SLOPE: 135
>   STYLE: Tropical hills
> • **MAKAI COURSE**
>   27 holes 3208/3149/3157 yds.
>   STYLE: Trees, lakes, oceanside

Jones came back to Princeville in 1989 to create what is now recognized as the most challenging golf course in all Hawaii, the Prince Course. Laid upon 390 acres of land formerly owned by a nineteenth-century Hawaiian prince, and with a USGA rating of 75.6 from the championship tee, the course is a masterpiece of design talent and imagination. The architect has utilized the diverse elements offered by nature—verdant ravines, rocky streams and waterfalls, and Hawaii's most exotic flora and fauna—to design a series of memorable signature holes. You might choose "Burma Road," the 547-yard, par-5 tenth ravine hole, as your favorite nightmare. Or you might elect "Eagle's Nest," the 358-yard, par-4 twelfth, with a tee elevated a hundred feet above a slender fairway to an amphitheater green surrounded by water and tropical foliage.

In this jungle fantasy, do not let your imagination take you too far: the yardages indicated above are from the middle of five tees, and play from the two back tees is limited to single-digit handicappers only. Since its opening in 1990, the Prince has been acclaimed as the best course in Hawaii. It has inspired such adjectives as "awesome," "fantastic," and "fabulous." With reverence for its royal heritage, we prefer to call it "magnificent." *Golf Digest* ranked it as the best new resort course of 1990.

MAKAI COURSE (ABOVE), PRINCE COURSE (BELOW)

KAUAI LAGOONS GOLF CLUB

`9`

P.O. BOX 3330, LIHUE, HI 96766 (808)246-5078, (800)634-6400 *(5 mins. from Lihue Airport)*
ACCOMMODATIONS: WESTIN KAUAI (808)245-5050

Kauai Lagoons has two extremely picturesque eighteen-hole courses: the Kiele Course and the Lagoons Course. Opened in 1989, both were designed by Jack Nicklaus and are maintained at his standards. Kiele was rated the best new resort course for 1990 by *Golf Digest*, while *Golf* magazine listed the Lagoons Course as one of the top ten new places to play in 1990. Kiele quickly earned a reputation for its superior par 3s. The 219-yard fifth, for example, plays over a ravine harboring a luxuriant rain forest. The second nine holes are built alongside the harbor entrance and offer many picture taking opportunities. The thirteenth requires a 207-yard shot over the ocean! The Lagoons Course, with its gently rolling fairways and well-contoured greens, presents an easier challenge to players of all levels.

> **KAUAI LAGOONS GOLF CLUB**
> ACCESS: No restrictions
> SEASON: All year   HIGH: Feb.
> GREEN FEES: $$$$$ (includes cart)
> REDUCED FEES: HG
> RESERVATIONS: 1 month
> WALKING: No   RANGE: Yes
> • **KIELE COURSE**
>   18 holes   Par 72   7070/6164/5417 yds.
>   USGA: 71.4
>   STYLE: Tropical, hills
> • **LAGOONS COURSE**
>   18 holes   Par 72   6942/6108/5607 yds.
>   USGA: 70.9
>   STYLE: Tropical, lakes

M O L O K A I

KALUAKOI GOLF COURSE

`10`

KALUAKOI RD., KEPUHI BEACH, MAUNALOA, HI 96770 (808)552-2739 *(20 mi. W of Kaunakakai)*
ACCOMMODATIONS: KALUAKOI HOTEL AND GOLF CLUB (808)552-2555

> **KALUAKOI GOLF COURSE**
> 18 holes   Par 72   6564/6187/5461 yds.
> USGA: 70.3   SLOPE: 122
> STYLE: Oceanside
> ACCESS: No restrictions
> SEASON: All year   HIGH: Nov.-Mar.
> GREEN FEES: $$
> RESERVATIONS: 1 month
> WALKING: No   RANGE: Yes

Sometimes called "The Hidden Secret" of Hawaii, Kaluakoi was designed by Ted Robinson. While a third of its holes are right on the ocean with trade winds commonly affecting shots, the back nine offers a beautiful mountain perspective of the entire resort. The course is well-bunkered (eighty-eight sandtraps) and counts four two-tiered greens and numerous water hazards. No. 6 requires two shots over water to the green, and No. 16 tees off over a deep ravine.

O A H U

KO OLINA GOLF CLUB

`11`

92-1220 ALII-NUI DR., EWA BEACH, HI 96707 (808)676-5300 *(25 mi. from downtown Honolulu)*
ACCOMMODATIONS: HOTEL IHILANI (OPENS LATE 1992)

Ko Olina's Ted Robinson-designed course, host of the LPGA Hawaiian Open, is a newcomer on Oahu. Inaugurated in 1990, it is located just off the ocean, and water is the dominant feature. Multiple lakes, streams, and waterfalls come into play on eight holes of this championship layout, and one-third of the seventy-two traps are pot bunkers. The par-4 eighteenth is 484 yards long from the men's championship tees and has been rated the toughest finishing hole on the LPGA Tour.

> **KO OLINA GOLF CLUB**
> 18 holes   Par 72   6867/6252/5358 yds.
> USGA: 69.3   SLOPE: 131
> STYLE: Tropical, lakes
> ACCESS: No restrictions
> SEASON: All year   HIGH: Nov.-Feb.
> GREEN FEES: $$$$$ (includes cart)
> REDUCED FEES: TW
> RESERVATIONS: 1 week
> WALKING: No   RANGE: Yes

SHERATON MAKAHA RESORT
12

84-626 MAKAHA VALLEY RD., WAIANAE, HI 96792 (808)695-9544 *(in Makaha)*
ACCOMMODATIONS: SHERATON MAKAHA RESORT (800)325-3535

MAKAHA COURSE
18 holes   Par 72   7091/6398/6002 yds.
USGA: 71.7   SLOPE: 138
STYLE: Flat nine, hilly nine
ACCESS: Priority to hotel guests
SEASON: All year
GREEN FEES: $$$$$ (includes cart)
REDUCED FEES: HG
RESERVATIONS: 2 weeks
WALKING: No   RANGE: Yes

This is a long and demanding Bill Bell course. The front nine is fairly flat and "dry," but the back nine brings hills and eight lakes into play. The greens are generous in size and can even be welcoming to some errant approaches, but they require excellent putting skills. Of course, even before you get on the green, you'll have to avoid Mahaka's one hundred bunkers. If not the sand, visitors always remember the great views of western Oahu's four-thousand-foot-high Waianae Mountains in the background.

OTHER EXCELLENT COURSES IN HAWAII

MAUI
- PUKALANI COUNTRY CLUB, East Maui (808)572-1314
- ROYAL KAANAPALI GOLF CLUB, Lahaina (808)661-3691
- SILVERSWORD GOLF COURSE, Kihei (808)874-0777

HAWAII
- WAIKOLOA VILLAGE GOLF CLUB, Waikoloa (808)883-9621

OAHU
- TURTLE BAY HILTON AND COUNTRY CLUB, Honolulu (808)293-8574

KAUAI
- KIAHUNA GOLF CLUB, Koloa (808)742-9595
- WAILUA GOLF COURSE, Lihue (808)245-8092

LANAI
- EXPERIENCE AT KOELE (800)321-4666

▲ RESTRICTIONS MAY APPLY   ■ HOTEL/RESORT GUESTS ONLY   ● OPEN WITHOUT RESTRICTIONS

CHAPTER TWO

THE WEST

With 1,300 miles of coastline stretching from the Canadian border to Mexico, and with elevations ranging from 14,410 feet at Mount Rainier in Washington to 282 feet below sea level at Death Valley National Monument, the western United States offer more diversity of geography and landscape than any other part of the country.

Leaving the gleaming waters and islands of Puget Sound and heading south, the traveling golfer will first encounter golf courses hidden in the volcanic wilderness of Oregon's Cascade Range. A few hundred miles to the south and west, the California coast begins to offer its rugged beauty and irresistible golfing attractions. And moving eastward to the sands of Nevada, our wandering golfer can turn his attention to the desert and more opportunities for memorable golf.

A diverse and imposing landscape is not the only attraction. This region is blessed with a climate that is the envy of outdoorsmen and golfers everywhere. With the exceptions of the higher mountain areas and the desert, golf is a year-round affair. The coastal regions enjoy the soothing influence of the Pacific Ocean, and while some may say that it gets a little wet up in Washington, the Evergreen State is heaven when it comes to golf courses. As for Southern California, the weather there needs no write-up. The Mediterranean-like flora that beautifies many of the region's courses is testimony enough to the climate.

Two places in the West are synonymous with golf. Palm Springs, a favorite winter retreat, demands a visit as soon as the winter blues hit home. But in the hearts of all devotees of the game, nowhere do land, sea, and climate unite more ideally than on the Monterey Peninsula, home of the famous Pebble Beach Golf Links and other marvelous golf courses.

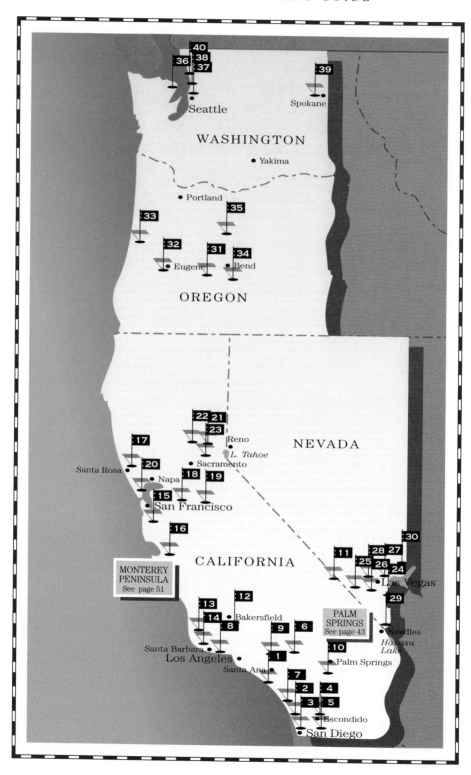

THE LINKS AT MONARCH BEACH

1

33080 NIGUEL RD., DANA POINT, CA 92677 (714)240-8247 *(45 mi. S of Los Angeles)*
ACCOMMODATIONS: THE RITZ CARLTON (714)240-2000

This Robert Trent Jones, Jr., design is a testimony to what a talented architect can do with a small, albeit lovely, piece of property. The course winds along a cliff overlooking the Pacific and offers magnificent views of the ocean and Monarch Beach. There is extensive bunkering—more severe on the shorter holes—and water comes into play on half. Truly a shotmaker's course, it demands accurate, if not always long, drives and thoughtful approaches. No. 12 is breathtaking: it tees off toward the ocean, then veers left to a large green with four-foot-high undulations. With ocean breezes, the course becomes a real tester.

> **THE LINKS AT MONARCH BEACH**
> 18 holes   Par 70   6224/5655/5046 yds.
> USGA: 67.2   SLOPE: 117
> STYLE: Rolling hills, oceanside
> ACCESS: Priority to hotel guests
> SEASON: All year   HIGH: May-Nov.
> GREEN FEES: $$$$ (includes cart)
> REDUCED FEES: WD, TW
> RESERVATIONS: 1 week
> WALKING: Yes   RANGE: No

LA COSTA RESORT AND SPA

2

COSTA DEL MAR RD., CARLSBAD, CA 92009 (619)438-9111, EXT. 4243 *(30 mi. N of San Diego)*
ACCOMMODATIONS: LA COSTA RESORT AND SPA (619)438-9111, EXT. 38

It is said that great players win on great courses, so you'll get an idea of just how good the two La Costa courses are by looking at some of the players who have won the Tournament of Champions here: Jack Nicklaus, Gary Player, and Lee Trevino, to name just a few. In this coastal valley of flowering hills, Joe Lee and Dick Wilson created challenges for the thinking man. The North Course, with nine water hazards and seventy-nine bunkers, requires accurate tee shots and proper club selection. The South Course brings twelve water hazards .and eighty-four bunkers into play! The Tournament of Champions course includes a selection of the best holes from each of the two tracks.

> **LA COSTA RESORT AND SPA**
> ACCESS: Hotel guests only
> SEASON: All year   HIGH: Feb.-Apr.
> GREEN FEES: $$$$
> REDUCED FEES: PK
> RESERVATIONS: Anytime
> WALKING: Yes   RANGE: Yes
> • **NORTH COURSE**
>   18 holes   Par 72   6987/6688/6269 yds.
>   USGA: 72.1   SLOPE: 129
>   STYLE: Traditional
> • **SOUTH COURSE**
>   18 holes   Par 72   6894/6524/6198 yds.
>   USGA: 72   SLOPE: 128
>   STYLE: Traditional

LA COSTA, NORTH COURSE: HOLE NO. 16

TORREY PINES GOLF COURSES

11480 N. TORREY PINES RD., LA JOLLA, CA 92037 (619)570-1234 *(18 mi. N of downtown San Diego)*
ACCOMMODATIONS: TORREY PINES INN (619)453-4420

TORREY PINES GOLF COURSES
ACCESS: No restrictions
SEASON: All year   HIGH: June-Oct.
GREEN FEES: $$$
REDUCED FEES: WD, TW
RESERVATIONS: 1 week
WALKING: Yes   RANGE: Yes
• SOUTH COURSE
18 holes   Par 72   7012/6706/6447 yds.
USGA: 72.2   SLOPE: 124
STYLE: Hills, oceanside
• NORTH COURSE
18 holes   Par 72   6659/6375/6104 yds.
USGA: 69.6   SLOPE: 116
STYLE: Hills, oceanside

Americans know Torrey Pines as the site of the PGA Tour's San Diego tournament. The locals know it as a civic treasure of which they are justly proud and fiercely protective. These courses are exceedingly fair but remain challenging enough for players of every level. The South Course is the tournament course and definitely the more difficult. No. 18, a reachable par 5 guarded by a pond in front, is a great hole for testing your nerve and ending a round. The most popular hole, No. 16 on the North Course, offers a dramatic view and the best shot challenge—206 yards downhill to a small green, with superb views of the ocean and coastline. These courses are the pride of the people of San Diego—and the envy of the rest of the world.

TORREY PINES: SOUTH COURSE

RAMS HILL COUNTRY CLUB

1881 RAMS HILL COUNTRY CLUB, BORREGO SPRINGS, CA 92004 (619)767-5124 *(60 mi. from Escondido)*
ACCOMMODATIONS: LA CASA DEL ZORRO (619)767-5323

RAMS HILL COUNTRY CLUB
18 holes   Par 72   6866/6328/5694 yds.
USGA: 70.9   SLOPE: 125
STYLE: Traditional
ACCESS: No restrictions
SEASON: Nov.-Sept.   HIGH: Nov.-Mar.
GREEN FEES: $$$$ (includes cart)
REDUCED FEES: HG, LS, TW, PK
RESERVATIONS: 3 days
WALKING: No   RANGE: Yes

There is an oasis-like feel to this championship course that Ted Robinson designed at the bottom of a valley in the Anza Borrego Desert State Park. Palm, olive, and eucalyptus trees border the lush fairways and seven sparkling lakes. A waterfall graces the par-4 No. 18, a dogleg that demands a second shot over water. Nine holes were recently added, and the director of golf is former PGA Champion Bob Rosburg.

TEMECULA CREEK INN   5

44501 RAINBOW CANYON RD., TEMECULA, CA 92390 (714)676-2405 *(50 mi. NE of San Diego)*
ACCOMMODATIONS: TEMECULA CREEK INN (800)96-CREEK

Temecula Creek has three nine-hole courses: the Creek and the Oaks, which opened in 1970, and the Stonehouse, which opened in 1990. The course is located in a resplendent country setting, with a great variety of trees, including plum and peach. Majestic mountains form the landscape, and at some points, large granite boulders border the course. The fairways present comfortable landing areas and water comes into play on only three holes, but there are more than sixty white silica sandtraps to penalize errant shots. The 555-yard, par-5 No. 9 on Stonehouse commands respect: it demands a firm approach shot over ninety yards of water, with an out-of-bounds behind the green.

TEMECULA CREEK INN
27 holes   3183/3192/3103 yds.
STYLE: Rolling hills, trees
ACCESS: No restrictions
SEASON: All year   HIGH: Winter
GREEN FEES: $$$
REDUCED FEES: WD, HG, LS, PK
RESERVATIONS: Nonguests 1 week
WALKING: Yes   RANGE: Yes

MORENO VALLEY RANCH GOLF CLUB   6

28095 JFK AVE., MORENO VALLEY, CA 92360 (714)924-4444 *(60 mi. E of Los Angeles)*

Pete Dye made use of a variety of terrain and added a few ingredients of his own while building this course. The Valley, Mountain, and Lake nines provide a combination of uphill and downhill holes, where mounds, pot bunkers, and railroad ties show up—sometimes unexpectedly. The signature hole is No. 7 on the Mountain Course: the 165-yard par 3 plays from one mountain to another; what lies in between, you don't want to know. Moreno Valley has fast, sloping greens, in addition to some great views of snowcapped sierras in the background. With tight fairways demanding accurate tee shots, this well-designed course was ranked by *Golf Digest* in 1990 as one of America's seventy-five best public courses.

MORENO VALLEY RANCH GOLF CLUB
27 holes   2878/2955/2952 yds.
STYLE: Hills, lakes
ACCESS: No restrictions
SEASON: All year   HIGH: Jan.-May
GREEN FEES: $$$ (includes cart)
REDUCED FEES: WD, TW
RESERVATIONS: 1 week
WALKING: No   RANGE: Yes

PALA MESA RESORT HOTEL   7

2001 OLD HWY. 395, FALLBROOK, CA 92028 (619)728-5881 *(45 mi. N of San Diego)*
ACCOMMODATIONS: PALA MESA RESORT HOTEL (800)722-4700 IN CA, (800)822-4600 OUTSIDE CA

The course at Pala Mesa is not especially long, but it demands controlled and accurate shotmaking. Nine holes travel along rolling and sometimes steep hills, while the other nine is heavily wooded with oak, sycamore, and pine. Accuracy is indeed at a premium on this splendid course. Landing areas average thirty yards in width, and some shrink to a mere twenty-five yards! Although the sixty sandtraps are not too penalizing, and only three holes have water hazards, you'll find that the manicured greens are kept at a dangerously fast 9 to 11 on the stimpmeter, not to mention the severe slopes on some of them. Pala Mesa offers a fine retreat for golf in a quiet and secluded setting.

PALA MESA RESORT HOTEL
18 holes   Par 72   6461/6172/5835 yds.
USGA: 70.1   SLOPE: 125
STYLE: Rolling hills, woods
ACCESS: No restrictions
SEASON: All year   HIGH: Feb.-June
GREEN FEES: $$$ (includes cart)
REDUCED FEES: WD, HG, TW
RESERVATIONS: 1 week
WALKING: No   RANGE: Yes

Ojai Valley Inn and Country Club

8

Country Club Rd., Ojai, CA 93023 (805)646-2420 *(25 mi. E of Santa Barbara)*
ACCOMMODATIONS: Ojai Valley Inn and Country Club (805)646-5511

Originally built in 1923, the Ojai Valley course was renovated in 1988 under the supervision of architect Jay Morrish. It has received a lot of attention, and rightfully so: the terrain offers considerable variety, from dense woods to steep hills. The design combines generous landing areas on long holes and tight ones on short holes, with several intimidating barrancas running across. The result is a shotmaker's course where good thinking and skillful execution yield better results than long shots. Large oaks border the fairways of this elegant and challenging layout, which has hosted numerous PGA events and is home to the Senior PGA Tour GTE West Classic.

Ojai Valley Inn and Country Club
18 holes   Par 70   6252/5909/5242 yds.
USGA: 68.9   SLOPE: 117
STYLE: Rolling hills, barrancas
ACCESS: Priority to hotel guests
SEASON: All year   HIGH: Late spring
GREEN FEES: $$$$
REDUCED FEES: HG
RESERVATIONS: Nonguests 1 day
WALKING: Yes   RANGE: Yes

Industry Hills Recreation and Conference Center

9

One Industry Hills Pkwy., City of Industry, CA 91744 (818)810-GOLF *(20 mi. E of Los Angeles)*
ACCOMMODATIONS: Industry Hills Recreation and Conference Center (818)965-0861

Industry Hills Recreation and Conference Center
ACCESS: Priority to members
SEASON: All year
HIGH: May-June/Sept.-Nov.
GREEN FEES: $$$ (includes cart)
REDUCED FEES: WD, PK
RESERVATIONS: 3 days
WALKING: No   RANGE: Yes
• **Babe Didrikson Zaharias Course**
18 holes   Par 71   6778/6124/5363 yds.
USGA: 70.3   SLOPE: 130
STYLE: Hills
• **Dwight D. Eisenhower Course**
18 holes   Par 72   7181/6262/5589 yds.
USGA: 70.9   SLOPE: 130
STYLE: Hills

The two championship eighteen-hole courses at Industry Hills were built on top of a former dump—a stunning transformation that is simply hard to believe. Both the Dwight D. Eisenhower Course (the "Ike"), rated one of the top twenty-five courses in the United States by *Golf Digest,* and the Babe Didrikson Zaharias Course (the "Babe") are outstanding challenges. These William Bell-designed layouts are long and demanding, but the generous plantings of shrubs and flowers, combined with views of the snowcapped mountains off to the east, make them a visual treat as well. One of the finest golf libraries in the country is located in the clubhouse. Another unique feature is the authentic Swiss funicular that carries golfers from one level of the course to the next.

PALM SPRINGS

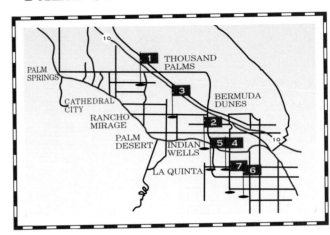

Two hours east of Los Angeles, America's winter golf capital stretches along twenty-five miles of Highway 10 from the city of Palm Springs to the city of Indio and encompasses the towns of Cathedral City, Rancho Mirage, Palm Desert, Indian Wells, and La Quinta. In these retirement and resort communities, golf has always been a way of life. Golf carts sporting automobile license plates can be spotted on the streets, and the traditional two-car garage is a two-and-a-half here. For visitors, a ride on the Palm Springs Aerial Tramway is a must. From the snowy, 8,500-foot summit of the San Jacinto Mountain, the entire valley seems a mosaic of small, square green patches—each containing one or more golf courses. At the latest count, more than eighty courses have been built over what used to be hot desert sand. The area is even said to experience its own microclimate due to the turf's cooling effect!

In recent years, the Palm Springs area has seen the development of a good number of resort and daily-fee courses. Some of them—such as the Stadium Course at PGA West and the Dunes and Citrus Courses at La Quinta—are spectacular creations.

Golf season in the California desert is year-round. However, because the summer months are quite hot (average daytime temperatures are above 100 degrees), summer golf is best played in the early morning and late afternoon. To compensate for the heat, green fees are usually reduced by half from June to September.

WESTIN MISSION HILLS RESORT GOLF CLUB

71-501 DINAH SHORE DR., RANCHO MIRAGE, CA 92270 (619)328-3198 *(10 mi. E of Palm Springs)*
ACCOMMODATIONS: WESTIN MISSION HILLS RESORT HOTEL (619)328-3198

Westin Mission Hills offers a Pete Dye championship course that is challenging for the average player and can even be tough for the pros. The Mission Hills fairways are wide, and you should not have any problem staying out of the penalizing pot bunkers (there are one hundred traps) or the thick Bermuda rough. After negotiating the few—but quite large—water hazards with railroad ties, you can still have plenty of fun on the spacious and severely undulated greens. The course is adorned with colorful floral displays, in case you decide it's time to concentrate on the scenery.

PETE DYE COURSE
18 holes Par 70   6706/6196/4841 yds.
USGA: 70.3   SLOPE: 126
STYLE: Desert
ACCESS: No restrictions
SEASON: All year   HIGH: Nov.-Apr.
GREEN FEES: $$$$$ (includes cart)
REDUCED FEES: HG, LS, PK
RESERVATIONS: 3 days
WALKING: No   RANGE: Yes

INDIAN WELLS GOLF RESORT

44-500 INDIAN WELLS LA., INDIAN WELLS, CA 92210 (619)346-4653 *(15 mi. E of Palm Springs)*
ACCOMMODATIONS: CALL RESORT FOR INFORMATION

> **INDIAN WELLS GOLF RESORT**
> ACCESS: Priority to hotel guests
> SEASON: All year   HIGH: Jan.-Mar./Oct.
> GREEN FEES: $$$$$ (includes cart)
> REDUCED FEES: WD, LS, TW, PK
> RESERVATIONS: Nonguests 2 days
> WALKING: No   RANGE: Yes
> • **EAST COURSE**
>   18 holes   Par 72   6662/6227/5521 yds.
>   USGA: 69.4   SLOPE: 110
>   STYLE: Desert, lakes
> • **WEST COURSE**
>   18 holes   Par 72   6478/6115/5387 yds.
>   USGA: 68.7   SLOPE: 109
>   STYLE: Desert, lakes

The two Indian Wells courses, designed by Ted Robinson, are among the most beautiful in the Palm Springs valley. Lush, undulating fairways are surrounded by lakes and outlined by panoramic views of the mountains. Each course has approximately 120 sandtraps—most of them difficult—including the feared and respected pot bunker variety. There are many excellent holes here, some of them particularly scenic and challenging. For example, the par-3 No. 13 on the West Course travels from an elevated tee to an island green and has the resort and mountains sitting beautifully in the background. No. 13—on the East Course, this time—is a par 4 that requires a tee shot to an unusual island fairway. No. 18, also on the East Course, is fronted by a large water hazard and makes a great par-5 finishing hole.

MARRIOTT'S DESERT SPRINGS RESORT AND SPA

74-855 COUNTRY CLUB DR., PALM DESERT, CA 92260 (619)341-1756 *(10 mi. E of Palm Springs)*
ACCOMMODATIONS: MARRIOTT'S DESERT SPRINGS RESORT AND SPA (619)341-2211

"Oasis golf at its best" may be the most appropriate way to describe the Palms and Valley Courses at Marriott's Desert Springs. Emerald-green fairways meander around glimmering lakes, with hundreds of mature palm trees and colorful flower beds adding to the landscape. Spectacular sierras, gray at the bottom and white on top, rise in the distance to paint a contrasting background to the courses. The Palms Course was nominated by *Golf Digest* as best new resort course in 1987, and the Valley Course was a runner-up in 1988. The Palms Course brings into play twelve water hazards. They create problems on at least nine holes, but it's the waterfall on the par-3 seventeenth that makes it one of the most picturesque

> **MARRIOTT'S DESERT SPRINGS RESORT AND SPA**
> ACCESS: Restrictions on tee times
> SEASON: All year   HIGH: Feb.-Sept.
> GREEN FEES: $$$$$ (includes cart)
> REDUCED FEES: HG, LS, TW, PK
> RESERVATIONS: Nonguests 3 days
> WALKING: No   RANGE: Yes
> • **PALMS COURSE**
>   18 holes   Par 72   6761/6381/5492 yds.
>   USGA: 70.2   SLOPE: 118
>   STYLE: Traditional
> • **VALLEY COURSE**
>   18 holes   Par 72   6679/6063/5330 yds.
>   USGA: 70.4
>   STYLE: Traditional

and challenging holes anywhere. Desert Springs also has a third and very popular attraction: "The Greens," a 350-yard, eighteen-hole putting course, designed by Ted Robinson, complete with rolling fairways, trees, rough, and water hazards.

LA QUINTA HOTEL GOLF CLUB (DUNES COURSE)

50-200 AVE. VISTA BONITA, LA QUINTA, CA 92253 (619)564-7610 *(20 mi. E of Palm Springs)*
ACCOMMODATIONS: LA QUINTA HOTEL GOLF AND TENNIS RESORT (619)564-4111

The Pete Dye-designed Dunes Course at La Quinta is not very long, but it plays a lot tougher than the scorecard indicates—for reasons that you will quickly discover. It is a Dye course, all right, with seven intimidating water hazards and a multitude of bunkers, most of them very difficult. It is the kind of course where you can see the ball bouncing off the railroad ties even before you hit it. The Dunes Course has hosted many tournaments, including the PGA Club professional Championship

DUNES COURSE
18 holes   Par 72   6861/5798/5024 yds.
USGA: 67   SLOPE: 129
STYLE: Desert
ACCESS: Priority to hotel guests
SEASON: All year   HIGH: Jan.-Apr.
GREEN FEES: $$$$$ (includes cart)
REDUCED FEES: HG, LS
RESERVATIONS: Nonguests 1 day
WALKING: No   RANGE: Yes

and the California State Open. In 1986, the PGA of America selected No. 17 as the toughest seventeenth hole in the country. Naturally, this exciting course is superbly maintained, and nestled against the majestic Santa Rosa Mountains, it is a visual feast as well.

LA QUINTA HOTEL GOLF CLUB (CITRUS COURSE)

50-503 JEFFERSON ST., LA QUINTA, CA 92253 (619)564-7620 *(20 mi. SE of Palm Springs)*
ACCOMMODATIONS: LA QUINTA HOTEL GOLF AND TENNIS RESORT (619)564-4111

La Quinta's Citrus Course, which opened in 1987, is a fairly flat layout that architect Pete Dye designed and carved out of a citrus orchard. Flat does not mean dull, and that's a guarantee with a Pete Dye track. The course has generous, contoured fairways, but the large bentgrass greens are protected by approximately eighty bunkers, most of

CITRUS COURSE
18 holes   Par 72   7135/6477/5106 yds.
USGA: 70.9   SLOPE: 123
STYLE: Desert, lakes, trees
ACCESS: Priority to hotel guests
SEASON: All year   HIGH: Oct.-May
GREEN FEES: $$$$$ (includes cart)
REDUCED FEES: LS
RESERVATIONS: Same day
WALKING: No   RANGE: Yes

them quite difficult to play out. Then there are the five lakes which come into play on holes Nos. 3, 6, 13, 14, and 18. As anyone could have guessed by now, railroad ties come with them, at no extra charge. The eighteenth hole makes sure that you won't leave the Citrus Course unimpressed: the long par 4 is the number two handicap hole. The entire left side of the green is flanked by a mesmerizing and perversely attractive water hazard.

PGA WEST (JACK NICKLAUS RESORT COURSE)

56-150 PGA BLVD., LA QUINTA, CA 92253 (619)564-7429 *(20 mi. SE of Palm Springs)*

At PGA West, Jack Nicklaus wanted to create a demanding layout—you would expect that from the six-time Masters champion—but he wanted an attractive course as well. He succeeded on both counts. Although not tremendously tight, the length and contouring will challenge players of all levels. The course is long and rolls considerably over mounds and breaks, incorporating desert vegetation, waste areas, and lakes along the way, with sharp drops off the fairway. On the par-5

JACK NICKLAUS RESORT COURSE
18 holes   Par 72   7126/6001/5070 yds.
USGA: 69.2   SLOPE: 122
STYLE: Desert links, water
ACCESS: No restrictions
SEASON: All year   HIGH: Jan.-Mar.
GREEN FEES: $$$$$ (includes cart)
REDUCED FEES: HG, LS, TW
RESERVATIONS: 1 day
WALKING: At times   RANGE: Yes

fifteenth, the island green is framed by the picturesque Santa Rosa Mountains in the background. Once again, Nicklaus succeeded in creating a visually dramatic golfing challenge.

PGA WEST (STADIUM COURSE)

56-150 PGA BLVD., LA QUINTA, CA 92253 (619)564-PGAW *(20 mi. E of Palm Springs)*

TPC STADIUM GOLF COURSE
18 holes   Par 72   7261/6164/5087 yds.
USGA: 71.2   SLOPE: 130
STYLE: Desert links, water
ACCESS: No restrictions
SEASON: All year   HIGH: Jan.-Mar.
GREEN FEES: $$$$$ (includes cart)
REDUCED FEES: HG, LS, TW
RESERVATIONS: 1 day
WALKING: At times   RANGE: Yes

When Pete Dye was commissioned to design the Stadium Course at PGA West, his orders were simple: build the toughest course in the world. He did. In fact, he was so successful in fulfilling his task that, when the course was added to the Bob Hope Desert Classic in 1987, the tour pros protested so loudly that it was subsequently dropped. Still, some pros liked it. That same year, at the 1987 Skins Game, Lee Trevino holed a 6-iron worth $175,000 at the rocky, island-green seventeenth. The course has eight lakes covering thirty-five acres of water, and its bunkers are the most talked about and photographed in the world of golf. The pit that borders the left of No. 16's green is twenty feet deep! PGA West's Stadium is an unbelievable course. With holes named "Double Trouble" (No. 5), "Amen" (No. 6), and "Eternity" (No. 11), just reading the scorecard requires nerves of steel (or at least graphite). From the white tees, the course is a lot of fun to play. It is fairly short, and a solid three-wood will do just fine off the tee. Shot placement, however, must be perfect. The greens are tournament-fast and true, and all you need to do is pretend that you're playing in the Skins Game.

TPC STADIUM GOLF COURSE, HOLE NO. 9

THE FIRST NINE HOLES CONCLUDE WITH A TESTY PAR 4: THE HOLE CAN BE PLAYED ANYWHERE FROM 450 YARDS TO 315 YARDS. REGARDLESS, THE APPROACH SHOT MUST CATCH A GREEN EXTREMELY WELL DEFENDED BY BUNKERS ON THE LEFT AND WATER ON THE RIGHT.

HOLE NO. 9, "REFLECTION"

HOLES

HOLE NO. 7, "BLACK HOLE"

DESERT DUNES GOLF CLUB

19300 PALM DR., DESERT HOT SPRINGS, CA 92240 (619)329-2941 *(9 mi. from Palm Springs)*

Robert Trent Jones, Jr.'s, work at Desert Dunes received immediate acclaim. Only two years after its opening in 1989, it was already listed by *Golf Digest* as one of the seventy-five best public courses in the nation. Jones succeeded in creating a natural course, incorporating many desert features from the surrounding areas. The layout is inspired by traditional Scottish links, but the local sand dunes and mature tamarisk trees give it a real desert look. The 517-yard, par-5 sixteenth, for example, combines a large lake with rocks, a waterfall, mesquite bushes, sand, and cactus; the result is a memorable and playable challenge.

> **DESERT DUNES GOLF CLUB**
> 18 holes Par 72 6876/6205/5359 yds.
> USGA: 69.3 SLOPE: 121
> STYLE: Desert links
> ACCESS: No restrictions
> SEASON: All year HIGH: Nov.-Apr.
> GREEN FEES: $$$$$ (includes cart)
> REDUCED FEES: LS, TW
> RESERVATIONS: 1 week
> WALKING: No RANGE: Yes

FURNACE CREEK INN AND RANCH RESORT

DEATH VALLEY, CA 92328 (619)786-2301 *(140 mi. W of Las Vegas)*
ACCOMMODATIONS: FURNACE CREEK INN AND RANCH RESORT (619)786-2345

In the heart of Death Valley, at 214 feet below sea level, sits the lowest golf course in the world. Furnace Creek, built in 1930, is a cool oasis of greenery in the middle of the stark dryness of the desert. The course is actually very pretty, with many water hazards and a beautiful grove of mature palm trees bordering several holes. It is not a long course, but it is very pleasant to play, especially given the unusual setting. Of special interest to golf "historians," Furnace Creek was one of the first all-grass courses in southern California. This little gem should not be confused with the "Devil's Golf Course," a sightseeing attraction of craggy black rocks just a few miles away!

> **FURNACE CREEK GOLF COURSE**
> 18 holes Par 70 6036/5830/5203 yds.
> USGA: 66.6 SLOPE: 101
> STYLE: Traditional
> ACCESS: Priority to hotel guests
> SEASON: All year HIGH: Feb.-Mar.
> GREEN FEES: $$
> RESERVATIONS: 3 months
> WALKING: Yes RANGE: Yes

RIO BRAVO RESORT GOLF CLUB

11200 LAKE MING RD., BAKERSFIELD, CA 93306 (805)872-5000 *(12 mi. E of Bakersfield)*
ACCOMMODATIONS: RIO BRAVO RESORT (805)872-5000

Rio Bravo's course, built on rolling terrain in the foothills of the Tehachapi Mountains, offers two challenges. First is the diversity of shots it demands—uphill, downhill, and sidehill, there is never a dull moment. No. 11, a par-5 uphill and sidehill, measures 616 yards from the blue markers. It is nicknamed "Big Bertha." The other test comes from the large, bentgrass greens, the pride of the superintendent, who will challenge you to find any better in the U.S. With lateral water hazards on Nos. 7 and 8 and some well-placed bunkers, this Robert Muir Graves design has hosted many California Opens and PGA Tour qualifyings since it opened in 1982.

> **RIO BRAVO RESORT GOLF CLUB**
> 18 holes Par 72 7018/6555/5704 yds.
> USGA: 70.9 SLOPE: 122
> STYLE: Hills
> ACCESS: Hotel guests only
> SEASON: All year HIGH: Mar.-May
> GREEN FEES: $$$ (includes cart)
> REDUCED FEES: HG, TW
> RESERVATIONS: 1 year
> WALKING: No RANGE: Yes

LA PURISIMA GOLF COURSE

13

3455 STATE HWY. 246, LOMPOC, CA 93436 (805)735-8395 *(40 mi. N of Santa Barbara)*

La Purisima is a championship layout situated on three hundred acres of gently rolling hills near the beautiful Lompoc Valley in Santa Barbara County. Architect Robert Muir Graves did not carve the course out of the terrain; instead, he simply laid it according to the natural features of the ranch land. Oak and eucalyptus border the course, and three lakes add to the beauty. Built with the goal of "pure golf" in mind, it is a difficult course kept in tournament shape. *California Golf* ranked it number two in the state.

LA PURISIMA GOLF COURSE
18 holes Par 72   7105/6657/5763 yds.
USGA: 72.8   SLOPE: 132
STYLE: Rolling hills
ACCESS: No restrictions
SEASON: All year   HIGH: Summer
GREEN FEES: $$$
REDUCED FEES: WD, LS, TW
RESERVATIONS: 1 week
WALKING: Yes   RANGE: Yes

SANDPIPER GOLF COURSE

14

7925 HOLLISTER AVE., GOLETA, CA 93117 (805)968-1541 *(8 mi. N of Santa Barbara)*

SANDPIPER GOLF COURSE
18 holes   Par 72   7053/6645/5766 yds.
USGA: 72.5   SLOPE: 126
STYLE: Oceanside
ACCESS: No restrictions
SEASON: All year   HIGH: June-Oct.
GREEN FEES: $$$
REDUCED FEES: WD, TW, PK
RESERVATIONS: 1 week
WALKING: Yes   RANGE: Yes

The Sandpiper course is built right on the ocean just outside Santa Barbara. The clubhouse offers a panoramic view of the Pacific, the fairways, and the lake on No. 18. Bill Bell designed this championship course in 1982, and it has since been consistently ranked as one of the nation's top public courses. Favorite holes include No. 11, a steep, downhill par 3 with an oceanside green, No. 13, a par 5 that requires a third shot over a deep, oceanside barranca, and the par-3 No. 18 over a lake. It is so scenic and so good that it is often compared to Pebble Beach itself.

HALF MOON BAY GOLF LINKS 15

2000 FAIRWAY DR., HALF MOON BAY, CA 94019 (415)726-4438 *(25 mi. S of San Francisco)*

HALF MOON BAY GOLF LINKS
18 holes   Par 72   7116/6447/5694 yds.
USGA: 71   SLOPE: 130
STYLE: Hills, oceanside
ACCESS: No restrictions
SEASON: All year   HIGH: Summer
GREEN FEES: $$$$$ (includes cart)
REDUCED FEES: WD, TW
RESERVATIONS: 1 week
WALKING: No   RANGE: No

The Half Moon Bay Golf Links is situated on land bordering the Pacific Ocean, with coastal hills as a backdrop in the east. The Arnold Palmer-designed course runs through an attractive mix of Cape Cod and northern California-style homes that seem quite natural in this misty setting. The course is long and demanding at times, combining hills, barrancas, and water hazards to test a golfer's skill. The par-3 seventeenth and the par-4 eighteenth are reminiscent of the famous Pebble Beach Golf Links fifty miles down the coast.

PASATIEMPO GOLF CLUB 16

18 CLUBHOUSE RD., SANTA CRUZ, CA 95060 (408)459-9155 *(75 mi. S of San Fransisco)*

This masterful layout was designed in 1929 by Scottish architect Alistair MacKenzie, who eventually retired in a home alongside the course. He is also credited with designing Cypress Point, just a few miles down the coast, and Augusta National, in Georgia. The classic course, built on rolling, mountainside hills, has beautiful views of Monterey Bay and the Santa Cruz Mountains. Fairways are somewhat narrow and framed by big oak trees, while the greens are large and well-protected by deep-faced bunkers. MacKenzie declared No. 16 to be his "favorite hole in all of golf."

PASATIEMPO GOLF CLUB
18 holes   Par 71   6483/6154/5647 yds.
USGA: 71.4   SLOPE: 134
STYLE: Rolling hills, trees
ACCESS: Restrictions on weekends
SEASON: All year   HIGH: Summer
GREEN FEES: $$$$
REDUCED FEES: WD, TW
RESERVATIONS: 1 week
WALKING: Yes   RANGE: Yes

PASATIEMPO: HOLE NO. 9

The Monterey Peninsula

Located on the Pacific coast about 120 miles south of San Francisco, the Monterey Peninsula has the unique privilege of being home to seven great golf courses in an area just a few miles wide. After leaving Highway 101, this seaside garden of golf is accessible by driving down a private and scenic toll road, the Seventeen Mile Drive. The road first winds its way through wooded hills of pine and eucalyptus, then follows the jagged shoreline of the peninsula alongside the beach and the crashing ocean surf. Soon, each turn of the road reveals another gem of a course: the Links at Spanish Bay, the two courses at the Monterey Peninsula Country Club, Spyglass Hill, Poppy Hills Golf Course, the

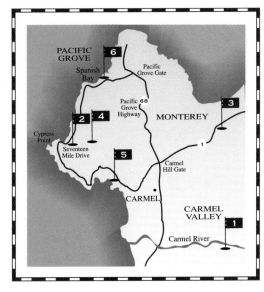

Cypress Point Club, and the legendary and world-famous Pebble Beach Golf Links. With the exception of the Monterey Peninsula Country Club and Cypress Point Club courses, all of these championship layouts are accessible to the public.

Just outside Pebble Beach's gate, the quaint village of Carmel-by-the-Sea offers delightful shopping and dining, and a short drive down the coast leads to the spectacular and magical vistas of Big Sur. The peninsula benefits from temperate, Mediterranean-like weather: temperatures average a cool 57 degrees during the winter months, but afternoons are warm, and golf can be enjoyed all year. Still, surprises abound. Fog can be a frequent summer companion, and occasional winter storms descend off the Pacific from the northwest to transform the normally peaceful links into grueling but no less beautiful golfing experiences.

Carmel Valley Ranch Golf Club   1

1 Old Ranch Rd., Carmel, CA 93923 (800)4-Carmel *(6 mi. E of Carmel)*
ACCOMMODATIONS: Carmel Valley Ranch Resort (408)625-9500

Set high in the warm hills above Carmel, this Pete Dye course rises and falls, bends left and right, and offers shotmaking challenges of every kind. The front nine is rather narrow and flat compared with the back. After the turn, there are some severe changes of elevation, and it becomes a game of uphill, downhill, and sidehill lies. Carmel Valley is often overshadowed by the likes of nearby Pebble Beach, but it remains a fine test in its own right. The course is kept in immaculate condition, and the surrounding hills are simply enchanting.

Carmel Valley Ranch Golf Club
18 holes   Par 70   6515/6055/5582 yds.
USGA: 67.8   SLOPE: 119
STYLE: Hills
ACCESS: Hotel guests only
SEASON: All year   HIGH: Apr.-Oct.
GREEN FEES: $$$$ (includes cart)
REDUCED FEES: TW, PK
RESERVATIONS: Recommended
WALKING: No   RANGE: Yes

SPYGLASS HILL GOLF COURSE

STEVENSON DRIVE, PEBBLE BEACH, CA 93953 (408)624-3811
ACCOMMODATIONS: PEBBLE BEACH RESORTS (800)654-9300

SPYGLASS HILL GOLF COURSE
18 holes Par 72 6810/6277/5556 yds.
USGA: 73.1 SLOPE: 135
STYLE: Oceanside, woods
ACCESS: No restrictions
SEASON: All year HIGH: Aug.-Nov.
GREEN FEES: $$$$$ (includes cart)
REDUCED FEES: HG, TW, PK
RESERVATIONS: Nonguests 1 day
WALKING: Yes RANGE: Yes

This Robert Trent Jones design was beautiful but controversial when it opened in 1963. Alterations have settled the controversy, but the beauty remains just the same. No. 1, the "Treasure Island" hole, starts deep in the woods and terminates six hundred yards later with an island green lost in a sea of sand. The next few holes are some of the most memorable anywhere: they play around sandy areas right by the Pacific Ocean. The par-4 fourth, for example, has a green tucked between natural grassy mounds covered with dreaded ice plant. For added fun, the putting surface slopes away from incoming approach shots. With the sixth hole, the course returns to the protection of Del Monte Forest's hillsides. Most fairways are tight, and pine trees often seem to stand in the line of play. Spyglass is long, technical, and some think it is too unforgiving; but one thing is sure: it remains one of Robert Trent Jones's best achievements and, certainly, one of the most difficult and beautiful tests of golf that the public can play .

OLD DEL MONTE GOLF COURSE

1300 SYLVAN RD., MONTEREY, CA 93940 (408)373-2436 *(1 mi. from downtown Monterey)*
ACCOMMODATIONS: CALL GOLF COURSE FOR INFORMATION.

OLD DEL MONTE GOLF COURSE
18 holes Par 72 6278/6007/5431 yds.
USGA: 68.7 SLOPE: 119
STYLE: Traditional
ACCESS: No restrictions
SEASON: All year HIGH: Mar.-Oct.
GREEN FEES: $$$
REDUCED FEES: HG, LS, TW
RESERVATIONS: 2 months
WALKING: Yes RANGE: No

Founded in 1897, the Old Del Monte Golf Course is the oldest golf course on the Monterey Peninsula—and the oldest course in operation west of the Mississippi. Located inland, it is a lot easier than the famous courses down the road. It has small greens, rather narrow fairways, and no water hazards, but it is adorned with beautiful California oak and Monterey pine. There are splendid views of the foothills, and the course record—62—is co-held by Ben Hogan, Walter Hagen, and Ken Venturi.

THE POPPY HILLS GOLF COURSE

3200 LOPEZ RD., PEBBLE BEACH, CA 93953 (408)625-2154

In 1986, Robert Trent Jones, Jr., was commissioned to create yet another world-class course on the Monterey Peninsula. Apparently, Jones, Jr., did not want his creation to pale in comparison to his father's Spyglass masterpiece, and he made sure to use the hills and pine trees to the proper effect. The fairways climb, descend and bend through the wooded terrain, and lots of sand can be found by the unsuspecting player. In addition

THE POPPY HILLS GOLF COURSE
18 holes Par 72 6865/6288/5433 yds.
USGA: 71.7 SLOPE: 134
STYLE: Hills, woods
ACCESS: No restrictions
SEASON: All year HIGH: Mar.-Oct.
GREEN FEES: $$$$$
RESERVATIONS: 1 month
WALKING: Yes RANGE: Yes

the greens are larger and more undulating than on the Peninsula's other courses, so that putting is more of a factor here. Poppy Hills has now replaced Cypress Point in the rotation of the AT&T Pebble Beach National Pro-Am. The course is already ranked among the very best in California and the United States. Indeed, as the still young layout matures, it will surely earn the same recognition as its distinctive and famous neighbors.

PEBBLE BEACH GOLF LINKS: HOLE NO. 18

PEBBLE BEACH GOLF LINKS

SEVENTEEN MILE DR., MONTEREY, CA 93953 (408)624-3811
ACCOMMODATIONS: PEBBLE BEACH RESORTS (800)654-9300

PEBBLE BEACH GOLF LINKS
18 holes   Par 72   6799/6357/5197 yds.
USGA: 72.7   SLOPE: 139
STYLE: Oceanside, links
ACCESS: No restrictions
SEASON: All year   HIGH: Aug.-Nov.
GREEN FEES: $$$$$ (includes cart)
REDUCED FEES: HG, TW, PK
RESERVATIONS: Nonguests 1 day
WALKING: Yes   RANGE: Yes

Jack Nicklaus has called Pebble Beach his favorite course. Many think it is the best in the country and certainly the most beautiful. It is a regular in *Golf Digest*'s prestigious listing of America's hundred greatest courses, locking in a spot in the top ten. Golf history has been made here, too. The first two U.S. Opens on the course were won by Jack Nicklaus and Tom Watson, and most of us recall Watson's chip-in at No. 17 on his way to winning the 1982 Open title. Pebble Beach sits by Carmel Bay and probably has the most scenic setting in all of golf. The course is difficult, but no matter how you play, it is the golfer's experience of a lifetime.

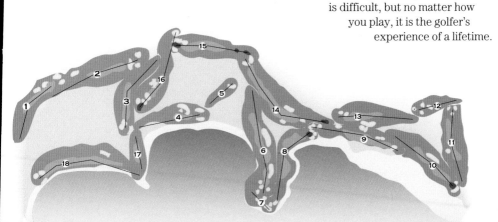

THE LINKS AT SPANISH BAY

SEVENTEEN MILE DR., MONTEREY, CA 93953 (408)624-3811
ACCOMMODATIONS: PEBBLE BEACH RESORTS (800)654-9300

Three of golf's most prominent figures—Tom Watson, former USGA president Sandy Tatum, and Robert Trent Jones, Jr.—collaborated in designing Spanish Bay, and the result is one of the finest links courses in America. The land available to the designers was perfect links terrain: a gently rolling, oceanside, windswept area of sand dunes and marshes. All that was needed were the knowledge, experience, and inspiration of these three golf personalities to create the right course for the right place.

> **THE LINKS AT SPANISH BAY**
> 18 holes Par 72   6820/6078/5287 yds.
> USGA: 70.8   SLOPE: 133
> STYLE: Scottish links
> ACCESS: No restrictions
> SEASON: All year   HIGH: Aug.-Nov.
> GREEN FEES: $$$$$ (includes cart)
> REDUCED FEES: HG, TW, PK
> RESERVATIONS: Nonguests, 2 months
> WALKING: Yes   RANGE: Yes

The Scottish influence can be observed everywhere on the course. The small greens are nestled between dunes, pot bunkers hide behind grassy mounds, and tees, fairways, and greens were seeded with fescue grasses to provide the firm playing surface found on the old-world links.

To play Spanish Bay requires the imagination and ability to fashion shots through the wind and along the rolling dunes. Patience is also of the essence here. As on many Scottish courses (and life in general!), a fine shot can fall prey to the unexpected—in this instance a gust of wind, a bad bounce off a mound, or a thicket of heavy grass. The oceanside holes at Spanish Bay offer splendid views of the crashing Pacific, and surfers are almost within reach of a solid drive. The inland holes are bordered by tall pine, which bring to the course the elegant look of a classic.

THE LINKS AT SPANISH BAY

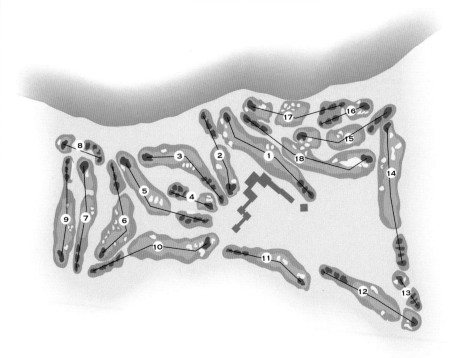

FOUNTAINGROVE RESORT AND COUNTRY CLUB   17

1525 FOUNTAINGROVE PKWY., SANTA ROSA, CA 95403 (707)579-GOLF *(5 min. NE of Santa Rosa)*
ACCOMMODATIONS: FOUNTAINGROVE RESORT AND COUNTRY CLUB (707)544-5100

Located in Sonoma County's wine country, Fountaingrove was built on the grounds of a former ranch. The picturesque course is routed around a large lake, wetlands, and a series of hills wooded with mature oaks. The beauty of this natural site inspires reverence; in fact, Nos. 13 through 16 are called "Amen Corner." But perhaps the seventeenth says it best. This intimidating, 220-yard par 3 plays down from a hill, over a finger of the lake, and onto a small, dangerous waterside green.

FOUNTAINGROVE COUNTRY CLUB
18 holes   Par 72   6797/6380/5644 yds.
USGA: 70.9   SLOPE: 128
STYLE: Rolling hills
ACCESS: Restrictions on weekends
SEASON: All year   HIGH: Apr.-Oct.
GREEN FEES: $$$$ (includes cart)
REDUCED FEES: WD, TW, PK
RESERVATIONS: 1 week
WALKING: No   RANGE: Yes

CHARDONNAY CLUB   18

2555 JAMESON CANYON RD., NAPA, CA 94558 (707)257-8950 *(50 mi. NE of San Francisco)*

The Chardonnay Club became an immediate favorite in northern California when it opened in 1987. Architect Algie Pulley, Jr., made the bold decision to route a links-style course through the local vineyards. The result is an exciting and difficult layout that also brings in hilly terrain, lakes, and rock outcroppings. A creek runs throughout, and trouble abounds everywhere. The course's twenty-seven holes are being expanded to thirty-six. Eighteen will become private, but the newly named East Course (formerly the Lakes and Meadows Courses) will remain open to the public.

EAST COURSE
18 holes   Par 71   6884/6024/5162 yds.
USGA: 68.8   SLOPE: 115
STYLE: Links, rolling hills
ACCESS: Restrictions on tee times
SEASON: All year   HIGH: June-Oct.
GREEN FEES: $$$ (includes cart)
REDUCED FEES: WD, LS, TW, PK
RESERVATIONS: Nonmembers 1 week
WALKING: No   RANGE: Yes

CHARDONNAY CLUB

SILVERADO COUNTRY CLUB AND RESORT

1600 ATLAS PEAK RD., NAPA, CA 94558 (707)257-0200 *(52 mi. NE of San Francisco)*
ACCOMMODATIONS: SILVERADO COUNTRY CLUB AND RESORT (800)532-0500

SILVERADO COUNTRY CLUB AND RESORT
ACCESS: Hotel guests only
SEASON: All year   HIGH: Apr.-Oct.
GREEN FEES: $$$$$ (includes cart)
REDUCED FEES: HG, LS, TW, PK
RESERVATIONS: At time of hotel booking
WALKING: Members only   RANGE: Yes
• **NORTH COURSE**
    18 holes   Par 72   6896/6351/5857 yds.
    USGA: 70.9   SLOPE: 126
    STYLE: Traditional
• **SOUTH COURSE**
    18 holes   Par 72   6632/6213/5672 yds.
    USGA: 70.5   SLOPE: 124
    STYLE: Traditional

SILVERADO COUNTRY CLUB

Silverado's two eighteen-hole courses were designed by Robert Trent Jones, Jr. Stately oak, redwood, and two-hundred-year-old eucalyptus trees line the fairways of these park-like layouts. Although the North Course is longer, the South Course has some virtues of its own: it goes around hillier terrain, and its fairways and greens are more contoured—sometimes severely so. The eighteenth hole is a five-hundred-yard, par-5 dogleg with a huge bunker across the front of the green. The impressive Silverado Mansion, built in 1870, overlooks the putting surface.

BODEGA HARBOUR GOLF LINKS

20

21301 HERON DR., BODEGA BAY, CA 94923 (707)875-3538 *(65 mi. N of San Francisco)*

The town of Bodega Bay, about an hour and a half north of San Francisco on the beautiful Sonoma coast, is already known as the location for Alfred Hitchcock's film, *The Birds*. It is also the site of an exciting golf course designed by Robert Trent Jones, Jr.: the Bodega Harbour Golf Links. The first four holes take the player straight uphill to the course's highest elevation. Getting there, however, is painfully earned. Many pot bunkers, sidehill lies, and severely contoured greens make par an elusive

HOLE NO. 5: VIEW FROM HELL'S CORNER

goal on this stretch. No. 4 is an adventure in itself. At 371 yards from the men's tee, it requires a long and accurate uphill drive to a small landing area framed by sandtraps and rock outcrops. The approach shot then plays steeply uphill to a narrow green with trouble on the right. At No. 5 come the rewards—at last! The tee offers spectacular vistas of the gorgeous Bodega Bay and miles of rugged Pacific coastline. The hole itself is a 448-yard, par-5, double dogleg that twists its way downhill. A conservative drive will avoid the bunkers and mounds of "Hell's Corner," setting up the ball for easy downhill second and third shots. After adding up the score on the first four holes, a birdie might come in handy here. Don't let the view distract you, though. The back nine has softer contours and larger greens, but there are thirty-eight bunkers and plenty of difficult approaches. The last three holes bring a dramatic conclusion to this unique course. Playing over a seaside marsh behind the beach, the intimidating Nos. 16, 17, and 18, known as "The Pit," require shots with good carry and great accuracy. Playing The Pit in par is a crowning achievement to an exhilarating round of golf. Beware Mother Nature, however. This is northern California, and fog or wind can add unexpected twists to this wonderfully scenic and challenging course.

BODEGA HARBOUR HOLE NO. 5
THE DOWNHILL FIFTH HOLE IS 491 YARDS LONG FROM THE CHAMPIONSHIP TEES. FOLLOWING A STRAIGHT, 200-YARD DRIVE TO THE CORNER PLATEAU,

THE GREEN CAN BE REACHED IN TWO WITH A WELL-STRUCK FAIRWAY WOOD SHOT. BUT WATCH OUT! A FIELD OF BUNKERS GUARDS THE TARGET 90 YARDS AHEAD OF THE PUTTING SURFACE.

BODEGA HARBOUR GOLF LINKS
18 holes Par 70 6220/5630/4749 yds.
USGA: 69.2 SLOPE: 125
STYLE: Hills, oceanside
ACCESS: Restrictions on tee times
SEASON: All year HIGH: May-Oct.
GREEN FEES: $$$
REDUCED FEES: WD, LS, TW, PK
RESERVATIONS: 2 months
WALKING: Yes RANGE: No

NORTHSTAR-AT-TAHOE

21

HWY. 267 AND NORTHSTAR DR., TRUCKEE, CA 96160 (916)587-0290 *(40 mi. W of Reno, NV)*
ACCOMMODATIONS: NORTHSTAR-AT-TAHOE (800)533-6787

NORTHSTAR-AT-TAHOE
18 holes   Par 72   6897/6337/5470 yds.
USGA: 69.3   SLOPE: 130
STYLE: Tree-lined fairways, lakes
ACCESS: No restrictions
SEASON: May-Oct.   HIGH: July-Aug.
GREEN FEES: $$$
REDUCED FEES: HG, LS, TW, PK
RESERVATIONS: 3 weeks
WALKING: At times   RANGE: Yes

Northstar-at-Tahoe was designed by California architect Robert Muir Graves. On the championship course's front nine, players enjoy wide fairways but encounter heavily contoured greens. However, on the back nine they find tight fairways beautifully lined with pine and aspen trees, but easier greens. Mountain streams and ponds come into play on fourteen holes! No. 17 has a huge chasm running the length of the fairway, and your best drive will be needed to clear it. At an elevation of six thousand feet, the course was built on an old Basque sheepherding area, and remnants of buildings from the early 1900s are still around.

EDGEWOOD TAHOE GOLF COURSE

22

HWY. 50 AND LAKE PKWY., STATELINE, NV 89449 (702)588-3566 *(60 mi. from Reno)*
ACCOMMODATIONS: CALL GOLF COURSE FOR INFORMATION

EDGEWOOD TAHOE GOLF COURSE
18 holes   Par 72   7491/6544/5749 yds.
USGA: 70.9   SLOPE: 128
STYLE: Woods, lakes
ACCESS: No restrictions
SEASON: May-Sept.   HIGH: June-Sept.
GREEN FEES: $$$$$ (includes cart)
RESERVATIONS: 2 weeks
WALKING: Yes   RANGE: Yes

This wonderful golf course was created by George Fazio on beautiful meadows adjoining Lake Tahoe. Opened in 1968, the course has received many honors, including membership in the exclusive *Golf Digest* top hundred. The extremely scenic and difficult layout is heavily wooded, with several varieties of pine lining the fairways; lakes and streams come into play on twelve holes. No. 17 is a par 3 that uses Lake Tahoe's beach as a hazard, and No. 18 has a green tucked between a pond and the lake itself. Four sets of tees make the challenge suitable to all, and everyone can share the sight of the majestic Sierra Nevada Mountain Range. Edgewood is a mandatory stop in the Tahoe area.

N
E
V
A
D
A

INCLINE VILLAGE GOLF RESORT

23

955 FAIRWAY BLVD., INCLINE VILLAGE, NV 89450 (702)832-1144 *(30 mi. SW of Reno)*

INCLINE VILLAGE GOLF RESORT
ACCESS: Restrictions on tee times
SEASON: May-Nov.   HIGH: July-Aug.
GREEN FEES: $$$$$ (includes cart)
REDUCED FEES: TW
RESERVATIONS: Within season
WALKING: Yes   RANGE: Yes
• **CHAMPIONSHIP COURSE**
18 holes   Par 72   6910/6446/5350 yds.
USGA: 70.5   SLOPE: 124
STYLE: Mountain, water
• **EXECUTIVE COURSE**
18 holes   Par 58   3513/3002 yds.
USGA: 56.6   SLOPE: 94
STYLE: Mountain, water

At an altitude of 6,400 feet, Incline Village's 6,910 yards from the back tees is less daunting than at sea level, but Robert Trent Jones, Sr., made up for the thin air when he built this Championship Course. A genius at tempting and taunting golfers, he designed the course's sloping greens to accommodate defensive pin positions; then, for good measure, he framed them with water. On a cheerier note, there's the eighteen-hole, par-58 Executive Course nearby. Designed in 1971 by Jones, Jr., it offers the illusion of relief—until the numerous water hazards come into play. Both courses are classics, and there are wonderful views of Lake Tahoe to keep you sane.

THE LEGACY GOLF CLUB

24

130 PAR EXCELLENCE DR., HENDERSON, NV 89016 (702)897-2200 *(7 mi. SE of Las Vegas)*

THE LEGACY GOLF CLUB
18 holes   Par 72   7150/6211/5340 yds.
USGA: 69.1   SLOPE: 118
STYLE: Desert links
ACCESS: No restrictions
SEASON: All year
HIGH: Feb.-May/Sept.-Nov.
GREEN FEES: $$$$ (includes cart)
REDUCED FEES: WD, LS
RESERVATIONS: 2 months with credit card
WALKING: No   RANGE: Yes

The Legacy, designed by Arthur Hills and opened in 1989, is located in Green Valley, an exclusive suburb of Las Vegas. The style here is clearly Scottish, and Hills created undulating fairways dotted with mounds and seeded with a blend of selected grasses. In sections of the rough, two-foot-deep "love grass" contrasts beautifully with the surrounding desert landscape, especially the lava rock of the nearby Black Mountains. The difficult Nos. 11, 12, and 13 form the "Devil's Triangle," where Las Vegas visitors can try their luck.

THE LEGACY

ANGEL PARK GOLF CLUB   25

100 S. RAMPART BLVD., LAS VEGAS, NV 89128 (702)254-GOLF *(10 mi. W of the Strip)*

ANGEL PARK GOLF CLUB
ACCESS: No restrictions
SEASON: All year   HIGH: Mar.-May
GREEN FEES: $$$ (includes cart)
REDUCED FEES: LS, TW
RESERVATIONS: 2 weeks with credit card
WALKING: No   RANGE: Yes
- **PALM COURSE**
  18 holes   Par 71   6743/5634/4790 yds.
  USGA: 66.7   SLOPE: 114
  STYLE: Hills
- **MOUNTAIN COURSE**
  18 holes   Par 71   6722/5751/5147 yds.
  USGA: 67.8   SLOPE: 116
  STYLE: Hills

Nestled against the breathtaking Spring Mountain and Red Rock Canyon, the courses at Angel Park overlook Las Vegas. Designed by Arnold Palmer, the Palm Course and the Mountain Course both use approximately fifty bunkers and five lakes as obstacles. The Palm Course's eighth is a par-5 double dogleg that plays over two canyons, while on the Mountain Course, it is the 529-yard No. 17 that features the canyon carry-over. Opened in 1989 and 1990, the courses are still maturing, while a tree-planting program continues. Another attraction is the 1,392-yard championship putting course, with bunkers, a creek, lakes, and waterfalls affecting play.

DESERT INN GOLF CLUB   26

3145 LAS VEGAS BLVD. S., LAS VEGAS, NV 89109 (702)733-4290 *(in Las Vegas)*
ACCOMMODATIONS: DESERT INN HOTEL AND CASINO (702)733-4444

This celebrated Las Vegas layout first opened in 1952 and was redesigned in 1983. The course has a rich tradition. Through the years, many celebrities have played here, including famous entertainers, Tour professionals, and United States Presidents. It is also the only place to annually host PGA, Senior PGA, and LPGA Tour events. The eighteen holes are located near the Strip, but because they are heavily wooded with mature trees, it is hard to tell that you are in the desert. With many trees, sharp doglegs, an abundance of ocean-sand bunkers, and seven water holes, the course can be quite challenging. In fact, No. 7 has been rated one of the most difficult par 3s on the PGA and Senior PGA Tours.

DESERT INN GOLF CLUB
18 holes   Par 72   7111/6632/5809 yds.
USGA: 73   SLOPE: 127
STYLE: Traditional
ACCESS: Priority to hotel guests
SEASON: All year
HIGH: Jan.-June/Sept.-Nov.
GREEN FEES: $$$$$ (includes cart)
REDUCED FEES: HG, LS, TW, PK
RESERVATIONS: Guests 1 year
WALKING: No   RANGE: Yes

DUNES HOTEL CASINO AND COUNTRY CLUB   27

3650 LAS VEGAS BLVD. S., LAS VEGAS, NV 89109 (702)737-4748 *(in Las Vegas)*
ACCOMMODATIONS: DUNES HOTEL CASINO AND COUNTRY CLUB (800)243-8637

The Dunes Country Club's eighteen-hole championship course, nicknamed the "Emerald Green," was designed by Bill Bell in 1965. The course plays long due to the little roll allowed by the lush fairways. There are five large lakes, with water coming into play on six holes. Palm trees add to the beauty as well as to the difficulty of this oasis-like golf course. The eighty bunkers are reasonably easy, and the greens are generally large, but the course is still challenging. The 444-yard, par-4, dogleg-right eighteenth is a great finishing hole.

DUNES COUNTRY CLUB COURSE
18 holes   Par 72   7078/6533/6163 yds.
USGA: 71.2   SLOPE: 125
STYLE: Traditional
ACCESS: No restrictions
SEASON: All year   HIGH: Jan.-Nov.
GREEN FEES: $$$$$ (includes cart)
REDUCED FEES: WD, HG, PK
RESERVATIONS: 3 months
WALKING: No   RANGE: No

PAINTED DESERT

5555 PAINTED MIRAGE WAY, LAS VEGAS, NV 89129 (702)645-2568 *(in Las Vegas)*

Located only seventeen miles from the Las Vegas Strip, Painted Desert's target-style course was designed by Jay Morrish and opened in 1987. The course is aptly named, for the desert is a predominant feature, with rocks, dunes, and waste areas bordering almost every hole. There is also a fair—and sometimes unfair—amount of sand: the 490-yard, par-5 fifth counts no less than eighteen bunkers, while the 395-yard, par-4 ninth features "only" sixteen. Water comes into play on four holes. At the short but spectacular par-4 No. 13, your tee shot must carry Lone Mountain Lake; on the other side, the diminutive fairway reminds you of the true meaning of the words "target golf."

PAINTED DESERT
18 holes   Par 72   6840/6323/5711 yds.
USGA: 70.9   SLOPE: 121
STYLE: Desert, target-style
ACCESS: No restrictions
SEASON: All year
HIGH: Sept.-May/Dec.-Jan.
GREEN FEES: $$$ (includes cart)
REDUCED FEES: LS, TW
RESERVATIONS: 5 days
WALKING: No   RANGE: Yes

EMERALD RIVER RESORT AND COUNTRY CLUB

1155 W. CASINO DR., LAUGHLIN, NV 89029 (702)298-0061 *(86 mi. S of Las Vegas)*

The banks of the Colorado River and some desert bluffs studded with cactus provide the setting for Emerald River's spectacular golf course. Some traditional-style holes run by the river, but farther up, on the bluffs, the course changes to target-style fairways. In between, two par 3s, each with a seventy-five-foot drop, give the player a restful but memorable pause. Dick Ault and Tom Clark designed a tough one here—and a slope rating of 144 from the back tees is there to prove it. In fact, Emerald River is the toughest course in Nevada, and one of five tied for eighth most difficult in the southwest. However, higher handicappers should take advantage of the four tee-box system to really enjoy themselves. They can play the course at about 5,900 yards from the forward/middle tees.

EMERALD RIVER GOLF COURSE
18 holes   Par 72   6809/6296/5205 yds.
USGA: 70.7   SLOPE: 136
STYLE: Desert
ACCESS: No restrictions
SEASON: All year   HIGH: Feb.-May/Sept.-Nov.
GREEN FEES: $$$$ (includes cart)
REDUCED FEES: WD, HG, LS, PK
RESERVATIONS: 1 week
WALKING: No   RANGE: Yes

PEPPERMILL PALMS GOLF COURSE

1137 MESQUITE BLVD., MESQUITE, NV 89024 (800)621-0187, EXT. 3777 *(76 mi. NE of Las Vegas)*
ACCOMMODATIONS: PEPPERMILL RESORT HOTEL AND CASINO (800)621-0187

William Hull used every opportunity offered by the desert terrain to lay out the course at Peppermill. The landscape includes steep hills, deep canyons, and desert rock sculptures—a rather inhospitable environment for fairways and greens. The architect softened the layout by adding twenty-seven acres of lakes and big palm trees to create a lush golf oasis. The front nine is fairly open, but the back nine is narrow and takes no prisoners. The par-3 fourteenth is a complete

PEPPERMILL PALMS GOLF COURSE
18 holes   Par 72   7022/6284/5162 yds.
USGA: 71.2   SLOPE: 130
STYLE: Desert, steep hills
ACCESS: No restrictions
SEASON: All year
GREEN FEES: $$$ (includes cart)
REDUCED FEES: WD, HG
RESERVATIONS: Nonguests 1 week
WALKING: No   RANGE: Yes

carry over a deep canyon, while the 547-yard, par-5 fifteenth tees off from a hill 150 feet above the fairway! Peppermill's verdant expanses contrast strikingly with the stark desert surroundings. They served as the site of the 1991 Nevada State Seniors Championship.

TOKATEE GOLF CLUB 31

54947 McKENZIE HWY., BLUE RIVER, OR 97413 (503)822-3220, (800)452-6376 *(47 mi. E of Eugene)*

TOKATEE GOLF CLUB
18 holes   Par 72   6817/6245/5651 yds.
USGA: 69.7   SLOPE: 119
STYLE: Woods
ACCESS: No restrictions
SEASON: Feb.-Nov.   HIGH: Summer
GREEN FEES: $$
RESERVATIONS: Within season
WALKING: Yes   RANGE: Yes

Tokatee, a Chinook word meaning "place of restful beauty," sits in the foothills of the magnificent McKenzie River Valley. It is surrounded by mountain peaks, including the snow-capped Three Sisters in the distance. The course was the dream of Nat Giustina, a Eugene lumberman who loved the splendid river setting and who also loved golf. This is golf at its most natural, with simple design elements provided by the site: there are only eighteen bunkers on the course, but there are also fifteen lakes and over ten thousand towering pine trees! Rated several times by *Golf Digest* as one of America's top twenty-five public courses, this extremely scenic layout offers an inviting combination of pleasurable golf and exceptional surroundings.

EMERALD VALLEY GOLF COURSE 32

83293 DALE KUNI RD., CRESWELL, OR 97426 (503)895-2174 *(9 mi. S of Eugene)*
ACCOMMODATIONS: EMERALD VALLEY RESORT (503)895-2147

Opened in 1967, Emerald Valley is built on frontage land along the Willamette River, in the foothills of the Cascade Mountains. The eighteen-hole championship course is set in heavily wooded terrain, with the river and three additional ponds coming into play on seven holes, along with twenty-three moderately difficult bunkers. The par-4 fifth, at 438 yards from the championship tees displays some of Emerald Valley's muscle. It demands a second shot across an arm of the river, which cuts

EMERALD VALLEY GOLF COURSE
18 holes   Par 72   6873/6388/5803 yds.
USGA: 71.4   SLOPE: 126
STYLE: Woods, lakes
ACCESS: No restrictions
SEASON: All year   HIGH: May-Aug.
GREEN FEES: $$
REDUCED FEES: WD, LS, TW
RESERVATIONS: 1 week
WALKING: Yes   RANGE: Yes

diagonally across the fairway. The narrow, tree-lined fairways average only thirty-five yards in width, and the slightly elevated, fast, bentgrass greens add to an already severe test. The course is maintained in excellent condition and can be played year round.

SALISHAN GOLF LINKS ▪33▪
GLENEDEN BEACH , OR 97388 (503)764-3632 *(100 mi. SW of Portland)*
ACCOMMODATIONS: SALISHAN LODGE (503)764-2371

SALISHAN GOLF LINKS
18 holes   Par 72   6439/6246/5693 yds.
USGA: 71.5   SLOPE: 127
STYLE: Woods, oceanside
ACCESS: No restrictions
SEASON: All year   HIGH: May-Nov.
GREEN FEES: $$
REDUCED FEES: LS, PK
RESERVATIONS: 2 weeks
WALKING: Yes   RANGE: Yes

Graced with the natural beauty for which Oregon is famous, Salishan's front nine is wooded and tight, but the back nine brings in natural links terrain and ocean views. Only twenty-seven sandtraps dot the course, but some of them are in true Scottish fashion: small, deep pot bunkers that will test the best of your sand game. The rough, well-fed by Pacific rainstorms, can be heavy, and when the ocean wind kicks in, it all adds up to a tough course, especially if played from the back tees.

SUNRIVER LODGE AND RESORT ▪34▪
P.O. BOX 3609, SUNRIVER, OR 97707 (800)962-1769 *(20 mi. S of Bend)*
ACCOMMODATIONS: SUNRIVER LODGE AND RESORT (503)593-1221

Sunriver's South Course, a 1968 creation of architect Fred Federspiel, starts along a giant meadow, travels into the woods, then rejoins the meadow at the last two holes. All greens are elevated and protected with mounds, so that accurate iron shots are essential. The par-3 sixteenth plays straight toward the majestic, snowcapped Mt. Bachelor. The North Course was designed by Robert Trent Jones, Jr., and it opened in 1981. Jones plotted his course among great ponderosa pine and around seven glimmering lakes. This beautiful and intricate course has many doglegs that offer perpetual shotmaking dilemmas! Sunriver is rated as one of America's top resort courses.

SUNRIVER LODGE AND RESORT
ACCESS: No restrictions
SEASON: Apr.-Oct.   HIGH: June-Aug.
GREEN FEES: $$$
REDUCED FEES: HG, LS, TW, PK
RESERVATIONS: Nonguests 1 day
WALKING: Yes   RANGE: Yes
• **SOUTH COURSE**
  18 holes   Par 72   6960/6522/5847 yds.
  USGA: 70.8   SLOPE: 125
  STYLE: Lakes, woods
• **NORTH COURSE**
  18 holes   Par 72   6880/6274/5446 yds.
  USGA: 70.2   SLOPE: 125
  STYLE: Lakes, woods

KAH-NEE-TA RESORT ▪35▪
100 MAIN ST., WARM SPRINGS, OR 97761 (503)553-1112 *(100 mi. SE of Portland)*
ACCOMMODATIONS: KAH-NEE-TA RESORT (800)831-0100

KAH-NEE-TA RESORT GOLF COURSE
18 holes   Par 72   6288/5418 yds.
USGA: 69.7   SLOPE: 115
STYLE: Desert, water
ACCESS: No restrictions
SEASON: All year   HIGH: June-Sept.
GREEN FEES: $$
REDUCED FEES: LS
RESERVATIONS: 2 weeks
WALKING: Yes   RANGE: Yes

Kah-Nee-Ta is located on the Warm Springs Indian reservation, and according to its head professional, it is the place where "eagles soar and birdies fly." Well, on No. 17, it is aquatic life, not birds, that you may encounter: the 517-yard, par-5 hole demands a carry over the seventy-yard-wide Warm Springs River. On the finishing hole, the river runs hard along the right side of the fairway—well within range of a slice. All along, though, the views of the rim rocks above and around the course are quite spectacular.

W
A
S
H
I
N
G
T
O
N

PORT LUDLOW GOLF COURSE

36

9483 OAK BAY RD., PORT LUDLOW, WA 98365 (206)437-9178 *(40 mi. NW of Seattle)*
ACCOMMODATIONS: THE RESORT AT PORT LUDLOW (206)437-2222

PORT LUDLOW GOLF COURSE
18 holes   Par 72   6787/6262/5598 yds.
USGA: 71.6   SLOPE: 135
STYLE: Hills, woods, lakes
ACCESS: Priority to hotel guests
SEASON: All year   HIGH: May-Oct.
GREEN FEES: $$$
REDUCED FEES: WD, HG, LS, TW, PK
RESERVATIONS: Nonguests 3 days
WALKING: Yes   RANGE: Yes

Port Ludlow, a Robert Muir Graves design, is cut from the Olympic Peninsula's primeval forest, with sublime vistas of Puget Sound and the Cascade Range. Hilly, wooded fairways are dotted with eleven water hazards, including rustic ponds and lakes. Cedar stumps, a legacy of a century of logging, create unique obstacles. No. 17 is probably the region's most photographed hole; the 150-yard par 3 is fronted by a lake; a large stump, covered with foliage, forms an island in the middle.

PORT LUDLOW GOLF COURSE: HOLE NO. 17

HARBOUR POINTE GOLF CLUB

37

11817 HARBOUR POINTE BLVD., MUKILTEO, WA 98275 (206)355-6060 *(20 mi. N of Seattle)*

Designed by renowned architect Arthur Hills, Harbour Pointe Golf Club opened in 1989. The layout harmoniously blends rolling meadows, lakes, and marshland. The narrow front nine is literally surrounded by water. Every hole has some wet stuff lurking somewhere! The back nine is tree-lined, with water only on the tenth. Golfers are particularly fond of the wonderful view of Puget Sound at No. 11—whenever they make it that far! Harbour Pointe is difficult for the average player but still enjoyable. *Golf* magazine rated it one of 1990's best new public-access courses.

HARBOUR POINTE GOLF CLUB
18 holes   Par 72   6880/6052/5460 yds.
USGA: 70.4   SLOPE: 128
STYLE: Rolling hills, lakes, marsh
ACCESS: No restrictions
SEASON: All year   HIGH: June-Oct.
GREEN FEES: $$
REDUCED FEES: WD
RESERVATIONS: 5 days
WALKING: Yes   RANGE: Yes

KAYAK POINT GOLF COURSE　　　38
15711 MARINE DR., STANWOOD, WA 98292 (206)652-9676 *(30 mi. N of Seattle)*

This outstanding course covers 250 acres of steep and heavily wooded hills along the shores of Puget Sound. Carved out of a forest of fir and alder, this and natural layout grants players gorgeous views of the sound and the Olympic and Cascade Mountains. With narrow fairways, steep hills, and thousands of trees, Kayak Point can be quite a challenge. That fact was duly recognized by the rules committee: for amateurs, a modified lost-ball rule is in effect— you drop a ball where it left for the woods and take a penalty stroke. The course is ranked by *Golf Digest* as one of the fifty best public courses in the United States.

KAYAK POINT GOLF COURSE
18 holes　Par 72　6719/6109/5409 yds.
USGA: 70.2　SLOPE: 129
STYLE: Hills, woods
ACCESS: No restrictions
SEASON: All year　HIGH: May-Oct.
GREEN FEES: $
REDUCED FEES: WD, LS
RESERVATIONS: 1 week, anytime if prepaid
WALKING: Yes　RANGE: Yes

INDIAN CANYON GOLF COURSE　　　39
W. 4304 WEST DR., SPOKANE, WA 99204 (509)747-5353 *(5 mins. from downtown Spokane)*

Indian Canyon opened in 1935, a time when six thousand yards was considered an average length for a golf course. Don't let the short yardage (or lack of water hazards) fool you, however. The course is heavily wooded, and with its tight, hilly fairways, it plays a lot harder than the scorecard might indicate. For example, No. 5 is 403 yards long, uphill all the way, and it reaches to a severely sloped green. The first and the tenth both overlook the city of Spokane, and the view is terrific. In the last ten years, Indian Canyon has hosted both the Men's and Women's Public Links Championships. It also ranks in *Golf Digest's* best twenty-five public courses.

INDIAN CANYON GOLF COURSE
18 holes　Par 72　6255/5943/5355 yds.
USGA: 69.3　SLOPE: 123
STYLE: Rolling hills, woods
ACCESS: No restrictions
SEASON: Apr.-Nov.　HIGH: July
GREEN FEES: $
REDUCED FEES: TW
RESERVATIONS: 1 day, 1 week for weekends
WALKING: Yes　RANGE: Yes

SEMIAHMOO GOLF AND COUNTRY CLUB　　　40
8720 SEMIAHMOO PKWY., BLAINE, WA 98230 (206)371-7005 *(2 hours N of Seattle)*
ACCOMMODATIONS: INN AT SEMIAHMOO (206)371-2000

Named after a tribe of Indians that inhabited the area long ago, Semiahmoo is located only one mile from the Canadian border. Here, the design team of Arnold Palmer and Ed Seay has created eighteen individual holes in a pristine forest of evergreen and alder. The course's aesthetics and challenge are enhanced by bright white sandtraps and four blue lakes that contrast beautifully with the surrounding greenery. Palmer made the layout enjoyable for all by providing four sets of tees, but the 128 slope rating from the middle tees indicates clearly that there is more to this course than meets the eye, regardless of how beautiful it is. While putting on the third green, be sure to look for the resident family of bald eagles! *Golf Digest* gave Semiahmoo its 1987 best new resort course distinction. It is also a *Golf* magazine Silver Medal winner.

SEMIAHMOO INN AND COUNTRY CLUB
18 holes　Par 72　7005/6435/5288 yds.
USGA: 71.4　SLOPE: 128
STYLE: Woods, lakes
ACCESS: Restrictions on tee times
SEASON: All year　HIGH: May-Oct.
GREEN FEES: $$$
REDUCED FEES: HG, LS, TW
RESERVATIONS: 1 week, 1 day for weekends
WALKING: Yes　RANGE: Yes

A L A S K A

ANCHORAGE GOLF COURSE

41

3651 O'MALLEY RD., ANCHORAGE, AK 99516 (907)522-3363 *(5 mi. S of downtown Anchorage)*

Set in the foothills of the Chugach Mountains on the south side of town, this golf course offers a view of the city of Anchorage in the foreground and, on a clear day, a beautiful view of Mt. McKinley in the distance. If you've forgotten your geography, McKinley, at 20,320 feet, is the highest point in North America. The course itself is no pushover. Designed by Bill Newcomb and opened in 1986, it combines narrow fairways, woods, lakes, and small, contoured greens to create a difficult challenge. If that were not enough, wandering moose can occasionally become moving obstacles.

ANCHORAGE GOLF COURSE
18 holes   Par 72   6616/6115/4848 yds.
USGA: 69.2   SLOPE: 125
STYLE: Woods, lakes
ACCESS: No restrictions
SEASON: May-Oct.   HIGH: June-Aug.
GREEN FEES: $$
RESERVATIONS: 1 week
WALKING: Yes   RANGE: Yes

OTHER EXCELLENT COURSES IN THE WEST

CALIFORNIA

- ■ THE ALISAL RANCH GOLF COURSE, Solvang (805)688-4215
- ● ANCIL HOFFMAN GOLF COURSE, Carmichael (916)482-5660
- ■ THE GOLF CLUB AT QUAIL LODGE, Carmel (408)624-2770
- ● LAGUNA SECA GOLF CLUB, Monterey (408)373-3701
- ● LAKE SHASTINA GOLF RESORT, Weed (916)938-3205
- ▲ MARRIOTT'S RANCHO LAS PALMAS RESORT, Rancho Mirage (619)568-2727
- ▲ PALM DESERT RESORT AND COUNTRY CLUB, Palm Desert (619)345-2791
- ● TUSTIN RANCH GOLF CLUB, Tustin (714)730-1611

NEVADA

- ● NORTHGATE GOLF CLUB, Reno (702)747-7577
- ● LAKE RIDGE GOLF COURSE, Reno (702)825-2200

OREGON

- ● BLACK BUTTE RANCH, Black Butte Ranch (503)595-6689
- ● EASTMORELAND GOLF COURSE, Portland (503)775-2900
- ● HERON LAKES GOLF COURSE, Portland (503)289-1818

WASHINGTON

- ● ALDERBROOK GOLF AND YACHT CLUB, Union (206)898-2560
- ● McCORMICK WOODS GOLF COURSE, Port Orchard (206)895-0130

ALASKA

- ● MOOSE RUN GOLF COURSE, Ft. Richardson (907)428-0056

▲ RESTRICTIONS MAY APPLY   ■ HOTEL/RESORT GUESTS ONLY   ● OPEN WITHOUT RESTRICTIONS

THE ROCKY MOUNTAIN STATES

This is national park and national monument country: Yellowstone National Park, the oldest and most famous in the nation's park system, lays like a giant, covering more than two million acres of land in parts of Idaho, Montana, and Wyoming. In Utah, Arches, Zion, and Bryce Canyon National Parks display their unusual rock formations and spectacular colors. To the south, Colorado National Park reaches to the sky with 107 peaks at altitudes exceeding 11,000 feet! Golfers and their playgrounds seem insignificant in the shadows of this awesome landscape.

Fortunately for all of us, many of the golf courses built in these scenic regions benefit from their majestic backgrounds. All five of the Rocky Mountain states offer great courses in superb scenery, and Colorado in particular distinguishes itself as a major golfing region. The best known golf architects of our time have come to the Sky High State to meet the challenge of mountain course design: Robert Trent Jones, Jr., at the Arrowhead Golf Club, Jack Nicklaus at Breckenridge, and Pete Dye at the 9,700-foot-high Copper Mountain Resort course. Impressed by the land's tremendous proportions, they have created masterpieces worthy of the magnificent surroundings. Colorado golf embodies the essence, beauty, and drama of the Rockies.

Just a few words of caution about Rocky Mountain golf: a ball will fly up to 20 percent farther in the thin, dry air of these high elevations, so give the foursome ahead of you plenty of room before hitting! Needless to say, golf here is mostly a late-spring to early-autumn event; the rest of the year is devoted to skiing. Always bring a good sweater, and, above all never forget a camera and plenty of film.

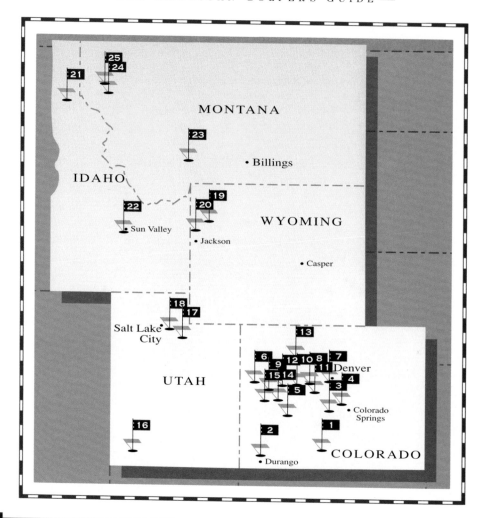

GREAT SAND DUNES COUNTRY CLUB

5303 HWY. 150, MOSCA, CO 81146 (719)378-2357 *(200 MI. FROM DENVER)*
ACCOMMODATIONS: GREAT SAND DUNES COUNTRY INN (719)378-2356

The Great Sand Dunes Country Club is located at the base of the Sangre de Cristo Mountain Range in southern Colorado. Cut among towering cottonwood, cedar, and golden aspen trees, this 1990 Scottish-type layout has desert-style features and elevated greens with a small creek running through six holes. Besides the excellent golf, players can feast their eyes on the Great Sand Dunes National Monument, seven 14,000-foot-high snowcapped peaks, and the third-largest buffalo herd in America, grazing right by the course.

GREAT SAND DUNES COUNTRY CLUB
18 holes   Par 72   6816/6353/5840 yds.
USGA: 68   SLOPE: 119
STYLE: Scottish links
ACCESS: No restrictions
SEASON: Apr.-Nov.   HIGH: June-Aug.
GREEN FEES: $$
REDUCED FEES: LS
RESERVATIONS: 1 month
WALKING: Yes   RANGE: Yes

TAMARRON RESORT AT DURANGO, COLORADO

2

40292 U.S. HWY. 550 N., DURANGO, CO 81302 (303)259-2000 *(18 mi. N of Durango)*
ACCOMMODATIONS: TAMARRON RESORT (303)259-0955

At just under 6,900 yards, Tamarron is not too long, given the thin air, but as its slope rating indicates, it's no pushover. In fact, it is always mentioned as one of the state's toughest. It's a thinking golfer's course: the design places a premium on accuracy and proper club selection. The fairways meander among canyons and sheer rock cliffs, flower-sprinkled meadows, and stands of oak, aspen, and ponderosa pine. *Golf Digest* has rated it one of the top seventy-five resort courses in the country.

TAMARRON RESORT
18 holes   Par 72   6885/6340/5350 yds.
USGA: 70.6   SLOPE: 139
STYLE: Mountain
ACCESS: Priority to hotel guests
SEASON: Apr.-Nov.   HIGH: Apr.-Aug.
GREEN FEES: $$$$ (includes cart)
REDUCED FEES: LS, PK
RESERVATIONS: 2 days
WALKING: No   RANGE: Yes

TAMARRON RESORT GOLF COURSE

THE BROADMOOR

1 LAKE AVE., COLORADO SPRINGS, CO 80906 (719)577-5790, (719)577-5791 *(66 mi. S of Denver)*
ACCOMMODATIONS: THE BROADMOOR (719)634-7711

3

THE BROADMOOR
ACCESS: Hotel guests only
SEASON: All year   HIGH: May-Aug.
GREEN FEES: $$$
REDUCED FEES: PK
RESERVATIONS: 1 day
WALKING: No   RANGE: Yes
- **EAST COURSE**
  18 holes   Par 72   7218/6555/5920 yds.
  USGA: 71.4   SLOPE: 122
  STYLE: Traditional
- **WEST COURSE**
  18 holes   Par 72   6937/6109/5505 yds.
  USGA: 70.3   SLOPE: 128
  STYLE: Traditional
- **SOUTH COURSE**
  18 holes   Par 72   6781/6108/5609 yds.
  USGA: 68.5   SLOPE: 131
  STYLE: Rolling hills

For fanatics of golf architecture, there are fewer places in the world that will give you greater pleasure than the Broadmoor. Three great architects have made their mark here. For absolute purists, there is the East Course, designed in 1918 by Donald Ross, who left us a beautiful mountain legacy. Full-grown pines enhance the scenery, and the natural setting lent itself well in constructing a challenging course. Then there is the West Course, with nine holes done in 1950 and nine in 1965—all by Robert Trent Jones, Sr., who also did some redesigning on the East Course. Finally, in 1976, the team of Arnold Palmer and Ed Seay made their contribution with the South Course, the toughest of the three, making the Broadmoor the largest—and certainly one of the finest—golf properties in Colorado.

PINE CREEK GOLF CLUB

PINE CREEK GOLF CLUB

9850 DIVOT TRAIL, COLORADO SPRINGS, CO 80920 (719)594-9999 *(60 mi. S of Denver)*

PINE CREEK GOLF CLUB
18 holes   Par 72   6980/6579/5314 yds.
USGA: 70.5   SLOPE: 127
STYLE: Hills, Scottish links
ACCESS: No restrictions
SEASON: All year   HIGH: May-Aug.
GREEN FEES: $$
REDUCED FEES: WD, LS
RESERVATIONS: 3 days
WALKING: Yes   RANGE: Yes

This Richard Phelps design was inspired by Scottish links. It incorporates four lakes and four dry creek washes to create a true masterpiece of beauty, strength, and strategy. The par-5 fifteenth, for example, plays over and around Pine Creek and demands nothing but the best shots to reach in regulation. The track climbs as high as seven thousand feet, at which point one can get some astonishing views of the surrounding mountain ranges; then it tumbles down to the bottom of the valley and Pine Creek.

SKYLAND COUNTRY CLUB

385 COUNTRY CLUB DR., CRESTED BUTTE, CO 81224 (303)349-6131 *(30 mi. N of Gunnison)*
ACCOMMODATIONS: CALL COUNTRY CLUB FOR INFORMATION (800)628-5496

SKYLAND COUNTRY CLUB
18 holes   Par 72   7208/6635/5747 yds.
USGA: 69.8   SLOPE: 121
STYLE: Scottish links, woods
ACCESS: No restrictions
SEASON: May-Oct.   HIGH: June-Aug.
GREEN FEES: $$$$ (includes cart)
REDUCED FEES: LS, TW, PK
RESERVATIONS: 1 week
WALKING: No   RANGE: Yes

Skyland has a two-faced layout, but, happily, both faces are very attractive. The course, designed by Robert Trent Jones, Jr., and open since 1984, runs along one of the prettiest valleys in all of Colorado, with four trout streams cutting through the pine and aspen. The first nine is wooded, while the back nine assumes a more links-like form that encourages bump-and-run shots under the wind. No. 13's nine-thousand-foot elevation commands a spectacular view of the valley.

RIFLE CREEK GOLF CLUB   6

3004 HIGHWAY 325, RIFLE, CO 81650 (303)625-1093 *(20 mi. W of Glenwood Springs)*

RIFLE CREEK GOLF CLUB
18 holes   Par 72   6241/5751/5131 yds.
USGA: 67   SLOPE: 117
STYLE: Desert, mountain
ACCESS: No restrictions
SEASON: Mar.-Nov.   HIGH: May-Sept.
GREEN FEES: $
REDUCED FEES: No
RESERVATIONS: 1 week
WALKING: Yes   RANGE: Yes

A combination of Rocky Mountain beauty and some unique sandstone cliff formations give Rifle Creek its high desert atmosphere and sensational scenery. The course is surrounded by foothills and farmland, and the entire valley can be admired from the tee at No. 7. On the back nine, the Rifle Creek, a mountain stream named for an old trapper's abandoned gun, runs through the course, creating several water hazards.

PLUM CREEK GOLF AND COUNTRY CLUB   7

331 PLAYERS CLUB DR., CASTLE ROCK, CO 80104 (303)688-2611 *(15 mi. S of Denver)*

A Pete Dye Scottish-links-type championship course located in the upper plains of Colorado, Plum Creek is a difficult track with target fairways and small greens protected by numerous bunkers. Dye designed this stadium-style course to accommodate the viewing needs of tournament spectators. The most memorable hole is No. 16, a 402-yard par 4 that plays into the prevailing wind. It has water on the right all the way to the green and an out-of-bounds on the left.

PLUM CREEK GOLF AND COUNTRY CLUB
18 holes   Par 72   6633/5915/4881 yds.
USGA: 70.3   SLOPE: 126
STYLE: Scottish links
ACCESS: No restrictions
SEASON: All year   HIGH: July-Aug.
GREEN FEES: $$$ (includes cart)
REDUCED FEES: WD, LS
RESERVATIONS: 1 week
WALKING: No   RANGE: Yes

PLUM CREEK GOLF AND COUNTRY CLUB

COPPER CREEK GOLF CLUB

8

104 WHEELER PL., COPPER MOUNTAIN, CO 80443 (303)968-2882 *(75 mi. W of Denver)*
ACCOMMODATIONS: COPPER MOUNTAIN RESORT (303)968-2882

COPPER CREEK GOLF CLUB
18 holes Par 70 6094/5742/4392 yds.
USGA: 65.1 SLOPE: 115
STYLE: Mountain, water
ACCESS: Priority to hotel guests
SEASON: May-Oct. HIGH: July-Aug.
GREEN FEES: $$$ (includes cart)
REDUCED FEES: HG, LS, TW, PK
RESERVATIONS: Nonguests 4 days
WALKING: No RANGE: Yes

At an altitude of 9,650 feet, Copper Creek is the highest eighteen-hole golf course in North America! The course is situated in a valley enclosed by snowcapped mountain peaks reaching 13,000 feet in the sky. Pete Dye redesigned the layout in 1986 and routed the fairways through brooks and ponds. The course's modest length is compensated by its incomparable beauty. The great pine forest and the abundance of wildflowers add vibrant color to a valley that is one of the most scenic in the world.

BRECKENRIDGE GOLF CLUB

9

200 CLUBHOUSE DR., BRECKENRIDGE, CO 80424 (303)453-9104 *(3 mi. N of Breckenridge)*

It's true that the ball flies farther in the thin mountain air, but at 7,279 yards from the blue tees, this Jack Nicklaus course is a real backbreaker. The course is owned and operated by the city of Breckenridge, and, in fact, it is the only Nicklaus-designed municipal golf course in the world. Like most of his layouts, this one gives the advantage to players who can hit high, soft, and accurate approaches. The course appears fairly open and offers sensational views of four mountain ranges in the distance. The extensive use of wetlands, grassy mounds, and strategic bunkering reminds you that this course was designed by the master himself.

BRECKENRIDGE GOLF CLUB
18 holes Par 72 7279/5980/5066 yds.
USGA: 69.9 SLOPE: 138
STYLE: Meadows, wetlands
ACCESS: No restrictions
SEASON: June-Oct. HIGH: July-Aug.
GREEN FEES: $$$
REDUCED FEES: LS,TW
RESERVATIONS: 2 days
WALKING: At times RANGE: Yes

KEYSTONE RANCH

10

P.O. BOX 75 KR, DILLON, CO 80435 (303)468-4250 *(76 mi. W of Denver)*
ACCOMMODATIONS: KEYSTONE RESORT (800)222-0188, (303)468-2316

KEYSTONE RANCH
18 holes Par 72 7090/6521/5720 yds.
USGA: 69.9 SLOPE: 130
STYLE: Mountain
ACCESS: Priority to hotel guests
SEASON: June-Sept. HIGH: July-Aug.
GREEN FEES: $$$$ (includes cart)
REDUCED FEES: HG, LS, TW
RESERVATIONS: Nonguests 1 day
WALKING: No RANGE: Yes

Keystone was built on an old cattle ranch in a beautiful high valley, and many of the original buildings are preserved. Robert Trent Jones, Jr., who designed the course, made discreet but efficient use of Trout Creek, the local mountain stream. It comes into play quietly and with great effect. At 9,300 feet above sea level, the majestic mountain views are as memorable as the course itself.

ARROWHEAD GOLF CLUB

11

10850 W. SUNDOWN TR., LITTLETON, CO 80125 (303)973-9614 *(30 mi. SW of Denver)*

Site of one of the most spectacular displays of stone formations in the Rockies, Roxborough Park is also the home of the incredibly picturesque Arrowhead Golf Club. The cathedrals of sandstone through which the course is routed were formed 250 million years ago during an era of great land upheaval. Settlers arrived in the area in the late 1800s. In 1877, Jackson, an official photographer for the Hayden expedition, stood at the edge of one of the huge rocks and captured with his camera this unforgettable landscape. The original plate from the "Jackson Photo Site" is now kept in the Library of Congress.

> **ARROWHEAD GOLF CLUB**
> 18 holes Par 70 6682/6249/5521 yds.
> USGA: 68.9 SLOPE: 129
> STYLE: Mountain
> ACCESS: No restrictions
> SEASON: Apr.-Nov. HIGH: June-Aug.
> GREEN FEES: $$$$ (includes cart)
> REDUCED FEES: LS, TW
> RESERVATIONS: 1 week
> WALKING: No RANGE: Yes

In 1970, Robert Trent Jones, Jr., was given the great opportunity and responsibility of laying a golf course in this wondrous natural theater. Jones responded by drawing a series of holes as memorable as the setting itself. The result is a fairly difficult course that uses the stone formations, scrub oaks, and several large lakes to protect par. At the corner of the 398-yard, par-4 dogleg fifteenth, the player stands right at the Jackson Photo Site. However, don't let a sense of history cloud your judgment. As the yardage book mentions, the rocks are 187 feet high at this point, and attempting a shot over them could get you in trouble!

The splendid Arrowhead course has received the highest praise from golf's best known critics. Best of all, though, Arrowhead instills in every golfer—and nongolfer, for that matter—an immediate respect for the symbiotic relationship between golf course and nature.

ARROWHEAD HOLE NO. 15
From the regular tees, the hole is only 361 yards long, and negotiating the spectacular dogleg should not be too difficult, but try to hit your approach shot close to the flag. The green is 92 feet long and hides many breaks and unhappy surprises!

Arrowhead Golf Club: Hole No. 11

EAGLE-VAIL GOLF CLUB

BOX 5660, AVON, CO 81620 (303)949-5267 *(7 mi. W of Vail)*

EAGLE-VAIL GOLF CLUB
18 holes Par 72   6819/6142/4856 yds.
USGA: 68.6   SLOPE: 123
STYLE: Mountain, lakes
ACCESS: No restrictions
SEASON: May-Oct.   HIGH: June-Aug.
GREEN FEES: $$
REDUCED FEES: LS, TW
RESERVATIONS: 2 days
WALKING: At times   RANGE: Yes

Australian touring pro Bruce Devlin teamed with architect Robert von Hagge to design this scenic, 6,819-yard course, which features a double green on the front side (Nos. 3 and 6) inspired by the famed double greens at St. Andrews. Many tees overlook the fairways by fifty feet or more and numerous streams and creeks run across the course. Among the most beautiful finishing holes in the Rockies are the final four, which wind into the mountains. A nice par-3 course is also available to junior golfers.

SHERATON STEAMBOAT GOLF CLUB

2000 CLUBHOUSE DR., STEAMBOAT SPRINGS, CO 80477 (303)879-1391 *(165 mi. NW of Denver)*
ACCOMMODATIONS: SHERATON STEAMBOAT RESORT (303)879-2220

SHERATON STEAMBOAT GOLF CLUB
18 holes   Par 72   6906/6276/5647 yds.
USGA: 70   SLOPE: 129
STYLE: Woods, water
ACCESS: Priority to hotel guests
SEASON: May-Oct.   HIGH: July-Sept.
GREEN FEES: $$$$ (includes cart)
REDUCED FEES: HG, LS, TW
RESERVATIONS: 1 month
WALKING: At times   RANGE: Yes

Robert Trent Jones, Jr., was in top form when he designed this course, which opened in 1974. Jones made good use of Fish Creek, and, as a result, the course is blessed with some of the finest water holes in the region. The greens are large, presenting a wide choice of pin placements, which adds to the variety and interest of the course. Also, like any outstanding layout, it presents a fair challenge to players of every skill level. Just pick the right set of tees to play from, and Steamboat Springs will show you a very enjoyable day of golf.

BEAVER CREEK GOLF CLUB

103 OFFERSON RD., AVON, CO 81620 (303)949-7123 *(100 mi. W of Denver)*
ACCOMMODATIONS: CALL GOLF CLUB FOR INFORMATION.

Beaver Creek doesn't demand brute strength as much as pinpoint accuracy and clear thinking. In short, it is a very good test of shotmaking capability. The course's most prominent feature—and the most hazardous—is a hard-running creek that winds throughout the course, leaving bogeys and double bogeys in its wake. The four-hundred-yard, par-4 dramatic finishing hole, another Robert Trent Jones, Jr., masterpiece, requires a second shot over Beaver Creek, with the mountains and Beaver Creek Village in the background.

BEAVER CREEK GOLF CLUB
18 holes   Par 70   6500/6100/5300 yds.
USGA: 67   SLOPE: 128
STYLE: Hills, woods
ACCESS: Hotel guests only
SEASON: May-Oct.   HIGH: June-Sept.
GREEN FEES: $$$$ (includes cart)
REDUCED FEES: No
RESERVATIONS: At time of hotel booking
WALKING: No   RANGE: Yes

SINGLETREE GOLF CLUB

SINGLETREE GOLF CLUB 15

1265 BERRY CREEK RD., EDWARDS, CO 81632 (303)926-3533 *(125 mi. W of Denver)*
ACCOMMODATIONS: SONNENALP HOTEL AND COUNTRY CLUB (303)476-5656

SINGLETREE GOLF CLUB
18 holes   Par 71   7059/6423/5293 yds.
USGA: 69.8   SLOPE: 134
STYLE: Mountain
ACCESS: Priority to hotel guests
SEASON: Mar.-Nov.   HIGH: June-Sept.
GREEN FEES: $$$$ (includes cart)
REDUCED FEES: HG, LS, TW
RESERVATIONS: Nonguests 1 day
WALKING: At times   RANGE: Yes

Singletree is part of Sonnenalp, a resort with a Bavarian heritage and a tradition of quality. For golfers, that translates into a splendid layout, rated by *Golf Digest* as one of the top fifty resort courses in the U.S. Designed by Jay Morrish and Bob Cupp, it rolls along alpine meadows filled with wildflowers and natural grasses. Mountain streams and waterfalls complete the idyllic setting but also account for the high slope rating.

GREEN SPRING GOLF COURSE 16

588 N. GREEN SPRING DR., WASHINGTON, UT 84780 (801)673-7888 *(2 mi. N of St. George)*

GREEN SPRING GOLF COURSE
18 holes   Par 71   6717/6293/5042 yds.
USGA: 69.3   SLOPE: 118
STYLE: Hills, desert
ACCESS: No restrictions
SEASON: All year   HIGH: Feb.-May
GREEN FEES: $$
REDUCED FEES: HG, LS, PK
RESERVATIONS: 1 week
WALKING: Yes   RANGE: Yes

Green Spring, designed by Gene Bates with an assist from Johnny Miller, opened in late 1989 to rave reviews, and the praise hasn't stopped yet. The course winds through the colored desert, and from the back tees it is a tough and dramatic test of golf. The fairways and areas around the greens are a series of rolling mounds that resemble an angry seascape set in the shadow of Pine Valley Mountain.

JEREMY RANCH GOLF CLUB

17

8770 N. JEREMY RD., PARK CITY, UT 84060 (801)531-9000 *(8 mi. W of Park City)*

JEREMY RANCH GOLF CLUB
18 holes   Par 72   7103/6251/5283 yds.
USGA: 72.9   SLOPE: 130
STYLE: Mountain, water
ACCESS: Restrictions on tee times
SEASON: Apr.-Nov.   HIGH: May-Sept.
GREEN FEES: $$$ (includes cart)
RESERVATIONS: 1 week
WALKING: After 4:00 p.m.   RANGE: Yes

The Jeremy Ranch Golf Club is a championship course situated at 6,200 feet in the mountains of Utah. Opened in 1981, the Arnold Palmer-Ed Seay design brings into play several streams and ponds to create water hazards on no less than fourteen holes. Players have their choice of four or, in some cases, five tees to hit from. Jeremy Ranch's greatest strength is the variety offered by its eighteen exceptionally different holes. With its well-contoured greens and its extensive bunkering (129 sandtraps!), the course is quite difficult. *Golf Digest* keeps rating it as one of Utah's top five.

PARK MEADOWS GOLF CLUB

2000 MEADOWS DR., PARK CITY, UT 84068 (801)649-2460 *(25 mi. E of Salt Lake City)*

To describe Park Meadows briefly, one could just say that it is a Jack Nicklaus course, opened in 1983, located at an altitude of seven thousand feet, and ranked in 1989 by *Golf Digest* as number one in the state of Utah. However, that would not do complete justice to this terrific layout. It is a difficult but enjoyable, true links-type course, combining generous driving areas with some severe, greenside bunkering and even some traditional Scottish double greens. The par-5 No. 15 offers a choice of two fairways. As any Scot could tell you, however, trying the island-fairway shortcut to the green could be a foolish decision.

PARK MEADOWS GOLF CLUB
18 holes   Par 72   7338/6666/5816 yds.
USGA: 70.6   SLOPE: 124
STYLE: Scottish links
ACCESS: No restrictions
SEASON: Apr.-Oct.   HIGH: June-Sept.
GREEN FEES: $$ (includes cart)
REDUCED FEES: WD, LS, PK
RESERVATIONS: 1 week
  (2 months with credit card)
WALKING: At times   RANGE: Yes

PARK MEADOWS: THE GREEN AT NO. 17

JACKSON HOLE GOLF AND TENNIS CLUB

19

5800 SPRING GULCH RD., JACKSON, WY 83001 (307)733-3111 *(10 mi. N of Jackson)*

JACKSON HOLE GOLF COURSE
18 holes   Par 72   7168/6783/6036 yds.
USGA: 70.3   SLOPE: 124
STYLE: Woods, water
ACCESS: No restrictions
SEASON: Apr.-Oct.   HIGH: June-Aug.
GREEN FEES: $$
REDUCED FEES: TW
RESERVATIONS: One week in advance
   before June, anytime thereafter
WALKING: Yes   RANGE: Yes

The spectacular view of the Grand Tetons is the dominant feature at Jackson Hole. The layout lies on the flat and open valley floor, and the Gros Ventre River flows through the grounds, bringing water trouble on twelve holes. Robert Trent Jones, Jr., redesigned the course in 1967, which now features elevated and contoured greens and sixty-five well-placed bunkers. Trees line the fairways, but there is plenty of room to hit the driver on every hole.

JACKSON HOLE

TETON PINES GOLF CLUB

TETON PINES GOLF CLUB
3450 N. CLUBHOUSE DR., JACKSON, WY 83001 (307)733-1733 *(12 mi. W of Jackson)*
ACCOMMODATIONS: TETON PINES COUNTRY CLUB (800)238-2223

TETON PINES GOLF CLUB
18 holes   Par 72   7400/6888/5486 yds.
USGA: 71   SLOPE: 125
STYLE: Mountain, water
ACCESS: Restrictions on tee times
SEASON: May-Oct.   HIGH: July-Aug.
GREEN FEES: $$$
REDUCED FEES: HG, LS, TW
RESERVATIONS: Anytime in season
WALKING: At times   RANGE: Yes

ARNOLD PALMER AT TETON PINES

There are two memorable features on this 1987 Arnold Palmer-Ed Seay championship course: the splendid views of the Teton Mountain Range a few miles away and the abundance of water—forty-two acres of meandering streams and lakes, to be precise. You can measure yourself against the 634-yard, par-5 seventh with its thin peninsula green or against the 221-yard, par-3 twelfth, which travels completely over water to a swale-type putting surface. Good luck. We should mention that there are two sets of middle tees to lighten things up a bit, and, of course, the magnificent scenery is always there to save the day.

I
D
A
H
O

COEUR D'ALENE RESORT

900 FLOATING GREEN DR., COEUR D'ALENE, ID 83814 (208)667-4653 *(35 mi. W of Spokane, WA)*
ACCOMMODATIONS: COEUR D'ALENE RESORT (800)688-5253

21

Of all the courses recently opened in America, the Coeur d'Alene Resort in western Idaho has been one of the most talked about. Even before its completion, the island green on No. 14 attracted a lot of curiosity, and understandably so: the green is laid upon a 15,000-square-foot floating pontoon that weighs several thousand tons and is reachable only by boat. The green can be towed anywhere from seventy-five to 175 yards away from land. The self-contained vessel has its own trees, flower beds, bunkers, and recyclable water system.

> **COEUR D'ALENE RESORT GOLF COURSE**
> 18 holes   Par 71   6309/5899/5490 yds.
> USGA: 68.2   SLOPE: 117
> STYLE: Mountain, lakes
> ACCESS: Priority to hotel guests
> SEASON: Apr.-Nov.   HIGH: June-Sept.
> GREEN FEES: $$$$$ (includes cart)
> REDUCED FEES: HG, PK
> RESERVATIONS: Nonguests 3 days
> WALKING: No   RANGE: Yes

Gimmickry can easily disqualify a course in the eyes of purists, but there is none of that at Coeur d'Alene. The lake has been called by *National Geographic* one of the five most beautiful in the world, and its densely forested slopes make a perfect setting for a splendid, natural golf course. Architect Scott Miller designed the layout to take advantage of this special place, and players are rewarded with beautiful lake views from every hole. There are large greens and multiple tees to make the course enjoyable for players of all levels. The lake itself only comes into play on three holes, but one of them is the fourteenth, and that boat ride alone is worth a detour to Idaho.

THE LOCAL RULE ALLOWS PLAYERS ONLY TWO ATTEMPTS AT HITTING THE FLOATING GREEN. AFTER THAT, ONE MUST DROP A BALL AT THE DESIGNATED AREA ON THE ISLAND.

COEUR D'ALENE RESORT: THE FLOATING GREEN ON NO. 14

ELKHORN RESORT

ELKHORN RD., SUN VALLEY, ID 83353 (208)622-3309 *(70 mi. N of Twin Falls)*
ACCOMMODATIONS: ELKHORN RESORT AND LODGE (800)635-9356

22

Elkhorn was built on Indian territory overlooking the beautiful Sun Valley. It is some of the most spectacular land in America, and when it came time to create a world-class course, Robert Trent Jones, Jr., was called in. Opened in 1973, Elkhorn is a wonderfully hilly course, especially on the front nine, with water coming into play in the form of trout streams and ponds on the back nine. The course is situated at an elevation of six thousand feet, and although the ball will fly a great distance

ELKHORN RESORT
18 holes Par 72 7101/6524/5701 yds.
USGA: 70.3 SLOPE: 128
STYLE: Hills, water
ACCESS: Restrictions on tee times
SEASON: Apr.-Oct. HIGH: June-Sept.
GREEN FEES: $$$ (includes cart)
REDUCED FEES: HG, LS, TW, PK
RESERVATIONS: Nonguests 2 days
WALKING: At times RANGE: Yes

in the thin air, it can play quite long. Elkhorn is ranked "the number one" course in Idaho, and *Golf Digest* rates the resort among the top fifty in the United States.

MONTANA

BIG SKY GOLF CLUB

1 LONE MOUNTAIN TR., BIG SKY, MT 59716 (406)995-4706 *(40 mi. S of Bozeman)*
ACCOMMODATIONS: BIG SKY SKI AND SUMMER RESORT (406)995-4211

23

A 360-degree view of the surrounding majestic mountain range will explain the derivation of this magnificent course's name. Big Sky Golf Club, only eighteen miles from the Yellowstone National Park boundary, shares many of the characteristics of its grand neighbor: the scenery combines incredible views with peaceful alpine meadows, fresh mountain air, and an abundance of wildflowers. The appearance of an occasional elk completes the natural and idyllic setting. This fine

BIG SKY GOLF CLUB
18 holes Par 72 6748/6115/5374 yds.
USGA: 66 SLOPE: 105
STYLE: Mountain
ACCESS: No restrictions
SEASON: May-Sept. HIGH: July-Aug.
GREEN FEES: $$
REDUCED FEES: PK
RESERVATIONS: 1 month
WALKING: Yes RANGE: Yes

and relaxed atmosphere makes for an enjoyable round of golf for everyone. Wisely, Arnold Palmer chose this spot to design his only course in Montana. The layout is not too difficult, although the back nine, which brings a creek into play, presents some testy moments. The 210-yard, par-3 twelfth, for example, bordered by the creek on one side and a marsh on the other, may convince you to temporarily concentrate on the scenery and fascinating wildlife.

EAGLE BEND GOLF CLUB

279 EAGLE BEND DR., BIGFORK, MT 59911 (406)837-5400 *(20 mi. S of Kalispell)*

24

EAGLE BEND GOLF CLUB
18 holes Par 72 6758/6237/5398 yds.
USGA: 69.6 SLOPE: 119
STYLE: Hills, lakes
ACCESS: No restrictions
SEASON: Apr.-Oct. HIGH: June-Sept.
GREEN FEES: $$
REDUCED FEES: TW
RESERVATIONS: Anytime with credit card
WALKING: Yes RANGE: Yes

If you are a player who is easily distracted, this may not be the right course for you. Set near beautiful Flathead Lake, the course offers water and mountain views that are simply remarkable, not to mention the sightings of eagles, moose, deer, and other wildlife. Eagle Bend offers quite a golfing challenge, too. One of the most memorable holes is the fifteenth, a long par 3 well-guarded by bunkers and the Flathead River.

BUFFALO HILL GOLF CLUB
25

1176 N. MAIN ST., KALISPELL, MT 59901 (406)756-4545 *(in Kalispell city limits)*

BUFFALO HILL GOLF CLUB
ACCESS: No restrictions
SEASON: Apr.-Nov.   HIGH: June-Aug.
GREEN FEES: $$
REDUCED FEES: HG, LS
RESERVATIONS: 2 days
WALKING: Yes   RANGE: Yes
• **CHAMPIONSHIP 18 COURSE**
   18 holes   Par 72   6525/6247/5258 yds.
   USGA: 70.2   SLOPE: 128
   STYLE: Rolling hills, woods
• **CAMERON 9**
   9 holes   Par 35   3001/2950 yds.
   USGA: 68   SLOPE: 122
   STYLE: Hills, tree-lined fairways

The first nine holes at Buffalo Hill, the Cameron 9, date back to the 1930s. The architect is unknown, but the wide fairways and tiny greens are typical of the style in favor at that time. In 1978, Robert Muir Graves added the Championship 18, a modern but classic test of golf with majestic views of the Rocky Mountains and golf challenges at every corner. The course cuts a path among stands of old, tall willow and birch trees, while the picturesque Stillwater River meanders through the course more than the wayward golfer may like. The Championship 18 has been ranked by *Golf Digest* as one of the best courses in Montana.

OTHER EXCELLENT COURSES IN THE ROCKY MOUNTAIN STATES

COLORADO
● BATTLEMENT MESA GOLF CLUB, Battlement Mesa (303)285-7274
● COAL CREEK GOLF COURSE, Louisville (303)666-7888
● GRANDOTE GOLF AND COUNTRY CLUB, La Veta (719)742-3122
● HYLAND HILLS GOLF CLUB, Westminster (303)428-6526
● POLE CREEK GOLF CLUB, Winter Park (303)726-8847
▲ PTARMIGAN, Ft. Collins (303)226-6600
● RIVERDALE GOLF COURSE, Brighton (303)659-6700

IDAHO
● SUN VALLEY GOLF RESORT, Sun Valley (208)622-2251

MONTANA
● WHITEFISH LAKE GOLF COURSE, Whitefish (406)862-4000

UTAH
● PARK CITY MUNICIPAL GOLF COURSE, Park City (801)521-2135
● WOLF CREEK RESORT, Eden (801) 745-3365

WYOMING
● KENDRICK GOLF COURSE, Sheridan (307)674-8148

▲ RESTRICTIONS MAY APPLY   ■ HOTEL/RESORT GUESTS ONLY   ● OPEN WITHOUT RESTRICTIONS

— CHAPTER FOUR—

THE SOUTHWEST

To the average nongolfer, the Southwest is a barren land of deserts and deep canyons framed by stark mountains. To us, the enlightened practitioners of The Game, it has become a fertile ground where patches of green courses have taken root and multiplied. A combination of year-round sunshine with low humidity, rugged but picturesque landscapes, and the unique flora of saguaro cactus, ocotillo bushes, and wildflowers has created an original setting for the practice of golf.

Arizona, the Grand Canyon State, boasts more than two hundred golf courses, of which approximately two-thirds are accessible to the public. The sprawling Phoenix-Scottsdale urban area, also known as "The Valley of the Sun," is one of America's premier winter golf destinations. To the north, the red rocks of Sedona, and to the South, the old west country surrounding Tucson, are also the sites of innovative desert-style golf course architecture.

New Mexico offers a more spiritual experience. In this land, vast expanses of desert and cloud-reaching mountains embody the spirit of the Indian culture and bring back to golfers that sense of isolation and serenity that is such an inherent part of the game.

And then there is Texas. Texas is big golf country: the largest of the forty-eight contiguous states offers practically every kind of environment for the game. Some say that the best golf in the Lone Star State is to be found in the hills and lakes surrounding the city of Austin, but there are also some great layouts in the Houston and Dallas areas. Perhaps we should let the people of Texas decide for themselves. Having produced more than their share of golf greats—Ben Hogan, Lee Trevino, and Ben Crenshaw, to name just a few—they ought to know.

SHERATON TUCSON EL CONQUISTADOR

1

10555 N. LA CANADA RD., TUCSON, AZ 85737 (602)742-7300 *(15 mi. NW of Tucson)*
ACCOMMODATIONS: SHERATON TUCSON EL CONQUISTADOR GOLF AND TENNIS RESORT (602)742-7000

SHERATON TUCSON EL CONQUISTADOR
ACCESS: Restrictions on Sunset Course
SEASON: All year   HIGH: Jan.-Mar.
GREEN FEES: $$$$ (includes cart)
REDUCED FEES: HG
RESERVATIONS: Nonguests 2 days
WALKING: Yes   RANGE: Yes
- **SUNRISE COURSE**
  18 holes   Par 72   6715/6178/5255 yds.
  USGA: 69   SLOPE: 113
  STYLE: Desert
- **SUNSET COURSE**
  18 holes   Par 72   6763/6340/5394 yds.
  USGA: 69.8   SLOPE: 116
  STYLE: Desert

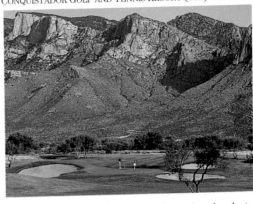

There's a nine-hole course right on the property at Sheraton Tucson El Conquistador, but a few miles away are the thirty-six holes at the El Conquistador Country Club (formerly Canada Hills), and they pose a classic desert test. Set against a backdrop of mountains and towering cactus, the Sunrise Course and the Sunset Course have narrow fairways and many two-tiered greens, putting an emphasis on a properly placed approach shot. The club has hosted several regional tournaments as well as the 1987 Oldsmobile Scramble, and par held up very well against the pros' efforts. The nine-hole Resort Course is often disregarded in favor of the other two, but, in fact, it's rather tough. Fairways are narrow, and one hole has an island green. The Sunset Course is restricted to guests staying at the resort, but the Sunrise and Resort Courses are available to nonguests.

SHERATON TUCSON EL CONQUISTADOR

VENTANA CANYON GOLF AND RACQUET CLUB

6200 N. CLUBHOUSE LA., TUCSON, AZ 85715 (800)828-5701, EXT. 356 *(NE area of Tucson)*
ACCOMMODATIONS: LOEWS VENTANA CANYON RESORT (800)234-5117,
VENTANA CANYON GOLF AND RACQUET CLUB (800)828-5701

Architect Tom Fazio may be best known for his oceanside courses, but the two eighteen-hole desert layouts he created here are real beauties. The Canyon Course sits at the base of the Catalina Mountains and plays through a series of washes and into Esperanto Canyon. The classic par-5 finishing hole, which travels toward the mountain, has a green that sits at the base of the hotel; it is flanked by water in back and on the right and guarded by a desert wash across the front. The Mountain Course offers still more beautiful desert scenes—and more great golf! No. 3 is a short, downhill par 3 that requires nothing more than a well-struck wedge to reach the green. The operative word here is "well-struck," for a mediocre shot will end in a sea of rocks, cactus, and other unpleasant desert realities. The Mountain Course was rated by *Golf Digest* as one of the best new resort courses of 1986. Ventana Canyon has hosted several PGA Tour shootouts, and the pros love the courses as much as amateurs do. A note about access: the Canyon Course is open to guests at the Loews Ventana Canyon Resort and to outside visitors on an availability basis. To enjoy the Mountain Course, however, you must stay at the resort's Ventana Canyon Golf and Racquet Club.

VENTANA CANYON
ACCESS: Restrictions (see description)
SEASON: All year HIGH: Feb.-May
GREEN FEES: $$$$$ (includes cart)
REDUCED FEES: LS, PK
RESERVATIONS: Nonguests 1 day
WALKING: No RANGE: Yes
• **CANYON COURSE**
  18 holes Par 72 6818/6282/4919 yds.
  USGA: 71.3 SLOPE: 129
  STYLE: Hills, desert
• **MOUNTAIN COURSE**
  18 holes Par 72 6948/6356/4789 yds.
  USGA: 70.7 SLOPE: 131
  STYLE: Hills, desert

CANYON COURSE: HOLE NO. 14

CANYON COURSE, HOLE No. 13

THIRTEENTH IS A SIDEHILL PAR 3 NORMALLY PLAYED WITH A SHORT IRON. FROM THE LADIES TEES IT'S ONLY 127 YARDS LONG, BUT THE ROCKS AND CACTUS ON THE RIGHT, AND THE STAGGERED BUNKERS UNDER THE GREEN'S LEFT SIDE, ARE MERCILESS.

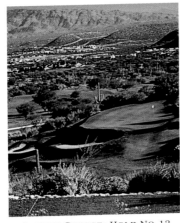

CANYON COURSE: HOLE No. 13

CANYON COURSE: HOLE No. 12

CANYON COURSE: HOLE No. 12

THE TWELFTH HOLE ON THE CANYON COURSE MEASURES 498 YARDS FROM THE MIDDLE TEES. THE FAIRWAY UNDULATES UPHILL, AND GETS UNCOMFORTABLY NARROW AT TIMES. THE GREEN ITSELF IS 128 FEET DEEP, SO PLAN YOUR THIRD SHOT ACCORDINGLY.

THE WESTIN LA PALOMA

3800 E. SUNRISE DR., TUCSON, AZ 85718 (800)842-7814 *(12 mi. N of Tucson)*
ACCOMMODATIONS: THE WESTIN LA POLOMA (800)876-3683

3

Jack Nicklaus designed a three nine-hole combination at The Westin La Paloma. On the Hills, Ridge, and Canyon Courses, a variety of tees allows players of all levels to enjoy a game of golf tailored to their individual abilities. All three are true target-style courses *and* true desert courses. Not a single water hazard is to be found; instead, Nicklaus made imaginative use of large bunkers, mounds, and swales, while retaining the desert

JACK NICKLAUS SIGNATURE GOLF COURSE
27 holes   2991/2464/3020 yds.
STYLE: Desert
ACCESS: Hotel guests only
SEASON: All year   HIGH: Jan.-May
GREEN FEES: $$$$$ (includes cart)
REDUCED FEES: LS
RESERVATIONS: 1 month
WALKING: No   RANGE: Yes

wildlife habitats. With a concern for preserving the natural environment, during the development of this course, nine thousand cactus trees were saved and transplanted into other areas of the resort grounds. If you have a low tolerance for frustration, be wary of the 211-yard, par-3 eighth on the Canyon. To reach the wide green tucked behind a tremendous sand bunker, you'll have to hit long and precise over a portion of the Sonoran Desert—a true test of your shotmaking and your nerve. Although the difficulty can be unrelenting, you'll still find plenty to enjoy at this magnificent location. The courses are extremely picturesque and display all the beautiful landscapes of the desert. *Golf Digest* has rated The Westin La Paloma as one of the country's top resort courses.

CANYON COURSE: HOLE NO. 5

GREAT GOLFING DESTINATION
THE VALLEY OF THE SUN

More than a dozen communities make up "The Valley of the Sun." Phoenix, Scottsdale, and the adjacent towns of Paradise Valley, Tempe, Mesa, and Sun City join to form this sprawling region of nearly two million people. What draws such numbers to the southwestern desert? The weather, of course, is a great attraction: the sun shines 320 days of the year, and temperatures average in the mid-60s in the winter and the mid-80s in the summer. Generally, however, the cool mornings are fresh and invigorating, and later in the day, the hot temperatures are seldom uncomfortable, thanks to extremely low humidity.

TROON NORTH

But there is more than a wonderful climate in The Valley of the Sun. In and around the area, nature has created a most interesting and compelling display: the Sonoran Desert. Stark mountains and colorful mesas mix with forest-like expanses of saguaro cactus, scrubby bushes, and wildflowers. Golf has become a way of life here, and well over one hundred courses provide opportunities to enjoy desert golf at its best.

The Valley of the Sun is located in the heart of Arizona. To the north, the Grand Canyon is four hours away by car; to the south, the old western town of Tucson and the spectacular Saguaro National Monument await your visit.

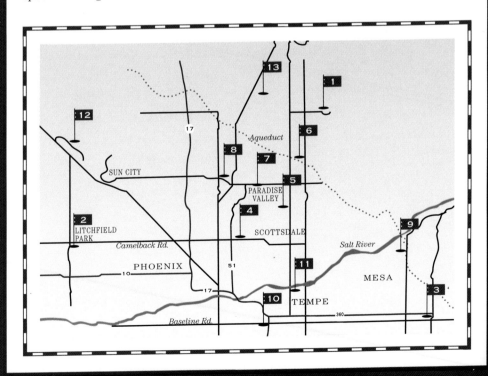

TROON NORTH GOLF CLUB

10320 E. DYNAMITE BLVD., SCOTTSDALE, AZ 85255 (602)585-7700

Due partly to the gently rolling nature of the eroded desert land and partly to recent regulations restricting water usage in desert communities, a new concept in golf architecture has evolved: the "desert links." As in Scotland, desert fairways follow the natural contours of the terrain. In these rugged landscapes, however, greens may be nestled against rock outcrops instead of sand dunes, and you may be required to carry over a small rocky canyon, or *arroyo*, instead of a ditch full of Scottish heather.

TROON NORTH GOLF CLUB
18 holes   Par 72   7008/6472/5008 yds.
USGA: 71.8   SLOPE: 132
STYLE: Desert
ACCESS: Priority to property owners
SEASON: All year   HIGH: Dec.-Apr.
GREEN FEES: $$$$$ (includes cart)
REDUCED FEES: LS
RESERVATIONS: 1 week
WALKING: No   RANGE: Yes

Desert courses vary in another significant way: the weather. It rains a lot less in the Sonoran Desert than on the Firth of Forth; as a result, conservation-conscious architects have sometimes reduced the fairways to targets that don't seem much bigger than a tam o' shanter. At least while playing in the desert, you won't encounter any Nordic gales.

Troon North is one of the finest examples anywhere of the desert-links style. Jay Morrish and Tom Weiskopf have routed the course around the high Sonoran Desert near the famous Pinnacle Peak. The layout takes players around rock outcroppings, over desert washes, and through a small forest of saguaro cactus. Even though the landscape is fairly uniform, every hole here is different and memorable. The course is thoroughly enjoyable without any gimmicks or unnatural features. Several elevated tees, some as high as fifty feet above the desert floor, grant players superb views of the entire layout and the surrounding desert. Troon North has received a lot of praise since its opening in 1990. Some call it the best desert course around, period.

TROON NORTH

Wigwam Resort

451 N. Litchfield Rd., Litchfield Park, AZ 85340 (800)327-0396, ext. 1530
ACCOMMODATIONS: Wigwam Resort (800)327-0396

This outstanding resort offers three different eighteen-hole courses set in a seventy-five-acre oasis of orange and palm trees. The courses are traditional in style and fairly flat, with a lot of trees and water hazards—not what you'd expect in a desert region. The original Gold Course, designed by Robert Trent Jones, Sr., is a long and hard affair where water and bunkers are plentiful: eleven holes have lakes or streams, and the ninety-six bunkers are mostly large. Stretching to 7,074 yards, this highly regarded course is a great leveler—a pure test of skill, intelligence, and ability.

WIGWAM RESORT
ACCESS: Priority to hotel guests
SEASON: All year   HIGH: Jan.-Mar.
GREEN FEES: $$$ (includes cart)
REDUCED FEES: LS, PK
RESERVATIONS: 2 days
WALKING: At times   RANGE: Yes
- **GOLD COURSE**
  18 holes   Par 72   7074/6504/5657 yds.
  USGA: 71.7   SLOPE: 128
  STYLE: Traditional, parkland
- **BLUE COURSE**
  18 holes   Par 70   5960/5178 yds.
  USGA: 69.3   SLOPE: 119
  STYLE: Traditional
- **WEST COURSE**
  18 holes   Par 72   6965/6307/5808 yds.
  USGA: 69.2   SLOPE: 112
  STYLE: Lakes, streams

Jones also did the Blue Course, a tree-lined track running in the same parkland setting as the Gold, but shorter and wider. It is an excellent alternative for less accomplished players. The West Course, a Red Lawrence design, makes extensive use of a stream that winds its way through the layout. There are also five good-size lakes that come into play, one with dramatic effect on the long eighteenth hole. The Wigwam is a classic resort of the Southwest, and over the years it has been visited by many famous and wealthy guests. After an extensive renovation program, the resort has recently received a Silver Medal award from *Golf* magazine.

Superstition Springs Golf Club

6542 E. Baseline Rd., Mesa, AZ 85206 (602)890-9009

SUPERSTITION SPRINGS GOLF CLUB
18 holes   Par 72   7005/6405/5328 yds.
USGA: 71   SLOPE: 123
STYLE: Desert links
ACCESS: No restrictions
SEASON: All year   HIGH: Jan.-Apr.
GREEN FEES: $$$$ (includes cart)
REDUCED FEES: LS
RESERVATIONS: 1 week if prepaid
WALKING: No   RANGE: Yes

Architect Greg Nash did first-rate work at Superstition Springs. He incorporated considerable mounding, numerous grass bunkers, and several lakes into his design and created a truly enjoyable course. Nominated by *Golf Digest* as one of the best public courses in 1987, it offers excellent challenge and diversity. The layout meanders around water hazards and massive sandtraps, and it is graced with beautiful trees all along the way. Since the course's opening in 1986, the par-4 No. 9 has twice been voted Arizona's favorite hole; this scenic, 425-yard test requires a drive over water and sandtraps to a narrow fairway, then a medium iron to an undulating, irregular-shaped green, with the southern-plantation-style clubhouse as a backdrop.

ARIZONA BILTMORE COUNTRY CLUB

24TH ST. AND MISSOURI, PHOENIX, AZ 85016 (602)955-9655
ACCOMMODATIONS: ARIZONA BILTMORE HOTEL (602)955-6600, (800)528-3696

The Biltmore has a reputation for keeping its two eighteen-hole courses in top shape year round. Designed by William Bell and opened in 1929, the Adobe Course is long and flat, but don't be lulled into thinking it's a pushover. The fairways are lined with trees, and water hazards are well-placed, with greenside bunkers on every hole. The shorter Links Course, a Bill Johnston layout added almost fifty years later, has a completely different style. As its name suggests, it features rolling terrain, and the view from the par-3 fifteenth offers a dazzling vista of downtown Phoenix. The Links Course is shorter in yardage than the Adobe but its narrower fairways and five lakes have ruined many scores just the same. Local lore claims that Clark Gable lost his wedding band on the Adobe Course, which is a lot better than losing, say, a putter that's on a hot streak.

ARIZONA BILTMORE COUNTRY CLUB
ACCESS: Priority to hotel guests
SEASON: All year   HIGH: Jan.-May
GREEN FEES: $$$$ (includes cart)
REDUCED FEES: LS, TW
RESERVATIONS: 5 days with credit card
WALKING: No   RANGE: Yes
• **ADOBE COURSE**
  18 holes   Par 72   6767/6455/6094 yds.
  USGA: 70   SLOPE: 116
  STYLE: Traditional, trees, water
• **LINKS COURSE**
  18 holes   Par 71   6300/5726/4912 yds.
  USGA: 66.6   SLOPE: 115
  STYLE: Hills, links

TPC OF SCOTTSDALE

TOURNAMENT PLAYERS CLUB OF SCOTTSDALE

17020 N. HAYDEN RD., SCOTTSDALE, AZ 85255 (602)585-3600
ACCOMMODATIONS: SCOTTSDALE PRINCESS (602)585-4848

TPC OF SCOTTSDALE
ACCESS: No restrictions
SEASON: All year
HIGH: Feb.-May/ Sept.-Nov.
GREEN FEES: $$$$
REDUCED FEES: LS
RESERVATIONS: 1 week
WALKING: Desert Course only
RANGE: Yes
• **STADIUM COURSE**
  18 holes   Par 71   6992/6508/5567 yds.
  USGA: 71   SLOPE: 124
  STYLE: Desert links
• **DESERT COURSE**
  18 holes   Par 71   6552/5908/4715 yds.
  USGA: 68.4   SLOPE: 109
  STYLE: Desert links

Scottsdale resident Tom Weiskopf and his partner, Jay Morrish, designed the two eighteen-hole courses at the Tournament Players Club of Scottsdale. The Stadium Course, with its huge grass stadium mounds, is widely regarded as one of the better TPC designs. Like the original TPC at Sawgrass, this course has an island green—at the par-5 No. 15—which is reachable in two shots if a player feels very strong or very lucky. The best hole on the course might just be the 303-yard, par-4 seventeenth. Weiskopf and Morrish are known for their trademark drivable par 4s, and this one is a beauty. The Desert Course has considerably lower green fees and includes an easy forty bunkers, especially in comparison to the Stadium Course's fairly difficult seventy-two.

MARRIOTT'S CAMELBACK GOLF CLUB

7847 N. MOCKINGBIRD LA. NW, SCOTTSDALE, AZ 85253 (800)24-CAMEL
ACCOMMODATIONS: MARRIOTT'S CAMELBACK INN (800)24-CAMEL

There are two championship courses at Camelback. The original Padre Course isn't long, but it is testing. Architect Red Lawrence lined the narrow fairways with palms and eucalyptus but included tricky doglegs left and right. To ease the pain, all eighteen holes are landscaped with blooming, multi-colored flowerbeds. Discretion is the better part of valor off the tees here. The Indian Bend Course, designed by Jack Snyder, runs through a natural wash area and has a links feel to it. The rolling fairways and well-defended greens put an emphasis on accurate approach shots. Generally, it is less difficult than the Padre Course, but the 432-yard, par-4, dogleg-right No. 1, which plays to an elevated green, is a tough starting hole.

MARRIOTT'S CAMELBACK GOLF CLUB
ACCESS: No restrictions
SEASON: All year   HIGH: Jan.-Mar.
GREEN FEES: $$$$ (includes cart)
REDUCED FEES: LS, PK
RESERVATIONS: 1 week
WALKING: No   RANGE: Yes
- **PADRE COURSE**
  18 holes   Par 71   6559/6019/5626 yds.
  USGA: 67.7   SLOPE: 113
  STYLE: Trees, mountains
- **INDIAN BEND COURSE**
  18 holes   Par 72   7014/6486/5917 yds.
  USGA: 70   SLOPE: 115
  STYLE: Desert links

STONECREEK, THE GOLF CLUB

4435 E. PARADISE VILLAGE PKWY. S., PARADISE VALLEY, AZ 85032 (602)953-9110

The services of Arthur Hills and Associates were retained to redesign Stonecreek in 1989. A Scottish links-type course, it lies upon rolling terrain, with ponds and creeks coming into play on seventeen holes. No. 6 is a par 4, with water on the front and to the right of the green and out-of-bounds on both sides of the fairway. Special efforts are made to keep the large and undulating greens fast, and the spirit of the game is preserved with a traditional dress code and fast-play policy.

STONECREEK, THE GOLF CLUB
18 holes   Par 71   6839/6280/5098 yds.
USGA: 70.2   SLOPE: 126
STYLE: Scottish links
ACCESS: Priority to members
SEASON: All year   HIGH: Jan.-Apr.
GREEN FEES: $$$$ (includes cart)
REDUCED FEES: LS
RESERVATIONS: Nonmembers 3 days
WALKING: No   RANGE: Yes

THE POINTE CLUB ON LOOKOUT MOUNTAIN

11111 NORTH 7TH ST., PHOENIX, AZ 85020 (602)866-9816
ACCOMMODATIONS: THE POINTE AT TAPATIO CLIFFS (602)866-7500

Architect Bill Johnston has routed this scenic course along the slopes and arroyos of the majestic Phoenix Mountain Preserve. In describing the challenge at Lookout Mountain, two holes come to mind: No. 9, a testy but beautiful par 3, with the green nestled into the shrubby desert hillside, and the fourteenth, a par-4 dogleg with a minimum carry of 175 yards to the fairway, followed by a wedge to the green. A courageous player may attempt to reach the green directly with a long

**THE POINTE CLUB
ON LOOKOUT MOUNTAIN**
18 holes   Par 72   6617/5834/4552 yds.
USGA: 69   SLOPE: 125
STYLE: Hills, desert
ACCESS: Priority to hotel guests
SEASON: All year   HIGH: Feb.-May
GREEN FEES: $$$$$ (includes cart)
REDUCED FEES: LS, PK
RESERVATIONS: Nonguests 2 days
WALKING: No   RANGE: Yes

drive from the tee! Saguaro cactus, mesquite bushes, ironwood trees, and wildflowers add to the scenery on the course, which the PGA Tour players have dubbed their "Champagne Stop."

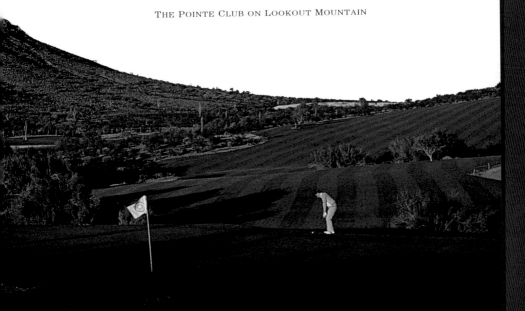

THE POINTE CLUB ON LOOKOUT MOUNTAIN

"Golf Reveals Character. Play Accordingly"

Common courtesy and respect for fellow players, the golf course, and the traditions of the game is what makes golf such a lasting enjoyment for all. Here is a quick reminder of basic golf etiquette:

◆ Replace divots on tees and fairways
◆ Fix ballmarks on the greens (yours and any forgotten ones)
◆ Rake bunkers after sandshots
◆ Avoid damaging the greens by carelessly dropping flagstick or clubs
◆ Avoid damaging the course when taking practice swings
◆ If you use a power-cart, avoid driving close to greens and tee areas
◆ Keep the course free of litter
◆ Play promptly, and always remember to enjoy your game!

Red Mountain Ranch Country Club

6425 E. Teton, Mesa, AZ 85205 (602)985-0285

Located in the high desert foothills, Red Mountain Ranch presents magnificent red-rock formations that sharply contrast with the bright green of Pete Dye's superb course. Everything you'd expect is here: target-style landing areas, sand and grass bunkers, multi-tiered greens, and the signature Dye railroad ties. Water comes into play on three holes, with great effect on the par-3 No. 11 and its semi-island green. There is also distinctive desert vegetation everywhere and a sparkling, four-acre lake to reflect the splendid sunsets.

RED MOUNTAIN RANCH COUNTRY CLUB
18 holes Par 72 6977/6080/4982 yds.
USGA: 67.8 SLOPE: 121
STYLE: Desert
ACCESS: Restrictions on tee times
SEASON: All year HIGH: Jan.-Apr.
GREEN FEES: $$$ (includes cart)
REDUCED FEES: WD, LS, TW
RESERVATIONS: Nonmembers 3 days
WALKING: Yes RANGE: Yes

The Pointe Golf Club on South Mountain

7777 S. Pointe Pkwy., Phoenix, AZ 85234 (602)438-1413
ACCOMMODATIONS: The Pointe Resort (602)438-9000

The Pointe on South Mountain is a short but tight, hilly course built on ninety acres of Sonoran Desert adjacent to the Phoenix Mountain Preserve Park. One can see as far as forty miles from some of the elevated tees, and these views of The Valley of the Sun are, needless to say, spectacular. The target-golf layout was designed to play over and around the desert's natural features. The 461-yard, par-5 No. 13 plays through a picturesque desert canyon. The approach shot must cross the "Jailhouse Steps," a field of unappealing desert rocks staggered in a grand staircase fashion. The greens are well-contoured and protected by mounds instead of heavy bunkering. The Pointe hosted the ESPN 1989 Legends of Sports Tournament.

THE POINTE GOLF CLUB ON SOUTH MOUNTAIN
18 holes Par 70 6000/4999/4410 yds.
USGA: 67.3 SLOPE: 112
STYLE: Desert, hills
ACCESS: No restrictions
SEASON: All year HIGH: Jan.-Apr.
GREEN FEES: $$$$ (includes cart)
REDUCED FEES: LS, TW, PK
RESERVATIONS: 1 month with credit card
WALKING: No RANGE: No

THE KARSTEN GOLF COURSE AT ASU

1125 E. RIO SALADO PKWY., TEMPE, AZ 85281 (602)921-8070

Pete Dye was commissioned to create The Karsten Golf Course at Arizona State University. Opened in 1989, the course has already established a national reputation for championship-caliber golf and has been retained as the host of several tournaments. It is a demanding Scottish-links-type course in the Dye tradition, with mounds and bulkheaded water hazards. Two lakes come into play on five holes. The par-4 ninth, the par-3 sixteenth, and the par-4 eighteenth have been rated as three of the most challenging holes in the state by the Arizona Golf Association and *Arizona Golf Journal*. The course can be played from four different sets of tees, providing a fair challenge for everyone.

> **THE KARSTEN GOLF COURSE AT ARIZONA STATE UNIVERSITY**
> 18 holes   Par 72   7057/6272/4760 yds.
> USGA: 69.9   SLOPE: 120
> STYLE: Desert links
> ACCESS: No restrictions
> SEASON: All year   HIGH: Jan.-Apr.
> GREEN FEES: $$$$ (cart included)
> REDUCED FEES: LS, TW
> RESERVATIONS: 5 days
> WALKING: At times   RANGE: Yes

HILLCREST GOLF CLUB

20002 STAR RIDGE DR., SUN CITY WEST, AZ 85375 (602)975-1000

Hillcrest's championship course runs through 179 acres of undulating terrain and glimmering lakes. It is located in a valley, and many elevated tees

offer nice views of the entire layout. No. 13, which plays up a hill, is considered one of the best holes in the state. Although the course is fairly open, it requires accurate iron play to steer clear of the many yawning sandtraps and lurking water hazards. Since its opening in 1979, this Greg Nash course has matured beautifully, and most holes are adorned with fully grown palm, olive, and pine trees. Multiple tee placements allow Hillcrest to accommodate players of all skill levels, and many tournaments have been hosted here.

> **HILLCREST GOLF CLUB**
> 18 holes   Par 72   6960/6421/5880 yds.
> USGA: 69.8   SLOPE: 116
> STYLE: Rolling hills, lakes
> ACCESS: No restrictions
> SEASON: All year   HIGH: Jan.-Apr.
> GREEN FEES: $$$ (includes cart)
> REDUCED FEES: LS, TW
> RESERVATIONS: 3 days
> WALKING: No   RANGE: Yes

TATUM RANCH GOLF CLUB

29888 N. TATUM RANCH DR., CAVE CREEK, AZ 85331 (602)252-1230

The setting at Tatum Ranch is postcard-perfect: natural desert scenery, mountains in the background, and beautiful mesquite and Palo Verde trees. Robert Cupp laid out the course, which opened in 1987, making full use of the ideal site to create his challenge. The course counts only thirty-six bunkers and one lake. While some of the traps are quite difficult, Cupp relied mainly

> **TATUM RANCH GOLF CLUB**
> 18 holes   Par 72   6870/6357/5609 yds.
> USGA: 70.0   SLOPE: 120
> STYLE: Desert
> ACCESS: No restrictions
> SEASON: All year   HIGH: Oct.-May
> GREEN FEES: $$$ (includes cart)
> REDUCED FEES: LS, TW
> RESERVATIONS: 6 days
> WALKING: No   RANGE: Yes

on the natural roll of the land and some subtle mounding to test the golfer. He also made attractive use of the mesquite bushes to border the fairways and a visit to the local flora could prove quite damaging to your score. Tatum Ranch is a natural-looking course with the peaceful atmosphere and quality of a private country club.

SEDONA GOLF RESORT

THE SEDONA GOLF RESORT

7260 HIGHWAY 179, SEDONA, AZ 86336 (602)284-9355 *(8 mi. S of Sedona)*

Ninety miles north of Phoenix lies a natural wonder of the American Southwest: the red rocks of Sedona. At Oak Creek Canyon, these million-year-old natural fortresses, with their beautiful red turrets and spires, stand in striking contrast to the backdrop of the Coconino National Forest's emerald-green foothills.

Since the mid-sixties, Sedona has been the home of a large and active colony of artists. These colorful rocks and foothills hide many dream houses born in the minds of innovative architects. Golf course designers and players—artists in their own right—could not continue to ignore this magnificent site.

Sedona was put on the golf map in 1988 with the opening of The Sedona Golf Resort. Renowned architect Gary Panks put his imagination to work and came up with a design that enhances the breathtaking views of the monumental mesas. For variety and scale, he incorporated five lakes and a few small waterfalls throughout the layout, while natural desert areas create unusual obstacles and blend the course into the scenery. Wildlife abounds around Sedona; it is not uncommon to spot coyotes, white-tailed deer, and eagles—those of the flying kind, that is...

THE SEDONA GOLF RESORT
18 holes   Par 71   6642/6126/5030 yds.
USGA: 68.1   SLOPE: 124
STYLE: Desert, mountain
ACCESS: No restrictions
SEASON: All year   HIGH: Spring and fall
GREEN FEES: $$$ (includes cart)
REDUCED FEES: TW
RESERVATIONS: 2 weeks
WALKING: Yes   RANGE: Yes

OCOTILLO GOLF CLUB `5`
3751 S. CLUBHOUSE DR., CHANDLER, AZ 85248 (602)275-4355 *(15 mi. SE of Phoenix)*

Although it is located in the desert, Ocotillo is far from being a typical desert course. There is water on twenty-three of the Blue, White, and Gold Courses' twenty-seven holes! One may assume that designer Ted Robinson tried to scare golfers away. Quite the contrary. Thanks to four sets of tees and a forgiving design, the water hazards can easily be avoided on most holes. The difficulty stems more from multi-tiered greens and the delicate club judgment that is required. There are scenic views of mountains, and the course is extremely enjoyable to play. Ocotillo hosted the 1991 PGA Tour qualifiers and received very favorable reviews from the pros.

OCOTILLO GOLF CLUB
27 holes   2960/2890/3068 yds.
STYLE: Rolling hills, lakes
ACCESS: No restrictions
SEASON: All year   HIGH: Jan.-Mar.
GREEN FEES: $$$$ (includes cart)
REDUCED FEES: LS
RESERVATIONS: 2 days to 1 week
WALKING: At times   RANGE: Yes

PINON HILLS GOLF COURSE `6`
2101 SUNRISE PKWY., FARMINGTON, NM 87401 (505)326-6066 *(180 mi. from Albuquerque)*

The dominant characteristic of Pinon Hills is its diversity—at least in terms of desert terrain. Designed by Ken Dye and opened in 1989, the course's bluegrass fairways roll and jump over plateaus and arroyos, ending with large, multi-tiered greens. There are also sixty-four sandtraps to deal with, and roughs seeded with a mix of fescue, rye, and bluegrass. Pretty to look at, but hard to get out of! An outstanding hole is No. 6, a par 3 over a rough sandstone canyon. It plays anywhere between 100 and 157 yards. But the signature hole, another par 3, is the fifteenth, which tees off from the top of a sandstone cliff to a green surrounded by more spectacular rock formations. Many beautiful views of Colorado's La Plata Mountains add to the enjoyment of the course.

PINON HILLS GOLF COURSE
18 holes   Par 72   7249/6736/5522 yds.
USGA: 70.9   SLOPE: 130
STYLE: Desert
ACCESS: No restrictions
SEASON: All year   HIGH: Summer
GREEN FEES: $
RESERVATIONS: 1 week
WALKING: Yes   RANGE: Yes

N E W   M E X I C O

UNIVERSITY OF NEW MEXICO GOLF COURSE `7`
3601 UNIVERSITY BLVD. SE, ALBUQUERQUE, NM 87131 (505)277-4546 *(in Albuquerque)*

The University of New Mexico's eighteen-hole South Course, site of many tournaments, sits on a hill that overlooks the city of Albuquerque to the west and mountains to the east. At times, the layout is steep, and desert terrain comes into play on many holes. The greens, very large and contoured, present a tough challenge; this is also true of the bunkers, many of which are deep and steep. The tee shot on the par-4 No. 10 is uphill to a plateau; from there, it doglegs sharply to the right and drops downhill to the green. Despite these elements, this Red Lawrence-designed course is fair and can be played by golfers of all abilities. The nine-hole North Course, designed by William Tucker, has many mature trees which lend it a park-like atmosphere. The course has some long holes and small, target-style putting surfaces.

UNIVERSITY OF NEW MEXICO SOUTH COURSE
18 holes   Par 72   7253/6480/6167 yds.
USGA: 70.3   SLOPE: 121
STYLE: Rolling hills, desert
ACCESS: No restrictions
SEASON: All year   HIGH: May-Sept.
GREEN FEES: $
REDUCED FEES: TW
RESERVATIONS: On Thurs. for Sat.-Fri.
WALKING: Yes   RANGE: Yes

COCHITI LAKE GOLF COURSE 8

5200 COCHITI HWY., COCHITI LAKE, NM 87041 (505)465-2239, (505)465-2230 *(35 mi. S of Santa Fe)*

COCHITI LAKE GOLF COURSE
18 holes Par 72   6500/6000/5300 yds.
USGA: 68.3 SLOPE: 115
STYLE: Mountain, woods
ACCESS: No restrictions
SEASON: All year HIGH: May-Aug.
GREEN FEES: $
REDUCED FEES: WD
RESERVATIONS: 1 week
WALKING: Yes RANGE: Yes

Cochiti Lake is located on a reservation owned by the Cochiti Pueblo Indians. The foothills offer a quiet setting for this Robert Trent Jones, Jr., course, which *Golf Digest* ranked number one in New Mexico and as one of the top twenty-five public courses in the nation. This wooded track presents many mountain-style holes, including Nos. 9 and 12, which both have tees perched on a cliff a hundred feet above the fairway. Great vistas of surrounding mountain ranges complement a superior golf experience.

INN OF THE MOUNTAIN GODS 9

BOX 259, RTE. 4, MESCALERO, NM 88340 (800)446-2963 *(130 mi. NE of El Paso, TX)*
ACCOMMODATIONS: INN OF THE MOUNTAIN GODS (505)257-5141

INN OF THE MOUNTAIN GODS
18 holes Par 72   6819/6416/5459 yds.
USGA: 70.1 SLOPE: 128
STYLE: Hills, woods, lakes
ACCESS: No restrictions
SEASON: Mar.-Nov. HIGH: May-Sept.
GREEN FEES: $$$
REDUCED FEES: HG
RESERVATIONS: Nonguests 2 weeks
WALKING: No RANGE: No

The magnificent land on which this dramatic course is built is considered sacred by the Apaches. Ted Robinson designed the eighteen-hole layout, and it is operated and maintained by the Mescalero Apache tribe. Thought of as one of the finest resort courses in America, the track plays through mountainous surroundings punctuated by the waters of Lake Mescalero. The 348-yard, par-4 No. 10 is sure to remain engraved in your memory: it plays to a unique island fairway before returning to firm land.

T
E
X
A
S

RIVERCHASE GOLF CLUB 10

700 RIVERCHASE DR., COPPELL, TX 75019 (214)462-8281 *(7 mi. NE of Dallas-Ft. Worth Airport)*
ACCOMMODATIONS: DOUBLETREE PARK WEST (214)869-4300

RIVERCHASE GOLF CLUB
18 holes Par 71   6593/6041/5125 yds.
USGA: 68.4 SLOPE: 114
STYLE: Lakes
ACCESS: No restrictions
SEASON: All year HIGH: Apr.-Oct.
GREEN FEES: $$$ (includes cart)
REDUCED FEES: WD, TW
RESERVATIONS: 7 days, weekends 2 days
WALKING: Yes RANGE: Yes

Set in a country landscape, Riverchase incorporates the Trinity River and eight lakes to create a course both challenging and aesthetically pleasing. Water comes directly into play on only five holes, but lateral water can be found on all eighteen. Nos. 5, 6, and 7 actually border the river itself. The course was designed by George Fazio and features abundant mounding on and around the fairways. The elevated and well-contoured greens are kept in top condition.

HYATT BEAR CREEK GOLF AND RACQUET CLUB **11**

W. AIRFIELD DR. AT BEAR CREEK CT., DFW AIRPORT, TX 75261 (214)615-6801
(inside Dallas-Fort Worth Airport)
ACCOMMODATIONS: HYATT REGENCY DFW HOTEL (214)453-1234

Standing in the middle of Bear Creek's large oak and cottonwood trees, it's hard to believe that these two eighteen-hole courses are on the grounds of the Dallas-Fort Worth Airport. Ted Robinson designed both, and they're similar in several ways. Water comes into play on ten holes on the West and seven on the East. Both have tree-lined fairways rolling over terrain that is uncommonly wooded and hilly for the area. The West Course's seventh is the number-one handicap; at 360 yards from the regular tees, this par 4 goes uphill and is framed by towering trees. On the East Course, No. 5 is a beautiful par 4 with an elevated landing area and a downhill second shot over a picturesque pond.

HYATT BEAR CREEK
ACCESS: Priority to hotel guests
SEASON: All year
HIGH: Apr.-June/Sept.-Oct.
GREEN FEES: $$$
REDUCED FEES: WD, LS, TW, PK
RESERVATIONS: Nonguests 3 days
WALKING: Yes   RANGE: Yes
- **EAST COURSE**
  18 holes   Par 72   6677/6261/5620 yds.
  USGA: 72.5   SLOPE: 121
  STYLE: Rolling hills, woods
- **WEST COURSE**
  18 holes   Par 72   6670/6282/5597 yds.
  USGA: 72.7   SLOPE: 125
  STYLE: Rolling hills, woods

FOUR SEASONS RESORT AND CLUB TOURNAMENT PLAYERS COURSE **12**

4150 N. MACARTHUR BLVD., IRVING, TX 75038 (214)717-0700, EXT. 2530 *(12 mi. NW of Dallas)*
ACCOMMODATIONS: FOUR SEASONS RESORT AND CLUB AT LAS COLINAS (214)717-0700

The Tournament Players Course at the Four Seasons Resort is the home of the Byron Nelson Classic. It was designed by Jay Morrish, with Byron Nelson and Ben Crenshaw as consultants. This stadium course is not long by championship standards and demands more finesse than raw power. A creek runs through the course and comes into play on nine holes. The sandtraps are small but deep, and the well-guarded greens are kept tournament fast. The course is always in first-class condition, and to get your swing ready for competition, there are two practice putting greens, a sandtrap practice area, and a full driving range.

TOURNAMENT PLAYERS COURSE
18 holes   Par 70   6767/5937/5337 yds.
USGA: 69.5   SLOPE: 124
STYLE: Rolling hills
ACCESS: Hotel guests only
SEASON: All year   HIGH: Apr.-Sept.
GREEN FEES: $$$$
REDUCED FEES: PK
RESERVATIONS: Guests 1 month
WALKING: No   RANGE: Yes

MARRIOTT'S GOLF CLUB AT FOSSIL CREEK

MARRIOTT'S GOLF CLUB AT FOSSIL CREEK 〔13〕

3401 CLUBGATE DR., FORT WORTH, TX 76137 (817)847-1900 *(15 mi. N of Dallas-Fort Worth Airport)*
ACCOMMODATIONS: CALL GOLF CLUB FOR INFORMATION

Arnold Palmer designed Fossil Creek's course and played the official first round here in 1987. The legendary player and architect was offered a wide range of design opportunities by the site—a limestone quarry full of cliffs and ravines. On fifteen holes, crystal-clear lakes and rock-ledged creeks enhance the challenge of the course and the great Texas scenery. The bentgrass greens are on the smaller side, and the thirty-nine white sand bunkers deliver an additional test. Palmer also designed a variety of tees to deliver a fair challenge to all levels of players. *Golf Journal,* the publication of the USGA, has featured No. 15 as one of the great holes of golf. This 394-yard par 4 is bordered by a creek on the entire right side, and the second shot must be played over a rocky ledge to an elevated green.

MARRIOTT'S GOLF CLUB AT FOSSIL CREEK
18 holes   Par 72   6865/6457/5066 yds.
USGA: 71.1   SLOPE: 121
STYLE: Steep hills, water
ACCESS: Restrictions on tee times
SEASON: All year   HIGH: Mar.-June
GREEN FEES: $$$ (includes cart)
REDUCED FEES: WD, LS, TW, PK
RESERVATIONS: 3 days
WALKING: No   RANGE: Yes

WATERWOOD NATIONAL RESORT AND COUNTRY CLUB 〔14〕

1 WATERWOOD PKWY., HUNTSVILLE, TX 77340 (409)891-5050 *(19 mi. E of Huntsville)*
ACCOMMODATIONS: WATERWOOD NATIONAL RESORT AND COUNTRY CLUB (409)891-5211

WATERWOOD NATIONAL RESORT AND COUNTRY CLUB
18 holes   Par 71   6872/6258/5029 yds.
USGA: 70.6   SLOPE: 134
STYLE: Woods, lakes
ACCESS: No restrictions
SEASON: All year   HIGH: Apr.-Oct.
GREEN FEES: $$
REDUCED FEES: WD, HG, LS, PK
RESERVATIONS: 1 month
WALKING: Yes   RANGE: Yes

Waterwood is located on a secluded site in the middle of the Sam Houston National Forest, and it borders the 90,000-acre Lake Livingston. The course is the brainchild of architects Pete Dye and Bill Coore, and its 134 slope rating from the middle tees gives you an indication of the trouble ahead. Those who have survived it say that every hole is memorable. But then again, after trying to carry the ball 225 yards over water to No. 13's peninsula green, you would remember it, too.

MILL CREEK GOLF AND COUNTRY CLUB   15
OLD MILL RD., SALADO, TX 76571 (817)947-5141, (817)947-5698 *(45 mi. N of Austin)*
ACCOMMODATIONS: INN, TOWNHOUSES, AND CONDOS (817)947-5141

Six holes play directly over the Salado Creek at this course, which was redesigned in 1981 by Robert Trent Jones, Jr. Bermuda-grass fairways are rather generous and tempt you to get the driver out of the bag more often than you really need to, and Jones's large, cloverleaf sandtraps—one of his signatures—are here to catch the errant drives. You do need your driver on No. 4, however: the tee shot is played over an arm of the Salado Creek to the corner of the 398-yard, par-4

MILL CREEK GOLF COURSE
18 holes   Par 71   6486/6052/5250 yds.
USGA: 70   SLOPE: 124
STYLE: Tree-lined fairways, water
ACCESS: Priority to hotel guests
SEASON: All year   HIGH: Spring
GREEN FEES: $$$
REDUCED FEES: WD, PK
RESERVATIONS: Nonguests 2 days
WALKING: No   RANGE: Yes

dogleg. The second shot, played to an elevated green, goes over—and often into—the creek itself. Having attempted a fine, high lofted shot over the creek, any number of sandtraps lie in wait to capture deviant trajectories. The course is graced with large oak and elm trees and bluebonnets in the springtime. Mill Creek is famous for its unique heart-shaped green on No. 3.

TOURNAMENT PLAYERS COURSE AT THE WOODLANDS   16
1730 S. MILLBEND DR., THE WOODLANDS, TX 77380 (713)367-7285 *(25 mi. N of Houston)*
ACCOMMODATIONS: THE WOODLANDS RESORT (800)433-2624, (800)533-3052 (IN TX)

TPC AT THE WOODLANDS
18 holes   Par 72   7045/6387/5302 yds.
USGA: 70.5   SLOPE: 127
STYLE: HW, LK
ACCESS: No restrictions
SEASON: All year
HIGH: Jan.-June/Sept.-Nov.
GREEN FEES: $$$$ (includes cart)
REDUCED FEES: WD, LS, TW
RESERVATIONS: Anytime
WALKING: Yes   RANGE: Yes

HOLE NO. 13

Designed by the team of Bruce Devlin and architect Bob von Hagge, this may be the most natural of all the TPC layouts. The course winds through heavily wooded terrain, which makes for well-defined and isolated fairways. As one would expect at a TPC course, there is substantial mounding around the greens, mostly to facilitate tournament viewing. Lakes come into play on ten holes to help spice up the show. The island green on the par-5 thirteenth is a favorite of spectators, although it may prove to be rather daunting when you attempt it. The Tournament Players Course at The Woodlands is the home of the PGA Tour Independent Insurance Agent Open. The North Golf Course, a semi-private eighteen-hole course, is also available to guests of the Woodlands.

BARTON CREEK

8212 BARTON CLUB DR., AUSTIN, TX 78735 (512)329-4616 *(10 mi. W of downtown Austin)*
ACCOMMODATIONS: BARTON CREEK RESORT AND CONFERENCE CENTER (800)527-3220, (512)329-4000

BARTON CREEK
ACCESS: Hotel guests only
SEASON: All year   HIGH: Spring and fall
GREEN FEES: $$$$$
REDUCED FEES: See description
RESERVATIONS: Recommended
WALKING: No   RANGE: Yes
• **FAZIO COURSE**
  18 holes   Par 72   6956/6513/5095 yds.
  USGA: 70.5   SLOPE: 122
  STYLE: Hills, woods, water
• **LAKESIDE COURSE**
  18 holes   Par 71   6622/6046/5063 yds.
  USGA: 67.7   SLOPE: 112
  STYLE: Hills, woods, water
• **CRENSHAW-COORE COURSE**
  18 holes   Par 71   6678/6066/4843 yds.
  STYLE: Hills, woods, water

LAKESIDE COURSE

These are some of the finest courses in Texas. The Fazio course at Barton Creek is familiar to television viewers as the site of the Legends of Golf tournament. It takes dramatic advantage of the rolling land of the Texas hill country, including a waterfall-surrounded green on the par-3 No. 9, and a hundred-foot drop on the majestic No. 10. The Lakeside Course, designed by Arnold Palmer, features some spectacular holes built along a high bluff over Lake Travis. The new Crenshaw-Coore Course, opened in 1991, is Ben Crenshaw's first design in his hometown, and it's a beauty. Crenshaw, the ultimate traditionalist, and his partner, Bill Coore, designed generous fairways and greens that give players of every skill level an abundance of strategic options. The par-3 No. 17 requires a short iron over a deep gorge. A note about access and green fees: all three courses are reserved for guests of the hotel and conference center. The Fazio Course is more expensive, and the other two offer reduced rates for weekday play.

TAPATIO SPRINGS RESORT AND COUNTRY CLUB

WEST JOHNS RD., BOERNE, TX 78006 (512)537-4197 *(20 mi. N of San Antonio)*
ACCOMMODATIONS: TAPATIO SPRINGS RESORT (512)537-4611

The Tapatio Springs Championship Course is nestled in Texas hill country, with large oak trees bordering—and sometimes interfering—with the rolling fairways. The course is not very long, and golfers will enjoy a pleasant experience in a country setting. The spring-fed creek comes into play repeatedly, and you won't have to wait long before getting your water balls out of the bag: much of the 346-yard No. 2 is bordered on the left by the

CHAMPIONSHIP COURSE
18 holes   Par 72   6472/6122/5179 yds.
USGA: 69.5   SLOPE: 116
STYLE: Hills, water
ACCESS: Hotel guests only
SEASON: All year   HIGH: Spring
GREEN FEES: $$$ (includes cart)
RESERVATIONS: 6 months
WALKING: No   RANGE: Yes

creek, which cuts sharply into the fairway to form a semi-island green. No. 12 offers a panoramic view of the entire valley. Tapatio Springs also has a nine-hole executive course.

HORSESHOE BAY RESORT

19

HORSESHOE BAY BLVD., HORSESHOE BAY, TX 78654 (800)531-5105, *(45 mi. W of Austin)*
ACCOMMODATIONS: HORSESHOE BAY RESORT (512)598-2511

The Horseshoe Bay Resort is located in the heart of Texas, alongside beautiful lake LBJ. Guests of the resort have the privilege of experiencing three courses of heroic proportion that Robert Trent Jones built among granite rocks in valleys wooded with oak, cedar, and persimmon trees. Slickrock, the original course, opened in 1973. It runs through rolling and wooded terrain studded with stone outcroppings and presents plenty of water trouble. A waterfall runs completely across No. 14's fairway! Ramrock, opened in 1981, is regarded as one of the most difficult layouts in Texas. It combines steep hills with eight water holes to create a challenge that even tour players fear and respect. To complete Jones's Texas trilogy, Applerock was opened in 1985 on high hills overlooking the lake. This third course presents considerable changes in elevation and some serious bunkering. Horseshoe Bay is for people who love Robert Trent Jones and golf!

HORSESHOE BAY RESORT
STYLE: Hills, lakes
ACCESS: Hotel guests only
SEASON: All year   HIGH: May-Sept.
GREEN FEES: $$$$$
REDUCED FEES: WD, PK
RESERVATIONS: 1 week
WALKING: No   RANGE: Yes
• **SLICKROCK**
  18 holes   Par 72   6839/6358/5843 yds.
  USGA: 70.2   SLOPE: 117
• **APPLEROCK**
  18 holes   Par 72   6999/6536/5480 yds.
  USGA: 71.5
• **RAMROCK**
  18 holes   Par 71   6946/6408/5305 yds.
  USGA: 72

PECAN VALLEY GOLF COURSE

20

4700 PECAN VALLEY DR., SAN ANTONIO, TX 78223 (512)333-9018 *(5 mi. S of downtown San Antonio)*

PECAN VALLEY GOLF COURSE
18 holes   Par 72   7163/6614/5651 yds.
USGA: 71   SLOPE: 128
STYLE: Rolling hills, water
ACCESS: No restrictions
SEASON: All year   HIGH: Mar.-June/Oct.
GREEN FEES: $$
RESERVATIONS: 2 weeks
WALKING: Yes   RANGE: Yes

Pecan Valley hosted the fiftieth PGA Championship in 1968. During that tournament, Arnold Palmer hit a 230-yard shot on No. 18 to within five feet of the pin, then missed the putt that would have put him in a playoff with Julius Boros. The Salado Creek winds through the entire course, and ten holes have water hazards. All fairways are tree-lined; in fact, the course is filled with beautiful pecan, oak, ash, and mesquite.

SHANGRI-LA

SHANGRI-LA RESORT

21

RTE. 3, AFTON, OK 74331 (918)257-4204, (800)331-4060 *(75 mi. N of Tulsa)*
ACCOMMODATIONS: SHANGRI-LA RESORT (918)257-4204

SHANGRI-LA RESORT
ACCESS: Priority to hotel guests
SEASON: All year   HIGH: May-Sept.
GREEN FEES: $$$ (includes cart)
REDUCED FEES: WD, LS, PK
RESERVATIONS: Nonguests 2 weeks
WALKING: At times   RANGE: Yes
• **BLUE COURSE**
  18 holes   Par 72   7012/6435/5975 yds.
  USGA: 70.5   SLOPE: 115
  STYLE: Rolling hills, lakes
• **GOLD COURSE**
  18 holes   Par 70   5932/5431/5109 yds.
  USGA: 66.3   SLOPE: 97
  STYLE: Rolling hills, lakes

The two recently renovated eighteen-hole courses at Shangri-La are built on gently rolling terrain and have tree-lined fairways and views of a lake. The longer and more hilly Blue Course, with large, undulating greens, is definitely the toughest. Water interferes with play on four holes. The 521-yard, par-5 fourteenth has a green sitting across a sizable lake, and your drive and second shot had better be good. The Gold Course plays shorter and perhaps a bit more open but brings a lot more water into play: drives, second shots, and approaches have to be played over the H_2O, and a round on this course is usually a lot of fun. The par-4 eighteenth demands a long second shot across a cove to a far, semi-island green.

OTHER EXCELLENT COURSES IN THE SOUTHWEST

ARIZONA

■ THE BOULDERS, Carefree (800)553-1717
● FOOTHILLS GOLF CLUB, Phoenix (602)460-4653
■ THE PHOENICIAN, Scottsdale (602)423-2450
▲ RANCHO DE LOS CABALLEROS, Wickenburg (602)684-5484
● TPC AT STARPASS, Tucson (602)622-6060
● TUCSON NATIONAL RESORT, Tuscon (602)575-7540

NEW MEXICO

● ANGEL FIRE COUNTRY CLUB, Angel Fire (505)377-3055

OKLAHOMA

● PAGE BELCHER GOLF COURSE, Tulsa (918)446-1529

TEXAS

● BEAR CREEK GOLF WORLD, Houston (713)859-8188
● CHASE OAKS GOLF CLUB, Plano (214)517-7777
■ LAKEWAY INN, A CONFERENCE RESORT, Austin (512)261-7572
● RANCHO VIEJO AND COUNTRY CLUB, Brownsville (512)350-4000
● RAYBURN COUNTRY CLUB, Sam Rayburn (409)698-2958

▲ RESTRICTIONS MAY APPLY   ■ HOTEL/RESORT GUESTS ONLY   ● OPEN WITHOUT RESTRICTIONS

Dana,

Here's hoping you're on
the mend of things very
soon. Thanks so much for
everything – you're a great
host!

Love Jim

CHAPTER FIVE

THE MIDWEST

Golfing adventures may not come to mind when thinking of the Midwest. Farmland and grain silos, yes. The Great Lakes, naturally. Even the Sears Tower—but golf? Probably not. Well, that's all right. Anyone can make a mistake.

Indeed, a quick review of the Midwest uncovers some enlightening facts about golf in this region: no less than twenty-two of *Golf Digest*'s seventy-five best public courses are located here, and many more contenders are busy making improvements so that they, too, might be included on the coveted list. Indiana, Illinois, Michigan, Minnesota, Ohio, and Wisconsin offer a true roster of high-quality courses open to the public. The great city of Chicago is famous for providing local golf fans with a greater choice of high-quality, public-access courses than any other big metropolis in the country! There are also superb golf resorts in the Midwest. Many are concentrated in the northwest corner of Michigan's lower peninsula, an area once devoted only to skiing and now known as "America's Summer Golf Capital." Wisconsin's southeast corner is also coming on strong as a serious contender in the golf resort scene.

Midwesterners have earned the privilege of having such an abundance of golf. After all, winters can be long and painful in the Great Lakes area. In the early chill of a March morning, the sight of contingents of golf fanatics flocking to the famous courses at Chicago's Cog Hill only proves that the people of the Midwest have as much character as their courses do.

EDGEWOOD GOLF COURSE

1

N. ELM ST., FARGO, ND 58102 (701)232-2824 *(in Fargo)*
ACCOMMODATIONS: CALL GOLF COURSE FOR INFORMATION

EDGEWOOD GOLF COURSE
18 holes   Par 71   6369/6045/5176 yds.
USGA: 68.4   SLOPE: 122
STYLE: Rolling hills, water
ACCESS: No restrictions
SEASON: Apr.-Oct.   HIGH: June-Aug.
GREEN FEES: $
REDUCED FEES: WD, TW
RESERVATIONS: 3 days
WALKING: Yes   RANGE: Yes

When in North Dakota, do as the North Dakotans do: play Edgewood's golf course. This Robert Bruce Harris design is situated on a river and runs across thick lines of oak, elm, and maple trees. Although only twenty-five sandtraps are scattered throughout, you'll still be tested by the course. Golfers praise the variety of holes here, and the lakes, ponds, and brooks make for a most picturesque setting. Contoured greens and rolling hills add to the challenge. Edgewood is kept in excellent shape by a dedicated staff.

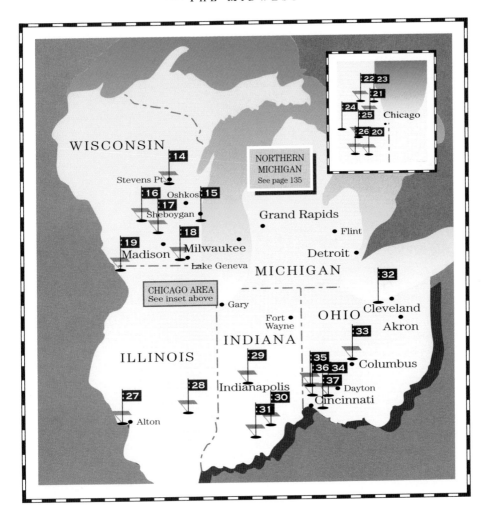

MEADOWBROOK GOLF COURSE

2

3625 JACKSON BLVD., RAPID CITY, SD 57702 (605)394-4191 *(12 mi. from Mt. Rushmore)*
ACCOMMODATIONS: CALL GOLF COURSE FOR INFORMATION

Located twelve miles from Mount Rushmore on the flood plain of Rapid Creek—which comes into play on nine holes—this long and challenging layout is known for its wonderful variety of mature trees, including weeping birch, black walnut, and elm, and for views of the surrounding Black Hills. Its real strength, however, lies in its par 5s, the toughest of which is the 590-yard sixth, a double dogleg with a creek cutting across the fairway twice. *Golf Digest* has rated Meadowbrook one of the top fifty public courses in the country.

> **MEADOWBROOK GOLF COURSE**
> 18 holes   Par 72   7054/6520/5603 yds.
> USGA: 70.7   SLOPE: 133
> STYLE: Trees, water
> ACCESS: No restrictions
> SEASON: All year   HIGH: June-Aug.
> GREEN FEES: $
> RESERVATIONS: 1 day
> WALKING: Yes   RANGE: Yes

SOUTH DAKOTA

N E B R A S K A

HERITAGE HILLS GOLF COURSE

6000 CLUBHOUSE DR., McCOOK, NE 69001 (308)345-5032 *(225 mi. W of Omaha)*

3

HERITAGE HILLS GOLF COURSE
18 holes   Par 72   6715/6095/5475 yds.
USGA: 69.8   SLOPE: 127
STYLE: Scottish links, ravines
ACCESS: No restrictions
SEASON: All year   HIGH: June-Aug.
GREEN FEES: $
REDUCED FEES: WD
RESERVATIONS: Recommended
WALKING: Yes   RANGE: Yes

This links-style course is a fine example of lay-of-the-land golf course design. Although virtually treeless, the undulating terrain, gaping bunkers, native prairie grasses, and speedy greens pose problems enough for the average golfer—and when the wind blows, look out! The signature hole is No. 11, a four-hundred-yard dogleg left, with four bunkers pinching the landing area and a deep swale in front of the green. *Golf Digest* has rated it one of the top seventy-five public courses in the country.

K A N S A S

TERRADYNE RESORT HOTEL AND COUNTRY CLUB

1400 TERRADYNE DR., ANDOVER, KS 67002 (316)733-5851 *(8 mi. E of Wichita)*
ACCOMMODATIONS: TERRADYNE RESORT HOTEL (316)733-2582

4

**TERRADYNE RESORT HOTEL
AND COUNTRY CLUB**
18 holes   Par 71   6704/6215/5048 yds.
USGA: 71.6   SLOPE: 132
STYLE: Scottish-style links, water
ACCESS: Priority to hotel guests
SEASON: All year   HIGH: May-Sept.
GREEN FEES: $$
REDUCED FEES: HG
RESERVATIONS: 1 week
WALKING: Yes   RANGE: Yes

The flat plains of Kansas and links-style golf may not seem like a natural match, but head pro Grier Jones's layout is bound to convince you otherwise. Terradyne boasts enough sand (over one hundred bunkers), water, and wind—remember, this is Kansas—to justify its Scottish-sounding name. And you won't find a tougher opening hole anywhere—a 470-yard par 4 with water lurking just beyond the green. *Golf Digest* rated it the fourth-best course in the state.

DEER CREEK GOLF CLUB

7000 W. 133RD ST., OVERLAND PARK, KS 66209 (913)681-3100 *(15 mi. SW of Kansas City)*

5

Long known for its excellent private courses, the Kansas City area now has a championship-caliber public layout to match. Designed by Robert Trent Jones, Jr., Deer Creek challenges golfers with slender, tree-lined fairways, an abundance of bunkers, and water on thirteen holes. The toughest hole on a tight back nine, voted the most difficult par 3 in Kansas City, is No. 15, otherwise known as "Devastation," or the "shortest par 5 in town." The front nine is no cakewalk either, with Nos. 3 through 5 causing special headaches.

DEER CREEK GOLF CLUB
18 holes   Par 72   6890/6368/5981 yds.
USGA: 72.5   SLOPE: 128
STYLE: Hills, woods, water
ACCESS: No restrictions
SEASON: All year   HIGH: May-Oct.
GREEN FEES: $$$ (includes cart)
REDUCED FEES: WD, TW
RESERVATIONS: 2 days
WALKING: Yes   RANGE: Yes

LODGE OF THE FOUR SEASONS

STATE RD. HH, LAKE OZARK, MO 65049 (314)365-8532 *(100 mi. SW of St. Louis)*
ACCOMMODATIONS: LODGE OF THE FOUR SEASONS (800)843-5253

LODGE OF THE FOUR SEASONS
ACCESS: See description
SEASON: Mar.-Dec.   HIGH: May.-Sept.
GREEN FEES: $$$ (includes cart)
REDUCED FEES: WD, TW
RESERVATIONS: Nonguests 1 week
WALKING: No   RANGE: Yes
- **ROBERT TRENT JONES COURSE**
  18 holes   Par 71   6346/5772/5198 yds.
  USGA: 68.4   SLOPE: 124
  STYLE: Hills, woods
- **SEASONS RIDGE COURSE**
  18 holes   Par 72   6416/6020/4657 yds.
  USGA: 69.3   SLOPE: 124
  STYLE: Hills, woods

SEASONS RIDGE COURSE

Lodge of the Four Seasons offers forty-five holes of golf. The Robert Trent Jones Course is one of Jones's own personal favorites, and it is a beauty indeed. The course's narrow fairways roll over the Ozarks' hilly terrain and lead to very fast and elevated greens. There are dense woods all along the layout, but an occasional clearing allows great views of Lake of the Ozarks. Actually, you can take a very close look at the water when playing the No. 13 "Witches Cove," a par 3 with as much as two hundred yards of carry over the lake. To play the Robert Trent Jones Course, you must be a guest of the Lodge. Ken Kavanaugh is the architect for the new Seasons Ridge Course. Built in the foothills, it offers great views of the woods and lake around the Lodge. There is also a nine-hole executive course.

LODGE OF THE FOUR SEASONS, ROBERT TRENT JONES COURSE

MARRIOTT'S TAN-TAR-A RESORT AND GOLF CLUB `7`
STATE RD. KK, OSAGE BEACH, MO 65065 *(180 mi. W of St. Louis)*
OAKS: (314)348-4163, HIDDEN LAKES: (314)348-8527
ACCOMMODATIONS: MARRIOTT'S TAN-TAR-A RESORT (314)348-3131

> **OAKS COURSE**
> 18 holes   Par 71   6442/6002/3943 yds.
> USGA: 70.1   SLOPE: 133
> STYLE: Hills, woods, lakes
> ACCESS: No restrictions
> SEASON: All year   HIGH: May-Oct.
> GREEN FEES: $$$ (includes cart)
> REDUCED FEES: WD, HG, LS, TW, PK
> RESERVATIONS: 1 week
> WALKING: No   RANGE: Yes

Tan-Tar-A's twenty-seven holes put a premium on accuracy and strategy rather than distance. The eighteen-hole Oaks Course features tree-lined fairways, gorgeous lake views, and water on thirteen holes. No. 4, a downhill par 4 with a lake guarding the green, is typical: choose the right club to lay up with, and you'll have a short iron into the green; stray off the narrow fairway, and you'll be staring at double bogey. The nine-hole Hidden Lakes Course is less demanding but offers the same terrific views of the Ozarks.

IOWA

AMANA COLONIES GOLF COURSE `8`
RTE. 1, BOX 8500, AMANA, IA 52203 (800)383-3636, (319)622-6222 *(30 mi. SW of Cedar Rapids)*

> **AMANA COLONIES GOLF COURSE**
> 18 holes   Par 72   6824/6194/5228 yds.
> USGA: 70   SLOPE: 126
> STYLE: Hills, woods, water
> ACCESS: No restrictions
> SEASON: Apr.-Nov.   HIGH: May-Sept.
> GREEN FEES: $$
> REDUCED FEES: WD, TW
> RESERVATIONS: 1 month, longer with
>   credit card
> WALKING: At times   RANGE: Yes

Amana Colonies is laid out on three hundred acres of 130-year old forest. The rolling hills and heavily wooded surroundings offer unrivaled scenery, and the course was rated by *Golf* magazine as one of the top ten new public access courses of 1990. The fairways are fairly wide and forgiving, but the ponds, creeks, ravines, and well-bunkered greens take their toll along the way.

MINNESOTA

IZATYS GOLF AND YACHT CLUB `9`
MILLE LACS LAKE, RTE. 1, ONAMIA, MN 56359 (800)533-1728 *(90 mi. N of Minneapolis/St. Paul)*
ACCOMMODATIONS: IZATYS GOLF AND YACHT CLUB (800)533-1728

> **IZATYS GOLF AND YACHT CLUB**
> 18 holes   Par 72   6481/5961/4939 yds.
> USGA: 69.7   SLOPE: 127
> STYLE: Woods, lakes
> ACCESS: No restrictions
> SEASON: Apr.-Oct.   HIGH: June-Sept.
> GREEN FEES: $$
> REDUCED FEES: LS, TW
> RESERVATIONS: Anytime
> WALKING: Yes   RANGE: Yes

On the shores of Mille Lacs Lake, the second largest in the state and known for beautiful sunsets, this layout was restructured by Dye Designs. Izatys features tree-lined fairways, contoured greens, and creeks, marshes, and ponds that affect twelve holes. The 225-yard, par-3 No. 16 has water to the right of the green and a huge fan bunker discouraging players from bailing out to the left—not surprisingly, this hole is nicknamed "The Drink."

EDINBURGH USA
10

8700 EDINBROOK CROSSING, BROOKLYN PARK, MN 55443 (612)424-7060 *(10 mi. NW of Minneapolis)*
ACCOMMODATIONS: CALL GOLF COURSE FOR INFORMATION

Unlike a lot of farmland courses which can be flat and uninteresting at times, this Robert Trent Jones, Jr., layout has plenty of wooded areas, gaping bunkers, and water hazards. The open, links-style front nine is followed by a tight back nine that is distinguished by a great golf hole: the seventeenth. This picturesque par 4 has an island fairway and a spectacular peninsula green. Another memorable feature at Edinburgh is the huge putting surface that serves the ninth, the eighteenth, and the practice area. It is one of the largest greens in the world. Named by *Golf Digest* as one of the fifty best public courses in the country, Edinburgh USA has been the site of the LPGA Northland Classic for three years running.

> **EDINBURGH USA**
> 18 holes Par 72   6701/6335/5255 yds.
> USGA: 71.3 SLOPE: 127
> STYLE: Woods, water
> ACCESS: Priority to members
> SEASON: Apr.-Oct.   HIGH: June-Sept.
> GREEN FEES: $$
> REDUCED FEES: TW, PK
> RESERVATIONS: 4 days
> WALKING: Yes RANGE: Yes

BUNKER HILLS GOLF COURSE
11

HWY. 242 AND FOLEY BLVD., COON RAPIDS, MN 55433 (612)755-4141 *(20 mi. N of Minneapolis)*

The Bunker Hills courses are located in the middle of a 1,400-acre regional park. The site is a glacial-deposit area covered with natural sand dunes, pine, and desert wildflowers, all of which account for much of the appeal. Redesigned in 1990, this thirty-six hole complex gets high marks for scenery. In fact, some call it the most beautiful course in Minnesota. It offers golfers four nine-hole layouts: the gently rolling, well-bunkered East and West Courses, the long, heavily wooded North Course, and an executive nine.

> **BUNKER HILLS GOLF COURSE**
> 27 holes   3234/3340/3194 yds.
> STYLE: Rolling hills, woods
> ACCESS: No restrictions
> SEASON: Apr.-Oct.   HIGH: June-Aug.
> GREEN FEES: $
> REDUCED FEES: WD, LS
> RESERVATIONS: 3 days
> WALKING: Yes RANGE: Yes

MADDEN'S ON GULL LAKE
12

8001 PINE BEACH PENINSULA, BRAINERD, MN 56401 (218)829-2811 *(12 mi. N of Brainerd)*
ACCOMMODATIONS: MADDEN'S ON GULL LAKE (800)642-5363

> **MADDEN'S ON GULL LAKE**
> ACCESS: Priority to hotel guests
> SEASON: Apr.-Oct.   HIGH: Apr.-Oct.
> GREEN FEES: $$
> REDUCED FEES: HG, TW, PK
> RESERVATIONS: 1 day
> WALKING: Yes RANGE: Yes
> • **PINE BEACH EAST COURSE**
>   18 holes   Par 72   5920/5498 yds.
>   USGA: 67.2 SLOPE: 102
>   STYLE: Tree-lined fairways
> • **PINE BEACH WEST COURSE**
>   18 holes   Par 67   5086/4725 yds.
>   USGA: 62.3 SLOPE: 92
>   STYLE: Tree-lined fairways

Madden's has two eighteen-hole courses, the Pine Beach East and West, and a nine-hole course thoughtfully named The Social 9. These courses have been around for a while—since 1928, to be precise. The elegant Norway pine and large, mature, northern red oak attest to that. The East Course offers views of the beautiful Gull Lake, but you will mostly remember it for the 618-yard, par-6 No. 6. A birdie five is always fun to get. To pick up some more birdies, and for some relaxing golf, The Social 9 is the thing. Par is 28, and the course "stretches" 1,341 yards. All forty-five holes at Madden's are exceptionally well-maintained, and the quality shows everywhere.

MAJESTIC OAKS COUNTRY CLUB

701 BUNKER LAKE BLVD., HAM LAKE, MN 55304 (612)755-2142 *(15 mi. N of Minneapolis)*

MAJESTIC OAKS COUNTRY CLUB
ACCESS: No restrictions
SEASON: Apr.-Nov.   HIGH: June-Aug.
GREEN FEES: $
REDUCED FEES: TW
RESERVATIONS: 4 days
WALKING: Yes   RANGE: Yes
• **PLATINUM COURSE**
   18 holes   Par 72   7013/6357/5268 yds.
   USGA: 70.4   SLOPE: 126
   STYLE: Tree-lined fairways
• **GOLD COURSE**
   18 holes   Par 72   6366/5879/4848 yds.
   USGA: 68.6   SLOPE: 117
   STYLE: Water hazards

Majestic oaks are exactly what you'll see here on the twenty-year-old Platinum Course—along with deer, fox, and "killer" geese (don't ask!). Designed by Charles Maddox, Sr., and ranked by *Golf Digest* as one of the top seventy-five public courses in the country, this lovely layout embraces wooded areas and marshy lowlands. With plenty of water and lots of deep bunkers guarding the contoured greens, average golfers will have to play their best to keep it in the 90s. The less hazardous and relatively flat Gold Course is shorter and features narrow fairways, ponds, and swampland. The par-5 No. 16 has a tee shot guarded by a maple tree on the left and bunkers on the right, with a creek running down the entire left side. Not to be outdone, the par-4, 400-yard No. 14 features water crossing the fairway 280 yards out, with the green guarded by trees on the left, and water protecting the right. A nine-hole executive layout brings the total number of holes at Majestic Oaks to forty-five.

SENTRYWORLD GOLF COURSE

14

601 MICHIGAN AVE. N., STEVENS POINT, WI 54481 (715)345-1600 *(180 mi. NW of Milwaukee)*

SENTRYWORLD GOLF COURSE
18 holes   Par 72   7055/5826/5197 yds.
USGA: 69.8   SLOPE: 133
STYLE: Tree-lined fairways, lakes
ACCESS: No restrictions
SEASON: Apr.-Oct   HIGH: May-Aug.
GREEN FEES: $$$ (includes cart)
REDUCED FEES: LS
RESERVATIONS: Anytime in season
WALKING: At times   RANGE: Yes

The brainchild of John Joanis, chairman of the Sentry Insurance Co., this exquisitely demanding Robert Trent Jones, Jr., layout is characterized by large, contoured greens, yawning, freeform bunkers, and an abundance of trees, rocks, and water. The most photographed hole on the course is the par-3 sixteenth, or "Flower Hole," which gets its name from the ninety thousand flowers arranged in beds around the green.

SentryWorld was rated by *Golf Digest* in 1983 as the best new public course in America, and the superintendent and his crew are among the busiest in the whole country!

SENTRYWORLD

BLACKWOLF RUN

1111 W. RIVERSIDE DR., KOHLER, WI 53044 (414)457-4446 *(50 mi. N of Milwaukee)*
ACCOMMODATIONS: THE AMERICAN CLUB (800)344-2838

After its opening in 1988, Blackwolf Run was immediately acclaimed as one of the finest tests of golf in the Midwest, and it received *Golf Digest*'s best new public course nomination for that year. Today, Blackwolf Run offers two splendid and exciting eighteen-hole courses. Pete Dye skillfully carved the terrain of an ancient glacial tract and molded the meadowlands, valleys, and small lakes into two layouts known as the River Course and the Meadow Valleys Course.

> **BLACKWOLF RUN**
> ACCESS: No restrictions
> SEASON: Apr.-Oct.   HIGH: June-Sept.
> GREEN FEES: $$$
> REDUCED FEES: HG, TW, PK
> RESERVATIONS: Nonguests 1 month
> WALKING: Yes   RANGE: Yes
> • **RIVER COURSE**
>   18 holes   Par 72   6991/6101/5090 yds.
>   USGA: 70.9   SLOPE: 137
>   STYLE: Steep hills, water
> • **MEADOW VALLEYS COURSE**
>   18 holes   Par 72   7142/6169/5065 yds.
>   USGA: 70.4   SLOPE: 132
>   STYLE: Hills, water

The River Course is hilly, and its fairways tumble over dramatic changes in elevation. The Sheboygan River flows at the bottom of the course and can be seen from twelve holes—but water actually threatens on fourteen! No. 5 is the favorite. This par 4 has a set of tees elevated as high as fifty feet above the river, and the hole is simply and appropriately named "Made in Heaven."

The Meadow Valleys Course may be a bit less dramatic and less bruising to a golfer's ego, but it still is a stern test of golf. Dye went for a links-style design. He created only eight water holes but incorporated seventy sandtraps, including many pot bunkers. On the Meadow Valleys, the par-3 fifteenth is the most memorable. Nicknamed "Mercy," it plays anywhere from 103 to 227 yards. Regardless, the tee shot must carry over a valley, all the way to an immense, 15,700-square-foot green.

During design and construction, every effort was made to preserve the natural surroundings. A large variety of trees line the courses, and prairie and bluegrass roughs blend harmoniously with the manicured fairways. Both courses at Blackwolf Run are exhilarating to play, but their difficulty cannot be underestimated. Four sets of tees are provided, but even from the forward-middle tees, the River Course has a slope rating of 137 while the Meadow Valleys is rated at 132. The back tees are reserved for single handicappers... and dreamers.

BLACKWOLF RUN, MEADOW VALLEYS COURSE: HOLE No. 12

LAWSONIA GOLF COURSE 16

HWY. 23, GREEN LAKE, WI 54941 (414)294-3320 *(96 mi. NW of Milwaukee)*

LAWSONIA GOLF COURSE
ACCESS: No restrictions
SEASON: Apr.-Nov.   HIGH: June-Sept.
GREEN FEES: $$
REDUCED FEES: HG, LS, TW, PK
RESERVATIONS: Anytime
WALKING: At times   RANGE: Yes
• **LINKS COURSE**
   18 holes   Par 72   3399/3249/2687 yds.
   USGA: 71.5   SLOPE: 128
   STYLE: Traditional
• **WOODLANDS COURSE**
   18 holes   Par 72   6618/6186/5106 yds.
   USGA: 70.1   SLOPE: 129
   STYLE: Hills, woods

With the recent opening of a fourth nine, Lawsonia's long-established operation, which overlooks Green Lake, now has two markedly different eighteen-hole layouts. Rated by *Golf Digest* as one of the top seventy-five public courses in the country, the original eighteen-hole layout, newly dubbed the Links Course, debuted in 1930 and features large, elevated greens, a slew of steep-sided bunkers, and gently rolling, bentgrass fairways. The newer Woodlands Course is set in thick woods above the lake and, with an old stone quarry and many sweeping views, is considered one of the most beautiful in the state.

OLYMPIA VILLAGE 17

1350 ROYALE MILE RD., OCONOMOWOC, WI 53066 (800)558-9573 *(20 mi. NW of Milwaukee)*
ACCOMMODATIONS: OLYMPIA VILLAGE (800)558-9573

OLYMPIA VILLAGE
18 holes   Par 71   6482/6215/5862 yds.
USGA: 70.1   SLOPE: 114
STYLE: Rolling hills, tree-lined fairways
ACCESS: No restrictions
SEASON: Apr.-Oct.   HIGH: June-Aug.
GREEN FEES: $$
REDUCED FEES: WD, HG
RESERVATIONS: 1 week
WALKING: Weekdays   RANGE: Yes

Olympia Village offers a typical midwestern course. It may not have any particularly unique characteristics, but it is a solid, well-maintained layout with plenty of bunkers and sizable, contoured greens. The rolling, tree-lined fairways are relatively narrow, and things get even tighter on the back nine, where a meandering creek comes into play on every hole. But the prettiest hole on the course is the par-3 fifth, which is all carry over a pond to a green surrounded by willows.

GENEVA NATIONAL GOLF CLUB 18

1221 GENEVA NATIONAL AVE. S., LAKE GENEVA, WI 53147 (414)245-7010 *(45 mi. S of Milwaukee)*
ACCOMMODATIONS: INTERLAKEN RESORT AND COUNTRY SPA (414)248-9121

Geneva National retained the services of legendary players Arnold Palmer and Lee Trevino to design its two eighteen-hole courses. The Palmer Course is carved out of heavily wooded hills overlooking Lake Como. Many holes run across streams and deep ravines, and the entire course blends effortlessly with the natural landscape. Five sets of tees allow the course to play anywhere from championship to recreational length. The Trevino Course is a reflection of the champion's personality: his course is meant to be fun for anyone who loves golf. The holes are forgiving for

GENEVA NATIONAL GOLF CLUB
ACCESS: No restrictions
SEASON: Apr.-Oct.
GREEN FEES: $$$$ (includes cart)
REDUCED FEES: WD
RESERVATIONS: 2 weeks with credit card
WALKING: No   RANGE: Yes
• **PALMER COURSE**
   18 holes   Par 72   7193/6138/4922 yds.
   STYLE: Hills, woods
• **TREVINO COURSE**
   18 holes   Par 72   7120/6254/5193 yds.
   STYLE: Hills, woods

amateur players, but alternate routes from tee to green allow the pros to demonstrate their "stuff." A third course, designed by Gary Player, is planned for Geneva National's outstanding golf complex.

EAGLE RIDGE INN AND RESORT

19

10 CLUBHOUSE DR., GALENA, IL 61036 (815)777-2500 *(6 mi. E of Galena)*
ACCOMMODATIONS: EAGLE RIDGE INN (800)892-2269

> **EAGLE RIDGE INN AND RESORT**
> ACCESS: Priority to resort guests
> SEASON: Apr.-Nov. HIGH: May-Sept.
> GREEN FEES: $$$$ (includes cart)
> REDUCED FEES: LS, TW, PK
> RESERVATIONS: Nonguests 1 week
> WALKING: No RANGE: Yes
> • **NORTH COURSE**
>   18 holes Par 72 6836/6381/5578 yds.
>   USGA: 70.9 SLOPE: 129
>   STYLE: Steep hills, woods, water
> • **SOUTH COURSE**
>   18 holes Par 72 6762/6361/5609 yds.
>   USGA: 71.1 SLOPE: 130
>   STYLE: Steep hills, woods, rocks

Eagle Ridge's traditional hotel sits beautifully on a cliff overlooking Lake Galena. Set among the rolling and wooded hills of the Mississippi River Valley, the resort and its courses have received a lot of praise over the years: *Golf* magazine rates Eagle Ridge one of the best golf resorts in the world, and *Golf Digest* has ranked both the North and South courses in the top seventy-five resort courses in America. Eagle Ridge's North, designed by Roger Packard in 1977, is quite hilly. It offers a long, scenic vista of the valley, while creeks, bunkers, and large oak and walnut trees complete the scenery. The South, which Larry Packard laid out in 1984, incorporates spectacular rock ledges and cliffs, a welcome distraction from the creek that interferes with eleven of the holes. As their slope ratings indicate, both courses are quite testing. In 1991, a brand new nine-hole ratings indicate layout was added, the East, bringing Eagle Ridge's total to forty-five holes.

TAMARACK GOLF CLUB

20

24032 ROYAL WORLINGTON DR., NAPERVILLE, IL 60564 (708)904-4653 *(30 mi. SW of Chicago)*

Tamarack is a good example of a challenging layout fashioned out of limited materials. The course used to be farmland, so it is relatively flat and open. However, what it lacks in rolling terrain and trees, it makes up for with an impressive amount of sand and water. More than seventy large, deep bunkers define the fairways and guard the greens. But it is water, which comes into play on fifteen holes, that is likely to be most troublesome to the average golfer. The combination of sand and water creates a diabolical effect on the seemingly endless No. 12, a 613-yard par 5 with *seventeen* bunkers and a treacherous creek that crosses the fairway twice.

> **TAMARACK GOLF CLUB**
> 18 holes Par 70 6955/6331/5016 yds.
> USGA: 70.9 SLOPE: 125
> STYLE: Lakes, sandtraps
> ACCESS: Restrictions on weekends
> SEASON: Apr.-Oct. HIGH: June-Aug.
> GREEN FEES: $$$ (includes cart)
> REDUCED FEES: WD
> RESERVATIONS: 1 week
> WALKING: At times RANGE: Yes

GOLF CLUB OF ILLINOIS

1575 EDGEWOOD DR., ALGONQUIN, IL 60102 (708)658-4400 *(35 mi. NW of Chicago)*

GOLF CLUB OF ILLINOIS
18 holes   Par 71   7011/6558/5617 yds.
USGA: 71.8   SLOPE: 127
STYLE: Links style, target fairways
ACCESS: No restrictions
SEASON: Mar.-Nov.   HIGH: June-Aug.
GREEN FEES: $$
REDUCED FEES: WD, TW
RESERVATIONS: 1 week
WALKING: Yes   RANGE: Yes

In the rolling farmlands northeast of Chicago, there is a golf course that happily blends an innovative design with the vast landscape and great skies of the Midwest. The course also demonstrates strong character; perhaps, for that reason, the club decided to pay tribute to Illinois' most famous adopted son, Abraham Lincoln. Its logo displays the venerable statesman's profile. This course is the Golf Club of Illinois.

After studying the site, architect Dick Nugent decided in favor of a Scottish-inspired layout. His choice turned out to be well-suited to the terrain and appropriate to the local windy conditions. The dominant features are the target-style fairways and greens, which force players into some dramatic and intimidating carries over tall prairie grasses.

The course can be arduous at times. The fifteenth, nicknamed "Grant's March," runs 678 yards from the back tees! Playing slightly uphill and into the prevailing wind, it demands successive shots to three separate landing areas (optimists would say "three shots to successive landing areas"). Grant's March was named by *Golf* magazine as one of "the new untouchables." At the Golf Club of Illinois, each hole is named after its main characteristics. With appellations such as "Iroquois Mounds," "Sandsnake," and "Algonquin Climb," you get a good idea of the fun ahead, even before you hit your first tee shot. But rest assured, the course is equipped with five sets of tees and can be enjoyed by all.

The Golf Club of Illinois was named one of the top ten new public courses by *Golf Digest* in 1988 and one of the top five public golf courses in the Chicago area by the *Chicagoland Golfer*. If Abe's spirit doesn't keep you honest, this course sure will!

HOLE NO. 9: RAHILLY'S SANCTUARY

HOLES

#1	LINCOLN TRAIL		#10	ADLAI'S DRAW
#2	SHALLOW GALLOWS		#11	SANDSNAKE
#3	IROQUOIS MOUNDS		#12	DALEY DILEMMA
#4	LOCH LINDSAY		#13	FEATHERIE
#5	BROAD SHOULDERS		#14	ALGONQUIN CLIMB
#6	MUSKET SHOT		#15	GRANT'S MARCH
#7	SHAWNEE WALK		#16	RAILSPLITTER FITZ
#8	ABE'S ELBOW		#17	ST. CHRISTOPHER'S CROSSING
#9	RAHILLY'S SANCTUARY		#18	SANDBURG DUNES

HOLE NO.13: FEATHERIE

KEMPER LAKES GOLF AND TENNIS CLUB 22

OLD MCHENRY RD., LONG GROVE, IL 60047 (708)540-3450 *(45 min. N of Chicago)*

> **KEMPER LAKES GOLF CLUB**
> 18 holes   Par 72   7217/6265/5638 yds.
> USGA: 71.7   SLOPE: 135
> STYLE: Woods, lakes
> ACCESS: No restrictions
> SEASON: Apr.-Oct.   HIGH: May-Aug.
> GREEN FEES: $$$$$ (includes cart)
> RESERVATIONS: 1 week
> WALKING: No   RANGE: Yes

Kemper Lakes is one of the finest public golf facilities in the world. The course, built on 325 acres of lakes, meadows, and forests, made golfing news when it hosted the 1989 PGA Championship. On the sharp dogleg No. 18, Greg Norman hit his drive straight to the green over the corner lake—in violation of architects Ken Killian and Dick Nugent's design intentions. A "Norman" tree has since been added to dampen long hitters' enthusiasm for the hole. The 567-yard, par-5 seventh contributes to Kemper Lakes' reputation as a tough course as well as one of the best conditioned. Bunkered on both the left and right sides of the landing area, with water lining the entire left side, any hope of hitting the green in two shots is practically eliminated. Nevertheless, Craig Stadler holds a course record of 64.

KEMPER LAKES

PINE MEADOW GOLF CLUB `23`

1 PINE MEADOW LA., MUNDELEIN, IL 60060 (708)566-GOLF *(30 mi. N of Chicago)*

PINE MEADOW GOLF CLUB
18 holes   Par 72   7141/6614/5335 yds.
USGA: 71.7   SLOPE: 129
STYLE: Tree-lined fairways, lakes
ACCESS: Restrictions on weekends
SEASON: Mar.-Nov.   HIGH: Summer
GREEN FEES: $$$
REDUCED FEES: TW
RESERVATIONS: 2 weeks
WALKING: Yes   RANGE: Yes

Restored in 1986 after lying dormant for almost twenty years, Pine Meadow was named America's best new public course in 1986, and it is ranked among *Golf Digest*'s top twenty-five public courses in the U.S. The layout displays a large number of sand and grass bunkers, and three lakes. Needless to say, a premium is placed on straight drives and accurate approach shots. Golfers who skip their morning coffee get a wake-up call on No. 3, a dogleg left that plays almost two shots tougher than par.

CANTIGNY GOLF AND TENNIS `24`

27 W. 270 MACK RD., WHEATON, IL 60187 (708)668-3323 *(30 mi. W of Chicago)*

CANTIGNY 18-HOLE COURSE
18 holes   Par 72   6709/6267/5421 yds.
USGA: 65.7   SLOPE: 127
STYLE: Rolling hills, trees, water
ACCESS: No restrictions
SEASON: Apr.-Oct.   HIGH: Apr.-Oct.
GREEN FEES: $$$
RESERVATIONS: 1 week
WALKING: Yes   RANGE: Yes

The former estate of Colonel Robert McCormick, longtime publisher and editor of the *Chicago Tribune,* Cantigny has two golf courses, an outstanding eighteen-hole layout and a less demanding nine-hole course. Named the best new public course in 1989 by *Golf Digest,* the championship course is a wonderful but difficult test, with virtually every hole being double bogey material. The track is not especially long but tee-to-green accuracy is essential: thick oak and hardwood trees line the fairways, while seventy-plus bunkers and a dozen lakes are guaranteed to bring spray-and-pray golfers to their knees. Cantigny's outstanding holes are too numerous to mention, but No. 18 must be the only golf hole in the country with a bunker shaped like Dick Tracy's profile. To sweeten your experience, 100,000 flowers dot the course and its surroundings. Cantigny is one of the top public facilities in the Chicago area.

FOREST PRESERVE NATIONAL `25`

16300 S. CENTRAL AVE., OAK FOREST, IL 60452 (708)535-3377 *(20 mi. SW of Chicago)*

FOREST PRESERVE NATIONAL
18 holes   Par 72   7170/6690/5535 yds.
USGA: 72.5   SLOPE: 129
STYLE: Tree-lined fairways, large greens
ACCESS: No restrictions
SEASON: Mar.-Nov.   HIGH: Mar.-Nov.
GREEN FEES: $
REDUCED FEES: WD, TW
RESERVATIONS: No reservations
WALKING: Yes   RANGE: Yes

Chicago golfers are lucky indeed. Forest Preserve National is the showcase of nine courses operated by the Forest Preserve District of Cook County. The National was designed by architects Ken Killian and Dick Nugent on almost three hundred acres of rolling forest south of Chicago, and it may be the finest municipal golf course in the world. The layout's distinctive characteristics are its huge greens, some of them sixty yards in depth, and its sixty-four massive, walled bunkers. Even with four sets of tees, the course is a difficult test of golf. Ranked by *Golf Digest* among the top twenty-five public courses, Forest Preserve is well worth a visit, but be warned—it can only be played on a first-come, first-served basis, so set your alarm clock early.

COG HILL GOLF AND COUNTRY CLUB, DUBSDREAD

COG HILL GOLF AND COUNTRY CLUB

26

12294 ARCHER AVE., LEMONT, IL 60439 (708)257-5872 *(32 mi. SW of Chicago)*

COG HILL GOLF AND COUNTRY CLUB
ACCESS: No restrictions
SEASON: All year   HIGH: Apr.-Sept.
GREEN FEES: $$ (courses 1, 2, and 3)
RESERVATIONS: 6 days, prepaid 3 months
WALKING: Courses 1, 2, and 3
RANGE: Yes
• **NO. 1 COURSE**
  18 holes   Par 71   6234/5717 yds.
  USGA: 69.2   SLOPE: 115
  STYLE: Traditional
• **NO. 2 COURSE**
  18 holes   Par 72   6295/5978/5755 yds.
  USGA: 68.4   SLOPE: 118
  STYLE: Traditional
• **NO. 3 COURSE**
  18 holes   Par 72   6298/5385 yds.
  USGA: 69.5   SLOPE: 115
  STYLE: Traditional
• **NO. 4 COURSE (DUBSDREAD)**
  18 holes   Par 72   6992/6366/5874 yds.
  USGA: 71.8   SLOPE: 138
  STYLE: Traditional
  GREEN FEES: $$$$ (includes cart)

With four eighteen-hole courses and an extensive practice area, Cog Hill is one of the best public golf facilities in the nation. Courses No. 1, No. 2, and No. 3 have enough sand, woods, and water to test the accomplished player without punishing the beginner. They tend to be gently rolling and wooded—sometimes very tight and sometimes open—with mostly elevated greens. But connoisseurs come here to play the Dick Wilson and Joe Lee-designed No. 4 Course, better known as "Dubsdread," site of the 1991 Western Open: a traditional-style course where all hazards are clearly visible, it demands long, accurate drives, laser-like irons, and a sure touch on the greens. Oh, and don't forget your sand wedge—though, with more than a hundred bunkers, you'll probably wish you had a camel instead. Green fees on the first three courses are about half as expensive as they are on Dubsdread, which has been ranked by *Golf Digest* among the top hundred courses in the country.

SPENCER T. OLIN COMMUNITY GOLF COURSE `27`
4701 COLLEGE AVE., ALTON, IL 62002 (618)465-3111 *(25 mi. N of St. Louis)*
ACCOMMODATIONS: HOLIDAY INN (618)462-1220

Opened in 1989, this course was designed by Arnold Palmer at the request of a longtime friend, businessman Spencer T. Olin. The course is situated in a two-hundred-acre community park, amid wildflowers and native prairie grasses. Each hole is unique in character, alternately mixing hills, woods, lakes, and meandering creeks in its design, while many waste bunkers spice up the challenge. A true test is the eighth hole. A 406-yard dogleg left, it plays to a fairway guarded by a lake along the left side and a ravine to the right. The second shot plays to a large green protected by the lake, along with two expansive, well-placed bunkers. The course's management is controlled by Arnold Palmer, and the quality of its conditioning surpasses that of many private clubs.

SPENCER T. OLIN COMMUNITY GOLF COURSE
18 holes Par 72 6941/6414/5059 yds.
USGA: 70.7 SLOPE: 126
STYLE: Rolling hills, lakes
ACCESS: No restrictions
SEASON: All year HIGH: Apr.-Oct.
GREEN FEES: $$ (includes cart)
REDUCED FEES: WD, HG, LS, TW, PK
RESERVATIONS: 1 week
WALKING: No RANGE: Yes

EAGLE CREEK RESORT `28`
EAGLE CREEK STATE PARK, FINDLAY, IL 62534 (217)756-3456, EXT. 714 *(150 mi. NE of St. Louis)*
ACCOMMODATIONS: CLARION INN AT EAGLE CREEK RESORT (217)756-3456

Rolling hills, steep ravines, and the manmade Lake Shelbyville make Eagle Creek's layout as scenic as it is challenging. Carved out of thick woods overlooking the lake, tight fairways coupled with large, undulating greens demand a precise, long game and a steady putting stroke. Although only two or three water hazards come into play, more than half the holes require a carry over a ravine to the fairway or green. The most memorable is the twelfth, a long, straightaway par-5 that has a spectacular view of the lake from the putting surface. In 1990, *Golf Digest* gave Eagle Creek an honorable mention for the best resort course of the year.

EAGLE CREEK RESORT
18 holes Par 72 6908/5901/4978 yds.
USGA: 68.6 SLOPE: 121
STYLE: Hills, woods, lakes
ACCESS: No restrictions
SEASON: All year HIGH: July-Sept.
GREEN FEES: $$ (includes cart)
REDUCED FEES: PK
RESERVATIONS: Nonguests 2 weeks
WALKING: At times RANGE: Yes

GOLF CLUB OF INDIANA `29`
6905 S. 525 E., LEBANON, IN 46052 (317)769-6388 *(16 mi. NW of Indianapolis)*

Only twenty minutes from downtown Indianapolis, the impeccably maintained Golf Club of Indiana is rural and very peaceful. The gently rolling layout is characterized by deceptively tight driving areas, more than seventy large bunkers, and water on fifteen holes. Typical is the par-4 fourth, with out-of-bounds left, a small pond right, and a second pond cradling the green. The course has been ranked by *Golf Digest* as one of the top seventy-five public courses every year since 1981.

GOLF CLUB OF INDIANA
18 holes Par 72 7084/6438/5498 yds.
USGA: 72.3 SLOPE: 130
STYLE: Rolling hills, water
ACCESS: No restrictions
SEASON: Mar.-Nov. HIGH: June-Aug.
GREEN FEES: $$
RESERVATIONS: Unlimited with credit card
WALKING: Yes RANGE: Yes

INDIANA

OTTER CREEK GOLF COURSE ⬛30

11522E 50N, COLUMBUS, IN 47203 (812)579-5227 *(5 mi. SE of Columbus)*

Laid out over 218 acres of lush, rolling country-side, with nary a condo or residential street in sight, this Robert Trent Jones, Sr., masterpiece has been rated by *Golf Digest* as one of the top twenty-five public courses—every year since it first opened in 1964! The small landing areas, the slipping greens, and ninety-plus bunkers test even the most accomplished golfer, which explains the USGA's penchant for holding amateur

> **OTTER CREEK GOLF COURSE**
> 18 holes Par 72 7258/6950/5690 yds.
> STYLE: Rolling hills, trees, water
> ACCESS: No restrictions
> SEASON: Mar.-Nov. HIGH: May-Sept.
> GREEN FEES: $$$
> REDUCED FEES: WD, TW, PK
> RESERVATIONS: Anytime
> WALKING: Yes RANGE: Yes

championships and Open qualifiers here. A memorable hole is the par-4, 327-yard No. 11, a sharp dogleg left which can be reached in one when the wind is favorable. However, the short cut requires a 257-yard carry over a creek, a pond, and a large bunker—as well as a lot of luck. A single hole-in-one has been recorded here in twenty-six years! Another great hole is the par-3 No. 13. Jones himself dubbed the water-surrounded green "Alcatraz," calling it the best hole he ever designed.

FRENCH LICK SPRINGS RESORT ⬛31

FRENCH LICK, IN 47432 (812)936-9300 *(108 mi. S of Indianapolis)*
ACCOMMODATIONS: FRENCH LICK SPRINGS GOLF AND TENNIS RESORT (800)457-4042

> **FRENCH LICK SPRINGS RESORT**
> ACCESS: Priority to hotel guests
> SEASON: All year HIGH: May-Oct.
> GREEN FEES: $$
> REDUCED FEES: LS, TW
> RESERVATIONS: 6 months
> WALKING: No RANGE: Yes
> • **VALLEY COURSE**
>   18 holes Par 70 6003/6003/5687 yds.
>   USGA: 68.0
>   STYLE: Traditional
> • **COUNTRY CLUB COURSE**
>   18 holes Par 70 6625/6291/5781 yds.
>   USGA: 70 SLOPE: 116
>   STYLE: Traditional

There are two courses at French Lick Springs. One is the player-friendly Valley Course, pleasant and scenic, with two brooks that come into play on seven holes and only sixteen sand-traps. The Donald Ross-designed Country Club Course is scenic, too, but much more demanding. At over 6,600 yards from the blues, it rolls along wooded hills and brings into play deep bunkers and contoured greens. No. 15, a 619-yard, straightaway par 5 that plays into the wind, will challenge every part of your game—length, accuracy, and putting touch. Indeed, with very few flat lies and more than its share of sloped putting surfaces, the course requires a well-rounded game to score decently. As a matter of fact, French Lick Springs has a long history of tournament golf, starting with the 1924 PGA Championship.

NORTHERN MICHIGAN

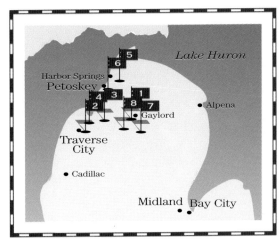

Flying over Michigan's lower peninsula and into Traverse City Cherry Capital Airport is a spiriting experience for anyone unfamiliar with this unique region of the United States. In the soft light of a late summer afternoon, the waters of Lake Michigan reflect the golden tones of the lowering sun, and the land is painted from a palette of rich greens dotted with hundreds of mirror-like lakes. As the plane nears the ground, hills, meadows, and forests reveal themselves, each displaying a different shade of green.

In just a few years, these pristine mountains and rich farmlands have been put on America's map of serious golf destinations. Within an hour's drive of Traverse City, several resorts offer a variety—and quality—of golf courses that is possibly unmatched anywhere in the country.

Big-name architects such as Robert Trent Jones and Jack Nicklaus, to mention just two, have left their imprint in these valleys and forests, and their legacies (still unfinished, one hopes) give us additional reasons to visit these beautiful and unspoiled lands.

In this self-declared "America's Summer Golf Capital," the season extends from mid-May to mid-October. On a typical summer's day, the sun will raise temperatures to the mid-eighties, but the humidity remains comfortably low. The latitude here affords golfers the additional pleasure of playing into the evening hours. Later on, the Northern Lights may dance in the clear night sky, announcing the coming of another day of great golfing adventures.

TREETOPS SYLVAN RESORT

TREETOPS SYLVAN RESORT: HOLE NO. 6

TREETOPS SYLVAN RESORT

3962 WILKINSON RD., GAYLORD, MI 49735 (517)732-6711 *(50 mi. from Traverse City)*
ACCOMMODATIONS: TREETOPS SYLVAN RESORT (800)444-6711

TREETOPS SYLVAN RESORT
18 holes   Par 71   7060/6399/4972 yds.
USGA: 72.6   SLOPE: 137
STYLE: Steep hills, woods
ACCESS: No restrictions
SEASON: Apr.-Oct.   HIGH: May-Sept.
GREEN FEES: $$$$ (includes cart)
REDUCED FEES: HG, TW, PK
RESERVATIONS: Anytime
WALKING: No   RANGE: Yes

From the tee of the famous par-3 No. 6 "Treetops" hole, the fairway drops 120 feet to the green, and the view extends for twenty miles over the gorgeous Pigeon River Valley. In the autumn, when the forest displays its fiery colors, the sight will surely break your concentration. This hole, and the other seventeen, are courtesy of master architect Robert Trent Jones. Each one is breathtaking in its own way, and the 146 championship slope rating may as well apply to the scenery. Treetops was selected as a runner-up for best new resort course by *Golf Digest* in 1987. Good news—forty-five additional holes are in the works!

HIGH POINTE GOLF CLUB

5555 ARNOLD RD., WILLIAMSBURG, MI 49690 (616)267-9900 *(5 mi. E of Traverse City)*

> **HIGH POINTE GOLF CLUB**
> 18 holes   Par 72   6819/6140/5258 yds.
> USGA: 69.4   SLOPE: 122
> STYLE: Hills, woods
> ACCESS: No restrictions
> SEASON: Apr.-Oct.   HIGH: July-Aug.
> GREEN FEES: $$$ (includes cart)
> REDUCED FEES: WD, HG, TW
> RESERVATIONS: Anytime
> WALKING: Yes   RANGE: Yes

Architect Tom Doak received a lot of praise after the opening of High Pointe in 1989. The course is built in an area surrounded by a state forest, and the beauty of the site alone justifies a detour. Tom Doak considered it "one of the world's most ideal sites for a golf course," and he certainly did justice to it. The front nine is routed through a mature cherry orchard and follows a fairly open, links-style design. The back is more hilly and tight. It travels through a pine plantation and includes some characteristic features of traditional Scottish layouts. Nos. 12 and 14 are definite visual treats, obviously designed with nature in mind. High Pointe is one of the few courses in America to have fairways seeded with fescue grass. This variety of turf provides a firm playing surface, and yet it requires less water, chemicals, and fertilizers than traditional seeds.

SHANTY CREEK RESORT

SHANTY CREEK RD., BELLAIRE, MI 49615 (616)533-6076 *(45 mi. NE of Traverse City)*
ACCOMMODATIONS: SHANTY CREEK RESORT (800)748-0249

Shanty Creek's guests and visitors have a choice of three eighteen-hole layouts: the popular Deskin Course, the Schuss Mountain Course, and the Legend Course. The best and most famous is the Arnold Palmer-designed Legend Course, listed by *Golf Digest* among the top fifty courses in the nation. Carved out of rolling woodlands overlooking Lake Bellaire, the Legend has been called the most scenic course in the state. Narrow fairways, strategically placed bunkers, and rugged surroundings do not allow for many errant shots. For sheer beauty, there is No. 7, a rather short par 5 that has a pond to the right of the landing area and Shanty Creek itself crossing in front of the green. This signature hole is tough to beat. The Schuss Mountain Course has gentler

> **SHANTY CREEK RESORT**
> ACCESS: No restrictions
> SEASON: May-Oct.   HIGH: July-Aug.
> GREEN FEES: $$$$$ (includes cart)
> REDUCED FEES: HG, TW, PK
> RESERVATIONS: Within season
> WALKING: At times   RANGE: Yes
> • **LEGEND COURSE**
>   18 holes   Par 72   6764/6269/4953 yds.
>   USGA: 71.5   SLOPE: 130
>   STYLE: Hills, creeks, woods
> • **SCHUSS MOUNTAIN COURSE**
>   18 holes   Par 72   6922/6394/5423 yds.
>   STYLE: Tree-lined fairways, water
> • **DESKIN COURSE**
>   18 holes   Par 71   6360/6019/4770 yds.
>   USGA: 70.4   SLOPE: 117
>   STYLE: Meadows

contours but is beautiful and challenging enough to be used for state tournaments. Finally, there is Deskin, the resort's original and most forgiving course, which offers fabulous lake views. Fees on both the Schuss Mountain and the Deskin are less expensive than on the Legend.

GRAND TRAVERSE RESORT

M-72 AT US-31, ACME, MI 49610 (616)938-1620 *(6 mi. NE of Traverse City)*
ACCOMMODATIONS: GRAND TRAVERSE RESORT (800)748-0303, (616)938-2100

If it looks like a bear and plays like a bear, it must be…a Jack Nicklaus course. The Bear Course, one of two eighteen-hole courses at Grand Traverse, was indeed designed by the man some have called the greatest golfer of all time, and it lives up to its name. The gently rolling terrain—the course winds through hardwood forests and orchards—belies the devilishness of its contoured greens and cavernous bunkers. The average golfer will certainly want to stick to the whites, which play a thousand yards shorter than the blues. The course, which is maintained to Nicklaus's standards, is kept in immaculate condition. The Resort Course is less difficult (and less expensive) but challenging in its own right. Architect Bill Newcomb laid out rolling fairways and undulating greens between evergreens and twelve water hazards that affect play on eleven holes. Of special interest is the par-3 No. 16, with its well-bunkered putting surface and backdrop of hardwood trees.

GRAND TRAVERSE RESORT
STYLE: Tree-lined fairways, water
ACCESS: No restrictions
SEASON: Apr.-Oct.   HIGH: June-Aug.
GREEN FEES: $$$$$ (includes cart)
REDUCED FEES: WD, HG, LS, TW
RESERVATIONS: Recommended
WALKING: No   RANGE: Yes
• **THE BEAR COURSE**
  18 holes Par 72 7177/6176/5281 yds.
  USGA: 71.9 SLOPE: 138
• **THE RESORT COURSE**
  18 holes Par 72 6741/6049/5139 yds.
  USGA: 69 SLOPE: 117

THE BEAR COURSE: HOLE N0. 5 (ABOVE LEFT), HOLE NO. 13 (ABOVE)

BOYNE HIGHLANDS RESORT

HIGHLANDS RD., HARBOR SPRINGS, MI 49740 (800)GO-BOYNE *(4 mi. from Harbor Springs)*
ACCOMMODATIONS: BOYNE HIGHLANDS RESORT (800)GO-BOYNE

Boyne Highlands offers golfers a choice of three championship layouts, each outstanding in its own way. The Robert Trent Jones-designed Heather Course has been rated among the top hundred in the country for a dozen years now. Open since 1965, this course is rolling and heavily wooded, with plenty of water, deep bunkers, and extra-large putting surfaces. It remains one of the best loved courses in the state. The scenic and demanding Moor Course, first played in 1974, is characterized by slippery, undulating greens, lots of sand and water, and a great par-5 finishing hole. Last but not least is the brand-new Donald Ross Memorial Course. This unique layout honors the father of American golf course architecture by bringing together eighteen of his best holes, including the seventeenth at Oakland Hills, three holes from Pinehurst No. 2, and two from Florida's Seminole. The course was named the best new resort course in the continental U.S. by *Golf Digest* in 1990. The Moor Course's green fees are slightly less expensive than the others, and it has reduced rates for twilight play.

BOYNE HIGHLANDS RESORT
ACCESS: No restrictions
SEASON: May-Oct.   HIGH: June-Sept.
GREEN FEES: $$$$ (includes cart)
REDUCED FEES: HG, LS, PK
RESERVATIONS: Nonguests 1 month
WALKING: No   RANGE: Yes
• **DONALD ROSS MEMORIAL COURSE**
  18 holes   Par 72   6840/6308/4977 yds.
  USGA: 70.7   SLOPE: 126
  STYLE: Traditional Donald Ross
• **MOOR COURSE**
  18 holes   Par 72   7179/6521/5459 yds.
  USGA: 71.3   SLOPE: 127
  STYLE: Woods, lakes
• **HEATHER COURSE**
  18 holes   Par 72   7218/6554/5263 yds.
  USGA: 71.2   SLOPE: 126
  STYLE: Woods, lakes

BOYNE HIGHLANDS RESORT, HEATHER COURSE

BOYNE MOUNTAIN RESORT

BOYNE MOUNTAIN RD., BOYNE FALLS, MI 49713 (616)549-2441 *(15 mi. S of Petoskey)*
ACCOMMODATIONS: BOYNE MOUNTAIN RESORT (800)GO-BOYNE

BOYNE MOUNTAIN RESORT
ACCESS: No restrictions
SEASON: May-Oct.   HIGH: June-Sept.
GREEN FEES: $$$$ (includes cart)
REDUCED FEES: HG, LS, TW, PK
RESERVATIONS: Nonguests 1 month
WALKING: No   RANGE: Yes
• **ALPINE COURSE**
  18 holes   Par 72   7017/6546/4986 yds.
  USGA: 71.4   SLOPE: 123
  STYLE: Rolling hills, woods
• **MONUMENT COURSE**
  18 holes   Par 72   7086/6377/4904 yds.
  USGA: 71.6   SLOPE: 132
  STYLE: Rolling hills, woods

MONUMENT COURSE

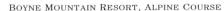

Boyne Mountain offers two eighteen-hole layouts. The first tee on the beautifully conditioned Alpine Course is situated some seven hundred feet above the pro shop. Splendid mountain views over the treetops and ponds are the rule, and the generous fairways encourage players to "tee it high and let it fly." Still, there is enough trouble in the form of bunkers and water hazards to keep the average golfer busy. The demanding Monument Course gets its name from plaques mounted on tee boulders—one at every hole—each in honor of a famous golf legend. Named a *Golf Digest* runner-up for the best new resort course in 1987, this layout boasts the same bird's-eye views along with one of the most intimidating finishing holes around: a 446-yard dogleg right, with weeds and bunkers squeezing the landing area and a contoured green completely surrounded by water. Boyne Mountain also offers the nine-hole Hemlock Course. Green fees on the Alpine Course are slightly less expensive.

BOYNE MOUNTAIN RESORT, ALPINE COURSE

GARLAND

COUNTY RD. 489, LEWISTON, MI 49756 (517)786-2211 *(25 mi. SE of Gaylord)*
ACCOMMODATIONS: GARLAND (800)968-0042

With sixty-three holes to play, this 3,500-acre resort offers more golf in a single location than any other facility in Michigan. The three eighteen-hole courses were designed by Garland's owner, Ron Otto, a single-digit golf amateur. There is nothing amateurish about the courses he designed, however: they offer terrific combinations of woods, water, and impeccable landscaping. The Monarch, opened in 1988, demands length and accuracy off the tee and has a great hole in No. 11—a long dogleg left, with woods from tee to green and a creek that must be carried with the second shot. If you're afraid of water, though, think twice before teeing it up at Swampfire. The wet stuff comes into play on fourteen holes, including ten out of the first eleven. No. 5, a medium-length par 3, features a 180-yard, horseshoe-shaped tee. The Reflections Course, shortest and newest of the three, has an equal number of par 5s, par 4s, and par 3s—a unique layout that stresses shotmaking and course-management skills. The par-36, nine-hole Herman's Nine course is the 1951 original work of Garland's founder, Herman Otto.

GARLAND
ACCESS: No restrictions
SEASON: May-Oct.   HIGH: May-Sept.
GREEN FEES: $$$ (includes cart)
REDUCED FEES: HG, TW, PK
RESERVATIONS: Anytime
WALKING: No   RANGE: Yes
- **THE MONARCH COURSE**
  18 holes   Par 72   7101/6056/4861 yds.
  USGA: 68.4   SLOPE: 126
  STYLE: Woods, water
- **SWAMPFIRE COURSE**
  18 holes   Par 72   6868/5937/4812 yds.
  USGA: 67.8   SLOPE: 123
  STYLE: Lakes
- **REFLECTIONS COURSE**
  18 holes   Par 72   6464/5966/4767 yds.
  USGA: 68.4   SLOPE: 116
  STYLE: Hills, woods, lakes

WILDERNESS VALLEY GOLF CLUB

7519 MANCELONA RD., GAYLORD, MI 49735 (616)585-7090 *(15 mi. SW of Gaylord)*

WILDERNESS VALLEY GOLF CLUB
ACCESS: No restrictions
SEASON: Apr.-Oct.   HIGH: June-Sept.
GREEN FEES: $$$ (includes cart)
REDUCED FEES: WD, HG, LS, TW
RESERVATIONS: 6 months
WALKING: Yes   RANGE: Yes
• **BLACK FOREST COURSE**
   18 holes   Par 18   7044/6496/5282 yds.
   USGA: 71.3   SLOPE: 129
   STYLE: Woods, hills
• **VALLEY COURSE**
   18 holes   Par 71   6485/6094/4889 yds.
   USGA: 68.6   SLOPE: 113
   STYLE: Woods

When it comes to great golf courses, northern Michigan suffers from an embarrassment of riches. With the brand-new Black Forest Course, to go with its pleasant Valley Course, Wilderness Valley has added another gem to the list. Designed by Tom Doak, the Black Forest Course is a devilish amalgam of lay-of-the-land architecture, length, and spectacular bunkering—and we mean spectacular. The hole most golfers are likely to remember is the 185-yard eighth, with a monstrous, forty-five-foot-high bunker fronting the green. You don't want to leave it short here. The architect's favorite is No. 10, a long, tree-lined par-5 with a pair of trees guarding either side of the green and a well-bunkered slope behind it. Ridges and valleys characterize the scenic terrain, and four sets of tees allow all levels of play.

WILDERNESS VALLEY GOLF CLUB

SAWMILL CREEK GOLF CLUB 　32

2401 CLEVELAND RD. W., HURON, OH 44839 (419)433-3789 *(62 mi. W of Cleveland)*
ACCOMMODATIONS: SAWMILL CREEK LODGE (419)433-3800

Sawmill Creek's flat, relatively open course is nestled among scenic wetlands along the shores of Lake Erie. Though deceptively easy at first glance, the average golfer will soon discover otherwise. Water, much of it marshland, maintains the pressure on thirteen holes. If you don't keep it in play off the tee—a tough proposition with a brisk lake breeze blowing—you'll be in for a long day. The approach shot at No. 12, a straightaway par 5 flanked by duck marshes, is played to a narrow, elevated green overlooking a natural wild fowl game preserve and Lake Erie.

SAWMILL CREEK GOLF CLUB
18 holes　Par 71　6781/6378/5416 yds.
USGA: 70.3　SLOPE: 128
STYLE: Marshland, water
ACCESS: No restrictions
SEASON: Apr.-Oct.　HIGH: June-Aug.
GREEN FEES: $$
REDUCED FEES: HG, LS, PK
RESERVATIONS: 1 year
WALKING: Yes　RANGE: No

BENT TREE GOLF CLUB 　33

350 BENT TREE RD., SUNBURY, OH 43074 (614)965-5140 *(10 mi. N of Columbus)*

BENT TREE GOLF CLUB
18 holes　Par 72　6800/6300/5300 yds.
STYLE: Tree-lined fairways, water
ACCESS: No restrictions
SEASON: Mar.-Dec.　HIGH: June
GREEN FEES: $$
REDUCED FEES: LS
RESERVATIONS: 1 week
WALKING: At times　RANGE: Yes

With rolling hills, tree-lined fairways, and ponds and lakes on nine holes, one could call Bent Tree a typical midwestern track. To be accurate, however, one should also mention the sixty-five white sand bunkers and the fast, undulated, bentgrass greens that have earned the course a *Golf Digest* nomination in 1989 as one of the top new public courses. One hole especially designed to test your skill, is the par-5 No. 15, with two water hazards on the left and a large trap in front of the green. With design, maintenance, and amenities comparable to a private club, one can only wish that all "typical" golf courses would be like Bent Tree.

WEATHERWAX GOLF COURSE 　34

5401 MOSIMAN RD., MIDDLETOWN, OH 45042 (513)425-7886 *(22 mi. S of Dayton)*

Golfers can play any combination of four different nines—Woodside, Meadows, Valley View, and Highlands—at this Arthur Hills-designed complex, and with three sets of tees per nine, the possibilities seem endless (we've provided figures in the box for two two-course combinations). The Woodside Course is the longest, the Meadows and Valley View Courses the most open, and the Highlands Course the tightest. The latter also has two of the top holes in the area: No. 1, a 455-yard par 4 with water running the length of the fairway, and No. 3, a 520-yard par 5 with water to the left and a gully to the right. Weatherwax has been called the best municipal course in the Cincinnati-Dayton area and has hosted many tournaments.

WEATHERWAX GOLF COURSE
ACCESS: No restrictions
SEASON: All year　HIGH: May-Sept.
GREEN FEES: $
RESERVATIONS: 1 week
WALKING: Yes　RANGE: Yes
• **WOODSIDE AND MEADOWS COURSES**
18 holes　Par 72　7174/6777/5669 yds.
USGA: 71.6　SLOPE: 112
STYLE: Traditional
• **VALLEY VIEW AND HIGHLANDS COURSES**
18 holes　Par 72　6756/6489/5253 yds.
USGA: 70.8　SLOPE: 117
STYLE: Traditional

JACK NICKLAUS SPORTS CENTER 35
3565 KINGS MILL RD., MASON, OH 45034 (513)398-7700 *(25 mi. N of Cincinnati)*
ACCOMMODATIONS: KINGS ISLAND INN (513)398-0115

JACK NICKLAUS SPORTS CENTER
ACCESS: No restrictions
SEASON: Mar.-Dec.   HIGH: June-Aug.
GREEN FEES: $$
REDUCED FEES: WD, TW
RESERVATIONS: 1 week
WALKING: No   RANGE: Yes
• **GRIZZLY COURSE**
  18 holes   Par 71   6850/6250/5301 yds.
  USGA: 70.5   SLOPE: 128
  STYLE: Trees, lakes
• **BRUIN COURSE**
  18 holes   3456 yds.
  STYLE: Trees, lakes

This is where Jack Nicklaus, with the help of Desmond Muirhead, first made his mark as a golf-course designer. The Grizzly Course is both challenging and impeccably maintained, with bentgrass fairways, plenty of trees and traps, and nine water hazards. The 546-yard eighteenth is what a great finishing hole should be; it has trouble on the left and right off the tee, a pond in front of the green to discourage long hitters from trying to get home in two, and four greenside bunkers to keep everyone else honest. The Bruin Course, another Nicklaus-Muirhead design, is an eighteen-hole executive course with seven par 4s and eleven par 3s.

BLUE ASH GOLF COURSE 36
4040 COOPER RD., CINCINNATI, OH 45241 (513)745-8577 *(15 mi. N of Cincinnati)*

Though hardly a monster in terms of length, Blue Ash has approximately sixty sandtraps, four lakes that come into play on seven holes, and a winding creek that affects play on nine holes—a combination that makes this rolling, traditional-style layout a stern test for the average golfer. The 160-yard eleventh, with trees to the right and a contoured green cradled by water, is a classic par 3: a good shot sets up a birdie putt, but a bad one leaves you staring at double bogey.

BLUE ASH GOLF COURSE
18 holes   Par 72   6643/6211/5125 yds.
USGA: 70.3   SLOPE: 122
STYLE: Traditional
ACCESS: Restrictions on tee times
SEASON: All year   HIGH: May-Aug.
GREEN FEES: $
RESERVATIONS: 5 days
WALKING: Yes   RANGE: No

THE VINEYARD 37
600 NORDYKE RD., CINCINNATI, OH 45255 (513)474-3007 *(11 mi. E of downtown Cincinnati)*

THE VINEYARD
18 holes   Par 71   6789/6254/4747 yds.
USGA: 70.6   SLOPE: 124
STYLE: Undulating greens, rolling hills
ACCESS: No restrictions
SEASON: Mar.-Nov.   HIGH: May-Sept.
GREEN FEES: $
REDUCED FEES: TW
RESERVATIONS: 5 days
WALKING: Yes   RANGE: No

Blessed with a beautiful setting on the site of an old vineyard, this gently rolling layout challenges the average golfer without aggravating him. Narrow fairways, lined with medium-sized trees in front and mature ones in back, put a premium on tee-to-green accuracy, while the seriously contoured greens—one three-tiered and one four-tiered—demand steady nerves and a deft touch. In 1987, *Golf Digest* named The Vineyard a runner-up as the best new public course in the U.S.

OTHER EXCELLENT COURSES IN THE MIDWEST

ILLINOIS
- ● LICK CREEK GOLF COURSE, Pekin (309)346-0077
- ▲ VILLAGE LINKS OF GLEN ELLYN, Glen Ellyn (708)469-8180

INDIANA
- ● EAGLE CREEK GOLF COURSE, Indianapolis (317)297-3366
- ● HULMAN LINKS GOLF COURSE, Terre Haute (812)877-2096

KANSAS
- ● ALVAMAR GOLF COURSE, Lawrence (913)842-1907

MICHIGAN
- ● BAY VALLEY HOTEL AND RESORT, Bay City (517)686-5400
- ● GRAND HAVEN GOLF CLUB, Grand Haven (616)842-4040
- ● MICHAWE HILLS GOLF CLUB, Gaylord (517)939-8911
- ● TIMBER RIDGE GOLF CLUB, East Lansing (517)339-8000

MINNESOTA
- ▲ BEMIDJI TOWN AND COUNTRY CLUB, Bemidji (218)751-9215
- ● BREEZY POINT RESORT, Breezy Point (218)562-7166

MISSOURI
- ● DOGWOOD HILLS GOLF COURSE, Osage Beach (314)348-3153
- ● QUAIL CREEK GOLF CLUB, South St. Louis (314)487-1988

NORTH DAKOTA
- ▲ MINOT COUNTRY CLUB, Minot (701)839-6169

OHIO
- ● AVALON LAKES GOLF COURSE, Warren (216)856-7211
- ● EAGLESTICKS GOLF CLUB, Zanesville (614)454-4900

SOUTH DAKOTA
- ● ELMWOOD GOLF COURSE, Sioux Falls (605)339-7092
- ▲ HILLCREST GOLF AND COUNTRY CLUB, Yankton (605)665-4522

WISCONSIN
- ● AMERICANA LAKE GENEVA RESORT, Lake Geneva (414)248-8811
- ● BROWN COUNTY GOLF COURSE, Oneida (414)497-1731
- ● BROWN DEER GOLF COURSE, Milwaukee (414)352-8080
- ● FOX HILLS RESORT, Mishicot (414)755-2831

▲ RESTRICTIONS MAY APPLY   ■ HOTEL/RESORT GUESTS ONLY   ● OPEN WITHOUT RESTRICTIONS

CHAPTER SIX

THE NORTHEAST

From the easternmost point in the U.S. on the coast of Maine, to the hills of western Pennsylvania, golfers have access to hundreds of courses with great character and natural beauty. In this part of the country, the land is varied and picturesque, and golf is loyal to the land. The mountains of Vermont and New Hampshire, the green hills of Massachusetts and Pennsylvania, the windy seashores of Cape Cod and Long Island—each offers a natural setting for beautiful golf courses. Indeed, architects such as Donald Ross were at work in these regions well before the decline of the great railroads could provide modern designers with an abundance of inexpensive construction materials...

The courses are mostly traditional in style, and scenery plays an important role in the design. Golf in the Northeast also follows nature's ever-changing seasons: this is the land where golfers can fill their eyes with the greenery of the newborn spring after Old Man Winter has finally retreated, and come back just a few months later to golf in the glory of autumn's fiery foliage.

In the Northeast, the wise golfer should avoid the proximity of the big cities, especially during weekends. Visitors might also be warned that, while New Englanders' hospitality is always dependable, the weather itself can be unsteady. In the northern part of the region, golf season opens a few weeks before Memorial Day and closes before families reunite for Thanksgiving dinner.

TOFTREES RESORT

1 COUNTRY CLUB LA., STATE COLLEGE, PA 16803 (800)458-3602 *(150 mi. from Pittsburgh)*
ACCOMMODATIONS: TOFTREES RESORT (800)458-3602

Open since 1969, Toftrees has hosted the
Pennsylvania PGA Championship for ten of the
last eleven years and has been rated by *Golf
Digest* as the top public and resort course in the
state. The demanding, well-wooded layout is
characterized by rolling fairways and large, undulating greens, with vantage points that grant
magnificent vistas of the surrounding mountains.
No two holes are alike, and golfers who let their
thoughts wander will quickly find themselves in
trouble. Especially scenic is No. 5, a long uphill dogleg left with a tremendous view from
the green. But Toftrees' most difficult hole is No. 9, requiring a two-hundred-yard carry
over water—for most golfers, the stuff of nightmares.

> **TOFTREES RESORT**
> 18 holes   Par 72   7018/6780/5567 yds.
> USGA: 73.3   SLOPE: 132
> STYLE: Rolling hills, woods, water
> ACCESS: No restrictions
> SEASON: Mar.-Nov.   HIGH: June-Aug.
> GREEN FEES: $$$ (includes cart)
> REDUCED FEES: WD, HG, LS, TW
> RESERVATIONS: 2 weeks
> WALKING: No   RANGE: Yes

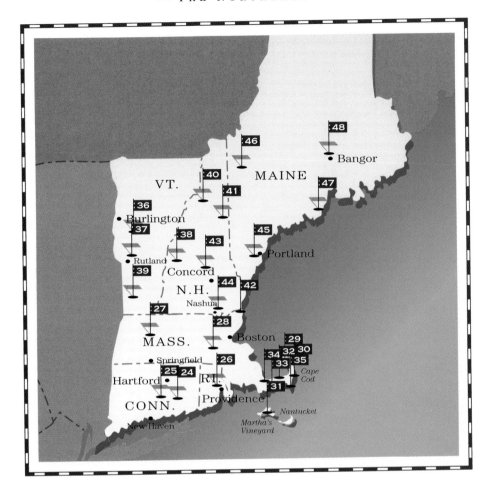

HERSHEY COUNTRY CLUB

2

1000 E. DERRY RD., HERSHEY, PA 17033 (717)533-2464 *(12 mi. E of Harrisburg)*
ACCOMMODATIONS: HOTEL HERSHEY (717)533-2171, HERSHEY LODGE (717)533-3311

HERSHEY COUNTRY CLUB
ACCESS: Hotel guests only
SEASON: Apr.-Nov.   HIGH: Apr.-Oct.
GREEN FEES: $$$
REDUCED FEES: WD
RESERVATIONS: Recommended
WALKING: No   RANGE: Yes
• **WEST COURSE**
   18 holes   Par 73   6860/6480/5908 yds.
   USGA: 71.3   SLOPE: 130
   STYLE: Rolling hills, woods
• **EAST COURSE**
   18 holes   Par 71   7061/6363/5645 yds.
   USGA: 70.5   SLOPE: 125
   STYLE: Rolling hills, ponds

With a classic style that features tight fairways, small, well-bunkered greens, and back-to-back par 5s, Hershey's West Course has been a favorite of golfers for more than sixty years now. It is a long but lovely, mature layout that challenges without causing undue misery. The newer, George Fazio-designed East Course rates a bit easier on the scorecard, but a hundred sandtraps and three manmade lakes swallow errant fairway woods and long iron shots with relish, while the speedy greens have been rumored to make grown men cry. The East Course has slightly lower green fees and stays open all year.

THE MOUNTAIN LAUREL RESORT GOLF CLUB

RTE. 534, WHITE HAVEN, PA 18661 (717)443-7424 *(90 mi. N of Philadelphia)*
ACCOMMODATIONS: THE MOUNTAIN LAUREL RESORT (800)458-5921, (717)443-8411

3

THE MOUNTAIN LAUREL RESORT GOLF CLUB
18 holes   Par 72   6798/6122/5631 yds.
USGA: 69.3
STYLE: Mountains
ACCESS: No restrictions
SEASON: Apr.-Nov.   HIGH: May-Aug.
GREEN FEES: $$ (includes cart)
REDUCED FEES: WD, TW, PK
RESERVATIONS: 2 weeks
WALKING: At times   RANGE: Yes

The Geoffrey Cornish-designed Mountain Laurel course has three distinct personalities. The first five holes are relatively open, while the middle eight bring a variety of water hazards into play. Finally, the last five wind in and out of tall trees. Particularly memorable are the ninth, a 548-yard par 5 with water flanking both sides of the landing area, and the tenth, a 360-yard par 4, which has a narrow, tree-lined fairway leading to an island green.

SHAWNEE INN

4

SHAWNEE-ON-DELAWARE, PA 18356 (717)421-1500, EXT. 1480 *(45 mi. N of Allentown)*
ACCOMMODATIONS: SHAWNEE INN (800)SHAWNEE

Located on an island in the middle of the
Delaware River, the Shawnee Inn course was
designed in 1906 by A. W. Tillinghast, the most
famous American golf course architect of his day,
and redone in 1960 by, among others, bandleader
Fred Waring, who bought the place in the 1940s.
Shawnee's three nines—the Red, the White, and
the Blue—are characterized by flat, tree-lined
fairways, lots of water and sand, and two par 3s

SHAWNEE INN
27 holes   3327/3063/3023 yds.
STYLE: Tree-lined fairways, water
ACCESS: No restrictions
SEASON: Apr.-Nov.   HIGH: May-Oct.
GREEN FEES: $$
REDUCED FEES: WD, HG, LS, TW, PK
RESERVATIONS: Guests 1 week
WALKING: No   RANGE: Yes

that play over the Delaware. Woe to the golfer who fails to carry the river: one woman's
ball was carried by the current so far that it took her 166 strokes to play it back on the
opposite bank, setting a Guiness World Record in the process.

SHAWNEE INN GOLF COURSE

HIDDEN VALLEY RESORT

5

1 CRAIGHEAD DR., HIDDEN VALLEY, PA 15502 (800)458-0175, EXT. 444 *(52 mi. SE of Pittsburgh)*
ACCOMMODATIONS: HIDDEN VALLEY RESORT (800)458-0175, (814)443-6454

THE GOLF CLUB AT HIDDEN VALLEY
18 holes   Par 72   6424/6071/4951 yds.
USGA: 69   SLOPE: 125
STYLE: Mountains, woods
ACCESS: Restrictions on tee times
SEASON: May-Nov.   HIGH: July-Aug.
GREEN FEES: $$$ (includes cart)
REDUCED FEES: WD, PK
RESERVATIONS: Nonguests 1 day
WALKING: Weekdays only   RANGE: Yes

Hidden Valley was nominated by *Golf Digest* as one of the best new resort courses of 1988. Set in a thick hardwood forest atop a three-thousand-foot mountain, this hilly track offers spectacular vistas of the surrounding Laurel Highlands (Arnold Palmer country). It's an enjoyable experience for the average golfer. No two holes run parallel, and you'll feel that you have the course to yourself. The modest length and many downhill holes almost guarantee good scores.

MOUNT AIRY LODGE

6

THE 18 BEST, MT. POCONO, PA 18344 (717)839-8811, EXT. 7086 *(90 mi. NE of New York City)*
ACCOMMODATIONS: MOUNT AIRY LODGE (800)441-4410, (717)839-8811

THE 18 BEST COURSE
18 holes   Par 72   7123/6426/5771 yds.
USGA: 71.4
STYLE: Hills, woods, water
ACCESS: Restrictions on tee times
SEASON: Apr.-Oct.   HIGH: May-Sept.
GREEN FEES: $$$
REDUCED FEES: WD, HG
RESERVATIONS: Guests 1 year
WALKING: No   RANGE: Yes

This popular resort, situated in the Poconos, advertises its course as "America's Most Challenging." Eleven years in the making, "The 18 Best" has everything: 7,123 yards of rolling terrain, mature oaks and maples, water on ten holes, and ninety-eight bunkers protecting the well-manicured, velvet greens. The result is an interesting mix of classic and extravagant holes well worth a detour. A nine-hole course is also available one mile away.

MOUNT AIRY LODGE: HOLES NO. 13, 14, AND 15

TAMIMENT RESORT

7

TAMIMENT, PA 18371 (717)588-6652 *(90 mi. from New York City)*
ACCOMMODATIONS: TAMIMENT RESORT (800)233-8105, (717)588-6652

TAMIMENT RESORT
18 holes   Par 72   6858/6599/5598 yds.
USGA: 71.4   SLOPE: 127
STYLE: Mountains, woods
ACCESS: Priority to hotel guests
SEASON: Apr.-Nov.   HIGH: June-Sept.
GREEN FEES: $$
REDUCED FEES: PK
RESERVATIONS: Nonguests 1 week
WALKING: At times   RANGE: No

One of the more established four-season resorts in the Poconos, Tamiment has a Robert Trent Jones, Sr., course entering its fifth decade of play. It is a deceptively gentle layout, with large, undulating greens and a good balance between long and short holes. Sweeping, twenty-mile vistas alternate with peaceful valley scenes. And while there are plenty of bunkers and water hazards, better players will find them only slightly more distracting than the scenery.

SKYTOP LODGE

8

1 SKYTOP, SKYTOP, PA 18357 (717)595-7401, EXT. 550 *(45 mi. NE of Allentown)*
ACCOMMODATIONS: SKYTOP LODGE (717)595-7401, EXT. 515

SKYTOP GOLF COURSE
18 holes   Par 71   6220/5800 yds.
USGA: 69.1   SLOPE: 118
STYLE: Mountains, tree-lined fairways
ACCESS: Priority to hotel guests
SEASON: Apr.-Nov.
HIGH: May/July-Aug.
GREEN FEES: $$
REDUCED FEES: HG
RESERVATIONS: 2 weeks
WALKING: After 3 p.m.   RANGE: No

Skytop is a classic example of a traditional, northeastern, mountain-style course: short, tight, and scenic. Designed by Robert White and opened in 1928, it abounds in gorgeous views (especially in autumn) and wildlife (deer, wild turkeys, and the occasional black bear). If the tree-lined fairways and thirty-odd bunkers are less than intimidating, the small putting surfaces surely make elusive targets. The finishing hole— with a creek pinching the landing area and an elevated green—is a beauty.

HOMINY HILL GOLF COURSE

9

92 MERCER RD., COLTS NECK, NJ 07722 (908)462-9223 *(50 mi. S of New York City)*

HOMINY HILL GOLF COURSE
18 holes   Par 72   7059/6470/5794 yds.
USGA: 71.7   SLOPE: 127
STYLE: Rolling hills, bunkers
ACCESS: No restrictions
SEASON: Mar.-Dec.   HIGH: May-Nov.
GREEN FEES: $$
REDUCED FEES: WD
RESERVATIONS: 5 days
WALKING: Yes   RANGE: No

Set in the Garden State's rolling farmland, this Robert Trent Jones course has consistently been ranked as one of the nation's top public courses since it opened in 1964. The layout places a premium on long, accurate drives, and the rough is dangerously deep. Over a hundred bunkers punctuate the fairways and protect the greens from inaccurate approach shots. The course was the site of the 1983 U.S. Men's Public Links Championship and the 1990 New Jersey Men's Amateur.

N
E
W

J
E
R
S
E
Y

MARRIOTT'S SEAVIEW RESORT, BAY COURSE

MARRIOTT'S SEAVIEW RESORT

RTE. 9, ABSECON, NJ 08201 (609)652-1800 *(6 mi. NE of Atlantic City)*
ACCOMMODATIONS: MARRIOTT'S SEAVIEW RESORT (609)652-1800

MARRIOTT'S SEAVIEW RESORT
ACCESS: Priority to hotel guests
SEASON: All year   HIGH: May-Nov.
GREEN FEES: $$$$ (includes cart)
REDUCED FEES: LS, PK
RESERVATIONS: Guests 1 month
WALKING: No   RANGE: Yes
• **PINES COURSE**
   18 holes   Par 71   6885/6394/5837 yds.
   USGA: 70.7   SLOPE: 128
   STYLE: Tree-lined fairways, heavily
   wooded, waste areas
• **BAY COURSE**
   18 holes   Par 71   6263/5981/5586 yds.
   USGA: 67.7   SLOPE: 111
   STYLE: Scottish links, oceanside

People come to Atlantic City to gamble, but for golf, the nearby Marriott's Seaview Resort guarantees two outstanding courses. The original nine at the Pines Course was built in the early 1930s. It plays to almost 6,900 yards from the tips, and its numerous doglegs travel through heavy woods highlighted by dogwoods and azaleas. The fairways and greens are also dotted by no less than 110 bunkers. The Bay Course, designed by Donald Ross in 1915, is situated on property bordering marshland and has the open look and feel of a links course. Often compared to Royal Dornoch in Scotland, it features small greens, pot bunkers, and quietly rolling terrain.

GREAT GORGE COUNTRY CLUB

RTE. 517, McAFEE, NJ 07428 (201)827-5757, (201)827-0718 *(47 mi. W of New York City)*
ACCOMMODATIONS: SEASONS RESORT (201)827-6000

GREAT GORGE COUNTRY CLUB
27 holes   2993/3068/3257 yds.
STYLE: Steep hills, water, rocks
ACCESS: No restrictions
SEASON: Mar.-Nov.
HIGH: May-June/Sept.
GREEN FEES: $$$ (includes cart)
REDUCED FEES: WD, TW
RESERVATIONS: 1 month
WALKING: No   RANGE: Yes

Great Gorge offers an unusual variety of interesting terrain. The Lake Nine is the longest of the three nine-hole courses that George Fazio designed here in 1971. As expected, water plays a major role on that stretch. The Rail Nine is slightly shorter and affords some nice views of the surrounding mountains. What makes Great Gorge so memorable, however, is the Quarry Nine, where spectacular and intimidating stone quarries overlook and encroach on several fairways.

GOLF HOUSE

United States Golf Association
Liberty Corner Road
Far Hills, NJ 07931
(908)234-2300

Mon-Fri: 9am to 5pm
Sat-Sun: 10am to 4pm
Closed Holidays

While in New Jersey, be sure to visit Golf House, the home of the USGA. Inside the stately mansion you will find interesting displays of champions' clubs, golf historical artifacts, exhibits on golf architecture and women in golf, and the Bobby Jones Library. Tours of the USGA testing facility and turf research center are also available.

RIVER OAKS GOLF CLUB 　12

201 WHITEHAVEN RD., GRAND ISLAND, NY 14072 (716)773-3336 *(7 mi. NW of downtown Buffalo)*

RIVER OAKS GOLF CLUB
18 holes　Par 72　7389/6588/5747 yds.
USGA: 71.6　SLOPE: 124
STYLE: Hills, woods, water
ACCESS: No restrictions
SEASON: Mar.-Nov.　HIGH: June-Aug.
GREEN FEES: $$
REDUCED FEES: WD
RESERVATIONS: Nonmembers 2 days
WALKING: Yes　RANGE: Yes

River Oaks is one of the top-ranked layouts in western New York State, and Gary Player was the course's original touring professional. The course sits off the scenic Niagara River and is surrounded by large oaks, maple trees, and beautiful estate homes. Desmond Muirhead designed River Oaks in 1970, incorporating brooks and lakes on nine holes and enough well-placed bunkers and high rough to make players think twice before attempting short cuts.

GLEN OAK GOLF COURSE 　13

711 SMITH RD., E. AMHERST, NY 14051 (716)688-5454 *(20 min. NE of Buffalo)*

Black Creek runs through the property at the Glen Oak course, which was laid out in 1970 by Robert Trent Jones. It's a fairly flat course, but fifteen holes have water, and when the wind whirls around the ponds, scores escalate very quickly. The par-3 signature hole, No. 8, is considered by players to be one of the toughest in the region— and while standing on the tee, one can easily get overwhelmed by the water all around. The greens crew affectionately

GLEN OAK GOLF COURSE
18 holes　Par 72　6730/6232/5561 yds.
USGA: 70.8　SLOPE: 122
STYLE: Tree-lined fairways, water
ACCESS: No restrictions
SEASON: Apr.-Nov.　HIGH: July-Aug.
GREEN FEES: $$ (includes cart)
REDUCED FEES: WD, TW
RESERVATIONS: 3 days
WALKING: No　RANGE: Yes

refers to the course as "The Game Farm" because of the numerous whooping cranes, fox, and deer which keep watch over the golfers' progress.

BRISTOL HARBOUR GOLF CLUB 　14

5500 SENECA POINT RD., CANANDAIGUA, NY 14424 (716)396-2460 *(30 mi. SE of Rochester)*
ACCOMMODATIONS: BRISTOL HARBOR (800)288-8248

Robert Trent Jones and son Rees collaborated on this 1972 course, nestled in the Finger Lakes region of New York State. Thanks to many significant changes in elevation, the site offers splendid views of both Canandaigua Lake and the nearby Bristol Hills. The layout features many water hazards: three streams, four ponds, and a lateral gorge that runs along five fairways on the back. The first nine holes are fairly open, but fairways get narrow after the turn. Accuracy is a must, and

BRISTOL HARBOUR GOLF CLUB
18 holes　Par 72　6700/6095/5482 yds.
USGA: 69.6　SLOPE: 121
STYLE: Steep hills, water, trees
ACCESS: Priority to hotel guests
SEASON: Apr.-Nov.　HIGH: June-Sept.
GREEN FEES: $$ (includes cart)
REDUCED FEES: LS
RESERVATIONS: 3 days
WALKING: No　RANGE: Yes

with sixty-seven sand bunkers ready to catch stray shots, a good sand game comes in very handy to score well. The wooded, dogleg-right, par-4 No. 14 is often mentioned as one of the finest holes in the state. From the regular tees, it takes a two-hundred-yard drive to reach the corner. At this point, it's 150 yards straight downhill to a green resting peacefully in a clearing of gorgeous trees. A course record of sixty-seven is held by none other than the master of masters himself—Jack Nicklaus.

LEATHERSTOCKING GOLF COURSE   15

NELSON AVE., COOPERSTOWN, NY 13326 (607)547-9853 *(26 mi. N of Oneonta)*
ACCOMMODATIONS: OTESAGA HOTEL (607)547-9931

LEATHERSTOCKING GOLF COURSE
18 holes   Par 72   6388/6006/5175 yds.
USGA: 69.3   SLOPE: 120
STYLE: Traditional
ACCESS: No restrictions
SEASON: Apr.-Oct.   HIGH: July-Aug.
GREEN FEES: $$$
REDUCED FEES: WD
RESERVATIONS: Anytime
WALKING: Yes   RANGE: No

Leatherstocking's course was designed in the early 1900s by architect Devereux Emmett. Short by modern standards, it sits by the side of Otsego Lake. The challenge comes from fairways with swales and dips and from elevated greens with tiers and undulations. The 520-yard, par-5 No. 18 plays from an island tee in Otsego Lake and requires an unnerving carry of 130 yards to the fairway. The course once had almost 150 bunkers; today, they number a "mere" hundred—small consolation if you happen to be in one.

KUTSHER'S COUNTRY CLUB   16

KUTSHER RD., MONTICELLO, NY 12701 (914)794-6000 *(90 mi. NW of New York City)*
ACCOMMODATIONS: KUTSHER'S COUNTRY CLUB (800)431-1273

Kutsher's is a demanding but fair test of golf, set in thick forests of maple, oak, beech, and ash. The fairways are narrow, and the generously contoured greens are difficult to read. Five ponds and a lake add to the challenge on six holes. The first hole is an easy par 4, but that's the only break you'll get on this tough mountain course. No. 4 is a tough one from the tee, since the fairway slopes down to the woods on the right. But the best holes can be found on the back nine. The

KUTSHER'S COUNTRY CLUB
18 holes   Par 72   7157/6638/5763 yds.
USGA: 71.2   SLOPE: 118
STYLE: Woods, rolling hills
ACCESS: No restrictions
SEASON: Apr.-Nov.   HIGH: June-Sept.
GREEN FEES: $$
REDUCED FEES: HG, PK
RESERVATIONS: 1 month
WALKING: No   RANGE: No

455-yard, par-4 No. 13 is a scenic beauty; the drive is from an elevated tee to a landing area guarded on the left by a pond; the green, set on a small rise, is sanctimoniously guarded by two large bunkers.

GROSSINGER'S COUNTRY CLUB   17

GROSSINGER HOTEL, GROSSINGER, NY 12734 (914)292-1450 *(100 mi. from New York City)*

Just like the Concord's Monster a short distance away, Grossinger's "Big G" course was designed by architect Joe Finger. Set in the verdant hills of the Catskills, the tree-lined fairways travel through some picturesque landscapes—and, at times, through some real trouble. The par-5 fourth is double-bogey land: a choice of several elevated tees sets you up for a long downhill drive that must carry over a distant brook; your second

THE BIG G
18 holes   Par 71   6791/6406/5836 yds.
USGA: 70.9   SLOPE: 131
STYLE: Rolling hills, lakes
ACCESS: No restrictions
SEASON: Apr.-Oct.   HIGH: Summer
GREEN FEES: $$
RESERVATIONS: 1 week
WALKING: No   RANGE: Yes

shot must be straight, as a large lake borders the entire left side of the fairway; the third shot is a 130-yard short iron to an island green with virtually no room for error. Throughout the round, hills, lakes and tree-lined fairways alternate to create one of the most scenic and demanding courses in the Catskills. Grossinger's also offers the easier but still fun and interesting Vista Nine course.

CONCORD GOLF CLUB

`18`

CONCORD RESORT HOTEL, KIAMESHA LAKE, NY 12751 (914)794-4000, EXT. 3324 *(87 mi. from Manhattan)*
ACCOMMODATIONS: CONCORD RESORT HOTEL (800)431-3850

Ranked among the nation's hundred best by *Golf Digest*, The Monster does not owe its name to its backbreaking length only. Although the course was designed to stretch as long as 7,700 yards from the back of the championship tees, it is seldom played from there and, in fact, does not need to. From the middle markers, the course is already very long and demands strategic ball placement on every shot.

There is not a single weak hole on this course. The first, a deceptively long and narrow 505-yard par 5, cuts among tall pines and sets the tone for the entire round. On No. 4, a hidden lake lies on the elevated landing area, ready to catch the ball after a blind and uphill tee shot. The lake then cuts diagonally through the fairway, requiring a lengthy and accurate second shot across. The third shot is still no gimme: it is a 150-yard iron approach to an elevated green. Bogey is an honorable score on this memorable 557-yard par 5. The 376-yard, par-4 tenth may be The Monster's most spectacular and intimidating hole. The elevated tee, located under the clubhouse, offers a beautiful view of the entire course. The drive must stay clear of the lake bordering the left side, but a hidden lake also protects the right. A long-iron second shot is then needed to reach the green, but it must first clear a treacherous creek in front of it.

The entire layout offers challenge and beauty, and while the emphasis is on long and straight tee shots, playing the course still requires all the clubs in the bag. In addition, the greens average more than 10,000 square feet in size, and three-putting is not uncommon here. Sitting among tall pines and surrounded by heavily wooded mountains, The Monster is a scenic as it is difficult. When architect Joe Finger set out to design the course in 1964, his mandate was to create a challenge that even the top professionals of the time would not conquer easily. Since its opening, this course has withstood the test heroically. Tough and beautiful, it remains one of the greatest courses of the Northeast.

The resort also offers the International, a short, hilly eighteen-hole layout. It is less intimidating but still gives golfers a last chance to warm up before attacking The Monster. A quick round can also be played at the nine-hole Challenger Course.

CONCORD GOLF CLUB
ACCESS: No restrictions
SEASON: Apr.-Nov.
GREEN FEES: $$$$$ (includes cart)
REDUCED FEES: WD, HG, LS, PK
RESERVATIONS: 7 months
WALKING: No   RANGE: Yes
• **MONSTER COURSE**
  18 holes   Par 72   7471/6989/6548 yds.
  USGA: 74.1   SLOPE: 137
  STYLE: Water hazards, woods
• **INTERNATIONAL COURSE**
  18 holes   Par 71   6619/5968/5554 yds.
  USGA: 69.5
  STYLE: Hills

THE CONCORD'S MONSTER: HOLE NO. 10

WATER COMES INTO PLAY ON HALF OF THE HOLES AT THE MONSTER. MANY TEE SHOTS AND SECOND SHOTS DEMAND PRECISE PLACEMENT, AND THE FIRST TIME VISITOR SHOULD MAKE SURE TO USE A YARDAGE BOOK, OR FACE A THREE-DIGIT SCORE...

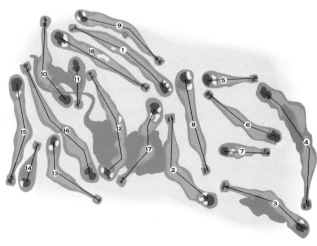

BETHPAGE STATE PARK

`19`

FARMINGDALE, NY 11735 (516)249-0700, (516)249-0701 *(35 mi. E of New York City)*

BETHPAGE, BLACK COURSE

BETHPAGE STATE PARK
ACCESS: No restrictions
SEASON: All year   HIGH: Mar.-Oct.
GREEN FEES: $
REDUCED FEES: WD, LS
RESERVATIONS: Not needed
WALKING: Yes   RANGE: Yes
• **BLACK COURSE**
18 holes   Par 71   7065/6556 yds.
USGA: 71.4   SLOPE: 134
STYLE: Traditional
• **GREEN COURSE**
18 holes   Par 71   6767/5903 yds.
USGA: 70.1   SLOPE: 117
STYLE: Traditional
• **RED COURSE**
18 holes   Par 70   6756/6537/6198 yds.
USGA: 71.6   SLOPE: 123
STYLE: Traditional
• **BLUE COURSE**
18 holes   Par 72   6684/6513/6213 yds.
USGA: 71.4   SLOPE: 121
STYLE: Traditional
• **YELLOW COURSE**
18 holes   Par 71   6316/6171/5966 yds.
USGA: 69.2   SLOPE: 114
STYLE: Traditional

Bethpage's Black Course is so good that, in an area that boasts some of the finest private courses in the country, it is a regular site for major local tournaments. It is simply a spectacular golf course, by any standard. The terrain is hilly and wooded, the fairways are narrow, and the rough is penal in the extreme. The bunkering here is as good as anywhere else. No. 5, for example, is a reachable par 5 with a bunker that splits the fairway. In the true tradition of the game, no carts are allowed on the Black Course, and better players will enjoy it most. Bethpage has four other eighteen-hole courses, all of them fine in their own right. The challenging Green Course features some elevated tees down to flat or rolling fairways. The Red Course is mostly flat but can play quite long. Rolling fairways and plenty of bunkers characterize the Blue Course. And the Yellow Course, considered the easiest of the five, is still quite interesting. It features nine doglegs, with a double dogleg at the par-5 No. 10. Each course here offers a true test for any golfer.

MARRIOTT'S WIND WATCH HOTEL AND GOLF CLUB

`20`

1717 VANDERBILT MOTOR PKWY., HAUPPAUGE, NY 11788 (516)232-9850 *(45 mi. E of New York City)*
ACCOMMODATIONS: MARRIOTT'S WIND WATCH HOTEL (516)232-9800

MARRIOTT'S WIND WATCH HOTEL AND GOLF CLUB
18 holes   Par 71   6405/6138/5135 yds.
USGA: 69.5   SLOPE: 129
STYLE: Tree-lined fairways, lakes
ACCESS: No restrictions
SEASON: All year   HIGH: May-Oct.
GREEN FEES: $$$
REDUCED FEES: HG, LS, TW, PK
RESERVATIONS: Nonguests 3 days
WALKING: No   RANGE: Yes

On Long Island's second-highest point, this Joe Lee course, redesigned in 1990, features the architect's trademark white sand bunkers— sixty-three in all. Wind Watch also encompasses about fifteen acres of lake and pond hazards that come into play on eleven holes. Fairways, some narrow, are lined with oak and maple, and steep hills enter the picture on a few occasions. Particularly challenging is the 338-yard, par-4 No. 16, which has water lining both sides, rock formations along the green, and a long bunker running parallel to the fairway.

MONTAUK DOWNS STATE PARK

S. FAIRVIEW AVE., MONTAUK, NY 11954 (516)668-1100 *(130 mi. E of New York City)*

MONTAUK DOWNS STATE PARK
18 holes   Par 72   6762/6289/5997 yds.
USGA: 70.5   SLOPE: 128
STYLE: Links
ACCESS: No restrictions
SEASON: Mar.-Dec.   HIGH: Summer
GREEN FEES: $
REDUCED FEES: WD, TW
RESERVATIONS: Not accepted
WALKING: Yes   RANGE: Yes

You have to travel all the way to the end of Long Island to play Montauk Downs, but it is well worth the effort. The course was redesigned in 1968 by Robert Trent Jones, and although it has some parkland, its sandy soil and rolling dunes make it close to a true links course. No. 11, for example, is a short par 4, where a solid 3-wood will leave you only a wedge away from the elevated and considerably protected green. With the wind blowing in your face, it looks, feels, and plays like the real thing.

SARANAC INN GOLF CLUB

HRC 1, BOX 16, UPPER SARANAC LAKE, NY 12983 (518)891-1402 *(18 mi. NW of Lake Placid)*
ACCOMMODATIONS: SARANAC INN GOLF CLUB (518)891-1402

Designed in 1903 by Willie and Seymour Dunn, Saranac's course is a step back in time that captures the links feel of the Dunns' native Scotland. Located on a mountain plateau, it offers stunning views of the high peaks of the Adirondacks. The Dunns kept the fairways generous in size, but the multi-tiered greens are extremely well-trapped, and the high fescue rough can be quite punishing. Play is limited to a hundred rounds a day, keeping the course as pristine as the surroundings.

SARANAC INN GOLF CLUB
18 holes   Par 72   6631/6453/5263 yds.
USGA: 73.4   SLOPE: 133
STYLE: Links
ACCESS: Priority to hotel guests
SEASON: May-Sept.   HIGH: July-Sept.
GREEN FEES: $$$ (includes cart)
REDUCED FEES: HG, PK
RESERVATIONS: 2 weeks
WALKING: No   RANGE: Yes

THE SAGAMORE RESORT

SAGAMORE RD., BOLTON LANDING, NY 12814 (518)644-9400 *(60 mi. S of Albany)*
ACCOMMODATIONS: THE SAGAMORE RESORT (800)358-3585

THE SAGAMORE RESORT GOLF COURSE
18 holes   Par 70   6706/6410/5265 yds.
USGA: 71.5   SLOPE: 128
STYLE: Rolling hills, woods
ACCESS: Priority to hotel guests
SEASON: May-Oct.   HIGH: June-Aug.
GREEN FEES: $$$$
REDUCED FEES: HG, PK
RESERVATIONS: At time of hotel booking
WALKING: No   RANGE: Yes

This classic Donald Ross golf course is located on enchanting upland meadows at the edge of the Adirondacks' evergreen forest, a mile from Lake George and the beautiful Sagamore Resort. The course, which Ross designed in 1928, was entirely restored to its former condition in 1985, with every detail rebuilt according to the master architect's original blueprints. It is routed through mountainside terrain heavily wooded with pine and birch, and Ross designed large, naturally elevated, and slippery greens protected by a few highly effective bunkers. Sagamore's course can play as long as 6,900 yards, but the challenge is all in finesse, demanding a complete mastering of the short irons, pitching, and chipping. At the conclusion of your game, you will be sure to rethink the 454-yard, par-4 thirteenth, which is as difficult as it is breathtaking. After a tough drive with water to the right and ahead of the green, the second shot is played uphill to a rolling green that Mr. Ross himself called "one undulating mass." It is a truly memorable hole. The course is kept in impeccable condition, worthy of its creator and the beautiful surroundings.

C
O
N
N
E
C
T
I
C
U
T

BLACKLEDGE COUNTRY CLUB 24

180 WEST ST., HEBRON, CT 06248 (203)228-0250 *(20 mi. SE of Hartford)*

The rolling Connecticut countryside and the thick trees lining the fairways give Blackledge its rustic look. Geoffrey Cornish created the course in 1963 and defined his layout by using the hills, trees, and four ponds. The fairways are comfortable in width, and the bentgrass greens are beautifully contoured. The third hole, a 439-yard par 4, incorporates two of the water hazards: you must hit your tee shot over water, and depending on the length of the drive, the second shot requires a 130 to 200-yard carry over another pond. The Cornish-Silva team is at work on nine additional holes.

BLACKLEDGE COUNTRY CLUB
18 holes   Par 72   6853/6416/5518 yds.
USGA: 70.7   SLOPE: 120
STYLE: Rolling hills, tree-lined fairways
ACCESS: No restrictions
SEASON: Mar.-Dec.   HIGH: Apr.-Oct.
GREEN FEES: $$
REDUCED FEES: WD, TW
RESERVATIONS: 5 to 7 days
WALKING: Yes   RANGE: Yes

LYMAN MEADOW GOLF CLUB 25

RTE. 157, MIDDLEFIELD, CT 06455 (203)349-8055 *(20 mi. S of Hartford)*

Lyman Meadow is part of a 250-year-old family-owned farm with a 27,000-tree apple, peach, and pear orchard adjacent to the course. The layout itself features the ponds, brooks, and rolling hills characteristic of the countryside, and each hole possesses a character all its own. The track begins with a difficult opening par 4, soon followed by the dogleg-right No. 3, also a challenging par 4, with a stream along the right side. In all, this 1968 Robert Trent Jones design brings into play streams and ponds on nine holes and a total of forty-seven bunkers. In addition, the greens average 5,500 square feet in surface, and the undulations bring an extra dimension to putting. To conclude your round, the par-5 No. 18 takes you uphill for a king-of-the-mountain finish. Lyman Meadow serves as a site for the Greater Hartford Open qualifying rounds.

LYMAN MEADOW GOLF CLUB
18 holes   Par 72   7011/6614/5812 yds.
USGA: 71.9   SLOPE: 127
STYLE: Rolling hills, ponds
ACCESS: No restrictions
SEASON: Mar.-Dec.   HIGH: June-Sept.
GREEN FEES: $$
REDUCED FEES: WD, PK
RESERVATIONS: 5 days
WALKING: Yes   RANGE: Yes

R
H
O
D
E

I
S
L
A
N
D

TRIGGS MEMORIAL GOLF COURSE 26

1533 CHALKSTONE AVE., PROVIDENCE, RI 02909 (401)272-GOLF *(2 mi. NW of Providence)*

Triggs Memorial is a championship course that Donald Ross laid out in 1927. Hills covered with Scottish heather are reminders of the architect's overseas origins, but the views of downtown Providence bring players quickly back to New England. In traditional Ross fashion, the fairways are wide, but ninety-five well-placed sandtraps patiently await any shots with sideway tendencies. The signature hole is the well-bunkered, 425-yard, par-4 No. 2 with its typical Scottish flavor. Triggs Memorial is considered a very difficult layout, and it hosts the annual Providence Open.

TRIGGS MEMORIAL GOLF COURSE
18 holes   Par 72   6590/6394/5320 yds.
STYLE: Traditional
ACCESS: No restrictions
SEASON: All year   HIGH: Apr.-Oct.
GREEN FEES: $
REDUCED FEES: WD
RESERVATIONS: 2 days
WALKING: Yes   RANGE: No

CRUMPIN-FOX CLUB

27

PARMENTER RD., BERNARDSTON, MA 01337 (413)648-9101 *(40 mi. N of Springfield)*

The Crumpin-Fox Club derives its name from the Bernardston-based Crump Soda Company which, in June of 1853, was purchased by Mr. Eli Fox. Over a century later, during construction of the course, Crump & Fox soda bottles were discovered on the site, giving a name to this outstanding course. Situated at the edge of the Berkshires, the layout features many elevated tees with breathtaking views of the distant mountains. The best time to visit is in late September when the fall foliage is at its peak. The 592-yard, par-5 No. 8 is a true gem: from the elevated tee, a player faces a dangerously narrowing fairway flanked on the entire left side by a lake. The safer the second shot, the more heroic the third shot will have to be. In 1991, Crumpin-Fox scored an honorable mention in the *Golf Digest* ranking of America's best new courses.

> **CRUMPIN-FOX CLUB**
> 18 holes   Par 72   7007/6508/5432 yds.
> USGA: 71.3   SLOPE: 136
> STYLE: Hills, woods, water
> ACCESS: No restrictions
> SEASON: Apr.-Nov.   HIGH: June-Aug.
> GREEN FEES: $$
> REDUCED FEES: PK
> RESERVATIONS: 2 days
> WALKING: Yes   RANGE: Yes

STOW ACRES COUNTRY CLUB

28

58 RANDALL RD., STOW, MA 01775 (508)568-8690, (508)568-1100 *(25 mi. W of Boston)*

Stow Acres is generally considered one of the best public golf facilities in the Boston area. The property dates back to a land grant from the King of England, and the rural setting is beautiful. The North Course is set in a stately pine forest, with some trees reaching as high as a hundred feet. It has hosted many events, and the 460-yard, par-4 No. 9 is rated one of the eighteen toughest in the Bay State. The older South Course is laid over rolling hills and incorporates several doglegs, five par 5s, and water on seven holes. On the 438-yard, par-4 sixteenth, the drive is hit from a chute of trees, followed by a second shot uphill to a large green. Both courses were designed by Geoffrey Cornish—the South in 1955, and the North in 1966.

> **STOW ACRES COUNTRY CLUB**
> ACCESS: No restrictions
> SEASON: Mar.-Dec.   HIGH: May-Oct.
> GREEN FEES: $$
> REDUCED FEES: WD, TW
> RESERVATIONS: 5 days
> WALKING: Yes   RANGE: Yes
> • **NORTH COURSE**
>   18 holes   Par 72   6909/6700/6400 yds.
>   USGA: 72.4   SLOPE: 124
>   STYLE: Woods, water
> • **SOUTH COURSE**
>   18 holes   Par 72   6520/6400/6100 yds.
>   USGA: 71.8   SLOPE: 120
>   STYLE: Rolling hills, water

BAYBERRY HILLS GOLF COURSE

29

W. YARMOUTH RD., W. YARMOUTH, MA 02673 (508)394-5597 *(Cape Cod)*

> **BAYBERRY HILLS GOLF COURSE**
> 18 holes   Par 72   7172/6523/5275 yds.
> USGA: 70.5   SLOPE: 125
> STYLE: Woods
> ACCESS: No restrictions
> SEASON: Apr.-Nov.   HIGH: June-Sept.
> GREEN FEES: $$
> REDUCED FEES: TW
> RESERVATIONS: 4 days
> WALKING: Yes   RANGE: Yes

This Geoffrey Cornish-Brian Silva design opened in 1987 and quickly established a reputation, not only as the longest course on the Cape, but also one of the best. The course, which features five sets of tees, winds through 205 heavily wooded acres, providing a nice sense of privacy. The 533-yard, par-5 No. 15 is the most noteworthy on the course. A grove of trees in the fairway forces the player to decide between a safe route for par or a gamble for birdie.

CAPE COD COUNTRY CLUB

THEATER RD., FALMOUTH, MA 02556 (508)563-9842, (508)563-6109 *(Cape Cod)*

CAPE COD COUNTRY CLUB
18 holes   Par 71   6404/6018/5423 yds.
USGA: 67.7   SLOPE: 118
STYLE: Traditional, tree-lined fairways
ACCESS: No restrictions
SEASON: All year   HIGH: July-Sept.
GREEN FEES: $$
REDUCED FEES: WD, TW
RESERVATIONS: 1 week
WALKING: Yes   RANGE: No

The Cape Cod Country Club course is surrounded by pine and oak, with picturesque views of the lovely Coonamessett Pond. This traditional course was designed by Donald Ross in the mid-1920s. With mostly small greens and some narrow fairways, it rewards accuracy over sheer force, yet it is demanding enough to have hosted three Massachusetts Opens. Seventy-one sand-traps dot the course, but only three holes have water. The 165-yard ninth is considered one of the most beautiful par 3s on Cape Cod.

FARM NECK GOLF CLUB

OAK BLUFFS, MA 02557 (508)693-3057 *(on Martha's Vineyard)*

FARM NECK GOLF CLUB
18 holes   Par 72   6806/6269/5506 yds.
USGA: 69.6   SLOPE: 126
STYLE: Rolling hills, oceanside
ACCESS: Restrictions in summer
SEASON: Apr.-Nov.   HIGH: July-Sept.
GREEN FEES: $$$
REDUCED FEES: LS
RESERVATIONS: 1 day
WALKING: Yes   RANGE: Yes

Located on Martha's Vineyard, Farm Neck is a bit out of the way, but its many ocean scenes make it a pleasure to play. The tight, well-trapped front nine is a 1976 Ted Robinson-Geoffrey Cornish design. It was joined in 1979 by the longer and more open back nine. In recent years, the club has hosted an annual hospital benefit tournament in which several PGA professionals come to play. A local rule requires "any ball moved or stolen by seagulls to be moved back to or replaced at the original lie."

FARM NECK GOLF CLUB

NEW SEABURY RESORT

NEW SEABURY RESORT `32`
P.O. BOX 550, NEW SEABURY, MA 02649 (508)477-9110 *(Cape Cod)*
ACCOMMODATIONS: NEW SEABURY RESORT (508)477-9111

NEW SEABURY RESORT
ACCESS: Restrictions on tee times
SEASON: All year   HIGH: Summer
GREEN FEES: $$$
REDUCED FEES: PK
RESERVATIONS: 1 day
WALKING: At times   RANGE: Yes
● **BLUE CHAMPIONSHIP COURSE**
 18 holes   Par 72   6909/6508/5764 yds.
 USGA: 70.8   SLOPE: 128
 STYLE: Oceanside, hills, trees
● **GREEN CHALLENGER COURSE**
 18 holes   Par 68   5939/5105 yds.
 USGA: 67.2
 STYLE: Oceanside, hills, trees

There are thirty-six holes at New Seabury, and each one is a beauty. The Blue Championship Course which hosted the 1985 Women's NCAA Championship, begins near the ocean, where it has a distinct links feel; then it climbs up through hilly, wooded terrain. The par-4 signature hole, No. 3, is surrounded by water on three sides. The Green Challenger Course is a shorter, easier layout that offers a fair test. But it can border on downright difficult when the wind picks up off the nearby ocean. Its narrow fairways place a premium on accuracy. Because of the warming effects of the Gulf Stream, golf can be played nearly year round at New Seabury.

CRANBERRY VALLEY GOLF COURSE `33`
183 OAK ST., HARWICH, MA 02645 (508)432-4653, (508)430-7560 *(20 mi. from Hyannis)*

CRANBERRY VALLEY GOLF COURSE
18 holes   Par 72   6745/6296/5518 yds.
USGA: 70.4   SLOPE: 123
STYLE: Tree-lined fairways
ACCESS: No restrictions
SEASON: Mar.-Dec.   HIGH: June-Nov.
GREEN FEES: $$
REDUCED FEES: TW
RESERVATIONS: 2 days, anytime
 if prepaid
WALKING: Yes   RANGE: Yes

Cranberry Valley, a scenic Robinson-Cornish creation, opened in 1974, and for its first ten years was ranked by *Golf Digest* as one of the top fifty public courses in the U.S. Its tree-lined, rolling fairways wind through marshland and cranberry bogs now reclaimed by nature. Many doglegs with bunkered corners add to the challenge. The par-4 No. 12 begins with a blind tee shot and travels down a sloping fairway to an elusive green protected by a pond in front and bunkers in back.

OCEAN EDGE GOLF COURSE

OCEAN EDGE RESORT

832 VILLAGES DR., BREWSTER, MA 02631 (508)896-5911 *(Cape Cod)*
ACCOMMODATIONS: OCEAN EDGE RESORT (508)896-2781

`34`

OCEAN EDGE RESORT
18 holes   Par 72   6665/6127/5098 yds.
USGA: 68.9   SLOPE: 127
STYLE: Rolling hills, tree-lined fairways
ACCESS: Restrictions on tee times
SEASON: All year   HIGH: July-Aug.
GREEN FEES: $$
REDUCED FEES: WD, LS, PK
RESERVATIONS: 1 week, 2 days
  for weekends
WALKING: No   RANGE: Yes

This Cornish and Silva design has emerged as one of the finest championship layouts in New England. It has hosted the New England PGA Championship each year since its opening in 1986. The length is not oppressive, but the course is tight, and the greens can be small, placing yet another demand on accuracy. The most challenging hole is the eighth. The green and the corner on that 601-yard-long dogleg left are guarded by steep pot bunkers. As the resort's name suggests, the clubhouse offers an outstanding ocean view.

THE CAPTAINS GOLF COURSE

1000 FREEMANS WAY, BREWSTER, MA 02631 (508)896-5100 *(Cape Cod)*

`35`

THE CAPTAINS GOLF COURSE
18 holes   Par 72   6794/6176/5388 yds.
USGA: 69.4   SLOPE: 126
STYLE: Rolling hills
ACCESS: No restrictions
SEASON: Mar.-Dec.   HIGH: June-Aug.
GREEN FEES: $$
REDUCED FEES: WD, TW
RESERVATIONS: 2 days, 2 months for
  foursomes if prepaid
WALKING: Yes   RANGE: Yes

The Captains course is located just a few miles outside of Brewster, a Cape Cod community with a rich maritime history. Geoffrey Cornish and Brian Silva did a beautiful job of routing the eighteen rolling fairways through a thick pine forest. Tight landing areas, large greens, and the strategic use of bunkers and hills make the course thoroughly challenging and enjoyable. The Captains is a first-class facility, ranked by *Golf Digest* in the top twenty-five public courses in the nation.

SUGARBUSH INN

36

WARREN, VT 05674 (802)583-2722 *(45 mi. S of Burlington)*
ACCOMMODATIONS: SUGARBUSH INN (802)583-2301

As good as golf is at Sugarbush, the scenery is even better. In fact, the views from this course are among the most spectacular in Vermont. The four-thousand-foot-high mountains looming in the background, and the gorgeous maple, pine, and oak trees are sure to delight you. Robert Trent Jones designed this gem and made good use of the heavily wooded, hilly land and natural water hazards. The fairways are narrow and con-toured, but the greens—as is so often the case with a Jones resort course—are generous. Locals say that if you learn to play on this course, you'll learn to use every club in the bag. By the way, don't forget to bring your camera. The panorama from No. 7 is one of the most photographed in the area, and the one from No. 11 is simply breathtaking: the hole plays steeply downhill to a green that sits nestled among trees.

> **SUGARBUSH GOLF COURSE**
> 18 holes   Par 70   6524/5886/5187 yds.
> USGA: 69   SLOPE: 122
> STYLE: Mountains, woods
> ACCESS: No restrictions
> SEASON: May-Oct.   HIGH: July
> GREEN FEES: $$
> REDUCED FEES: WD, TW
> RESERVATIONS: 1 day
> WALKING: Yes   RANGE: Yes

SUGARBUSH GOLF COURSE

THE KILLINGTON GOLF COURSE

37

VILLAGE LODGING CTR., KILLINGTON RD., KILLINGTON, VT 05751 (802)422-4100 *(84 mi. from Burlington)*
ACCOMMODATIONS: THE VILLAGES AT KILLINGTON RESORT (800)343-0762, (802)422-3101

THE KILLINGTON GOLF COURSE
18 holes   Par 72   6326/5876/5170 yds.
USGA: 70.2   SLOPE: 132
STYLE: Mountains, woods
ACCESS: Priority to hotel guests
SEASON: May-Oct.   HIGH: July-Aug.
GREEN FEES: $$
REDUCED FEES: PK
RESERVATIONS: Nonguests 5 days
WALKING: Yes   RANGE: No

Killington, a fine Cornish-Silva mountain course, puts pressure on your shotmaking and thinking, not on your power. Every hole offers options, and the key to scoring well is in picking those best suited to your game. The reachable, 485-yard, par-5 No. 11 is a good example. A bold 3-wood could yield an eagle...or double bogey. With great views, it is spectacular mountain golf, and course design at its best.

WOODSTOCK GOLF COURSE

WOODSTOCK INN AND RESORT

38

14 THE GREEN, WOODSTOCK, VT 05091 (802)457-2114 *(120 mi. N of Boston)*
ACCOMMODATIONS: WOODSTOCK INN AND RESORT (800)448-7900, (802)457-1100

Golf first came to Woodstock in 1895, but the present Robert Trent Jones course is considerably younger, having opened in 1969. The course winds along the base of the Kedron Valley, offering stunning views, particularly during the brilliant days of autumn. The fairways are slim, and greens are also on the small side. Kedron Brook winds through the course, coming into play on twelve holes. For additional fun, there are eighty deep sandtraps sprinkled around the layout. The best hole is prob-

WOODSTOCK INN AND RESORT
18 holes   Par 67   6001/5555/5202 yds.
USGA: 67   SLOPE: 117
STYLE: Tree-lined fairways, water
ACCESS: Priority to hotel guests
SEASON: May-Oct.   HIGH: July-Aug.
GREEN FEES: $$$
REDUCED FEES: HG
RESERVATIONS: Nonguests same day
WALKING: Yes   RANGE: Yes

ably No. 4, which requires a drive across the brook to a narrow landing area. The brook interferes again with the approach shot. It's a classic Trent Jones test of strategy.

STRATTON GOLF COURSE

STRATTON MOUNTAIN COUNTRY CLUB — 39

STRATTON MOUNTAIN, VT 05155 (802)297-1880 *(80 mi. N of Albany, NY)*
ACCOMMODATIONS: STRATTON MOUNTAIN RESORT (800)843-6867, (802)297-2200

Geoffrey Cornish designed three distinctive nines at Stratton mountain—the Lake, the Mountain, and the Forest. All three offer superb views of the surrounding ski area, and the annual Stratton Mountain LPGA Classic is held here. The course has narrow, bentgrass fairways that put a premium on shot placement. On the other hand, the greens are comfortably large and fairly flat. An enjoyable mix of long and short holes keeps play interesting for all golfers, but numerous contoured bunkers and trees interfere with many shots. In addition, water comes into play on at least half the holes. The best might be No. 5 on the Mountain Course; it is a very long par 5 where players must avoid three picturesque but dangerous streams.

STRATTON MOUNTAIN COUNTRY CLUB
27 holes   3066/3041/2978 yds.
STYLE: Rolling hills, trees, water
ACCESS: Restrictions on tee times
SEASON: May-Oct.   HIGH: July-Aug.
GREEN FEES: $$$
REDUCED FEES: HG, PK
RESERVATIONS: Nonguests 1 week
WALKING: At times   RANGE: Yes

N E W H A M P S H I R E

THE BALSAMS GRAND RESORT HOTEL `40`

THE BALSAMS, DIXVILLE NOTCH, NH 03576 (603)255-4961 *(120 mi. NW of Portland, ME)*
ACCOMMODATIONS: THE BALSAMS GRAND RESORT HOTEL (603)255-3400

The Donald Ross-designed Panorama Course at The Balsams offers a commanding view of Maine, Vermont, New Hampshire, and Canada. Except for the new championship tees, the course is unchanged from its 1912 design. Generous fairways welcome the tee shots, but the small greens often perch on nobs in classic Ross style. The 387-yard, par-4 No. 12 is a charmer; it tumbles down a seventy-five-foot drop, curves around a pond, and finishes with an elevated green. It's all natural golf, in a grand, traditional setting. The Balsams also offers the nine-hole, par-64 Coashaukee Course.

PANORAMA COURSE
18 holes   Par 72   6804/6097/5069 yds.
USGA: 68.9   SLOPE: 118
STYLE: Mountains
ACCESS: No restrictions
SEASON: May-Oct.   HIGH: July-Aug.
GREEN FEES: $$
REDUCED FEES: HG, PK
RESERVATIONS: 1 week
WALKING: Yes   RANGE: Yes

MT. WASHINGTON RESORT GOLF CLUB `41`

RTE. 302, BRETTON WOODS, NH 03575 (603)278-1000, EXT. 8540 *(25 mi. W of North Conway)*
ACCOMMODATIONS: MT. WASHINGTON HOTEL AND RESORT (603)278-1000

MT. WASHINGTON COURSE
18 holes   Par 71   6638/6154/5336 yds.
STYLE: Hills, woods
ACCESS: No restrictions
SEASON: May-Oct.   HIGH: July-Aug.
GREEN FEES: $
REDUCED FEES: WD, HG, TW, PK
RESERVATIONS: Anytime
WALKING: Yes   RANGE: No

The Mt. Washington Course, designed by Donald Ross, opened in 1912 and is considered by many the most scenic course in New England. Spectacular vistas of the White Mountains have attracted the likes of Babe Ruth, Gene Sarazen, and Ken Venturi to play here. The fairways wind through lovely, rolling terrain and offer ample landing areas. Greens vary in size and are protected by the wonderful bunkering that is one of Ross's hallmarks. The nine-hole Mt. Pleasant Course is a recently renovated Cornish-Silva design.

WENTWORTH BY THE SEA GOLF CLUB `42`

WENTWORTH RD., RTE. 1B, RYE, NH 03870 (603)433-5010 *(1 mi. from Portsmouth)*

WENTWORTH BY THE SEA GOLF CLUB
18 holes   Par 70   6179/5702/5145 yds.
USGA: 66.7   SLOPE: 121
STYLE: Oceanside, links
ACCESS: No restrictions
SEASON: Apr.-Nov.   HIGH: July-Sept.
GREEN FEES: $$
RESERVATIONS: 3 days, 2 days
for weekends
WALKING: At times   RANGE: No

Wentworth's unforgettably beautiful course makes the best use of the little seacoast that New Hampshire has. Half the holes are either on or overlook the Atlantic, and water also comes into play in the form of ponds and Witches Creek. Approximately a hundred sand bunkers dot the course. No. 7 is a stunning par 3 that extends into the Atlantic. The ocean is also a major factor on the par-5 eighth: you must carry it with your drive, then avoid it on the right all the way to the green.

THE COUNTRY CLUB OF NEW HAMPSHIRE `43`

KEARSARGE VALLEY RD., N. SUTTON, NH 03260 (603)927-4246 *(25 mi. NW of Concord)*
ACCOMMODATIONS: THE COUNTRY CLUB OF NEW HAMPSHIRE (603)927-4246

> **THE COUNTRY CLUB OF NEW HAMPSHIRE**
> 18 holes   Par 72   6727/6226/5396 yds.
> USGA: 69.6   SLOPE: 122
> STYLE: Woods, water
> ACCESS: No restrictions
> SEASON: Apr.-Nov.   HIGH: July-Sept.
> GREEN FEES: $$
> REDUCED FEES: WD, TW, PK
> RESERVATIONS: 1 week
> WALKING: Yes   RANGE: Yes

This William Mitchell design has twice been rated by *Golf Digest* as one of the seventy-five best public courses in America. It's a beautiful, well-routed course that winds through a valley at the base of the three-thousand-foot Mount Kearsarge. Thick woods line the undulating fairways, and lakes, brooks, and sandtraps are plentiful. The landing areas are ample, and the greens—some of the best in New Hampshire—are large, offering many good pin placements.

SKY MEADOW COUNTRY CLUB `44`

2 SKY MEADOW DR., NASHUA, NH 03062 (603)888-9000 *(35 mi. NW of Boston)*

> **SKY MEADOW COUNTRY CLUB**
> 18 holes   Par 72   6590/6036/5127 yds.
> USGA: 70.8   SLOPE: 128
> STYLE: Steep hills, water
> ACCESS: Priority to members
> SEASON: Apr.-Nov.   HIGH: June-Aug.
> GREEN FEES: $$$
> REDUCED FEES: WD
> RESERVATIONS: Recommended
> WALKING: No   RANGE: Yes

On a clear day, Sky Meadow, which is built on Nashua's highest elevation, boasts hundred-mile views, including a glimpse of the Boston skyline. But players shouldn't allow themselves to be distracted. This is a tight, target-style course that combines water hazards and steep hills—and there isn't much room for mistakes. No. 2 has an island green with swampy surroundings, and No. 11 plays seventy-five feet downhill from tee to green. Designed by William Amick, Sky Meadow has been open since 1989.

SABLE OAKS GOLF CLUB `45`

M A I N E

505 COUNTRY CLUB RD., S. PORTLAND, ME 04106 (207)775-6257 *(in Portland city limits)*
ACCOMMODATIONS: PORTLAND MARRIOTT HOTEL (800)752-8810

> **SABLE OAKS GOLF CLUB**
> 18 holes   Par 70   6359/6056/4786 yds.
> USGA: 70.2   SLOPE: 129
> STYLE: Rolling hills, woods, water
> ACCESS: No restrictions
> SEASON: Apr.-Nov.   HIGH: June-Aug.
> GREEN FEES: $$ (includes cart)
> REDUCED FEES: WD, LS, TW, PK
> RESERVATIONS: 1 month
> WALKING: No   RANGE: No

Geoffrey Cornish and Brian Silva did some excellent work on this target-style course, which opened in 1989. The gently rolling landscape is highlighted by numerous stands of pine, oak, and white birch, as well as ponds and streams. The 437-yard, par-4 No. 12 is quite memorable: on the second shot, the green rests ninety feet below the player; from there, you can admire the White Mountains of New Hampshire and the natural Maine countryside.

SUGARLOAF GOLF CLUB

RTE. 27, BOX 5000, CARRABASSETT VALLEY, ME 04947 (207)237-2000 EXT. 6812
(200 mi. NW of Boston)
ACCOMMODATIONS: CALL GOLF CLUB FOR INFORMATION

Deep in the mountains of western Maine, a true gem of a course awaits the New England golfer. Said to be one of Robert Trent Jones, Jr.'s, favorite designs, Sugarloaf was literally carved out of the colorful Maine woods and offers great vistas of the surrounding Bigelow Mountains. Each hole has a marked feeling of individuality and is completely separated from the others to preserve a sense of seclusion and wilderness. Tees elevated fifty feet or more over- look fairways lined by white birch trees. On the back nine, the

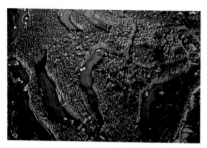

AN AERIAL VIEW OF SUGARLOAF

Carrabassett River rushes along and across the course, guided by walls of white rocks. Jones did not let nature do all the work, however: the layout is enhanced by numerous massive bunkers that effectively squeeze landing areas to a mere thirty yards in many places. Sets of multiple tees were built to tailor the course to every golfer's ability, and large, elevated, bentgrass greens add the final ingredient for a superb golf course.

Selecting a signature hole at Sugarloaf is unfair to the other ones. Still, perhaps Nos. 10, 11, and 14 are the most exciting. The 355-yard, par-4 tenth requires avoiding no less than seven bunkers; a huge one guards the left side of the fairway two hundred yards from the tee, and another deep trench runs across the front of the sloping green. And No. 11, a two-hundred-yard, downhill par 3, necessi- tates a long carry over the

SUGARLOAF GOLF CLUB
18 holes   Par 72   6900/6400/5400 yds.
USGA: 70.8   SLOPE: 137
STYLE: Mountains, woods, water
ACCESS: No restrictions
SEASON: May-Oct.   HIGH: July-Sept.
GREEN FEES: $$
REDUCED FEES: WD, HG, LS
RESERVATIONS: Nonguests 5 days
WALKING: Yes   RANGE: Yes

Carrabassett River from the men's tee. No. 14's second shot also requires a scary mid-iron shot over the foaming torrent. The elevat- ed green sits on the river's rocky bank, and a rear bunker discourages conservative overclubbing.

Since its opening in 1985, Sugarloaf has received much recogni- tion as one of the most scenic golf courses in the U.S.—if not the world. With a slope rating of 137 from the white tees, it is a very difficult test of golf but surely one of the most memorable. One word of caution: close encounters with moose may delay your round.

SUGARLOAF GOLF CLUB

SAMOSET RESORT GOLF CLUB · 47

ROCKPORT, ME 04856 (207)594-1431 *(89 mi. N of Portland)*
ACCOMMODATIONS: SAMOSET RESORT (800)341-1650

SAMOSET RESORT GOLF CLUB
18 holes Par 70 6384/6011/5385 yds.
USGA: 67.2 SLOPE: 118
STYLE: Oceanside
ACCESS: No restrictions
SEASON: Apr.-Nov. HIGH: July-Aug.
GREEN FEES: $$
REDUCED FEES: HG, LS
RESERVATIONS: Nonguests 2 days
WALKING: At times RANGE: Yes

HOLES NO. 7 & 16 DOUBLE GREEN

With ocean vistas from thirteen holes and seven fairways actually bordering the rocky coast of Penobscot Bay, Samoset has been described by *Golf Traveler* as "a golfer's paradise," and the "Pebble Beach of the East." A facetious writer even suggests that Pebble Beach should be referred to as the "Samoset of the West." In fact, the course, designed by Robert Elder in 1972, is pure Maine. Located in a century-old resort community, its signature hole, No. 7, is a par-5 dogleg left that hugs the shoreline, practically daring golfers to play over the ocean. But one must consider carefully the effect of capricious sea breezes before taking that chance. Two Scottish-style double greens add interest to the layout. No. 8 and No. 15 share a large putting surface with bunkers on all sides, while Nos. 7 and 16 share another one. A scenic fringe benefit is the 7/8-mile jetty that extends from the green, with one of the region's oldest lighthouses perched at its tip. The Samoset Golf Course has been the home of the Maine PGA Championships over the past seven years.

PENOBSCOT VALLEY COUNTRY CLUB · 48

366 MAIN ST., ORONO, ME 04473 (207)866-2423 *(5 mi. N of Bangor)*

PENOBSCOT VALLEY COUNTRY CLUB
18 holes Par 72 6301/5856 yds.
USGA: 69.6 SLOPE: 121
STYLE: Rolling hills, links
ACCESS: Four times a year
SEASON: Apr.-Nov. HIGH: Summer
GREEN FEES: $$
RESERVATIONS: 1 week
WALKING: Yes RANGE: Yes

Penobscot Valley was designed by Donald Ross and opened in 1924. The famous Scottish architect built the course on hilly terrain surrounded by thick woods, and the area is still rural today. The fairways run over severe undulations, and Ross created a serious challenge by combining the hills with very small and contoured greens. Errant shots will be caught by seventy sand-traps—if not by the heavy rough that blends deceptively into the landscape.

OTHER EXCELLENT COURSES IN THE NORTHEAST

CONNECTICUT
- BEL COMPO GOLF CLUB, Avon (203)678-1358
- RICHTER MEMORIAL PARK, Danbury (203)792-2552
- TUNXIS PLANTATION COUNTRY CLUB, Farmington (203)677-1367

DELAWARE
- ED "PORKY" OLIVER GOLF CLUB, Wilmington (302)571-9041
- ▲ GARRISON'S LAKE GOLF CLUB, Smyrna (302)653-9847

MASSACHUSETTS
- OAK RIDGE GOLF CLUB, Feeding Hills (413)786-9693
- SHAKER HILLS GOLF CLUB, Harvard (508)772-2227
- TACONIC GOLF CLUB, Williamstown (413)458-3997
- WACHUSETT COUNTRY CLUB, West Boylston (508)835-4453

MAINE
- KEBO VALLEY CLUB, Bar Harbor (207)288-3000

NEW HAMPSHIRE
- BRETWOOD GOLF COURSE, Keene (603)352-7626
- EASTMAN GOLF LINKS, Grantham (603)863-4500
- PORTSMOUTH COUNTRY CLUB, Greenland (603)436-9719

NEW JERSEY
- ▲ CRYSTAL SPRINGS GOLF CLUB, Hamburg (201)827-1444
- FLANDERS VALLEY GOLF COURSE, Flanders Valley (201)584-8964
- GREAT BAY RESORT AND COUNTRY CLUB, Somers Point (609)927-5071
- HOWELL PARK GOLF COURSE, Howell Township (908)938-4771

NEW YORK
- ▲ GARRISON GOLF CLUB, Garrison (914)424-3605
- SPOOK ROCK GOLF COURSE, Suffern (914)357-6466

PENNSYLVANIA
- BEDFORD SPRINGS GOLF COURSE, Bedford (814)623-8999
- ▲ LANCASTER HOST GOLF RESORT, Lancaster (717)397-7756
- POCONO MANOR INN AND GOLF CLUB, Pocono Manor (717)839-7111

RHODE ISLAND
- EXETER COUNTRY CLUB, Exeter (401)295-8212

VERMONT
- BASIN HARBOR CLUB, Vergennes (802)475-2309
- ▲ HAYSTACK GOLF CLUB, Wilmington (802)464-8301
- MOUNT SNOW COUNTRY CLUB, West Dover (802)464-5642

▲ RESTRICTIONS MAY APPLY   ■ HOTEL/RESORT GUESTS ONLY   ● OPEN WITHOUT RESTRICTIONS

CHAPTER SEVEN

THE MID-ATLANTIC STATES

Pleasant temperatures, an abundance of land naturally suited for golf courses, and a long tradition with the game place the Mid-Atlantic states in an enviable position when it comes to America's best golfing regions. The South Carolina Golf Club, the oldest recorded golf club in America, was founded in Charleston in 1786. Since then, the Mid-Atlantic States have been the closest witness to the development of the sport on the North American continent.

Clement weather may be what started it all. Golf season is year-round in most of South Carolina. In Virginia, it starts in March, but a New Year's Eve round of golf is not so unusual there, especially in the coastal areas. The Blue Ridge and Great Smoky Mountains of North Carolina are, of course, much cooler, but even there, golf is played in earnest from April to mid-November.

The diversity of geography, from mountains to semitropical islands, tells the rest of the story. Three distinct areas make up the Mid-Atlantic golf scene: the mountains to the west, with a collection of great resort courses around Asheville, North Carolina; the Atlantic Seaboard, with an almost continuous string of superb seaside courses from Chesapeake Bay to the Georgia state line; and, finally, the Sandhills, a unique area of central North Carolina.

In all the Mid-Atlantic, the greatest concentration of courses can be found around three well-known "golf hot spots": Myrtle Beach, a booming and popular South Carolina coastal destination; Hilton Head Island, a quieter and more isolated semitropical paradise; and the aforementioned Sandhills of North Carolina, home of the legendary Pinehurst Resort.

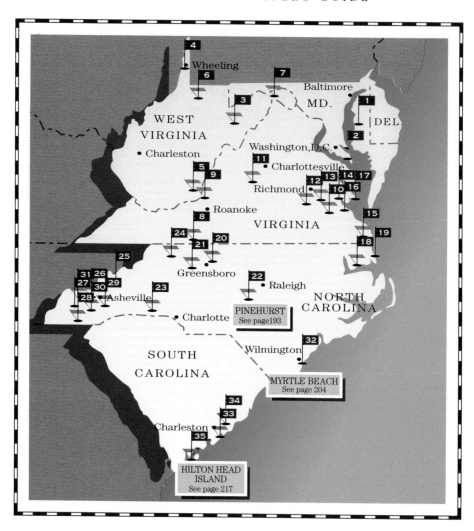

HARBOURTOWNE RESORT AND COUNTRY CLUB 🏴1

RTE. 33, ST. MICHAELS, MD 21663 (301)745-5183 *(70 mi. from Baltimore)*
ACCOMMODATIONS: HARBOURTOWNE RESORT (301)745-9066

**HARBOURTOWNE RESORT AND
COUNTRY CLUB**
18 holes   Par 70   6300/6100/5900 yds.
USGA: 68.5   SLOPE: 114
STYLE: Woods, lakes
ACCESS: Hotel guests only
SEASON: All year   HIGH: Spring-fall
GREEN FEES: $$
REDUCED FEES: WD
RESERVATIONS: 1 year
WALKING: No   RANGE: Yes

Pete Dye designed Harbourtowne's course in the early 1970s, a period when a number of people feel he did some of his best work. As with so many of his courses, he did a fine job with the small, well-guarded greens. At only 6,300 yards from the championship tees, the course relies mostly on narrow fairways and strategically placed hazards to protect par. Dye's signature holes are Nos. 15 and 17, but the long, narrow tenth is also a favorite. The Miles River runs nearby, offering many scenic views.

SWAN POINT

2

1 SWAN POINT BLVD., ISSUE, MD 20645 (301)259-2074 *(65 mi. SE of Washington, D.C.)*

SWAN POINT
18 holes Par 72 6761/6290/5009 yds.
USGA: 70.2 SLOPE: 125
STYLE: Woods, marshland
ACCESS: No restrictions
SEASON: All year HIGH: Apr.-June
GREEN FEES: $$
REDUCED FEES: LS
RESERVATIONS: 1 week, 2 days for weekends
WALKING: After 3 p.m. RANGE: Yes

Tucked along the banks of the Potomac River, Swan Point was sculpted out of a nine-hundred-acre piece of property covered with old pines and marsh areas. The green fees allow you to play the course, but the deer, osprey, heron, and even the eagle on No. 10 come free of charge. It is a beautiful course indeed, and Bob Cupp, formerly Jack Nicklaus's senior designer, made thoughtful use of the natural environment. Marshland is a common natural hazard at Swan Point, and it blends beautifully with the tall pine, giving the course its Carolinas look.

SWAN POINT: NO. 6, ISLAND HOLE

CANAAN VALLEY RESORT

3

RTE. 1, BOX 330, DAVIS, WV 26260 (304)866-4121, EXT. 2632 *(9 mi. S of Davis)*
ACCOMMODATIONS: CANAAN VALLEY RESORT (304)866-4121

CANAAN VALLEY RESORT GOLF COURSE
18 holes Par 72 6982/6436/5820 yds.
USGA: 71.4 SLOPE: 119
STYLE: Tree-lined fairways, water
ACCESS: No restrictions
SEASON: Apr.-Oct. HIGH: June-Sept.
GREEN FEES: $
REDUCED FEES: LS, PK
RESERVATIONS: Nonguests 2 weeks
WALKING: Yes RANGE: Yes

At 3,200 feet of elevation, Canaan Valley is one of the highest valleys east of the Mississippi River. Set in a six-thousand-acre state park and surrounded by unspoiled mountains and forests, the course is one of the most popular in West Virginia. This Geoffrey Cornish design combines wide, forgiving fairways with seven water hazards. The water comes in the form of ponds and brooks, and that, coupled with long yardages, makes for a challenging game. The valley's cool mountain climate is especially welcome during the summer.

WEST VIRGINIA

OGLEBAY

WHEELING, WV 26003 (800)624-6988 *(60 mi. SW of Pittsburgh)*
ACCOMMODATIONS: OGLEBAY (800)624-6988

4

OGLEBAY
ACCESS: No restrictions
SEASON: Mar.-Nov.   HIGH: May/Sept.
GREEN FEES: $$
REDUCED FEES: HG
RESERVATIONS: 2 months
WALKING: Yes   RANGE: Yes
- **SPEIDEL COURSE**
   18 holes   Par 71   7000/6085/5515 yds.
   USGA: 69   SLOPE: 118
   STYLE: Rolling hills, lakes
- **CRISPIN COURSE**
   18 holes   Par 71   5670/5100 yds.
   USGA: 66.6   SLOPE: 103
   STYLE: Rolling hills
- **PAR III COURSE**
   18 holes   1347 yds.

With two eighteen-hole layouts, as well as an eighteen-hole, par-3 course, Oglebay's complex has something special for all golfers. For the avid player in search of a real challenge, the seven-thousand-yard Speidel Course is the place to go. This Robert Trent Jones layout, which opened in 1971, offers rolling, bentgrass fairways and four lakes which come into play on four holes. But the strongest feature of this impressive course is the large, severely contoured greens, a real test for even the sharpest putter. Speidel, which hosted the West Virginia LPGA Classic for fourteen years, is especially glorious in the spring, when holes such as the thirteenth—a downhill par 3 over a lake—are enhanced by pink and white blossoms on the flowering crabapple trees. The Crispin Course is less difficult and less expensive, but it has enough personality to be a worthy companion to Speidel and label Oglebay a real golfing haven.

THE GREENBRIER

WHITE SULPHUR SPRINGS, WV 24986 (304)536-1110 *(70 mi. NW of Roanoke, VA)*
ACCOMMODATIONS: THE GREENBRIER (800)624-6070

THE GREENBRIER
ACCESS: Hotel guests only
SEASON: All year   HIGH: Apr.-Oct.
GREEN FEES: $$$
REDUCED FEES: LS, PK
RESERVATIONS: Recommended
WALKING: No   RANGE: Yes
- **GREENBRIER COURSE**
  18 holes   Par 72   6709/6311/5446 yds.
  USGA: 71.7   SLOPE: 133
  STYLE: Rolling hills, trees, water, sandtraps
- **LAKESIDE COURSE**
  18 holes   Par 70   6333/6068/5175 yds.
  USGA: 69   SLOPE: 120
  STYLE: Mountains, tree-lined fairways, water
- **OLD WHITE COURSE**
  18 holes   Par 70   6640/6353/5658 yds.
  USGA: 71.3   SLOPE: 126
  STYLE: Rolling hills, tree-lined fairways

Sam Snead's heart may lie a few miles away at the Homestead, but his glory years were spent at the Greenbrier. There are three eighteen-hole courses at this venerable resort, each with a style all its own. The Old White Course, designed by C. B. MacDonald and Seth Raynor, is the sentimental favorite. It dates back to 1910, and this is where young Sam Snead got most of his practice. You will surely remember the great views of the Allegheny Mountains, the severely sloped greens, and deep bunkers. The Greenbrier Course, reworked by Jack Nicklaus, is a tough track that proved its mettle in the 1979 Ryder Cup matches and several Senior PGA Tour events. Most of its bunkers are greenside, deep, and unforgiving. The Lakeside Course is shorter, but it is deceptively tough due to the narrow, tree-lined fairways. A stay at the Greenbrier brings back the glory and tradition of great golf resorts.

THE GREENBRIER: HOLE NO. 18

LAKEVIEW RESORT

6

RTE. 6, BOX 88A, MORGANTOWN, WV 26505 (304)594-2011 *(80 mi. S of Pittsburgh)*
ACCOMMODATIONS: LAKEVIEW RESORT (800)624-8300, (304)594-1111

Lakeview offers two beautiful, typical West Virginia layouts: lots of rolling and thickly wooded terrain adorned with colorful mountain laurel and dogwood trees. Although it has superb views of Cheat Lake, the Lakeview Course counts only one water hazard. No matter. The narrow, tree-lined fairways and strategically placed bunkers will give the average golfer all he or she can handle. And for big hitters who like to let it rip off the tee every now and then, the 620-yard, par-5 eighteenth is still waiting for someone to reach it in two. While the Mountainview Course is shorter and easier, it, too, offers golfers the same beautiful mountain setting and excellent conditioning.

LAKEVIEW RESORT
ACCESS: No restrictions
SEASON: All year   HIGH: Apr.-Oct.
GREEN FEES: $$
REDUCED FEES: WD, LS, PK
RESERVATIONS: Anytime
WALKING: No   RANGE: Yes
• **LAKEVIEW COURSE**
   18 holes   Par 72   6760/6357/5432 yds.
   USGA: 70.9   SLOPE: 124.9
   STYLE: Tree-lined fairways
• **MOUNTAINVIEW COURSE**
   18 holes   Par 72   6447/6152/5385 yds.
   USGA: 69.4   SLOPE: 116
   STYLE: Tree-lined fairways

CACAPON RESORT STATE PARK

7

RTE. 1, BOX 304, BERKELEY SPRINGS, WV 25411 (304)258-1022 *(25 mi. N of Winchester, VA)*
ACCOMMODATIONS: CACAPON RESORT STATE PARK LODGE (304)258-1022

CACAPON RESORT STATE PARK
18 holes   Par 72   6940/6410/5510 yds.
USGA: 70   SLOPE: 116
STYLE: Hills, woods, water
ACCESS: No restrictions
SEASON: All year   HIGH: Apr.-Oct.
GREEN FEES: $
REDUCED FEES: LS, PK
RESERVATIONS: Nonguests 1 week
WALKING: Yes   RANGE: Yes

Cacapon Mountain overlooks the six-thousand-acre state park in which this Robert Trent Jones-designed course is nestled, and the fairways seem, at times, to be overrun with deer and other wildlife! The championship 6,940-yard track is a good example of what Jones does best: all obstacles and trouble—including some seventy well-placed bunkers—are clearly visible, and if there are no overly difficult holes, there are no easy birdie holes either.

OLDE MILL GOLF RESORT

8

RTE. 1, BOX 84, LAUREL FORK, VA 24352 (703)398-2638 *(60 mi. SW of Roanoke)*
ACCOMMODATIONS: OLDE MILL GOLF RESORT (703)398-2211

OLDE MILL GOLF COURSE
18 holes   Par 72   6814/6185/5293 yds.
USGA: 69.5   SLOPE: 113
STYLE: Hills, water
ACCESS: No restrictions
SEASON: Mar.-Nov.
HIGH: Apr.-May/Sept.-Oct.
GREEN FEES: $$
REDUCED FEES: WD, TW, PK
RESERVATIONS: Within season
WALKING: At times   RANGE: Yes

A sixty-five-acre lake, two large ponds, and six creeks give players plenty of challenges on this course laid out by Ellis Maple. But sparkling white sandtraps, panoramic vistas of the countryside, and large groves of white pine, mountain laurel, rhododendron, and dogwood make this track a visual treat, as well. Bluegrass fairways are sculpted to various levels, while greens are often elevated and tiered. No. 10 is 150 feet above a peninsula fairway that juts into the larger lake. This beautiful view, coupled with the intimidating fairway, is a perfect example of Olde Mill's blend of challenging golf and scenic beauty.

V
I
R
G
I
N
I
A

THE HOMESTEAD

RTE. 220, HOT SPRINGS, VA 24445 (800)336-5771, (800)542-5734 IN VA *(65 mi. NW of Roanoke)*
ACCOMMODATIONS: THE HOMESTEAD HOTEL (703)839-5500

The Homestead is where Sam Snead got his start, and any combination of courses that can produce a Sam Snead is worth a trip from anywhere. Of the three eighteen-hole courses at this grand, traditional resort, the Cascades Course is undoubtedly the best. This classic mountain layout, often referred to as the "Upper Cascades" was designed by William Flynn in 1924, and it served as the site of the U.S. Women's Open in 1967 and the U.S. Men's Amateur in 1988. In something of an oddity, it ends with a par 3, but it is a remarkable par 3: the green sits a long-iron length away from the back tees, neatly tucked into the forest and overlooking a lake. The second course is the Lower Cascades, a Robert Trent Jones design that winds through thick woods and a valley. It's also a fine test, if somewhat overshad-owed by the Cascades Course. Last but not least, the Homestead Course is a wildly uphill-and-downhill affair that offers a great deal of fun. The course is located next to the magnificent old hotel and is the only one open all year. The Cascades and Lower Cascades Courses close from November to March.

THE HOMESTEAD
ACCESS: No restrictions
SEASON: All year   HIGH: Apr.-Oct.
GREEN FEES: $$$$ (includes cart)
REDUCED FEES: HG, LS, TW, PK
RESERVATIONS: 1 year
WALKING: No   RANGE: Yes
- **CASCADES COURSE**
  18 holes   Par 70   6566/6282/5448 yds.
  USGA: 71.6   SLOPE: 134
  STYLE: Mountains, woods, water
- **LOWER CASCADES COURSE**
  18 holes   Par 72   6619/6240/4726 yds.
  USGA: 70.4   SLOPE: 124
  STYLE: Rolling hills, creeks
- **THE HOMESTEAD COURSE**
  18 holes   Par 71   5957/5150 yds.
  USGA: 68.2   SLOPE: 115
  STYLE: Mountains, tree-lined fairways

KINGSMILL RESORT

10

1010 KINGSMILL RD., WILLIAMSBURG, VA 23185 (804)253-3906 *(40 mi. SE of Richmond)*
ACCOMMODATIONS: KINGSMILL RESORT (804)253-1703

Kingsmill Resort is home of the famous PGA Tour Anheuser-Busch Golf Classic and site of two superb eighteen-hole layouts. The tournament is played on the River Course, a Pete Dye creation with a 135 championship slope rating and a reputation for lack of clemency. The course runs through wooded territory and around four large ponds, concluding with three spectacular holes overlooking the James River. At the par-3 thirteenth, Dye constructed the tee on wooden posts that seem precariously anchored at the edge of Kingsmill Pond. From the platform, the hole plays 179 yards to a small green set against the hillside. On No. 17, remnants of Civil War fortifications lie on the left of the fairway, while the river runs tight along the entire right side. On the finishing hole, the tee shot is played over water, then the fairway rises gently toward the well-protected green. The Plantation Course, the brainchild of Arnold Palmer, is mostly routed through wooded areas, with water hazards that must be avoided on eight holes. The eighteenth green used to be on the River Course. If your first putt must go over the green's considerable swell, chances are it won't be your last. At Kingsmill, the fun doesn't end with the River and Plantation Courses. The Bray Links, an executive par-3 course built by Tom Clark along the James River, can be enjoyed by juniors as well as adults. The longest hole measures 110 yards; you won't need the whole set of clubs here, but a sharp wedge and putter could win you the admiration of the entire family.

KINGSMILL RESORT
ACCESS: No restrictions
SEASON: All year
GREEN FEES: $$$$$ (includes cart)
REDUCED FEES: HG, LS, TW
RESERVATIONS: Nonguests 1 day
WALKING: No   RANGE: Yes
- **RIVER COURSE**
  18 holes   Par 71   6776/6003/4588 yds.
  USGA: 69.5   SLOPE: 126
  STYLE: Woods, ponds
- **PLANTATION COURSE**
  18 holes   Par 72   6590/6109/4875 yds.
  USGA: 69.3   SLOPE: 115
  STYLE: Woods, ponds

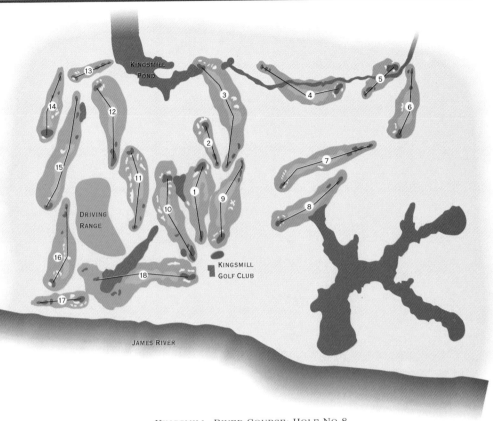

KINGSMILL
POND

13

14

12

3

2

4

5

6

15

11

7

1

9

10

8

DRIVING
RANGE

16

18

KINGSMILL
GOLF CLUB

17

JAMES RIVER

KINGSMILL, RIVER COURSE: HOLE NO. 8

WINTERGREEN RESORT

11

WINTERGREEN, VA 22958 (804)325-2200 *(40 mi. SW of Charlottesville)*
ACCOMMODATIONS: WINTERGREEN RESORT (804)325-2200

> **WINTERGREEN RESORT**
> ACCESS: No restrictions
> SEASON: All year   HIGH: June-Sept.
> GREEN FEES: $$$
> REDUCED FEES: WD, HG, PK
> RESERVATIONS: Nonguests 1 day
> WALKING: No   RANGE: Yes
> • **STONEY CREEK COURSE**
>   18 holes   Par 72   7005/6740/5500 yds.
>   USGA: 72.6   SLOPE: 126
>   STYLE: Trees, brooks
> • **DEVIL'S KNOB COURSE**
>   18 holes   Par 70   6576/6003/5101 yds.
>   USGA: 69.8   SLOPE: 119
>   STYLE: Mountains, streams

Wintergreen offers two fine courses—Devil's Knob, designed by Ellis Maples in 1976, and Stoney Creek, a Rees Jones creation which followed in1987. From an altitude of 3,850 feet, Devil's Knob is the highest course in the state, granting glorious vistas of the Shenandoah Valley. The Stoney Creek Course, set at a lower elevation with the dramatic background of the Blue Ridge Mountains, was a runner-up in the 1990 *Golf Digest* ranking of the best new resort course in the United States. Framed by sycamore, dogwood, and red bud oak, its front nine runs through a former cornfield, while the back nine is set amid deep groves of beech and pine. Brooks running down from the mountains traverse the layout. As is so often the case with him, Rees Jones created a design that fits into the natural contours of the terrain, and with excellent results. Witness the lovely, short downhill No. 12, which is cut into a thick pocket of trees and accented by a stream flowing to the left side of the hole. To complete their enjoyment while playing, golfers are at liberty to watch the many deer, wild geese and ducks that inhabit the property. Stoney Creek is open year round, but Devil's Knob closes during winter.

FORD'S COLONY COUNTRY CLUB

12

240 FORD'S COLONY DR., WILLIAMSBURG, VA 23188 (804)565-4130 *(30 mi. from Richmond)*
ACCOMMODATIONS: THE MANOR HOUSES (800)548-2978, (804)565-4340

> **FORD'S COLONY COUNTRY CLUB**
> 27 holes   3074/3163/3135 yds.
> STYLE: Rolling hills, tree-lined fairways
> ACCESS: No restrictions
> SEASON: All year
> HIGH: Apr.-June/Sept.-Oct.
> GREEN FEES: $$$$
> REDUCED FEES: WD, LS, TW
> RESERVATIONS: 1 month
> WALKING: At times   RANGE: Yes

Dan Maples designed three excellent nines here—the Red, the White, and the Blue. Set among native hardwood trees and ornamental landscaping, each utilizes several sets of tees but very little water and sand. Maples did, however, place his hazards for their best use. Touring pro Fuzzy Zoeller's favorite hole is the 452-yard, par-4 No. 7 on the Red. The tee shot is over a lake uphill to the landing area, while the second shot plays downhill to a large, sloping green. A fourth nine, the Gold, opened in 1991.

RIVER'S BEND COUNTRY CLUB `13`

11700 HOGAN'S ALLEY DR., CHESTER, VA 23831 (804)530-1000 *(20 mi. S of Richmond)*

The front nine at River's Bend follows a turn in the historic James River— hence the course's name—while the back nine travels through hilly terrain. Thick woods border the fairways, allowing for occasional glimpses of the river and passing ships, though you might want to pay more attention to the 112 sandtraps. There is a great variety of holes, and No. 10 offers a panoramic view of the course and the surrounding meadowlands. But it is the sight from the elevated eighteenth tee that you will find most exhilarating, if not intimidating. You will need a 180-yard carry to clear the marsh one-hundred feet below. Tour pro Bobby Wadkins contributed to this 1991 design by architect Steve Smyers.

RIVER'S BEND COUNTRY CLUB
18 holes   Par 71   6700/6200/5500 yds.
USGA: 69.3   SLOPE: 126
STYLE: Hills, woods, water
ACCESS: No restrictions
SEASON: All year   HIGH: Mar.-Oct.
GREEN FEES: $$
REDUCED FEES: WD, LS, TW
RESERVATIONS: Varies
WALKING: No   RANGE: Yes

GOLDEN HORSESHOE GOLF COURSE `14`

S. ENGLAND ST., WILLIAMSBURG, VA 23185 (804)220-7696 *(45 mi. E of Richmond)*
ACCOMMODATIONS: CALL FOR INFORMATION (800)HISTORY

Long before the infamous island green was built at the TPC at Sawgrass, Robert Trent Jones built one here, the 150-yard, par-3 sixteenth on the Gold Course. There are forty-five holes at the Golden Horseshoe—the Gold Course, the new Green Course, and an executive nine. The Gold Course is often mentioned as one of Jones's best designs. The fairways are narrow and the greens ample. Water comes into play on seven holes, and while the rough isn't severe, there are sixty-five sand bunkers to catch poor shots. The course is a scenic delight, and many people believe it has as strong a collection of par 3s as any course anywhere. In 1988, *Golf* magazine ranked the Williamsburg Inn and the Golden Horseshoe as one of the best resorts in America. The Green Course, designed by Rees Jones, opened in 1991.

GOLDEN HORSESHOE GOLF COURSE
ACCESS: No restrictions
SEASON: All year   HIGH: Spring and fall
GREEN FEES: $$$$
REDUCED FEES: HG, TW, PK
RESERVATIONS: Nonguests 1 day
WALKING: At times   RANGE: Yes
• GOLD COURSE
18 holes   Par 71   6700/6179/5159 yds.
USGA: 71.1   SLOPE: 131
STYLE: Hills, woods
• GREEN COURSE
18 holes   Par 72   7120/6244/5348 yds.
STYLE: Rolling hills

HELL'S POINT GOLF CLUB `15`

2700 ATWOODTOWN RD., VIRGINIA BEACH, VA 23456 (804)721-3400 *(20 mi. from Norfolk)*

HELL'S POINT GOLF CLUB
18 holes   Par 72   6766/6030/4844 yds.
USGA: 67.6   SLOPE: 123
STYLE: Tree-lined fairways, water
ACCESS: No restrictions
SEASON: All year   HIGH: June-Aug.
GREEN FEES: $$ (includes cart)
REDUCED FEES: WD, LS, TW, PK
RESERVATIONS: 1 week
WALKING: No   RANGE: Yes

Hell's Point is located in the midst of a pine and hardwood forest about a mile from the ocean. It opened in 1982 and was designed by Rees Jones. The track features a lake, marshland, canals, and sixty-one large, sculpted bunkers. Its verdant, undulating greens and tree-bordered fairways offer a variety of challenges to golfers of all levels, thanks to a set of four tees on every hole. The American Society of Golf Course Architects has rated Hell's Point one of the 130 best designed courses in the U.S.

THE TIDES LODGE, TARTAN COURSE

THE TIDES LODGE (TARTAN COURSE)   `16`
1 ST. ANDREWS LA., IRVINGTON, VA 22480 (804)438-6200 *(64 mi. E of Richmond)*
ACCOMMODATIONS: THE TIDES LODGE (804)438-6000

TARTAN COURSE
18 holes   Par 72   6566/6296/5731 yds.
USGA: 69.2   SLOPE: 116
STYLE: Tree-lined fairways, water hazards
ACCESS: No restrictions
SEASON: Mar.-Dec.   HIGH: Sept.-Oct.
GREEN FEES: $$
REDUCED FEES: HG, LS, TW, PK
RESERVATIONS: Anytime
WALKING: Yes   RANGE: Yes

Sir Guy Campbell, resident architect of St. Andrews Royal and Ancient in Scotland, completed the Tartan Course's original nine holes in 1959, and American architect George Cobb was called in to finish the second nine soon after. Elegant Virginia pines and large, venerable oaks hang over the tight fairways. The historic and majestic Carter Creek meanders throughout the property, and it must be carried over twice. Successfully negotiating the picturesque Tartan Course demands strategic thinking and straight, accurate drives; but in the springtime, the blossoming dogwoods, azaleas, and mountain laurels will probably absorb all your attention.

THE TIDES INN (GOLDEN EAGLE COURSE)   `17`
GOLDEN EAGLE DR., IRVINGTON, VA 22480 (804)438-5501 *(75 mi. E of Richmond)*
ACCOMMODATIONS: THE TIDES INN (804)438-5000, (800)843-3746

GOLDEN EAGLE COURSE
18 holes   Par 72   6963/6511/5384 yds.
USGA: 70.9   SLOPE: 126
STYLE: Hills, woods
ACCESS: Priority to hotel guests
SEASON: Mar.-Dec.
HIGH: Spring and fall
GREEN FEES: $$$
REDUCED FEES: WD, HG, PK
RESERVATIONS: Nonguests 1 day
WALKING: At times   RANGE: Yes

Consistently ranked by *Golf Digest* as one of the top courses in Virginia, the Golden Eagle has hosted both the 1987 and 1991 State Amateurs. It is built on gently rolling and densely wooded terrain, and, in the spring, the rough is highlighted by beautiful dogwoods and mountain laurel. One hundred and twenty bunkers place a high premium on accuracy, and Lake Irvington is a factor on four holes. The most memorable is the 463-yard, par-4 No. 5. It offers great views of the lake, and water comes into play repeatedly.

THE SOUND GOLF LINKS

18

ALBERMARLE PLANTATION, CLUBHOUSE DRIVE, HERTFORD, NC 27944 (919)426-5555
(22 mi. S. of Elizabeth City)

> **THE SOUND GOLF LINKS**
> 18 holes   Par 72   6504/5881/4723 yds.
> STYLE: Water, marshland, trees
> ACCESS: No restrictions
> SEASON: All year   HIGH: June-July
> GREEN FEES: $$
> REDUCED FEES: HG, LS
> RESERVATIONS: 6 months in advance
> WALKING: No   RANGE: Yes

The Sound Links is one of the fine examples of Dan Maple's ability to create a superb course without disturbing the natural environment. The wetlands and groves of birch, pine and moss-draped oaks were preserved all around the course to create hazards and attractive landscapes. Four holes directly border Albermarle Sound, providing plenty of challenge and splendid views. The track demands more accuracy than length, but its sheer beauty takes precedence over any other considerations.

THE SOUND GOLF LINKS: HOLE NO. 18

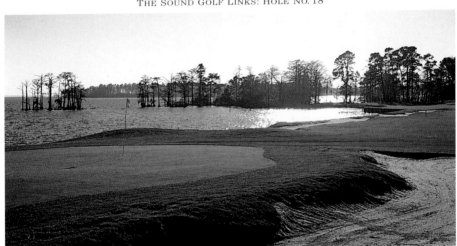

NAGS HEAD GOLF LINKS

19

5615 S. SEA CHASE DR., NAGS HEAD, NC 27959 (919)441-8073 *(104 mi. SE of Richmond)*
ACCOMMODATIONS: CALL NAGS HEAD FOR INFORMATION (800)548-9688

Nags Head is located on windswept land on the Outer Banks of North Carolina. Architect Bob Moore did not move a lot of earth to create this Scottish links course. The treeless, untamed terrain was just waiting for a thoughtful designer to lay down fairways and greens among the rolling dunes and wastelands. At just over 6,100 yards from the back, Nags Head's does not require a lot of muscle, but when the wind starts whipping from the adjacent Roanoke Sound, even teeing

> **NAGS HEAD GOLF LINKS**
> 18 holes   Par 71   6126/5717/4435 yds.
> USGA: 66.9   SLOPE: 126
> STYLE: Scottish links
> ACCESS: Priority to members
> SEASON: All year   HIGH: June-Aug.
> GREEN FEES: $$$ (includes cart)
> REDUCED FEES: LS, PK
> RESERVATIONS: 1 year
> WALKING: No   RANGE: Yes

off with "the old spoon" gives no guarantee of staying out of the natural, love-grass rough and the treacherous pot bunkers. Nags Head is one of the toughest and most picturesque golf courses on the Eastern Seaboard.

BRYAN PARK AND GOLF CLUB

6275 BRYAN PARK RD., BROWN SUMMIT, NC 27214 (919)375-2200 *(8 mi. NE of Greensboro)* **20**

> **BRYAN PARK AND GOLF CLUB**
> ACCESS: No restrictions
> SEASON: All year   HIGH: Spring-fall
> GREEN FEES: $
> REDUCED FEES: TW
> RESERVATIONS: 2 months with
> credit card
> WALKING: Yes   RANGE: Yes
> • **CHAMPIONS COURSE**
>   18 holes   Par 72   7135/6622/5395 yds.
>   USGA: 72.5   SLOPE: 125
>   STYLE: Rolling hills, woods, water
> • **PLAYERS COURSE**
>   18 holes   Par 72   7076/5260 yds.
>   USGA: 70.5   SLOPE: 120
>   STYLE: Rolling hills, woods, water

Bryan Park has two eighteen-hole layouts. The Champions Course, a Rees Jones design, received nominations by both *Golf Digest* and *Golf* magazine in their 1991 listings of the best new courses. The holes are routed through forests of tall pine and oak, and alongside the picturesque 1,700-acre Lake Townsend. The championship track features some strong par 4s, with only one reaching less that 400 yards. But the most memorable holes are the par-3 fourteenth, which can play as long as 230 yards over water, and the finishing hole, with a huge green set in an amphitheater. Jones also recently renovated the Players Course, an original 1974 George Cobb design. It rolls over scenic hills, covered with deciduous forests, and features nine water holes and extensive bunkering. Both courses host professional tournaments, and some of the pros call Bryan Park the best public golf facility in the country.

TANGLEWOOD PARK

HIGHWAY 158 WEST, CLEMMONS, NC 27012 (919)766-5082 *(13 mi. W of Winston-Salem)* **21**
ACCOMMODATIONS: TANGLEWOOD LODGE AND MANOR HOUSE (919)766-0591, EXT. 207

> **TANGLEWOOD PARK**
> ACCESS: No restrictions
> SEASON: All year   HIGH: Mar.-May
> GREEN FEES: $$
> REDUCED FEES: HG, TW
> RESERVATIONS: 1 week
> WALKING: At times   RANGE: Yes
> • **CHAMPIONSHIP COURSE**
>   18 holes   Par 72   7048/6538/5119 yds.
>   USGA: 72.3   SLOPE: 135
>   STYLE: Rolling hills, woods, water
> • **REYNOLDS COURSE**
>   18 holes   Par 72   6469/6061/5066 yds.
>   USGA: 68.5   SLOPE: 120
>   STYLE: Rolling hills, woods, water

Tanglewood's Championship Course has a rich history. It hosted the 1974 PGA Championship won by Lee Trevino, the Vantage Championship on the Senior PGA Tour, and the 1986 U.S. Public Links Championship. *Golf Digest* has consistently ranked it as one of the nation's top public courses, and the layout recently underwent a one-million-dollar restoration. The fairways and greens are generous, but the rough is deep. Water comes into play only three times, and while there is an abundance of fine holes, the 424-yard, par-4 fourteenth is one of the best in the United States. A lake runs the length of the entire left side, the landing area is small, and the green is elevated and well-protected by sand. Robert Trent Jones also designed the Reynolds Course, which is somewhat easier but every bit as deserving of praise. Together, they make a formidable pair.

PINEHURST AND THE NORTH CAROLINA SANDHILLS

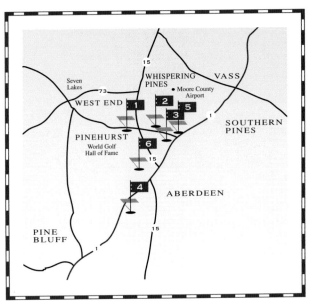

Millions of years ago, a forgotten ice age created a unique geological formation known as the North Carolina Sandhills. It now occupies the southern part of the state, halfway between the city of Charlotte and the Atlantic Ocean. In this area, thick pine forests cover the rolling, sandy terrain, and the clean smell of evergreen permanently fills the air. Average temperatures hover in the mid-60s, offering a pleasant compromise between the north's freezing winters and the Deep South's sometimes oppressive heat.

James W. Tufts, a pharmacist from Boston, was looking to acquire land in the region, when, around 1895, he came across the Sandhills. He bought a few acres and began to develop a resort that would serve as a winter retreat for northerners eager to escape the cold. The resort was named Pinehurst, and it was to become one of golf's most famous destinations. Today, more than ever, Pinehurst is synonymous with golf. An elegant and sporty atmosphere is present everywhere, and golf reigns supreme in the shadow of tall Carolina pines. Pinehurst Resort and Country Club's own seven courses are open to the hotel's guests only, but many of the area's other twenty excellent courses welcome visitors.

THE PGA/WORLD GOLF HALL OF FAME

PGA Boulevard,
Pinehurst, NC 28374
(919)295-6651

OPEN: March through November
Seven days a week
9am to 5pm

A stay at Pinehurst would not be complete without a visit to the PGA/World Golf Hall of Fame. This imposing museum overlooks the fourth hole of Donald Ross's Pinehurst Course No. 2 masterpiece. The fascinating display of photographs and golf memorabilia instills in the souls of visitors a sense of history appropriate to Pinehurst's grand legacy.

PINEHURST RESORT AND COUNTRY CLUB

CAROLINA VISTA, PINEHURST, NC 28374 (800)634-9297 *(70 mi. SW of Raleigh)*
ACCOMMODATIONS: PINEHURST RESORT AND COUNTRY CLUB (800)634-9297

COURSE NO. 2, HOLE NO. 17

PINEHURST RESORT AND COUNTRY CLUB
ACCESS: Hotel guests only
SEASON: All year   HIGH: Spring and fall
GREEN FEES: $$$
REDUCED FEES: LS, PK
RESERVATIONS: Anytime
WALKING: At times   RANGE: Yes
- **PINEHURST NO. 1 COURSE**
  18 holes   Par 70   5733/5329 yds.
  USGA: 68.2   SLOPE: 114
  STYLE: Tree-lined fairways
- **PINEHURST NO. 2 COURSE**
  18 holes   Par 72   7020/6401/5966 yds.
  USGA: 71.4   SLOPE: 127
  STYLE: Traditional Donald Ross
- **PINEHURST NO. 3 COURSE**
  18 holes   Par 71   5619/5231 yds.
  USGA: 68.5   SLOPE: 112
  STYLE: Tree-lined fairways
- **PINEHURST NO. 4 COURSE**
  18 holes   Par 72   6890/6371/5726 yds.
  USGA: 71.5   SLOPE: 117
  STYLE: Rolling hills, tree-lined fairways
- **PINEHURST NO. 5 COURSE**
  18 holes   Par 72   6827/6355/5832 yds.
  USGA: 71   SLOPE: 123
  STYLE: Rolling hills, tree-lined fairways
- **PINEHURST NO. 6 COURSE**
  18 holes   Par 72   7098/6314/5400 yds.
  USGA: 71   SLOPE: 129
  STYLE: Rolling hills, tree-lined fairways
- **PINEHURST NO. 7 COURSE**
  18 holes   Par 72   7114/6216/4907 yds.
  USGA: 70.4   SLOPE: 130
  STYLE: Hills, water, mounds

Pinehurst Resort and Country Club is the only resort in the world that offers seven eighteen-hole courses. The 126 holes of championship golf are playable year-round, and Pinehurst's guests have the privilege of experiencing some of the finest golf architecture in North America.

Standing under the grand veranda at the beautiful, traditional clubhouse, five courses can be seen. Few argue, however, that the greatest of them is the No. 2 Course, Donald Ross's timeless masterpiece. No. 2 opened in 1907, but Ross continued to refine his creation for almost twenty years, even as work proceeded on four additional layouts. Set among tall pines on gently rolling land, Pinehurst No. 2 might just be the fairest and most elegant of America's

DONALD ROSS

great courses. Ross built wide fairways, allowing some margin of error off the tee. However, he rewarded strategically placed drives, as wandering tee shots are met by mounds and large bunkers inspired from his native Scotland. He made precise approaches an essential ingredient, as missing the subtly crowned greens would require the ability to recover with the most delicate and imaginative pitches, chips, and sand shots. Sam Snead once said of Pinehurst No. 2, "You've got to be able to hit every shot on this old girl," and Sam was right!

There are six more championship courses at Pinehurst. Nos. 1 and 3 are also Ross creations, and so is No. 4, which Robert Trent Jones, and then Rees Jones, were commissioned to renovate and modernize in 1973 and 1983, respectively. Pinehurst No. 5 was designed by Ellis Maples in 1928 and has been renovated several times since. George and Tom Fazio built Pinehurst No. 6 in 1980, three miles from the main clubhouse. It is a fairly long layout, with tight fairways traveling among splendid pine and cedar trees. And finally there is Pinehurst No. 7, another Rees Jones work, built in 1986 on hilly terrain with water hazards and Scottish-style swales and mounds.

For golf enthusiasts, a visit to Pinehurst's "Golfdom" is a must. They come here to play, learn, watch, and talk about the game. And walking among the tall pines at No. 2, the true meaning of the game is revealed to amateurs and professionals alike.

PINEHURST COURSE NO. 2: HOLE NO. 17

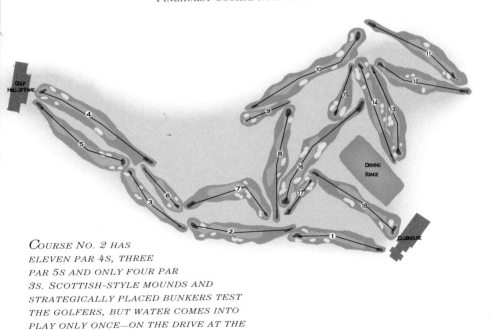

Course No. 2 has eleven par 4s, three par 5s and only four par 3s. Scottish-style mounds and strategically placed bunkers test the golfers, but water comes into play only once—on the drive at the par-5 sixteenth.

THE CLUB AT LONGLEAF: HOLE NO. 15

THE CLUB AT LONGLEAF

MIDLAND RD., PINEHURST, NC (919)692-6100 *(between Pinehurst and Southern Pines)*

2

THE CLUB AT LONGLEAF
18 holes   Par 71   6600/6073/4719 yds.
USGA: 67.3   SLOPE: 110
STYLE: Links, woods, water
ACCESS: No restrictions
SEASON: All year
HIGH: Mar.-May/Sept.-Oct.
GREEN FEES: $$$
REDUCED FEES: LS, TW
RESERVATIONS: 1 year
WALKING: No   RANGE: Yes

Built on the site of Starland Farm, a former horse-training estate, Longleaf's inspiration is all equestrian. The 1988 Dan Maples design incorporates the old, one-mile training track in its front nine, where links-style fairways are accented with steeplechase hedges and jumping rails. In contrast, the heavily wooded back nine features numerous elevation changes and a small lake, with water crossing Nos. 11, 12, 14, and 15. Regarded as one of the Pinehurst area's most popular lay-outs, Longleaf offers enjoyable golf year round.

MID PINES RESORT

1010 MIDLAND RD., SOUTHERN PINES, NC 28387 (919)692-2114 *(65 mi. S of Raleigh)*
ACCOMMODATIONS: MID PINES RESORT (800)323-2114

3

MID PINES RESORT
18 holes   Par 72   6515/6121/5592 yds.
USGA: 69.5   SLOPE: 122
STYLE: Tree-lined fairways
ACCESS: No restrictions
SEASON: All year   HIGH: Mar.-May
GREEN FEES: $$
REDUCED FEES: HS, LS
RESERVATIONS: 2 years
WALKING: At times   RANGE: Yes

Mid Pines is another example of the fine and enduring work of Donald Ross. The course has narrow fairways lined with towering old pines. The greens are elevated and crowned with subtle contouring, demanding impeccable approach shots. There is little water, but the combination of thick Bermuda rough and no less than a hundred bunkers protects par very effectively. The 411-yard, par-4, dogleg eighteenth plays back to the clubhouse in pure, classic Donald Ross style.

THE PINES GOLF RESORT

U.S. 1 S., PINEBLUFF, NC 28373 (800)334-4418, (919)281-
ACCOMMODATIONS: THE PINES GOLF RESORT (800)334-

In spite of its relatively modest yardage, the
Pines course benefits from an interesting and picturesque design. The layout travels over hills
interspersed with clusters of longleaf and loblolly
pine, colorful azaleas and dogwoods. There are
forty sandtraps to avoid, and you will certainly
want to stay clear from the cross-tie-supported
bunker at the eighteenth. Eight holes bring in
some kind of water trouble, but the toughest,
and certainly the most picturesque, is the par-3
eighth. Framed by towering pines, it requires a subs
tiered putting surface sitting peacefully across a refl

PINE NEEDLES RESORT

RIDGE RD., SOUTHERN PINES, NC 28388 (919)692-7111 (7
ACCOMMODATIONS: PINE NEEDLES RESORT (919)692-7

> **PINE NEEDLES RESORT**
> 18 holes   Par 71   6603/6235/5164 yds.
> USGA: 68.8   SLOPE: 120
> STYLE: Rolling hills, tree-lined fairways
> ACCESS: Hotel guests only
> SEASON: All year
> HIGH: Apr.-May/Sept.-Oct.
> GREEN FEES: $$
> REDUCED FEES: LS, PK
> RESERVATIONS: 1 day
> WALKING: No   RANGE: Yes

There's an old-time flavor to this
classic 1927 Donald Ross layout.
It's not especially long, but it is a
strategic test; the track winds
through avenues of tall pines and
over several changes in elevation.
Pine Needles is a course that
rewards solid shots as well as confi-
dent chipping and putting. Greens
are well bunkered—there are
forty-two sandtraps on the entire
course—and an approach played to
the wrong spot will flow off the
green, and put your short game to
the test. Ross, who also designed
Pinehurst No. 2 and Mid Pines in this
area, built some great par 3s here;
one of the prettiest and most photographed is the 134-yard No. 3. Its
small green is tightly surrounded by
five bunkers and a pond. Mrs. Peggy Kirk Bell, a fo
founders of the LPGA Tour, owns and operates thi

600 *(1 1/2 hrs. from Raleigh; 45 min. W of Fayetteville)*

THE PIT: HOLE NO. 9

WOODLAKE COUNTRY CLUB

150 WOODLAKE BLVD., VASS, NC 28394 (919)245-4686 *(50 mi. SW of Raleigh)*

22

WOODLAKE COUNTRY CLUB
28 holes   2972/3172/3026 yds.
STYLE: Hills, trees, water
ACCESS: No restrictions
SEASON: All year   HIGH: Mar.-May
GREEN FEES: $$$
REDUCED FEES: LS, PK
RESERVATIONS: 6 months
WALKING: No   RANGE: Yes

Ellis and Dan Maples designed Wood-
lake's twenty-eight holes. That's right,
twenty-eight. A practice hole was built here to let players warm up before tackling any of
the three enjoyable nine-hole courses: Lake Shore, Cypress Creek, and Cranes Cove. Wood-
lake is quite hilly, and its higher vantage points offer picturesque lake and forest views. Most
of the holes wind their way through large oak and tall pine, but some play right down by
the lake. Three island fairways create "interesting" shotmaking opportunities on each course.

HOUND EARS CLUB

HWY. 105 S. AND SHULLS MILL RD., BLOWING ROCK, NC 28605 (704)963-4321 *(90 mi. W of Charlotte)*
ACCOMMODATIONS: HOUND EARS CLUB (704)963-4321

23

HOUND EARS CLUB
18 holes   Par 72   6165/5639/4959 yds.
USGA: 65   SLOPE: 108
STYLE: Mountains, water
ACCESS: Hotel guests only
SEASON: Apr.-Oct.   HIGH: July-Aug.
GREEN FEES: $$
REDUCED FEES: LS, PK
RESERVATIONS: 2 days
WALKING: At times   RANGE: Yes

Narrow fairways of Kentucky bluegrass and
small, fast, bentgrass greens are the hallmarks of
this George Cobb-designed mountain course.
Water, in the form of either streams or ponds,
comes into play on seventeen holes. At 6,165
yards, the course is not long, but it can feel that
way if you aren't accurate with your drives and
approaches. The 110-yard, par-3 fifteenth is a
stunner: it plays one-hundred yards downhill to a
green surrounded by water and sand.

HOUND EARS CLUB: HOLE NO. 17

JEFFERSON LANDING `24`

HWY. 16/88, JEFFERSON, NC 28640 (919)246-4653 *(83 mi. NW of Winston-Salem)*
ACCOMMODATIONS: CALL GOLF CLUB FOR INFORMATION

JEFFERSON LANDING
18 holes   Par 72   7015/6389/4960 yds.
USGA: 69.4   SLOPE: 115
STYLE: Rolling hills, water hazards
ACCESS: Restrictions
SEASON: May-Nov.   HIGH: July-Aug.
GREEN FEES: $$
REDUCED FEES: WD, PK
RESERVATIONS: 8 days
WALKING: No   RANGE: Yes

Jefferson Landing's spectacular golf course opened in 1991. Tour pro Larry Nelson contributed to the design, set along the banks of Naked Creek and against one of the earth's oldest rivers, the New River. This beautiful site grants splendid views of the Blue Ridge Mountains and Mount Jefferson in the background. The creek plays a major factor in Nelson's layout. It must be crossed twelve times, and with the seven ponds that also come into play, there is water on fifteen holes.

MOUNT MITCHELL GOLF CLUB `25`

7590 HWY. 80 S., BURNSVILLE, NC 28714 (704)675-5454 *(55 mi. NE of Asheville)*

This golf club is situated in a valley below the 6,684-foot Mount Mitchell—the highest peak in the eastern U.S. The course, opened in 1975, was the first American design of Scottish architect Fred Hawtree. Despite its three-thousand-foot elevation, the course is fairly level. The South Toe River winds its way through lovely meadows surrounded by thick forests, and golfers are easily distracted by the magnificent views of the high mountains around. A favorite hole is the 450-yard, par-4 No. 14, a dogleg left that requires a second shot over the river, and onto a heavily trapped green.

MOUNT MITCHELL GOLF CLUB
18 holes   Par 72   6475/6110/5455 yds.
USGA: 68   SLOPE: 116
STYLE: Meadows, woods
ACCESS: No restrictions
SEASON: Apr.-Nov.   HIGH: July-Aug.
GREEN FEES: $$
REDUCED FEES: WD
RESERVATIONS: 2 weeks
WALKING: At times   RANGE: No

SPRINGDALE COUNTRY CLUB `26`

HWY. 276 SOUTH, CRUSO, NC 28716 (704)235-8451, (800)553-3027 *(28 mi. W of Asheville)*
ACCOMMODATIONS: SPRINGDALE COUNTRY CLUB (704)235-8451, (800)553-3027

SPRINGDALE COUNTRY CLUB
18 holes   Par 72   6812/6437/5421 yds.
USGA: 70.7   SLOPE: 121
STYLE: Mountains, water
ACCESS: Priority to hotel guests
SEASON: All year   HIGH: Apr.-Oct.
GREEN FEES: $
REDUCED FEES: HG, TW, PK
RESERVATIONS: 1 week
WALKING: At times   RANGE: Yes

SPRINGDALE: VIEW FROM THE 7TH TEE

Overlooking the Pisgah National Forest, with vistas stretching to Great Smoky Mountains National Park, pure mountain-style golf defines Springdale's personality. On half of the course, the sylvan fairways are crisscrossed with lively but treacherous, rocky streams. The 414-yard, par-4 No. 4, nicknamed "Springdale's Spasm," is a dogleg right with a narrow chute to the green on the second shot, and a creek running across the fairway just a hundred yards from the putting surface.

MAGGIE VALLEY RESORT AND COUNTRY CLUB 27

340 COUNTRY CLUB RD., MAGGIE VALLEY, NC 28751 (704)926-1616 *(35 mi. W of Asheville)*
ACCOMMODATIONS: MAGGIE VALLEY RESORT AND COUNTRY CLUB (800)438-3861

MAGGIE VALLEY
18 holes   Par 71   6284/6004/5222 yds.
USGA: 68.5   SLOPE: 118
STYLE: Rolling hills, water
ACCESS: Priority to hotel guests
SEASON: All year   HIGH: Apr.-Oct.
GREEN FEES: $$
REDUCED FEES: WD, HG, LS, TW, PK
RESERVATIONS: Nonguests 1 day
WALKING: After 2:30 p.m.   RANGE: Yes

Maggie Valley sits in pastoral meadows at the base of the Great Smoky Mountains, with fast-flowing creeks and streams meandering through the course. Springtime is particularly beautiful here, as wildflowers bloom throughout the property in a spontaneous display of yellows, blues, and reds. The front nine is fairly flat, but the second nine is hilly and demanding. The tee on the 556-yard, par-5 No. 18 offers a lovely view of the valley, but there is water and out-of-bounds on every shot.

HIGH HAMPTON INN 28

HWY. 107, CASHIERS, NC 28717 (704)743-2411, (704)743-5991 *(65 mi. SW of Asheville)*
ACCOMMODATIONS: HIGH HAMPTON INN (704)743-2411

HIGH HAMPTON COURSE
18 holes   Par 71   6012/5000 yds.
STYLE: Mountains, trees, water
ACCESS: Restrictions on tee times
SEASON: All year   HIGH: June-Aug./Oct.
GREEN FEES: $$
REDUCED FEES: HG, LS, TW, PK
RESERVATIONS: Recommended (1 day)
WALKING: Yes   RANGE: Yes

Set on a family estate 3,600 feet high in the Cashiers Valley of the Blue Ridge Mountains, High Hampton offers stunning panoramas of the surrounding forests, lakes, and mountains from almost every hole. It's a short course, but so scenic and well-designed that it's truly enjoyable for all. Most interesting is the 137-yard, par-3 No. 8, which plays to an island green and provides no margin for error. The course has no sandtraps, and even though there are more difficult courses you can play, few are as beautiful.

GREAT SMOKIES HILTON RESORT 29

1 HILTON DR., ASHEVILLE, NC 28806 (704)253-5874 *(in Asheville city limits)*
ACCOMMODATIONS: GREAT SMOKIES HILTON RESORT (704)254-3211

The Ridgerunner Course at Great Smokies Hilton is conveniently located within Asheville city limits, yet it features bracing Appalachian scenery. Designed by Willie B. Lewis in 1974, the course is built on 120 acres of grounds surrounding the hotel. Its mountain-style fairways are narrow and lined with beautiful trees. Brooks run alongside and together with several lakes and ponds, water comes into play on nine holes.

RIDGERUNNER COURSE
18 holes   Par 70   6000/5500/5200 yds.
USGA: 65.6   SLOPE: 106
STYLE: Mountains, water
ACCESS: No restrictions
SEASON: All year   HIGH: Spring-fall
GREEN FEES: $
REDUCED FEES: HG, LS, TW, PK
RESERVATIONS: Nonguests 2 days
WALKING: After 3 p.m.   RANGE: Yes

THE GROVE PARK INN AND COUNTRY CLUB 30

290 MACON AVE., ASHEVILLE, NC 28804 (704)252-2711 *(3 mi. from downtown Asheville)*
ACCOMMODATIONS: THE GROVE PARK INN (800)438-5800

GROVE PARK GOLF COURSE
18 holes   Par 72   6301/5925/4987 yds.
USGA: 67.5   SLOPE: 116
STYLE: Mountains, water
ACCESS: Hotel guests only
SEASON: All year   HIGH: Oct.
GREEN FEES: $$
REDUCED FEES: LS, PK
RESERVATIONS: 1 year
WALKING: Yes   RANGE: No

This region's oldest private-resort course, venerable Grove Park, was designed by Donald Ross and first opened in 1909. Arnold Palmer, Jack Nicklaus, Sam Snead, and many other famous professionals have played here over the years. The course was renovated in 1989, restoring the rolling fairways, rock gardens, and winding streams to a condition worthy of its great tradition. The inn itself, a historic landmark, is built of native boulders and, like the course, grants sensational vistas of the Blue Ridge Mountains.

WAYNESVILLE COUNTRY CLUB 31

COUNTRY CLUB DR., WAYNESVILLE, NC 28786 (704)452-4617 *(30 mi. W of Asheville)*
ACCOMMODATIONS: WAYNESVILLE COUNTRY CLUB INN (800)627-6250

The grand scenery of the Great Smoky Mountains highlight Waynesville's Carolina, Dogwood, and Blue Ridge nines. The courses wind through fertile valleys and thickets of trees at the edge of the Pisgah and Great Smoky Mountains National Forests. Architect Tom Jackson designed comfortable fairways and small, bentgrass greens that stress accurate approach shots and a good short game. On the Blue Ridge Course, Nos. 2 and 5 drop over fifty feet from tee to green, typifying the beauty of this memorable course.

WAYNESVILLE COUNTRY CLUB
27 holes   2575/2815/2678 yds.
STYLE: Mountains, trees, water
ACCESS: No restrictions
SEASON: All year   HIGH: May-Oct.
GREEN FEES: $$
REDUCED FEES: HG, TW
RESERVATIONS: 1 day
WALKING: At times   RANGE: No

THE CAPE GOLF AND RACQUET CLUB 32

535 THE CAPE BLVD., WILMINGTON, NC 28412 (919)799-3110 *(15 mi. S of Wilmington)*

THE CAPE GOLF AND RAQUET CLUB
18 holes   Par 72   6800/6200/5200 yds.
USGA: 70.5   SLOPE: 124
STYLE: Tree-lined fairways, marshland
ACCESS: No restrictions
SEASON: All year   HIGH: Mar.-Apr.
GREEN FEES: $$
REDUCED FEES: LS, TW, PK
RESERVATIONS: 6 months
WALKING: No   RANGE: Yes

The golfer who strays on The Cape's course might sympathize with the fate of Stede Bonnet, a famous pirate who, along with his crew, was hung from a tree that stands near the center of No. 10's fairway. There are water and marshes on sixteen holes, and extensive bunkering adds to the difficulty of the narrow fairways. Fortunately, the greens are generous in size, so much so that Nos. 15 and 17 share a double elevated putting surface.

MYRTLE BEACH

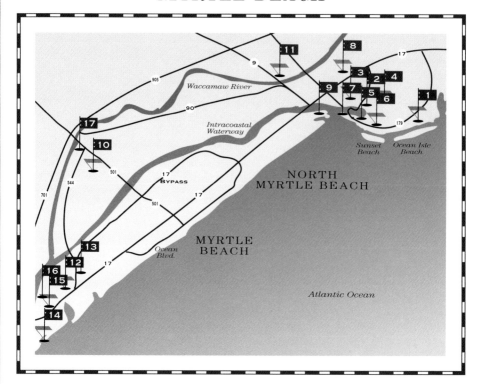

Of all the golfing destinations in the United States, the Myrtle Beach area has successfully established itself as Number One in terms of popularity. Each year, thousands of avid golfers fly or drive to this section of the Carolinas' seashore to indulge in their favorite pastime. Indeed, the business of Myrtle Beach is golf, and there is enough of that at the "Seaside Golf Capital of the World" to satisfy every golf addict's appetite.

The "Grand Strand," as it is also known, stretches along fifty miles of the Atlantic Coast from Ocean Isle Beach, North Carolina, down to Georgetown, South Carolina. This vast area of pine and oak forests, marshlands, and beaches counts close to seventy golf courses open to the public. In the last few years, the Myrtle Beach area has experienced an impressive transformation. It has forged a reputation for quality golf as much as quantity, and the top architects of the moment, including the likes of Jack Nicklaus, and Tom Doak, are busy adding their signature courses to the area's already large inventory of great courses.

Spring is the most popular time of year to visit the Grand Strand, but golf can be played year round. Even in the coldest months of December and January, daytime temperatures average about 55 degrees—well above a diehard golfer's threshold for comfort. In low season, tee-off times at the favorite courses are easier to get, and green fees and hotel rates are significantly lower.

A golf vacation at Myrtle Beach is simple to organize. Most hotels and courses are members of Myrtle Beach Golf Holiday, a local, nonprofit organization that coordinates hotel bookings and golf reservations. So go ahead, dial 1-800-845-4653, and head for "The Beach."

BRICK LANDING PLANTATION

RTE. 2, HWY. 179, OCEAN ISLE BEACH, NC 28459 (800)438-3006 *(15 mi. N of N. Myrtle beach)*
ACCOMMODATIONS: BRICK LANDING PLANTATION (800)438-3006, (800)222-9938 (IN NC)

When Brick Landing Plantation's championship course opened in 1987, it was called "brilliant" and "one of North Carolina's feistiest golf courses." It is the brainchild of architect H. Michael Brazeal, who succeeded beautifully in laying out a natural course among the tidal marshlands, lakes, and pine forests of Ocean Isle Beach. Don't let the short championship yardage fool you! There is water on seventeen holes, and you must either hit the ball straight or bring a lot of them with you. Nos. 1 and 18 play along the scenic Intracoastal Waterway—you can admire the cruising boats while sinking your last putt.

BRICK LANDING PLANTATION
18 holes   Par 72   6446/6121/4814 yds.
USGA: 69.4   SLOPE: 132
STYLE: Water, marshland, trees
ACCESS: Restrictions on tee times
SEASON: All year   HIGH: Apr./Oct.
GREEN FEES: $$$
REDUCED FEES: HG, LS
RESERVATIONS: 1 year
WALKING: No   RANGE: Yes

THE PEARL GOLF LINKS

RTE. 8, SUNSET LAKES BLVD., CALABASH, NC 28459 (919)579-8132 *(20 mi. N of Myrtle Beach)*

Sitting hard by the North Carolina coast, Pearl's two Dan Maples-designed courses—the East and the West—opened for play in 1987. The layouts offer a scenic combination of lakes, marshes, and subtropical trees and plants, all waiting to snare errant shots. Water comes into play on twenty-eight of the thirty-six holes, but a multitude of tees allows you to find the length of course best suited to your game. The most talked about hole is probably No. 17 on Pearl East. It's a rather long, dogleg par 4 that has two elevations and runs along the Calabash River. The Pearl Golf Links' fine collection of unique holes has attracted both the North Carolina Open and the North Carolina Amateur Championships.

THE PEARL GOLF LINKS
ACCESS: No restrictions
SEASON: All year   HIGH: Mar.-May/Oct.
GREEN FEES: $$$
REDUCED FEES: LS, TW
RESERVATIONS: 1 year
WALKING: No   RANGE: Yes
• **PEARL EAST**
  18 holes   Par 72   6749/6250/5125 yds.
  USGA: 70.8   SLOPE: 127
  STYLE: Water, marshland, trees
• **PEARL WEST**
  18 holes   Par 72   7008/6419/5188 yds.
  USGA: 71   SLOPE: 129
  STYLE: Water, marshland, trees

MARSH HARBOUR GOLF LINKS

201 MARSH HARBOUR RD., CALABASH, NC 29599 (800)552-2660 *(25 mi. N of Myrtle Beach)*

MARSH HARBOUR GOLF LINKS
18 holes   Par 71   6690/6000/4795 yds.
USGA: 70   SLOPE: 121
STYLE: Marshland, trees
ACCESS: No restrictions
SEASON: All year
HIGH: Feb.-May/Sept.-Nov.
GREEN FEES: $$$
REDUCED FEES: LS, PK
RESERVATIONS: 9 months
WALKING: No   RANGE: Yes

Marsh Harbour is rated by *Golf Digest* as one of the twenty-five best public courses in America, and it has the distinction of sitting right on the North and South Carolina borders. The course is built on elevated ground skirted by marshes, and it is one of the most beautiful in the area. Marsh Harbour's signature hole is the 510-yard No.17, which plays along and over wetlands to a target-style island fairway, then to a large green that is also surrounded by marshes and trees. The hole and the course are among the favorites on the Grand Strand.

SANDPIPER BAY GOLF AND COUNTRY CLUB

6660 SANDPIPER BAY DR., CALABASH, NC 28459 (800)356-5827 *(26 mi. N of Myrtle Beach)*

SANDPIPER BAY
18 holes   Par 71   6503/5923/4869 yds.
USGA: 69   SLOPE: 116
STYLE: Lakes, marshland
ACCESS: No restrictions
SEASON: All year   HIGH: Spring
GREEN FEES: $$
REDUCED FEES: LS, TW, PK
RESERVATIONS: 1 year
WALKING: No   RANGE: Yes

Another creation by prolific architect Dan Maples, Sandpiper Bay is built on wooded land alongside picturesque lakes and marshes. First opened in 1987, the course has rapidly become one of the Grand Strand's favorite stops. The traditional clubhouse stands beautifully among pines and lakes, with its classic veranda offering magnificent views from all four sides. From the regular tees, the course plays under six-thousand yards and its generous layout, with wide, well-manicured fairways, is pleasantly forgiving. If you like to "go at it" off the tee, Sandpiper is the place to do it. The bunkers are wide, but just like the water hazards, they are not overly obtrusive, and there is ample room to play around them. The design is well-balanced, and incorporates six par 3s, seven par 4s and five par 5s. Putting is also a pleasure, as Sandpiper's bentgrass greens are among the best on the Grand Strand. Altogether, there are nine large water hazards which golfers must share with the other local residents: the site of the course is part of a wildlife sanctuary where deer, alligators, herons, egrets, eagles, and—you guessed it—sandpipers, all frolic in the unspoiled scenery.

OYSTER BAY GOLF LINKS

HWY. 179, SUNSET BEACH, NC 28459 (800)552-2660, (803)272-6399 *(25 mi. from Myrtle Beach)*

OYSTER BAY GOLF LINKS
18 holes   Par 70   6695/6435/4630 yds.
USGA: 68.2   SLOPE: 119
STYLE: Lakes, marshland, trees
ACCESS: No restrictions
SEASON: All year
HIGH: Feb.-May/Sept.-Nov.
GREEN FEES: $$$
REDUCED FEES: LS
RESERVATIONS: 1 year
WALKING: No   RANGE: Yes

Architect Dan Maples got rave reviews for this 1983 creation. Water, in the form of lakes and marshes, comes into play on fifteen holes—most dramatically on the par-3 seventeenth, which is played from a tee to an island green, both of which are built atop a mound of oyster shells. The innovative and much photographed par-4 No. 13 also incorporates the shells into its design. The green, buttressed by the bright white oyster-shell wall, must be attacked over a gaping and unforgiving bunker. Oyster Bay ranks in *Golf Digest*'s prestigious list of the top fifty public courses in America.

SEA TRAIL PLANTATION

651 CLUBHOUSE RD., SUNSET BEACH, NC 28468 (919)579-4350 *(10 mi. N of Myrtle Beach)*
ACCOMMODATIONS: CLARION RESORT AT SEA TRAIL PLANTATION (800)624-6601

SEA TRAIL PLANTATION
ACCESS: No restrictions
SEASON: All year   HIGH: Mar.-May
GREEN FEES: $$$
REDUCED FEES: HG
RESERVATIONS: 1 year
WALKING: No   RANGE: Yes
• **DAN MAPLES COURSE**
   18 holes   Par 72   6751/6332/5090 yds.
   USGA: 71.9   SLOPE: 117
   STYLE: Rolling hills, woods, waste areas
• **REES JONES COURSE**
   18 holes   Par 72   6761/6334/4912 yds.
   USGA: 70.4   SLOPE: 126
   STYLE: Rolling hills, water hazards
• **WILLARD BYRD COURSE**
   18 holes   Par 72   6750/6263/4717 yds.
   SLOPE: 126
   STYLE: Water hazards

There are three signature courses at Sea Trail: the Dan Maples, the Rees Jones, and the Willard Byrd. They are built on rolling terrain, heavily wooded with dogwood and live oak, just a half mile from the ocean. The Maples layout, opened in 1985, features large waste areas, subtle, bent-grass greens, and water on ten holes. The par-5 fifteenth is typical of the course: a waste area runs down the left side, and heavy stands of trees guard the right. The Rees Jones Course, open since 1989, has elevated greens, water on eleven holes, and a great number of severe bunkers. No. 5, a 189-yard par 3, plays over water to a bulkheaded green with deep pot bunkers in the back. The newest of the three, the 1990 Willard Byrd Course, is characterized by the large lakes that come into play on thirteen holes.

OCEAN HARBOUR GOLF LINKS

10301 SOMMERSET LA., CALABASH, NC 28459 (919)579-3588 *(10 mi. N of North Myrtle Beach)*

OCEAN HARBOUR GOLF LINKS
18 holes   Par 72   7004/6148/5358 yds.
USGA: 70.4   SLOPE: 127
STYLE: Water, marshland, trees
ACCESS: No restrictions
SEASON: All year   HIGH: Spring and fall
GREEN FEES: $$$
REDUCED FEES: LS, TW, PK
RESERVATIONS: 1 year
WALKING: No   RANGE: Yes

Ocean Harbour's new course has garnered much praise since it opened in 1989—and deservedly so. It sits on a peninsula between the Calabash River and the Intracoastal Waterway, and a majority of its holes use water and marshland for obstacles and scenery. Fairways are narrow, often bordered with picturesque dogwoods, and the greens present demanding, contoured targets. *Golf* magazine recently named Ocean Harbour Golf Links one of the top new public courses in the world.

HEATHER GLEN GOLF LINKS

HWY. 17 S., LITTLE RIVER, SC 29566 (803)249-9000, (800)868-4536 *(5 mi. N of N. Myrtle Beach)*

Golf Digest voted Heather Glen the best new public course in 1987, and its reputation has only improved since. Set amid tall pine and oak, Willard Byrd and Clyde Johnston took great care to save as many trees as possible when building the twenty-seven hole layout. Heather, Scotch broom, small greens, and pot bunkers give the course its Scottish flavor. The fairways can get quite narrow at times, and ten water hazards affect play on an

HEATHER GLEN GOLF LINKS
27 holes   3127/3198/3183 yds.
STYLE: Scottish links, trees
ACCESS: No restrictions
SEASON: All year   HIGH: Spring
GREEN FEES: $$$
REDUCED FEES: LS, TW, PK
RESERVATIONS: 1 year
WALKING: No   RANGE: Yes

equal number of holes. No. 4 on the Second Nine Course is the home of the infamous "Devil's Mistress," a little, brick-faced pot bunker guarding the right front of the green.

HEATHER GLEN GOLF LINKS: HOLE NO. 18

TIDEWATER GOLF CLUB

4901 LITTLE RIVER NECK RD., N. MYRTLE BEACH, SC 29582 (803)249-3829 *(12 mi. N of Myrtle Beach)*

Tidewater was architect Ken Tomlinson's first effort —with three-time U.S champion Hale Irwin acting as player-consultant —yet it received *Golf Digest's* nomination as 1990's best new public course, and made *Golf* magazine's top-ten list of new public courses. Tidewater is located on a seaside peninsula with nine holes overlooking the Intracoastal Waterway and Cherry Grove Beach Inlet. The rest of the course is routed through a thick forest of virgin pine and oak, with four black water lakes. In his own words, Tomlinson "did not want to ruin such a beautiful piece of property," and he decided against any artificial obstacles or mounding. As a result, the holes follow the natural contours of the land, and afford exquisite views of the waterways, forests and marshlands. Five sets of tees are available on each hole, with enough positions to challenge the best players and the "not so best." Tidewater was the host of the 1990 and 1991 South Carolina State Open and the 1991 South Carolina State Amateur Tournament.

TIDEWATER GOLF CLUB
18 holes   Par 72   7020/6030/5100 yds.
USGA: 68.7   SLOPE: 118
STYLE: Woods, marshland, water
ACCESS: No restrictions
SEASON: All year   HIGH: Spring
GREEN FEES: $$$$$ (includes cart)
REDUCED FEES: LS
RESERVATIONS: 1 year
WALKING: No   RANGE: Yes

TIDEWATER GOLF CLUB: AERIAL VIEW

LEGENDS

The two Legends courses bring the best of Scotland and Ireland to Myrtle Beach. Both courses are built on treeless land, and considerable mounding and contouring has been used to recreate the look and challenge of the old-world links. Tom Doak designed the Heathland Course, which was rated by *Golf* magazine as one of the top ten new resort courses in 1990. The layout has huge putting surfaces, and the seventh was modeled after the green at St. Andrews' famous "Road Hole." The course has wide fairways, and you can hit it hard off the tee without fear of woods and water. But if the mounds and undulating dunes don't get you, the deep, sod-walled bunkers surely will. The Moorland Course is a tougher affair. P. B. Dye was called in to design this one, and the severity of the undulations is reminiscent of Ireland's great Ballybunion Old Course. There is water as well, and, true to the Dye tradition, you will get a chance to admire, if not experience, the bulkheads. The par-4 sixteenth at Moorland is a lot of fun: "Hell's Half Acre" is only 275 yards long, but a lake along the fairway and severe bunkers around the green can punish golf's best overachievers. The Parkland, a third course built around marsh areas, is about to open. It will complete the trilogy and make a visit to The Legends—and to its Scottish pub—a mandatory stop on the Grand Strand.

LEGENDS
ACCESS: No restrictions
SEASON: All year   HIGH: Apr.-May
GREEN FEES: $$$
REDUCED FEES: LS
RESERVATIONS: 1 year
WALKING: No   RANGE: Yes
- **HEATHLAND COURSE**
  18 holes   Par 71   6765/6190/5115 yds.
  USGA: 72   SLOPE: 121
  STYLE: Scottish links
- **MOORLAND COURSE**
  18 holes   Par 72   6832/5807/4939 yds.
  USGA: 72.8   SLOPE: 130
  STYLE: Scottish links

LEGENDS, MOORLAND COURSE

BUCK CREEK GOLF PLANTATION

701 BUCK'S TRAIL, LONGS, SC 29568 (800)344-0982, (803)249-5996 *(6 mi. W of North Myrtle Beach)*

Nominated for best new course by *Golf Digest* in 1990, Buck Creek was built on and around five hundred acres of protected wetlands. All twenty-seven holes, designed by Tom Jackson, wind through the undisturbed, low country setting. The Meadow, Cypress, and Tupelo nines bring lovely woods and lakes into play and present a variety of challenges, thanks to many elevated tees, extensive bunkering, and some consider-able undulations on the greens.

BUCK CREEK GOLF PLANTATION
27 holes   3010/3201/3105 yds.
STYLE: Woods, lakes, waste areas
ACCESS: No restrictions
SEASON: All year
HIGH: Mar.-Apr./Oct.-Nov.
GREEN FEES: $$$
REDUCED FEES: LS, PK
RESERVATIONS: 1 year
WALKING: No   RANGE: Yes

BLACKMOOR GOLF CLUB

HWY. 707, MURRELLS INLET, SC 29576 (803)650-5555 *(15 mi. S of Myrtle Beach)*

BLACKMOOR GOLF CLUB
18 holes   Par 72   6614/6217/4807 yds.
USGA: 69.3   SLOPE: 118
STYLE: Rolling hills, trees, wetlands
ACCESS: No restrictions
SEASON: All year   HIGH: Mar.-Apr.
GREEN FEES: $$$
REDUCED FEES: LS, PK
RESERVATIONS: 1 year
WALKING: No   RANGE: Yes

Once the largest rice plantation in the southeast, Blackmoor is now a Gary Player signature course that stresses playability while offering challenges for more accomplished golfers. The front nine is cut out of hardwood, pine, and wetlands that are lush with flowering plants, including orchids. The more challenging back nine has a Scottish flavor, with pot bunkers, mounds, and rolling terrain. There are eight water hazards and a few shallow traps, and No. 8 offers two routes to the green.

INDIGO CREEK

9480 HWY. 17 BYPASS, MURRELLS INLET, SC 29587 (803)650-0381 *(90 mi. NE of Charleston)*

INDIGO CREEK
18 holes   Par 72   6747/6167/4923 yds.
USGA: 69.1   SLOPE: 120
STYLE: Trees, water, marshland
ACCESS: No restrictions
SEASON: All year
HIGH: Mar.-Apr./Oct.-Nov.
GREEN FEES: $$
REDUCED FEES: LS, PK, TW
RESERVATIONS: 9 months
WALKING: At times   RANGE: Yes

Indigo Creek's golf course is located in the heart of South Carolina's low country plantation area and prides itself on a quality of service that reflects its traditional heritage. The course was designed by Willard Byrd and offers a pleasant challenge among tall pines, marshland, lakes, and flowers. On the par-3 eleventh, water must be carried 152 yards from the regular tees, and the green sits nicely among the trees, supported by railroad ties and flanked by a waste bunker. Wildlife abounds on and around the course.

INDIGO CREEK GOLF COURSE: AERIAL VIEW

PAWLEYS PLANTATION GOLF AND COUNTRY CLUB

HWY. 17 S., PAWLEYS ISLAND, SC 29585 (803)237-1736 *(35 mi. S of Myrtle Beach)*
ACCOMMODATIONS: PAWLEY'S PLANTATION VILLA RENTALS (800)545-5973

NOS. 13 AND 16 DOUBLE GREEN

PAWLEYS PLANTATION GOLF AND COUNTRY CLUB
18 holes   Par 72   7026/6522/5572 yds.
USGA: 72.5   SLOPE: 127
STYLE: Trees, marshland, lakes
ACCESS: Villa guests only
SEASON: All year
HIGH: Mar.-May/Sept.-Nov.
GREEN FEES: $$$
REDUCED FEES: LS, PK
RESERVATIONS: 1 year
WALKING: No   RANGE: Yes

Jack Nicklaus signature courses are generally something special, and this is no exception. Nicklaus blended an exciting design with the site's abundant gifts, including natural wetlands and towering pines. Water is here to both challenge and delight: thirteen water hazards appear on ten holes, but the lake views are breathtaking, especially in the early morning when steam rises slowly above the steely surface. A good number of bunkers show up, too, with varying degrees of difficulty. Among the course's memorable features are a double green and a dramatic split fairway. If No. 18 seems a little tight, you should tip your cap to the master player and architect who sacrificed width in order to preserve the stately old trees that border the hole.

RIVER CLUB

HWY. 17, PAWLEYS ISLAND, SC 29585 (803)237-8755 *(20 mi. S of Myrtle Beach)*
ACCOMMODATIONS: LITCHFIELD BY THE SEA (800)922-6348

Although the River Club course is built in a tall pine forest, the elevated clubhouse affords nice views of most of the layout. Players can hit the driver safely off the tee, but problems start with the eighty large bunkers that patch the course, some of them in very unfriendly locations. There is also water on ten holes, and large, well-contoured greens. All this explains why the Tom Jackson track was retained as the site of the 1987 Carolinas Open. An outstanding hole is the par-5 No. 18, a blessing for long hitters, who can cross water to a landing area and then reach the green in two shots. River Club is part of the Litchfield-by-the-Sea Resort Complex which offers two other affiliated golf courses for play: Litchfield Country Club and Willbrook Plantation Golf Club.

RIVER CLUB COURSE
18 holes   Par 72   6669/6283/4898 yds.
USGA: 69.7   SLOPE: 118
STYLE: Trees, water, sandtraps
ACCESS: No restrictions
SEASON: All year   HIGH: Spring
GREEN FEES: $$$
REDUCED FEES: LS
RESERVATIONS: 1 year
WALKING: At times   RANGE: Yes

THE HERITAGE CLUB

HERITAGE CLUB

RIVER RD., PAWLEYS ISLAND, SC 29585 (803)626-5121, (800)552-2660 *(20 mi. S of Myrtle Beach)*

HERITAGE CLUB
18 holes   Par 71   7100/6575/5325 yds.
USGA: 71.2   SLOPE: 122
STYLE: Trees, lakes, marshland
ACCESS: No restrictions
SEASON: All year   HIGH: Mar.-May
GREEN FEES: $$$
REDUCED FEES: LS
RESERVATIONS: 1 year
WALKING: No   RANGE: Yes

A great avenue of oaks leads to the colonial-style clubhouse at Heritage Club, giving visitors a preview of the beauty and challenge of the course. Built on the site of two eighteenth-century rice plantations, the layout is routed among centuries-old trees, with wetlands, lakes, and numerous fingered sandtraps to complete the challenge. Designed by developer Larry Young in 1986, the course is ranked in the top fifty of *Golf Digest*'s best public golf courses.

THE WITCH

1900 HWY. 544, CONWAY, SC 29526 (803)448-1300, (803)347-2706 *(10 mi. NW of Myrtle Beach)*

THE WITCH
18 holes   Par 71   6702/6011/4812 yds.
USGA: 68.3   SLOPE: 121
STYLE: Rolling hills, marshland
ACCESS: No restrictions
SEASON: All year   HIGH: Spring and fall
GREEN FEES: $$$
REDUCED FEES: HG, LS
RESERVATIONS: 1 year
WALKING: No   RANGE: Yes

There are no condos obstructing The Witch's five hundred acres of marshland and rolling, wooded terrain. There's just golf—and plenty of it. Four thousand feet of bridges were needed to span some of the natural obstacles. Three holes cross water hazards, and marshland comes into play on four holes—most notably the ninth, with a drive to a distant landing area and a second shot over the wetlands. The par-3 No. 17 is a rarity in the area; it drops thirty feet from tee to green. The Witch is the brainchild of architect Dan Maples.

HILTON HEAD ISLAND

Hilton Head Island, the second largest island on the Eastern Seaboard of the United States, was discovered in 1663 by English captain William Hilton. This twelve-mile-long, five-mile-wide collection of subtropical lowlands, forests, and marshes is located an hour away from Savannah, Georgia, and is separated from the mainland by the Intracoastal Waterway. Hilton Head is blessed with beautiful weather, and thanks to the warm influence of the Gulf Stream and the cooling effect of Atlantic breezes, island visitors can enjoy such year-round, outdoor activities as boating, fishing, biking, or just walking along the twelve miles of white, sandy beaches.

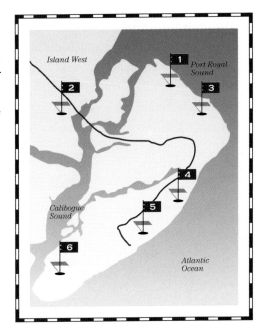

But, naturally, for us practitioners of The Game, it is golf that brings us to Hilton Head. The course that put the island on the map of great golfing destinations is the world-famous Harbour Town Golf Links (at Sea Pines Plantation), which Pete Dye and Jack Nicklaus teamed up to design in 1968. There are now a dozen courses open to the public on the island and several more at nearby locations. Although most of them are built on flat land, the combination of subtropical vegetation, freshwater lagoons, and tidal wetlands provides golf architects with all the necessary elements to exercise their creative talents.

In recent years, new layouts, such as the Arthur Hills Course at Palmetto Dunes and Gary Player's Hilton Head National, have received a lot of praise for their beauty and imaginative designs. So, if golf among moss-draped oaks, lagoons, and magnolias is your thing, then Hilton Head is your place.

OYSTER REEF GOLF CLUB

155 HIGH BLUFF RD., HILTON HEAD PLANTATION, SC 29926 (803)681-7717 *(35 mi. from Savannah)*

OYSTER REEF GOLF CLUB
18 holes   Par 72   7027/6440/5288 yds.
USGA: 71.2   SLOPE: 123
STYLE: Trees, water hazards
ACCESS: Restrictions on tee times
SEASON: All year   HIGH: Spring and fall
GREEN FEES: $$$$ (includes cart)
REDUCED FEES: LS, TW, PK
RESERVATIONS: 3 months with credit card
WALKING: No   RANGE: Yes

Oyster Reef is one of the longest championship layouts on Hilton Head. Opened in 1982, the Rees Jones course travels through thick Carolina pines and live oaks, onto the Intracoastal Waterway. No. 6 plays right by Port Royal Sound and opens up to a great view of the coast's other islands. Jones used an appreciable amount of mounding and bunkering, and even from the much shorter middle tees, Oyster Reef demands strategy as much as skill.

Hilton Head National Golf Club

HILTON HEAD NATIONAL GOLF CLUB
18 holes   Par 72   6643/6260/4649 yds.
USGA: 69.9   SLOPE: 119
STYLE: Links, woods, marshland
ACCESS: No restrictions
SEASON: All year   HIGH: Mar.-Apr./Oct.
GREEN FEES: $$$
REDUCED FEES: HG, LS, TW
RESERVATIONS: 3 months
WALKING: No   RANGE: Yes

This course provides a clear example of architect Gary Player's design philosophy: it has a minimum of hazards in the line of play, a wide selection of tees, and greens that are challenging without being unnerving. With mounds and tall grasses bordering the fairways, the course has the appearance and design of traditional links. It also travels along three hundred acres of dense woods and marshes, offering a wide variety of landscapes and challenges. Hilton Head National is one of the favorite courses on the island.

HILTON HEAD NATIONAL: HOLE NO. 16

PORT ROYAL RESORT

3

PORT ROYAL PLANTATION, HILTON HEAD ISLAND, SC 29928 (800)277-5588 *(40 mi. from Savannah)*
ACCOMMODATIONS: PORT ROYAL RESORT (800)277-5588

PLANTER'S ROW COURSE

Port Royal offers a choice of three plantation-style golf courses that meander around quiet lagoons and through gorgeous moss-draped oak and magnolia trees. Planter's Row was designed by Willard Byrd in 1985, and the greens were renovated in 1990. The course has a garden-like atmosphere, with many birdhouses, and even a gazebo along one fairway. There is an abundance of trees and wildflowers, and the narrow holes require constant precision. Robber's Row and Barony were both designed by George Cobb and opened in 1963. Robber's Row is a long and well-bunkered layout built on the marsh side of the plantation. Barony is shorter and more open, but features small greens and eleven water holes. Barony also incorporates colorful areas of wildflowers and gardens. These three shipyard courses are located on the site of Civil War battlegrounds, and the tee markers are metal renderings of war memorabilia and local history.

> **PORT ROYAL RESORT**
> ACCESS: No restrictions
> SEASON: All year   HIGH: Mar.-May/Oct.
> GREEN FEES: $$$$ (includes cart)
> REDUCED FEES: HG, LS, TW, PK
> RESERVATIONS: 2 months
> WALKING: At times   RANGE: Yes
> • **PLANTER'S ROW**
>   18 holes   Par 72   6520/6009/5126 yds.
>   USGA: 70.6   SLOPE: 126
>   STYLE: Tree-lined fairways, lagoons
> • **ROBBER'S ROW**
>   18 holes   Par 72   6711/6188/5299 yds.
>   USGA: 69.9   SLOPE: 124
>   STYLE: Tree-lined fairways, marshland
> • **BARONY**
>   18 holes   Par 72   6530/6038/5253 yds.
>   USGA: 69.2   SLOPE: 122
>   STYLE: Tree-lined fairways, gardens

PALMETTO DUNES RESORT

P.O. BOX 5849, HILTON HEAD ISLAND, SC 29938 (803)785-1138 *(40 mi. N of Savannah)*
ACCOMMODATIONS: PALMETTO DUNES RESORT (800)845-6130

ARTHUR HILLS COURSE AT PALMETTO DUNES

PALMETTO DUNES RESORT
ACCESS: No restrictions
SEASON: All year   HIGH: Apr./Oct.
GREEN FEES: $$
REDUCED FEES: LS, PK
RESERVATIONS: Nonguests 1 month
WALKING: No   RANGE: Yes

- **ROBERT TRENT JONES COURSE AT PALMETTO DUNES**
  18 holes   Par 72   6710/6148/5425 yds.
  USGA: 69.3   SLOPE: 119
  STYLE: Oceanside, trees, lagoons
- **ARTHUR HILLS GOLF CLUB AT PALMETTO DUNES**
  18 holes   Par 72   6651/6122/4999 yds.
  USGA: 69.3   SLOPE: 120
  STYLE: Rolling hills, woods, water
- **GEORGE FAZIO COURSE AT PALMETTO DUNES**
  18 holes   Par 70   6873/6239/5273 yds.
  USGA: 71.2   SLOPE: 123
  STYLE: Tree-lined fairways, lakes, waste areas
- **ARTHUR HILLS GOLF CLUB AT PALMETTO HALL PLANTATION**
  18 holes   Par 72   6918/6582/4956 yds.
  USGA: 70.5   SLOPE: 123
  STYLE: Marshland, waste areas, trees

Palmetto Dunes boasts four outstanding layouts, each named after its renowned designer. The Robert Trent Jones Course, the oldest of the four, features generous landing areas and well-trapped greens, which put a premium on accurate shotmaking over distance off the tee. At almost 6,900 yards from the tips, but with only two par 5s, the par-70 George Fazio Course (the youngest layout ever named to *Golf Digest*'s top hundred courses) demands distance off the tee *and* accuracy with the approach shot. The heavily wooded Arthur Hills Course at Palmetto Dunes combines the island's sand dunes and natural contours with the resort's lagoon system to create what many feel is the most challenging of the four layouts here. For the past four years, this track has hosted the Palmetto Dunes/Golf World Collegiate, a tournament which opposes the nation's top college teams. The latest addition to the resort is Palmetto Hall's Arthur Hills Course. It exemplifies the architect's classic lay-of-the-land approach, with naturally undulating fairways winding through and around thickets of oak, pine, and sparkling lakes.

SHIPYARD GOLF CLUB

SHIPYARD PLANTATION, HILTON HEAD ISLAND, SC 29928 (800)277-5588 *(40 mi.NE of Savannah)*
ACCOMMODATIONS: MARRIOTT HOTEL (803)842-2400

Shipyard's two original nine-hole courses, Galleon and Clipper, opened in 1969. The Brigantine nine was added in 1982. All three courses run along tall, handsome pines and stately live oaks, mixed with an abundance of magnolias and

wildflowers. But after encountering ponds and lagoons on twenty-five of the twenty-seven

SHIPYARD GOLF CLUB
27 holes   3035/2959/3132 yds.
STYLE: Trees, lagoons
ACCESS: No restrictions
SEASON: All year   HIGH: Apr.-May/Oct.
GREEN FEES: $$$$ (includes cart)
REDUCED FEES: HG, LS, PK
RESERVATIONS: 2 months
WALKING: At times   RANGE: Yes

holes, the maritime theme in each course's name takes on a new meaning. Shipyard has hosted many tournaments, and the head teaching professional is Ron Cerrudo of PGA Tour fame.

SEA PINES PLANTATION

P.O. BOX 7000, HILTON HEAD ISLAND, SC 29938 (803)671-2446 *(95 mi. S of Charleston)*
ACCOMMODATIONS: SEA PINES (800)845-6131

Harbour Town Golf Links at Sea Pines Plantation was designed by Pete Dye with the help of Jack Nicklaus. Since the first Heritage Classic was held here in 1969, it has racked up an impressive list of accolades, among them a selection by *Golf* magazine as the world's thirtieth greatest course. Early examples of the Dye trademarks—railroad ties, a strategic use of trees and bunkers, and small, firm greens—are already in evidence here, making this a great test of a golfer's shotmaking ability. Harbour Town's exceptionally demanding par 3s have been particularly acclaimed. Naturally, the course is mostly known for its picturesque and tough finishing hole; the 478-yard par 4 runs tightly along the salt marshes and waters of Calibogue Sound, while the landmark red and white lighthouse stands handsomely behind the green. Although Harbour Town gets most of the attention, Sea Pines has two other excellent designs by George Cobb—the Ocean and the Sea Marsh Courses—both of which are plenty scenic but more forgiving and less expensive than their famous neighbor.

SEA PINES PLANTATION
ACCESS: No restrictions
SEASON: All year   HIGH: Spring
GREEN FEES: $$$$$
REDUCED FEES: HG, LS, TW, PK
RESERVATIONS: Nonguests 2 weeks
WALKING: At times   RANGE: Yes
- **HARBOUR TOWN GOLF LINKS**
  18 holes   Par 71   6912/6119/5019 yds.
  USGA: 70   SLOPE: 126
  STYLE: Links, marshland, trees
- **SEA MARSH COURSE**
  18 holes   Par 72   6515/6169/5054 yds.
  USGA: 69   SLOPE: 117
  STYLE: Woods, marshland, lagoons
- **OCEAN COURSE**
  18 holes   Par 72   6614/6213/5284 yds.
  USGA: 70   SLOPE: 119
  STYLE: Woods, oceanside, lagoons

KIAWAH ISLAND INN AND VILLA

33

1 KIAWAH ISLAND DR., KIAWAH ISLAND, SC 29455 (803)768-2121 *(17 mi. SE of Charleston)*
ACCOMMODATIONS: KIAWAH ISLAND INN AND VILLA (803)768-2121

With three courses designed by Jack Nicklaus, Gary Player, and Tom Fazio, Kiawah was already high on the list of great golf resorts. But it got even better when Pete Dye designed the celebrated Ocean Course, site of the 1991 Ryder Cup matches. The Ocean Course winds along a two-and-a-half-mile stretch of beach, with every hole overlooking the Atlantic and ten actually bordering it. Allowing for the constant winds, Dye provided generous fairways but combined them with small, well-guarded, and contoured greens. The par-3 fifth, for example, plays through dunes and offers a sensational view of the ocean. No. 15, a par 4, has the sea down the right side and plays to a small putting surface tucked between pot bunkers and sand dunes. Although typical Carolina marshes and wetlands run through parts of the layout, the Ryder Cup Course certainly qualifies as one of the great links courses in America. Gary Player's Marsh Point Course is a shotmaker's dream. The fairways are narrow and the greens are small and nicely shaped. Water is a factor on thirteen holes. Jack Nicklaus's Turtle Point Course combines more narrow fairways, punishing rough, and relatively small and flat greens. Water comes into play on ten holes, and while the putting surfaces are well-protected by bunkers, they are generally open in front, allowing for run-up shots in the wind. Nos. 14, 15, and 16 play along the ocean and have the same links look as the Ocean Course. Tom Fazio's Osprey Point Course presents a different personality. Its fairways are generous and its greens range in size from tiny to impressive. The course is well-protected by sand, particularly where Fazio made his judicious use of native waste areas and dunes.

KIAWAH ISLAND INN AND VILLA
ACCESS: Priority to hotel guests
SEASON: All year   HIGH: Spring and fall
GREEN FEES: $$$$$ (includes cart)
REDUCED FEES: HG, LS
RESERVATIONS: Nonguests 1 day
WALKING: No   RANGE: Yes
- **OCEAN COURSE**
  18 holes   Par 72   7371/6244/5327 yds.
  STYLE: Oceanside links
- **MARSH POINT COURSE**
  18 holes   Par 72   6203/5841/5055 yds.
  USGA: 69.4   SLOPE: 120
  STYLE: Marsh, lakes, trees
- **TURTLE POINT COURSE**
  18 holes   Par 72   6919/6396/5285 yds.
  USGA: 71.5   SLOPE: 127
  STYLE: Oceanside, water hazards
- **OSPREY POINT COURSE**
  18 holes   Par 72   6678/5968/5122 yds.
  USGA: 68.8   SLOPE: 118
  STYLE: Lagoons, trees, waste bunkers

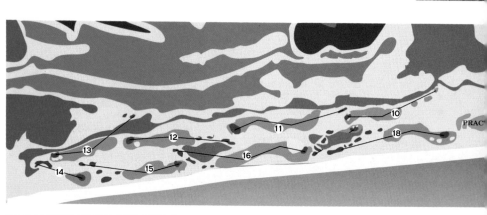

The Ocean Course, Site of the 1991 Ryder Cup

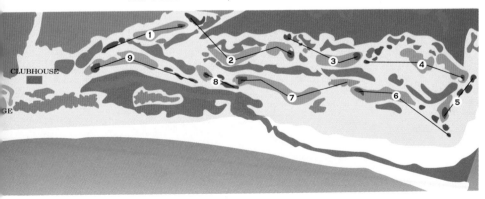

WILD DUNES

34

10,001 BACK BAY DR., ISLE OF PALMS, SC 29451 (803)886-6000, EXT. 2164 *(12 mi. NE of Charleston)*
ACCOMMODATIONS: DESTINATION WILD DUNES (800)845-8880, (803)886-6000

WILD DUNES
ACCESS: No restrictions
SEASON: All year   HIGH: Spring and fall
GREEN FEES: $$$$
REDUCED FEES: LS, PK
RESERVATIONS: 1 year
WALKING: No   RANGE: Yes
• **LINKS COURSE**
18 holes   Par 72   6722/6131/5280 yds.
USGA: 69.6   SLOPE: 124
STYLE: Links
• **HARBOR COURSE**
18 holes   Par 70   6446/5990/4774 yds.
USGA: 68.2   SLOPE: 117
STYLE: Links

Wild Dunes' two spectacular courses, the Links and the Harbor, were built by architect Tom Fazio on the Isle of Palms just outside of Charleston. The Links Course, ranked among the best in the world, was devastated by Hurricane Hugo in 1989. Now rebuilt and actually improved, it is highlighted by a fifty-foot-tall dune that winds through four of the holes. The course is also noted for its extensive mounding in both fairways and roughs. Nos. 17 and 18 are true oceanside, links-style holes and among the most photographed in the country. The Harbor Course was also extensively remodeled after the hurricane. It is slightly shorter and easier than the Links, but just as pretty.

FRIPP ISLAND OCEAN POINT GOLF LINKS

35

250 OCEAN PT. DR., FRIPP ISLAND, SC 29920 (803)838-2309 *(65 mi. from Savannah)*
ACCOMMODATIONS: FRIPP ISLAND RESORT (800)845-4100

The George Cobb-designed Ocean Point Golf Links borders the Atlantic on four holes, while the rest of the course is routed among multiple lagoons. No one will mistake Ocean Point for a monster, but there is a chance to "get wet" on ten of the eighteen holes, and it happens quite often when sea breezes pick up. The layout is built on flat terrain, but Cobb has added a good deal of mounding; and with some holes running through wooded areas, he's brought a lot of variety to the experience.

FRIPP ISLAND OCEAN POINT GOLF LINKS
18 holes   Par 72   6590/6060/4951 yds.
USGA: 69.4   SLOPE: 124
STYLE: Oceanside links, lagoons, woods
ACCESS: Hotel guests only
SEASON: All year   HIGH: Mar.-Aug.
GREEN FEES: $$
REDUCED FEES: LS, TW, PK
RESERVATIONS: 1 year
WALKING: At times   RANGE: Yes

Other Excellent Courses in the Mid-Atlantic States

Maryland
- ● Hog Neck Golf Course, Easton (301)822-6079

North Carolina
- ● Bald Head Island Club, Southport (919)457-7310
- ▲ Duck Woods Country Club, Kitty Hawk (919)261-2609
- ▲ Etowah Valley Country Club and Golf Lodge, Hendersonville (704)891-7141
- ▲ Fairfield Harbour, New Bern (919)638-8011
- ▲ Holly Forest Country Club, Sapphire (704)743-3441
- ● Keith Hills Country Club, Bules Creek (919)893-5051
- ● Oak Hollow Golf Course, Highpoint (919)883-3260

South Carolina
- ■ Arcadian Shores Golf Club, Arcadian Shores (803)449-5217
- ■ The Club at Seabrook, Charleston (803)768-2529
- ▲ Country Club of Callawassie, Hilton Head area (803)785-PUTT
- ■ Dunes Golf and Beach Club, Myrtle Beach (803)449-5914
- ● Fairfield Ocean Ridge Resort, Edisto Island (800)845-8500, ext. 5162
- ● Myrtle Beach National Golf Club, Myrtle Beach (803)448-2308
- ● Myrtle West Golf Club, Myrtle Beach (800)842-8390
- ■ Pine Lakes International Country Club, Myrtle Beach (803)449-6459

Virginia
- ● Birdwood Golf Course, Charlottesville (804)293-4653
- ● The Shenvalee Golf Resort, New Market (703)740-9930

▲ RESTRICTIONS MAY APPLY ■ HOTEL/RESORT GUESTS ONLY ● OPEN WITHOUT RESTRICTIONS

CHAPTER EIGHT

THE SOUTH

Fairways rolling under the shade of large, century-old mossy oaks; blooming, bright pink magnolias surrounding the greens…Golf is a tranquil and elegant affair in the South, where the warm climate and unhurried pace give golfers the time to savor the finer aspects of the game.

When it comes to southern golf, Georgia ranks supreme. Naturally, the Peach state occupies a special place in the hearts of golfers around the world as the home of golf's grand springtime tradition: The Masters Tournament at the Augusta National Golf Club. However, with its great variety of terrain—mountains, pine forests, marshlands, lakes, and miles of seashore—Georgia is also the home of over three hundred golf courses accessible to the public, many among the very best in the nation.

Southern hospitality can also be found in Kentucky and Tennessee, where the rolling, blue-grass fields and mountain foothills harbor many fine courses. In Arkansas, the visitor will find championship golf in the Hot Springs resort area, about an hour south of the state capital, Little Rock. Then comes the Deep South—Mississippi, Louisiana, and Alabama—where the touring golfer is easily lured away by the the lush greenery and semitropical climate of the Gulf shore.

All in all, the land of steamboats and plantations offers an array of beautiful golf with the special feeling that is associated with a different way of life. Gentleman and lady golfers should all taste the charm of the game as it is played in Grand Old South.

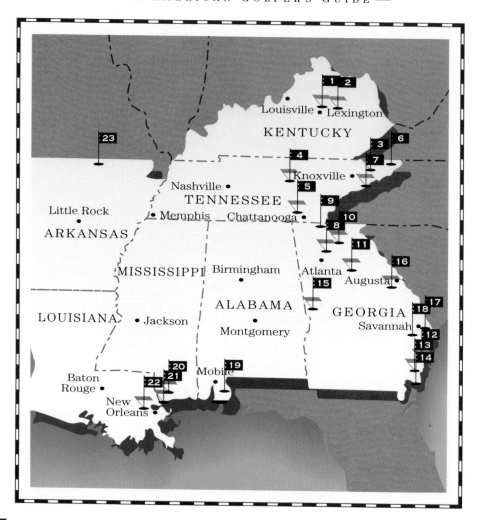

MARRIOTT'S GRIFFIN GATE RESORT

1

1720 NEWTOWN PIKE, LEXINGTON, KY 40511 (606)254-4101 *(5 mins. from downtown Lexington)*
ACCOMMODATIONS: MARRIOTT'S GRIFFIN GATE RESORT (606)231-5100

MARRIOTT'S GRIFFIN GATE RESORT
18 holes   Par 72   6801/6296/4979 yds.
USGA: 71.5   SLOPE: 128
STYLE: Traditional
ACCESS: Priority to hotel guests
SEASON: All year   HIGH: May-Oct.
GREEN FEES: $$$ (includes cart)
REDUCED FEES: WD, LS, TW, PK
RESERVATIONS: Guests 2 months
WALKING: No   RANGE: No

A regular stop of the Senior PGA Tour, this Rees Jones course has been acclaimed as one of the architect's best works. The relatively open front side affords pleasant views of nearby horse farms, and water comes into play on five holes. The back nine is a lot tighter, and winds through tall stands of oak, fir, and walnut. No. 10, a short par 5 with water on the left and yawning bunkers to the right, is reachable in two but exacts a toll from those who stray. *Golf Digest* has ranked Griffin Gate in the top seventy-five resort courses.

KEARNEY HILL GOLF LINKS

3403 KEARNEY RD., LEXINGTON, KY 40511 (606)253-1981 *(5 mi. from Lexington)*

KEARNEY HILL GOLF LINKS
18 holes   Par 72   6987/6501/5362 yds.
USGA: 70.5   SLOPE: 122
STYLE: Scottish links
ACCESS: No restrictions
SEASON: All year   HIGH: Apr.-Sept.
GREEN FEES: $
REDUCED FEES: TW
RESERVATIONS: 1 week
WALKING: Yes   RANGE: Yes

Situated in the heart of horse-farm country, this open, links-style course offers an interesting mix of Pete and P. B. Dye design techniques. Their signature railroad ties make an appearance on No. 16, and a liberal scattering of pot bunkers and strategically placed mounds keep long hitters on guard. Kearney Hill is rated among the top five courses in Kentucky, and it is one of only a handful in the state with bentgrass greens and fairways.

GRAYSBURG HILLS GOLF COURSE

RTE. 1, BOX 1415, CHUCKEY, TN 37641 (615)234-8061 *(12 mi. NE of Greeneville)*

GRAYSBURG HILLS GOLF COURSE
18 holes   Par 72   6804/6341/5562 yds.
USGA: 69.6   SLOPE: 119
STYLE: Rolling hills, lakes
ACCESS: No restrictions
SEASON: All year   HIGH: Apr.-Oct.
GREEN FEES: $
RESERVATIONS: 1 year
WALKING: Yes   RANGE: Yes

A pastoral setting with eighteen holes of Rees Jones-designed golf is what awaits visitors to Graysburg Hills. The course is set in a valley, with three large lakes in the middle. Extensive landscaping and the addition of fifty-four white silica sandtraps make the course very attractive. Graysburg Hills has many excellent holes, and one of the favorites is the downhill, par-3 eighth. It plays 177 yards to a bunkered green sitting prettily on a peninsula surrounded by the reflecting lake. An additional nine holes are being added.

STONEHENGE GOLF CLUB AT FAIRFIELD GLADE RESORT

FAIRFIELD BLVD., FAIRFIELD GLADE, TN 38555 (615)484-3731 *(75 mi. W of Knoxville)*
ACCOMMODATIONS: THE LODGE AT FAIRFIELD GLADE (800)251-6778

STONEHENGE COURSE
18 holes   Par 72   6549/6202/4900 yds.
USGA: 69.9   SLOPE: 121
STYLE: Mountains, trees
ACCESS: No restrictions
SEASON: Mar.-Dec.   HIGH: Apr.-Oct.
GREEN FEES: $$$ (includes cart)
REDUCED FEES: TW, PK
RESERVATIONS: Written 1 month,
  phone 5 days
WALKING: No   RANGE: Yes

In 1985, *Golf Digest* named this Joe Lee-designed course the country's best new resort course, and for the last six years, Stonehenge has hosted the Tennessee State Open. The layout runs over mountainous terrain, through thick stands of trees, and past dramatic rock outcroppings. There are great mountain and forest landscapes along the way, with lakes and streams in the foreground. Stonehenge is a beautiful but stern test of golf that better players will enjoy immensely.

FALL CREEK FALLS STATE PARK GOLF COURSE

RTE. 3, PIKESVILLE, TN 37367 (615)881-5706 *(75 mi. N of Chattanooga)*
ACCOMMODATIONS: FALL CREEK FALLS INN (615)881-3241

FALL CREEK FALLS STATE PARK GOLF COURSE
18 holes   Par 72   6706/6378/6060 yds.
USGA: 70.8   SLOPE: 121
STYLE: Rolling hills, woods
ACCESS: No restrictions
SEASON: Feb.-Dec.   HIGH: June-Aug.
GREEN FEES: $
REDUCED FEES: LS
RESERVATIONS: After Mar. 1
WALKING: Yes   RANGE: Yes

The Fall Creek Falls course is located in a state park that takes its name from nearby waterfalls, the highest east of the Rockies. *Golf Digest* rates Fall Creek Falls among the best fifty public courses in the nation. In this Joe Lee design, tight fairways cut through a forest of hardwood and pine, leading to large, elevated, and difficult greens. In spite of its location, there are no water hazards on the course, but seventy-four sand-traps are here to protect par.

ROAN VALLEY GOLF ESTATES

HWY. 421 S., MOUNTAIN CITY, TN 37683 (615)727-7931 *(22 mi. NW of Boone, NC)*

ROAN VALLEY GOLF ESTATES
18 holes   Par 72   6736/6078/4370 yds.
USGA: 68.9   SLOPE: 115
STYLE: Mountains, woods
ACCESS: Restrictions on tee times
SEASON: Apr.-Nov.   HIGH: June-Sept.
GREEN FEES: $$ (includes cart)
REDUCED FEES: LS
RESERVATIONS: Anytime
WALKING: At times   RANGE: Practice area

The Blue Ridge Mountains provide a gorgeous setting for Roan Valley's tumultuous layout, and thanks to its extensive landscaping, it seems as much nature park as golf course. The bluegrass fairways and bentgrass greens are impeccably maintained, and the wide variety of holes and hilly terrain demand the use of every club in the bag. On No. 12, a long downhill par 5, the green is two hundred feet below the tee. The site for the putting surface was blasted out of rock, leaving a dramatic, fifty-foot-high wall of solid rock behind the green and granite outcroppings on the side.

BENT CREEK GOLF RESORT

3919 E. PKWY., GATLINBURG, TN 37738 (615)436-3947, *(12 mi. E of Gatlinburg)*
ACCOMMODATIONS: BENT CREEK GOLF RESORT (615)436-2875

BENT CREEK GOLF RESORT
18 holes   Par 72   6084/5780/5053 yds.
USGA: 67.9   SLOPE: 123
STYLE: Mountains, woods, water
ACCESS: No restrictions
SEASON: All year   HIGH: Apr./July/Oct.
GREEN FEES: $$
REDUCED FEES: HG, LS, PK
RESERVATIONS: 1 year
WALKING: At times   RANGE: Yes

Opened in 1974, Bent Creek is one of Gary Player's earlier designs. The front nine is set in a picturesque valley, while the back nine is a traditional mountain layout. There are sweeping views of the peaks of the Great Smoky Mountains and a wide variety of trees, flowers, and wildlife. Thirteen holes have water hazards, including the winding and treacherous Bent Creek. One of the most difficult holes in Tennessee, No. 11, requires both a tee shot and an approach over the creek.

CHATEAU ELAN GOLF CLUB

8

6060 GOLF CLUB DR., BRASELTON, GA 30517 (404)658-1868 *(40 mi. NE of Atlanta)*

> **CHATEAU ELAN GOLF CLUB**
> 18 holes   Par 71   7030/5997/5278 yds.
> USGA: 68.9   SLOPE: 119
> STYLE: Rolling hills, trees, lakes
> ACCESS: No restrictions
> SEASON: All year   HIGH: Mar.-Nov.
> GREEN FEES: $$
> REDUCED FEES: TW
> RESERVATIONS: 1 week
> WALKING: At times   RANGE: Yes

Opened in 1989, Chateau Elan has already hosted several local and Georgia PGA events and has rapidly become one of the favorite courses in the state. The 7,030-yard layout winds around lakes and creeks, and beautiful dogwoods, azaleas, and flower beds are here to divert your senses. The course is fair, but eighty-seven bunkers punctuating the rolling fairways do not leave much room for bad strategy off the tee. A French chateau and a winery are on the site, and two additional eighteen-hole courses are being developed.

INNSBRUCK GOLF CLUB

9

BAHN INNSBRUCK, HELEN, GA 30545 (404)878-2100 *(89 mi. NE of Atlanta)*
ACCOMMODATIONS: IGLS RESORT VILLAS (404)878-2400

Innsbruck is located in the northeast Georgia mountains, and, as its name suggests, its design and architecture are inspired by the Austrian Alps. The course, which opened in 1987, is carved out of the mountain terrain and is routed among beautiful forests. Some steep hills come into play: the par-3 fifteenth drops 189 feet from tee to green and a water hazard sits across the front for some added fun. There are breathtaking views

> **INNSBRUCK GOLF CLUB**
> 18 holes   Par 72   6748/6216/5174 yds.
> STYLE: Mountain, woods
> ACCESS: Restrictions on tee times
> SEASON: All year   HIGH: Apr.-Oct.
> GREEN FEES: $$$ (includes cart)
> REDUCED FEES: WD, HG, LS
> RESERVATIONS: 1 month
> WALKING: No   RANGE: Yes

of verdant mountains, and the picturesque, Tyrolean-style clubhouse fits prettily in the landscape. Innsbruck consistently ranks as one of Georgia's best.

WHAT IS PAR?

The United States Golf Association rules book defines "Par" as "The score that an expert golfer would be expected to make for a given hole. Par means errorless play without flukes and under ordinary weather conditions, allowing two strokes on the putting green."

What this means to most of us would-be experts, is that we should reach the green in one shot on par 3s, in two shots on par 4s, and in three on par 5s. That is assuming, of course, that we average only two putts thereafter...

The USGA also suggests the following yardages to determine "par" on any given hole:

PAR	MENS YARDAGES	LADIES YARDAGES
3	up to 250	up to 210
4	251 to 470	211 to 400
5	471 and over	401 to 575
6		576 and over

STOUFFER PINEISLE RESORT

9000 HOLIDAY RD., LAKE LANIER ISLAND, GA 30518 (404)945-8922 *(45 mi. N of Atlanta)*
ACCOMMODATIONS: STOUFFER PINEISLE RESORT (404)945-8921

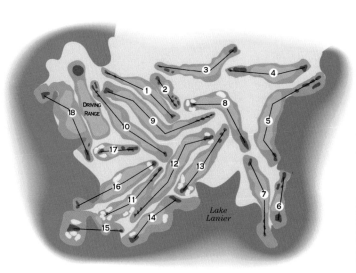

Since its opening in 1974, PineIsle has consistently ranked as one of the best courses in Georgia. Architects Gary Player and Ron Kirby brought together a superb site and a great design to make

STOUFFER PINEISLE RESORT
18 holes   Par 72   6527/6154/5297 yds.
USGA: 69.4   SLOPE: 117
STYLE: Woods, lakes
ACCESS: No restrictions
SEASON: All year   HIGH: Mar.-June
GREEN FEES: $$$
REDUCED FEES: WD
RESERVATIONS: 1 week
WALKING: At times   RANGE: Yes

PineIsle one of the most memorable courses in the South. The shores of Lake Lanier are hilly and covered with those lovely Georgia pines. Player and Kirby made wonderful use of the property, fashioning many holes that play from elevated tees and offer splendid views of the blue waters of the lake and the densely wooded countryside.

The first four holes travel through the pine forest and let you warm up before reaching down to the lake and the memorable par-5 fifth. Perhaps a bit too enthusiastically, this hole has been compared to Pebble Beach's famous No. 18. Here, too, players are "invited" to cut as much of the water as they dare from the tee, but unlike Pebble Beach, the hole is short enough to reward audacity and length by allowing a second shot directly to the green. Altogether, eight holes are routed along the lakeshore, and there is no safety until you get your putter out of the bag on No. 18. The finishing hole itself is a good score-destroyer and demands two successive water carries to reach the picturesque island green.

PineIsle is famous for having hosted the Nestlé World Championship from 1985 to 1989. The resort holds a Mobil 4-Star/AAA-4 Diamond rating.

PINEISLE: HOLE NO. 5

PINEISLE: HOLE NO. 5

THE HOLE STRETCHES BETWEEN 489 YARDS (CHAMPIONSHIP) AND 421 YARDS (LADIES). FROM THE REGULAR TEES, A DRIVE ACROSS THE LAKE TO THE LEFT SIDE OF THE FAIRWAY MUST CARRY THE WATER CLOSE TO 190 YARDS. TO ATTEMPT A "SAFE" SECOND SHOT TO THE GREEN, YOUR TEE SHOT SHOULD MEASURE AT LEAST 240 YARDS. EVEN FROM THAT POINT, THERE IS PLENTY OF WORK LEFT...

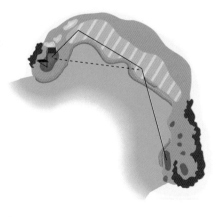

PORT ARMOR CLUB

1 PORT ARMOR PKWY., GREENSBORO, GA 30642 (404)453-4564 *(80 mi. E of Atlanta)*
ACCOMMODATIONS: INN ON THE GREEN (404)453-7366

According to *The Golf Reporter,* this lush, eighteen-hole layout ranks second in Georgia to Augusta National. Not a small feat, even for a course designed by former Jack Nicklaus senior architect Robert Cupp. The layout travels over gently rolling, lakeside terrain, and large, undulating greens sit peacefully

PORT ARMOR CLUB
18 holes   Par 72   6900/6300/5800 yds.
USGA: 70.6   SLOPE: 131
STYLE: Rolling hills, lakes
ACCESS: Hotel guests only
SEASON: All year   HIGH: Apr.-Sept.
GREEN FEES: $$
RESERVATIONS: 1 year
WALKING: After 5:00 p.m.   RANGE: Yes

amid tall Georgia pine. Three holes play along scenic Lake Oconee, and four more offer picturesque views of the reflecting waters. Four tees on each hole ensure a fair test for all golfers, and, thanks to Cupp's skillful design, the holes never seem repetitive. Port Armor is mainly private, but tee times are available to guests of the Inn on the Green.

ONE OF THE GUESTS
AT PORT ARMOR

PORT ARMOR CLUB

THE SEA ISLAND GOLF CLUB · 12

100 RETREAT AVE., ST. SIMONS ISLAND, GA 31522 (912)638-5118 *(75 mi. from Jacksonville, FL)*
ACCOMMODATIONS: THE CLOISTER (912)638-3611

THE SEA ISLAND GOLF CLUB
ACCESS: Restrictions on tee times
SEASON: All year   HIGH: Mar.-Apr.
GREEN FEES: $$$
REDUCED FEES: TW, PK
RESERVATIONS: 6 months
WALKING: Yes   RANGE: Yes
• **SEASIDE AND RETREAT**
  18 holes   Par 72   6659/6322/5760 yds.
  USGA: 69.7   SLOPE: 121
  STYLE: Oceanside, marshland
• **PLANTATION AND MARSHSIDE**
  18 holes   Par 72   6464/6064/5344 yds.
  USGA: 68.5   SLOPE: 117
  STYLE: Marshland, trees

The Sea Island Golf Club is part of the legendary five-star, five-diamond Cloister hotel, and it is located on the grounds of Retreat Plantation, a former cotton plantation at the southern tip of Sea Island. The site is lush with semitropical vegetation and beautiful flowers, and it offers some of the South's best golf.

The Sea Island Golf Club has four nine-hole courses: Plantation, Seaside, Retreat, and Marshside. The original two, Seaside and Plantation, were designed by English architects H. S. Colt and Charles Allison in 1929. They afford superb views of the sound and the ocean, and their great, moss-draped oaks and towering southern pines provide a visual feast for the player. Seaside, which Bobby Jones himself declared "one of the very best nines I have ever seen," features marshland, oceanside holes, and huge bunkers that defend large, elevated greens. Seaside's No. 4 is ranked by *Golf* magazine as one of the world's greatest holes. Off the tee, the player faces a drive across a yawning marsh, while on the other side, gaping bunkers sit ready to catch a conservative shot to the right. On Plantation, majestic oaks and pines line the fairways and recall the former grandeur of Retreat Plantation. Retreat was designed by Dick Wilson in 1960. It plays around two large lakes and concludes with an uphill march to the clubhouse along Avenue of the Oaks, a drive that is planted with seventy magnificent oaks from the antebellum era. Finally, there is the shorter and more intricate Marshside, a Joe Lee creation, which puts a premium on accuracy and nerve control. Note: during March and April, access to the courses is restricted to hotel guests only.

ST. SIMONS ISLAND CLUB · 13

100 KINGS WAY, ST. SIMONS ISLAND, GA 31522 (912)638-5130 *(65 mi. S of Savannah)*
ACCOMMODATIONS: THE CLOISTER (912)638-3611

ST. SIMONS ISLAND CLUB
18 holes   Par 72   6490/6114/5361 yds.
USGA: 70.1   SLOPE: 130
STYLE: Woods, marshland
ACCESS: No restrictions
SEASON: All year   HIGH: Mar.-June
GREEN FEES: $$
REDUCED FEES: LS, TW, PK
RESERVATIONS: 1 year
WALKING: After 4:30 p.m.   RANGE: Yes

St. Simons Island Club is operated by the nearby Cloister hotel in conjunction with the Sea Island courses. A fine Joe Lee design from 1976, the heavily wooded track involves large areas of marshland and nine lakes. Players hoping to score well here better be accurate, which is not easy when the wind picks up. The greens are welcoming in size but are heavily guarded by watery graves and sand. In all, eighty-eight fairway and greenside bunkers come into play, and negotiating some of the great par 5s can be a long and painful experience.

SEA ISLAND, SEASIDE NINE: HOLE NO. 4

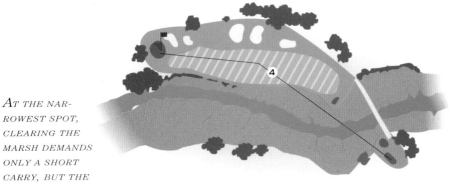

*AT THE NAR-
ROWEST SPOT,
CLEARING THE
MARSH DEMANDS
ONLY A SHORT
CARRY, BUT THE
BUNKERS ARE DIRECTLY IN THE
LINE OF FLIGHT, ABOUT 210 YARDS OUT. A
DRIVE TO THE LEFT SIDE OF THE FAIRWAY IS SAFE
FROM THE SAND, BUT REQUIRES A DARING 200 YARD WATER CARRY.*

OSPREY COVE: HOLE NO. 8

OSPREY COVE GOLF CLUB

14

123 OSPREY DR., ST. MARYS, GA 31558 (912)882-5575; (800)352-5575 *(30 mi. from Brunswick)*

> **OSPREY COVE GOLF CLUB**
> 18 holes Par 72 6791/6269/5263 yds.
> STYLE: Marshland, trees
> ACCESS: No restrictions
> SEASON: All year HIGH: Jan.-Apr.
> GREEN FEES: $$
> REDUCED FEES: WD, PK
> RESERVATIONS: 1 week
> WALKING: At times RANGE: Yes

OSPREY COVE

As the name suggests, the emphasis is on nature and wildlife at Osprey Cove. This beautifully maintained course on the Georgia-Florida border was designed by touring pro Mark McCumber. The links-style layout takes a scenic route through a pine forest, scattered lakes, and beautiful, extensive marshlands where deer, armadillo, and alligator are common sights. Thanks to wide fairways, it is not an overly severe test off the tee, but you must stay clear of the eighty-one gaping, steep-faced bunkers. Big, undulating greens add to the fun at Osprey Cove—a golf course with natural beauty and challenges that everyone can enjoy.

CALLAWAY GARDENS AND RESORTS

P.O. BOX 2000, PINE MOUNTAIN, GA 31822 (404)663-2281 *(70 mi. SW of Atlanta)*
ACCOMMODATIONS: CALLAWAY GARDENS AND RESORTS (800)282-8181

CALLAWAY GARDENS AND RESORTS
ACCESS: Restrictions on tee times
SEASON: All year   HIGH: Spring
GREEN FEES: $$$
REDUCED FEES: HG, LS, TW, PK
RESERVATIONS: Nonguests 1 day
WALKING: At times   RANGE: Yes
- **MOUNTAIN VIEW COURSE**
  18 holes   Par 72   7040/6605/5834 yds.
  USGA: 72.3   SLOPE: 124
  STYLE: Rolling hills, woods
- **GARDENS VIEW COURSE**
  18 holes   Par 72   6392/6108/5848 yds.
  USGA: 69.2   SLOPE: 121
  STYLE: Traditional
- **LAKE VIEW COURSE**
  18 holes   Par 70   6006/5452 yds.
  USGA: 69.4   SLOPE: 115
  STYLE: Lakes, trees

Callaway Gardens offers three scenic eighteen-hole courses and a nine-hole course. Rolling, tree-lined fairways and well-bunkered greens are the hallmarks of the Dick Wilson-designed Mountain View Course. The championship track, home of the Buick Southern Open, is a true test from the blues. Pros and 18-handicappers alike will want to think twice before hitting the driver on No. 6, a straightaway par 5 flanked by water from tee to green. Another superb hole is the 550-yard, par-5 No. 15, where water guards the entire right side of the fairway and forms an inlet in front of the green. The Joe Lee-designed Gardens View Course, an excellent test of shotmaking ability, runs along a trail of beautiful orchards and vineyards. The J. B. McGovern-Dick Wilson Lake View Course, Callaway's original, is known for its flowering landscape and the island tee at No. 5.

JONES CREEK GOLF CLUB 16

4101 HAMMONDS FERRY, EVANS, GA 30809 (404)860-4228, (800)445-3313 *(4 mi. W of Augusta)*

Often ranked as the top public course in Georgia, this 1986 Rees Jones design has already won rave reviews from pros and amateurs alike. The surroundings are heavily wooded, and the holes are sprinkled with sixty-five sand bunkers, four ponds, and numerous creeks. The most talked-about hole is the 513-yard, par 5 No. 13. A creek meanders lazily down the entire left side of the fairway before turning right and cutting across the front of the green. The hole is a true test of golfing skills.

> **JONES CREEK GOLF CLUB**
> 18 holes   Par 72   7008/6557/5430 yds.
> USGA: 71.9   SLOPE: 131
> STYLE: Rolling hills, tree-lined fairways
> ACCESS: No restrictions
> SEASON: All year   HIGH: Spring
> GREEN FEES: $$
> REDUCED FEES: WD
> RESERVATIONS: 10 days
> WALKING: At times   RANGE: Yes

SHERATON SAVANNAH RESORT AND COUNTRY CLUB 17

612 WILMINGTON ISLAND RD., SAVANNAH, GA 31410 (912)897-1612 *(9 mi. from Savannah)*
ACCOMMODATIONS: SHERATON SAVANNAH RESORT (800)325-3535

> **SHERATON SAVANNAH RESORT AND COUNTRY CLUB**
> 18 holes   Par 72   7000/6562/5438 yds.
> USGA: 71.7   SLOPE: 136
> STYLE: Traditional
> ACCESS: Priority to hotel guests
> SEASON: All year   HIGH: Spring and fall
> GREEN FEES: $$
> REDUCED FEES: LS, PK
> RESERVATIONS: Guests 6 months
> WALKING: No   RANGE: Yes

Originally designed by Donald Ross in 1927, and renovated by Willard Byrd in the 1960s, this is a true shotmaker's course, where players must deal with lakes and a stream on two-thirds of the holes. Sheraton Savannah also features lovely, undulating fairways and elevated, contoured greens that are strategically guarded by eighty-four bunkers—in the classic Ross style. The par-4 No. 15 is ranked one of the top eighteen holes in Georgia, thanks to water on the left and an out-of-bounds and traps on the right. The course has hosted the Georgia State Open for the last thirteen years.

SOUTHBRIDGE GOLF CLUB 18

415 SOUTHBRIDGE BLVD., SAVANNAH, GA 31405 (912)651-5455 *(8 mi. W of downtown Savannah)*

Rees Jones has been at work in the low swamplands outside of historic Savannah, and the result is the acclaimed Southbridge Golf Club. Opened in 1989, it has already been retained as a co-host site for the Georgia Open. It is cut out of heavily wooded terrain, and tall pines frame the undulating fairways with elegance. There are no weak holes at Southbridge, but No. 4 stands out from the rest. The over-water par 3 is guarded by an inconspicuous but deadly grass hollow—a feature that you won't easily forget once you experience it.

> **SOUTHBRIDGE GOLF CLUB**
> 18 holes   Par 72   6990/6458/5181 yds.
> USGA: 71.3   SLOPE: 129
> STYLE: Woods, lakes
> ACCESS: No restrictions
> SEASON: All year   HIGH: Mar.-May/Oct.
> GREEN FEES: $$
> REDUCED FEES: WD
> RESERVATIONS: 1 week
> WALKING: At times   RANGE: Yes

MARRIOTT'S GRAND HOTEL AT LAKEWOOD GOLF CLUB 19

SCENIC HWY. 98, POINT CLEAR, AL 36564 (205)990-6312 *(25 mi. E of Mobile)*
ACCOMMODATIONS: GRAND HOTEL (205)928-9201

MARRIOTT'S GRAND HOTEL AT LAKEWOOD GOLF CLUB

ACCESS: Hotel guests only
SEASON: All year   HIGH: Spring and fall
GREEN FEES: $$$ (includes cart)
REDUCED FEES: HG, PK
RESERVATIONS: At time of hotel booking
WALKING: No   RANGE: Yes

- **DOGWOOD COURSE**
  18 holes   Par 71   6676/6331/5596 yds.
  USGA: 70.5   SLOPE: 121
  STYLE: Traditional
- **AZALEA COURSE**
  18 holes   Par 72   6770/6292/5307 yds.
  USGA: 70.3   SLOPE: 124
  STYLE: Tree-lined fairways

The Lakewood Golf Club offers thirty-six holes of fine golf, set amid beautiful trees and numerous lagoons. The original eighteen, designed by Perry Maxwell, opened in 1946. In 1966, a third nine was designed by Joe Lee. Then, in 1986, nine more holes were added by Ron Garl, and a second eighteen was formed. The Dogwood Course, which is lined with huge, old oaks draped in Spanish moss, makes extensive use of doglegs. No. 10 is a par-4 dogleg with a corner formed by a tree that was downed by Hurricane Frederick— and which continues to grow. The Azalea Course is shorter, but it is fairly difficult due to narrow fairways and heavy rough.

MARRIOTT'S GRAND HOTEL, THE ISLAND GREEN

M
I
S
S
I
S
S
I
P
P
I

PINE ISLAND GOLF CLUB

20

P.O. BOX 843, OCEAN SPRINGS, MS 39564 (601)875-1674 *(1-1/2 mi. E of Ocean Springs)*

PINE ISLAND GOLF CLUB
18 holes   Par 71   6322/5863/4937 yds.
USGA: 67.6   SLOPE: 116
STYLE: Lakes, marshland, woods
ACCESS: Restrictions on tee times
SEASON: All year   HIGH: Feb.-Apr.
GREEN FEES: $
REDUCED FEES: LS
RESERVATIONS: 3 months
WALKING: At times   RANGE: Yes

Pine Island's course is built on three different islands, and it is a nature-lover's paradise. The Audubon Society occasionally uses the property for research, and the trees, lakes, and swamps abound with wildlife—and with surprises for the distracted golfer. Pete Dye's only creation in Mississippi requires a variety of conservative but skillful shots, as slices and hooks will likely end up in "gatorland." Water hazards lurk on all eighteen holes, and there are plenty of opportunities to get too close to nature.

DIAMONDHEAD

21

7600 COUNTRY CLUB CIRCLE, BAY ST. LOUIS, MS 39520 (601)255-3910 *(55 mi. E of New Orleans)*

CARDINAL COURSE:
HOLE NO. 15

Diamondhead's 6,400-acre resort property is built on the Mississippi Gulf Coast's highest elevation, and it offers two eighteen-hole courses. Brief and compact, the Cardinal Course, designed by Bill Adkins, has tight, wooded fairways and large, fast greens. It demands a subtle and careful application of power, and shot placement is essential for a decent score. The equally wooded Pine Course, designed by Earl Stone, is longer with smaller, leisurely greens and wider, more generous fairways. Both courses are equally challenging and will test different aspects of your game.

DIAMONDHEAD
ACCESS: No restrictions
SEASON: All year   HIGH: Feb.-May
GREEN FEES: $$
REDUCED FEES: LS, TW
RESERVATIONS: 2 days
WALKING: No   RANGE: Yes
• **CARDINAL COURSE**
   18 holes   Par 72   6831/6163/5065 yds.
   USGA: 70.6   SLOPE: 134
   STYLE: Traditional
• **PINE COURSE**
   18 holes   Par 72   6860/6421/5359 yds.
   USGA: 71.7   SLOPE: 130
   STYLE: Traditional

L
O
U
I
S
I
A
N
A

BELLE TERRE COUNTRY CLUB

22

111 FAIRWAY DR., LA PLACE, LA 70068 (504)652-5000 *(45 mins. from downtown New Orleans)*

BELLE TERRE COUNTRY CLUB
18 holes   Par 72   6850/6340/5590 yds.
USGA: 70.2   SLOPE: 125
STYLE: Marshland, water
ACCESS: Restrictions on tee times
SEASON: All year   HIGH: Mar.-June
GREEN FEES: $$$ (includes cart)
REDUCED FEES: WD
RESERVATIONS: 1 day
WALKING: At times   RANGE: Yes

Belle Terre means "beautiful land" in French, but the name does not seem appropriate for the site: the course was built around twenty-three swamps, bayous, and ponds, and there is less land here than water. Regardless of this mundane detail, Pete Dye created a challenging course, with some pretty detours into picturesque wooded areas. The finishing three holes, nicknamed "Last Chance," "Forever," and "Bayou Bend," provide several opportunities to wreck a good score, and are proof enough that *"Belle Eau"* would have been a better name for the course.

CHEROKEE VILLAGE SOUTH GOLF COURSE   23

P.O. BOX 840, CHEROKEE VILLAGE, AR 72525 (501)257-2555 *(150 mi. N of Little Rock)*
ACCOMMODATIONS: BEST WESTERN VILLAGE INN (501)856-2176

**CHEROKEE VILLAGE SOUTH
GOLF COURSE**
18 holes   Par 72   7058/6515/5270 yds.
USGA: 70   SLOPE: 123
STYLE: Mountains, woods
ACCESS: Restrictions on tee times
SEASON: All year   HIGH: May-Sept.
GREEN FEES: $
REDUCED FEES: PK
RESERVATIONS: Not accepted
WALKING: Yes   RANGE: Yes

Cherokee Village has two excellent golf courses, but only the South Course is available to visitors. The scenic track is laid out on expansive, mountainous terrain with nice views of the surrounding forests. The wide and friendly fairways roll up and down amid lots of red oak, and the tall-grass rough is sprinkled with an abundance of flowers. Only two holes have water: Nos. 1 and 11, yet, the hills and the appreciable yardage are enough to make Cherokee Village quite a golfing challenge.

A R K A N S A S

OTHER EXCELLENT COURSES IN THE SOUTH

ALABAMA
- ● BENT BROOK GOLF COURSE, Bessemer (205)424-2368
- ■ COTTON CREEK GOLF CLUB, Gulf Shores (205)968-7766
- ● LAGOON PARK GOLF COURSE, Montgomery (205)271-7000

ARKANSAS
- ▲ HOT SPRINGS COUNTRY CLUB, Hot Springs (501)624-2661
- ● MOUNTAIN RANCH COUNTRY CLUB, Fairfield Bay (501)884-3333
- ■ RED APPLE INN, Heber Springs (501)362-3111

GEORGIA
- ● BULL CREEK GOLF COURSE, Columbus (404)561-1614
- ● EAGLE WATCH GOLF CLUB, Woodstock (404)591-1000
- ■ THE HAMPTON CLUB, St. Simons Island (912)634-0255
- ● JEKYLL ISLAND GOLF RESORT, Jekyll Island (912)635-3464
- ● LAKE LANIER ISLANDS HOTEL AND GOLF CLUB, Lake Lanier (404)945-8787
- ▲ SEA PALMS RESORT, St. Simons Island (800)841-6268, (800)282-1226 in GA
- ● STONE MOUNTAIN GOLF COURSE, Stone Mountain (404)498-5715

LOUISIANA
- ▲ EASTOVER COUNTRY CLUB, New Orleans (504)245-7347
- ● SQUIRREL RUN GOLF COURSE, New Iberia (318)367-0863

MISSISSIPPI
- ■ ST. ANDREWS COUNTRY CLUB, Ocean Springs (601)875-7730
- ■ WINDANCE GOLF AND COUNTRY CLUB, Gulfport (601)832-4871

TENNESSEE
- ● BANEBERRY GOLF AND RESORT, White Pine (615)674-2500

▲ RESTRICTIONS MAY APPLY   ■ HOTEL/RESORT GUESTS ONLY   ● OPEN WITHOUT RESTRICTIONS

CHAPTER NINE

FLORIDA

The vision of Florida's sun-drenched beaches some-times overshadows this splendid state's other natural gifts: immense swamplands, thick forests of pine and oak, and endless stretches of rolling, coastal dunes. While the glorious weather allows for a multitude of outdoor activities and sports, it is no wonder that golf has become the Sunshine State's major attraction. By 1989, the opening of the acclaimed Emerald Dunes Golf Club in West Palm Beach had pushed Florida over the one-thousand-golf-course mark, and con-struction is continuing unabated into the early 1990s to meet the demands of residents and visitors from all over the world. The Doral, Walt Disney World, Sawgrass, PGA National, Palm Coast...Florida is the land of world-famous vacation golf resorts, and the choice is only getting bigger.

There is more good news. Gone is the time when Florida produced just those flat and watery "Florida-style" golf courses. Today, architects of local and international fame are at work transforming the land into great layouts with contours, beauty and charac-ter. There is also a strong interest in working with the existing terrain and preserving what nature has to offer: pinelands, marshlands, sand dunes, and, everywhere, a great variety of wildlife. Indeed, many Florida golf courses have become new habitats for numerous species of birds and aquatic animals that once only flourished on official preserves.

Florida has it all, year-round. Over one hundred of both the PGA, LPGA and Senior PGA Tour profes-sionals found out. They made it their home.

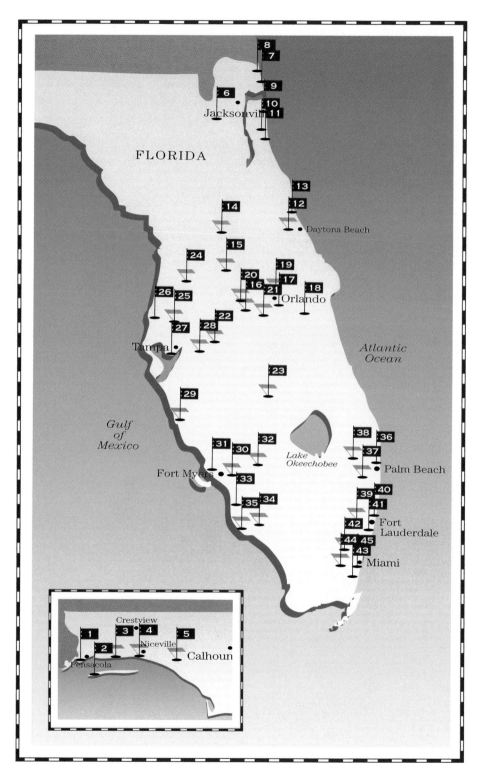

PERDIDO BAY RESORT

1 DOUG FORD DR., PENSACOLA, FL 32507 (904)492-1223 *(10 mi. SW of Pensacola)*
ACCOMMODATIONS: PERDIDO BAY RESORT (904)492-1213

PERDIDO BAY RESORT
18 holes   Par 72   7154/6782/5476 yds.
USGA: 72.2   SLOPE: 122
STYLE: Woods, water
ACCESS: Restrictions on tee times
SEASON: All year   HIGH: Feb.-May
GREEN FEES: $$
REDUCED FEES: WD, TW, PK
RESERVATIONS: Anytime
WALKING: No   RANGE: Yes

Although Perdido Bay is fairly flat and open, it has more than enough scenic appeal to keep the average golfer happy, even as his score mounts into the nineties. Lined with longleaf pine, dotted with bunkers, and made more difficult by lakes and streams, especially on the back side, the course also has a succession of tough par 4s. In fact, when the Pensacola Open was played here from 1978 to 1987, three holes were listed among the seventy-five toughest on the PGA Tour.

TIGER POINT GOLF AND COUNTRY CLUB

1255 COUNTRY CLUB RD., GULF BREEZE, FL 32561 (904)932-1333 *(10 mi. E of Pensacola)*

TIGER POINT GOLF AND COUNTRY CLUB
ACCESS: No restrictions
SEASON: All year   HIGH: Mar./Sept.
GREEN FEES: $$
REDUCED FEES: WD, PK
RESERVATIONS: 6 months with credit card
WALKING: No   RANGE: Yes
• TIGER POINT EAST COURSE
18 holes   Par 72   7033/6118/5242 yds.
USGA: 69.8   SLOPE: 137
STYLE: Links, water, oceanside
• TIGER POINT WEST COURSE
18 holes   Par 72   6744/6058/5343 yds.
STYLE: Lakes

The two courses at Tiger Point are among the Emerald Coast's most scenic. They offer an interesting design of links-style golf amid pine trees and waterways. Located on Santa Risa Sound, Tiger Point East was created by former U.S. Open champion Jerry Pate. Pate routed the links along the ocean, then through wetlands, lakes, and canals. Along the way, he dug deep greenside and fairway bunkers that can provide a few headaches. The course was the host of the 1988 Pensacola Open. The less expensive Tiger Point West also has pines, waterway-laced fairways, and a picture-perfect setting.

TIGER POINT: HOLE NO. 16

THE CLUB AT HIDDEN CREEK `3`

3070 PGA BLVD., NAVARRE, FL 32566 (904)939-4604, (800)239-2582 *(20 mi. E of Pensacola)*

As the youngest course to ever host a U.S. Open Qualifier, this Ron Garl-designed layout won't stay "hidden" much longer. Built on a subdivision just minutes away from the Gulf of Mexico, the course is impeccably maintained and has plenty of mature oak, pine, and elm trees in addition to twenty-two acres of sand.

THE CLUB AT HIDDEN CREEK
18 holes   Par 72   6844/6266/5206 yds.
USGA: 70.8   SLOPE: 137
STYLE: Hills, trees
ACCESS: Restrictions on tee times
SEASON: All year   HIGH: Jan.-Apr.
GREEN FEES: $$
REDUCED FEES: TW
RESERVATIONS: 4 days, more with deposit
WALKING: No   RANGE: Yes

Nowhere do they come together in more sinister fashion than on No. 11, a dogleg left with a beautiful old oak at the corner, and a three-hundred-yard bunker running up the left side of the fairway. The green itself is over 150 feet deep, and is supported by bulkheads rising from the huge sandtrap. The regular 137 slope rating gives a good indication of the course's difficulty. From the championship tees, the course rates a stern 143.

THE GOLF CLUB AT BLUEWATER BAY `4`

1950 BLUEWATER BLVD., NICEVILLE, FL 32578 (904)897-3241 *(6 mi. E of Niceville)*
ACCOMMODATIONS: BLUEWATER BAY (800)874-2128, (904)897-3613

If your game favors accuracy over sheer power, this twenty-seven-hole course is the one for you. The Tom Fazio design has tight fairways, small greens, and water hazards on fourteen holes, but the rough is minimal, and the fifty bunkers are not especially punishing. Some of the holes run through wooded areas, some are bordered by beautiful homes, but the most memorable offer superb views of the sparkling Bluewater Bay. A

THE GOLF CLUB AT BLUEWATER BAY
27 holes   2993/3137/3057 yds.
STYLE: Trees, lakes, marshland
ACCESS: No restrictions
SEASON: All year   HIGH: Feb.-Apr.
GREEN FEES: $$
REDUCED FEES: HG, LS, PK
RESERVATIONS: Nonguests 1 week
WALKING: After 1:00 p.m.   RANGE: Yes

particularly good hole is No. 6 on the Bay Course, a dogleg right with an approach shot that is played out before a stunning view of the water. The course is one of the best maintained in the Florida panhandle. It is the site of the Bluewater Bay International Tournament and has hosted the North Florida Amateur Championship.

SHALIMAR POINTE GOLF AND COUNTRY CLUB `5`

2 COUNTRY CLUB RD., SHALIMAR, FL 32579 (800)477-4TEE, (904)651-1416 *(45 mi. E of Pensacola)*

Along the shores of Choctawhatchee Bay, this Joe Finger course makes excellent use of water and has some of the whitest sand to be found anywhere. Pete Dye added some "refinements" to the course in 1985, in the form of omnipresent waste bunkers and bulkheaded water hazards. The short (335-yard), par-4 No. 14 is simply a great hole. A large waste bunker guards the right side of the landing area of the dogleg; water protects the corner and also flanks the right side of a dangerously undulating peninsula green—a great test of shotmaking and nerve.

SHALIMAR POINTE GOLF AND COUNTRY CLUB
18 holes   Par 72   6760/6313/5436 yds.
USGA: 69.9   SLOPE: 116
STYLE: Water, links, waste bunkers
ACCESS: No restrictions
SEASON: All year   HIGH: Mar.-Oct.
GREEN FEES: $$
RESERVATIONS: 6 months
WALKING: Weekdays after 12:00 pm
RANGE: Yes

RAVINES

6

2932 RAVINES RD., MIDDLEBURG, FL 32068 (904)282-7888 *(20 mi. SW of Jacksonville)*
ACCOMMODATIONS: INN AT RAVINES (904)282-1111

> **RAVINES**
> 18 holes   Par 72   6784/6132/5119 yds.
> USGA: 69.6   SLOPE: 125
> STYLE: Hills, woods
> ACCESS: Restrictions on tee times
> SEASON: All year   HIGH: Spring
> GREEN FEES: $$ (includes cart)
> REDUCED FEES: WD, LS, PK
> RESERVATIONS: 3 months
> WALKING: Members only   RANGE: Yes

Steep hills and sharp drops through heavily wooded terrain characterize the layout at Ravines. The course, built by Ron Garl and Mark McCumber along the meandering Black Creek, tumbles as much as one hundred feet in some places, creating opportunities for dramatic carries over the ravines. An incredible variety of trees, including moss-laden oaks, border the fairways, adding to the unspoiled beauty of the site. Ravines also has a fun eighteen-hole putting course: The Himalayas.

RAVINES

SUMMER BEACH RESORT

7

4700 AMELIA ISLAND PKWY., AMELIA ISLAND, FL 32034 (904)277-8015 *(30 mi. NE of Jacksonville)*
ACCOMMODATIONS: SUMMER BEACH RESORT (904)277-2525

> **SUMMER BEACH RESORT**
> 18 holes   Par 72   6681/6119/5741 yds.
> USGA: 69.1   SLOPE: 120
> STYLE: Trees, lakes, marshland
> ACCESS: Hotel guests only
> SEASON: All year   HIGH: Mar.-May
> GREEN FEES: $$$$ (includes cart)
> REDUCED FEES: LS
> RESERVATIONS: At time of hotel booking
> WALKING: No   RANGE: Yes

Summer Beach is the work of tour players Gene Littler and Mark McCumber. The front nine, mostly built around marshes, is beautifully complemented by the back nine, which is heavily laced with ponds and trees. Throughout the course, an abundance of flowers contribute to the colorful surroundings. The many ponds and wetlands create quite a few problems along the way. On the long par-5 No. 6, three marshes must be crossed before getting to an elevated green protected by a huge, ten-foot-tall, deep-faced bunker.

AMELIA ISLAND PLANTATION

HWY. A1A S., AMELIA ISLAND, FL 32034 (904)261-6161 EXT. 5381 *(32 mi. N of Jacksonville)*
ACCOMMODATIONS: AMELIA ISLAND PLANTATION (800)874-6878

AMELIA ISLAND PLANTATION
ACCESS: Hotel guests only
SEASON: All year   HIGH: Feb.-May
GREEN FEES: $$$$$ (includes cart)
REDUCED FEES: LS, TW, PK
RESERVATIONS: At time of hotel booking
WALKING: No   RANGE: Yes
• **LONG POINT CLUB COURSE**
  18 holes   Par 72   6775/6068/4927 yds.
  USGA: 69.5   SLOPE: 121
  STYLE: Woods, lakes, marshland,
  oceanside
• **OAKMARSH, OYSTERBAY, AND OCEANSIDE COURSES**
  27 holes   2978/2809/2572 yds.
  STYLE: Oceanside, marshland, trees

Amelia Island Plantation offers three nine-hole courses and a separate eighteen-hole layout. Each of the three nines has the tight fairways and small greens favored by Pete Dye, who designed the trio in 1972. The Oceanside nine may be the most memorable. Nos. 4, 5, and 6 wind along a looming dune ridge that overlooks the beach and the Atlantic. The holes combine spectacular views with challenging play, and the ocean wind is a major factor here. The Oysterbay nine meanders along salt-marsh creeks, with unusual wetland hazards and the occasional sunning alligator. No. 8 is rated one of Florida's more difficult holes: the blue tees are set back on an island in the middle of the marsh, and looking at the fairway from there is a humbling experience. The Oakmarsh nine features ancient, moss-draped oaks and palmetto thickets, and its eighth green is perched on a peninsula jutting into a lagoon. Amelia Island's other entry is the spectacular Tom Fazio-designed Long Point Club Course. The eighteen-hole layout, which opened in 1987 to great reviews, combines pristine oak and pine forests with marshland and acres of oceanfront dunes. The course rolls in and around the dense, subtropical vegetation, and lagoons complete the layout's magnificent and secluded setting. Some of the holes require playing over protected wetlands, where retrieving lost balls is prohibited. Two back-to-back, beachside par 3s add excitement and variety to this great course. Amelia Island has earned many awards, in cluding the coveted *Golf* magazine Gold Medal for golf resorts.

LONG POINT CLUB
*THE COURSE OFFERS MEMO-
RABLE MOMENTS ON BOTH
BEACHSIDE PAR-3S, NO. 6 AND
NO. 7 (OPPOSITE PAGE) RESPECTIVELY
166 AND 133-YARDS LONG, THEY'LL FORCE
YOU TO HIT ANYTHING FROM A NINE TO A ONE IRON,
DEPENDING ON THE WIND.*

TOURNAMENT PLAYERS CLUB AT SAWGRASS 9
110 TPC BLVD., PONTE VEDRA BEACH, FL 32082 (904)273-3235 *(15 mi. SE of Jacksonville)*
ACCOMMODATIONS: THE MARRIOTT AT SAWGRASS (904)285-7777

For a lot of people, the Stadium Course at the TPC at Sawgrass is synonymous with architect Pete Dye. A memorable moment came in 1982 after tour pro Jerry Pate sunk his short birdie putt on the eighteenth green to win the inaugural Tournament Players Championship. In celebration of a well-earned victory on this devilish new track, Pate took his stylish and famous dive into the bordering lake. Minutes later, he also tossed tour commissioner Deane Beman, an active contributor to the design, and Dye himself into the water to make sure they both understood his feelings—and those of his fellow tour pros—regarding their innovative design. Well, that was then, and this is now. A decade after its creation, the Stadium Course has matured into a fine and beautiful test of golf, requiring patience, daring, and skill. Ranked by *Golf* magazine's international panel of experts as one of the hundred greatest courses in the world, the TPC displays an array of imaginative features, such as diminutive target landing areas, immense waste bunkers, grassy mounds and knolls, and nerve-wracking putting surfaces. The surrounding landscape has also splendidly matured, and the impeccably manicured fairways run through a blend of lush, tropical foliage and elegant, tall pines. The grass "bleachers" bordering many parts of the track have a seating capacity of 20,000, and the most popular observation spot is around the infamous No. 17 island green. While *we* can play it from the short tees, the pros have to shoot at it from about 165 yards, and when the wind swirls over the lake, the scene can turn positively ugly. For an encore, No. 18 presents its own hair-raising view from the tee. It resembles Pebble Beach's finishing hole, except that, here, it is a 440-yard par 4 with a watery left side and not much space for a safe landing; meanwhile, the pesky grass mounds bordering the right side of the green seem to snicker at the approaching player. A great golf course, and a must for any golf lover...

The TPC experience continues with the Valley Course, opened in 1987, and home to the Senior Tournament Players Championship. Located adjacent to the Stadium, it has water on every single hole; but this time, Pete Dye was wiser: he consulted with Jerry Pate on the layout, thus ensuring himself a less eventful and drier exit from the scene.

Note: Guests of the Marriott at Sawgrass also have access to the Sawgrass Country Club (see following page) and the Marsh Landing and Oak Bridge eighteen-hole courses, all located within the Sawgrass community.

TPC AT SAWGRASS: HOLE NO. 17

**TOURNAMENT PLAYERS CLUB
AT SAWGRASS**
ACCESS: Hotel guests only
SEASON: All year   HIGH: Mar.-May
GREEN FEES: $$$$$
REDUCED FEES: LS, PK
RESERVATIONS: 1 month
WALKING: No   RANGE: Yes
• **TPC STADIUM COURSE**
   18 holes   Par 72   6857/6394/5034 yds.
   USGA: 71.9   SLOPE: 130
   STYLE: Water, waste areas, mounds
• **TPC VALLEY COURSE**
   18 holes   Par 72   6864/6092/5126 yds.
   USGA: 69   SLOPE: 122
   STYLE: Water, waste areas, mounds

ARCHITECT PETE DYE

SAWGRASS COUNTRY CLUB   10
1000 TPC BLVD., PONTE VEDRA BEACH, FL 32082 (904)285-7777 *(25 mi. from Jacksonville)*
ACCOMMODATIONS: THE MARRIOTT AT SAWGRASS (904)285-7777

Ed Seay's design of the twenty-seven holes at Sawgrass Country Club has been ranked by *Golf Digest* as one of the top hundred courses in the nation since 1977. A variety of water obstacles interfere with twenty-four holes of the East, West, and South nines. On top, over a hundred bunkers bring trouble to even the lowest handicappers. Some consider the East nine to be the toughest course in northern Florida. One of its highlights is

SAWGRASS COUNTRY CLUB
27 holes   3240/3198/3263 yds.
STYLE: Oceanside, trees, marshland
ACCESS: Hotel guests only
SEASON: All year   HIGH: Mar.-May
GREEN FEES: $$$$$
REDUCED FEES: LS, TW, PK
RESERVATIONS: Call club
WALKING: After 4:00 p.m.   RANGE: Yes

the par-4 No. 5, where a solid drive launched from an elevated tee lands on an area encircled by menacing marsh, sand, and water. With the ocean accentuating the background, the course is definitely a favorite among pros and amateurs alike.

PONTE VEDRA INN AND CLUB   11
200 PONTE VEDRA BLVD., PONTE VEDRA BEACH, FL 32082 (904)285-2044 *(15 mi. SE of Jacksonville)*
ACCOMMODATIONS: PONTE VEDRA INN AND CLUB (904)285-1111

PONTE VEDRA INN AND CLUB
ACCESS: Hotel guests only
SEASON: All year   HIGH: Mar.-May
GREEN FEES: $$$
REDUCED FEES: LS, PK
RESERVATIONS: At time of hotel confirmation
WALKING: No   RANGE: Yes
• OCEAN COURSE
18 holes   Par 72   6573/6055/5237 yds.
USGA: 68.9   SLOPE: 116
STYLE: Water hazards, bunkers
• LAGOON COURSE
18 holes   Par 70   5574/5261/4641 yds.
USGA: 64.9   SLOPE: 107
STYLE: Water hazards

Well before the PGA Tour moved to Ponte Vedra, there was some terrific golf going on at the Ponte Vedra Inn, and there still is. The Ocean Course, which dates back to 1929, is not terribly long, but it is enjoyable and challenging. And when the winds begin to swell off the Atlantic, it can be all the golf course anyone can handle. Of historic interest is the par-3 No. 9, which is claimed to be the first island hole ever. But the most memorable is the 516-yard, par-5 No. 3, which features many large mounds dotting the fairway and a well-bunkered, elevated green. Ponte Vedra also has the Lagoon Course, aptly named since there is a lagoon on practically every hole!

INDIGO LAKES HILTON GOLF AND TENNIS RESORT   15
312 INDIGO DR., DAYTONA BEACH, FL 32120 (904)254-3607 *(5 mi. W of downtown Daytona Beach)*
ACCOMMODATIONS: INDIGO LAKES HILTON GOLF AND TENNIS RESORT (904)258-6333

With a two-thousand-yard difference between the forward and back tees, and five sets of tees on each hole, Indigo Lakes is playable for golfers of every ability. The beautiful championship course is lined with pines and palms, and four nice lakes touch on eight holes. The track is also heavily bunkered—in fact, close to a hundred traps dot

INDIGO LAKES HILTON GOLF COURSE
18 holes   Par 72   7168/6176/5159 yds.
USGA: 69.4   SLOPE: 121
STYLE: Tree-lined fairways, lakes
ACCESS: Restrictions on tee times
SEASON: All year   HIGH: Oct.-Mar.
GREEN FEES: $$
REDUCED FEES: HG, LS
RESERVATIONS: Nonmembers 1 day
WALKING: No   RANGE: Yes

the course. When the six-thousand-square-foot greens are taken into account, it's easy to explain why the LPGA has selected Indigo Lakes as the site of its new headquarters and qualifying school.

MATANZAS WOODS GOLF CLUB

13

398 LAKEVIEW BLVD., PALM COAST, FL 32151 (904)446-6330 *(22 mi. N of Daytona Beach)*
ACCOMMODATIONS: SHERATON PALM COAST (904)445-3000

Ranked by *Golf* magazine in 1990 as one of Florida's top courses, Matanzas Woods exhibits all the attributes of a championship track. The Arnold Palmer-Ed Seay design blends lakes, ditches, mounded fairways, and expansive putting surfaces into a dense forest of tall pine. The par 5s are exceptional—most notably the 560-yard No. 4, with a lake guarding the front of the green. Matanzas has no parallel holes, and with its multitude of scenic delights, a round of golf there is as refreshing as a good walk in the woods. Matanzas Woods is one of four courses worthy of a visit at the sprawling Palm Coast development. The three other championship courses are Pine Lakes, another Arnold Palmer creation, Palm Harbor Golf Club, by architect Bill Amick, and finally, Cypress Knoll, a heavily mounded design by Gary Player, which opened in 1990.

MATANZAS WOODS GOLF CLUB
18 holes   Par 72   6985/6514/5407 yds.
USGA: 71   SLOPE: 121
STYLE: Tree-lined fairways, lakes
ACCESS: Restrictions on tee times
SEASON: All year   HIGH: Winter
GREEN FEES: $$$ (includes cart)
REDUCED FEES: LS, PK
RESERVATIONS: 5 days
WALKING: No   RANGE: Yes

SCENIC PINE LAKES, ONE OF FOUR COURSES AT THE PALM COAST COMPLEX

GOLDEN OCALA GOLF COURSE `14`

7300 U.S. HWY. 27 NW, OCALA, FL 32675 (904)629-6229 *(75 mi. N of Orlando)*

Golden Ocala is where one can play some of the world's most famous golf in just one location—all for a single green fee. In addition to ten Ron Garl-designed original holes, Golden Ocala has eight replicas of such notorious golf holes as Nos. 11 and 12 at Augusta National, No. 17—the Road Hole—at St. Andrews, the "Postage Stamp" at Royal Troon, and more from Muirfield and Baltusrol.

GOLDEN OCALA GOLF COURSE
18 holes   Par 72   6755/6247/5591 yds.
STYLE: Rolling hills, tree-lined fairways
ACCESS: No restrictions
SEASON: All year   HIGH: Jan.-Mar.
GREEN FEES: $$ (includes cart)
RESERVATIONS: 3 days
WALKING: No   RANGE: Yes

Each one is designed to warm the heart and test the skill of the serious golf nut. In 1990, *Golf Digest* rated Golden Ocala among the top seventy-five public courses in the country.

MISSION INN GOLF AND TENNIS RESORT `15`

10400 C.R. 48, HOWEY IN THE HILLS, FL 34737 (904)324-3885 *(35 mi. NW of Orlando)*
ACCOMMODATIONS: MISSION INN GOLF AND TENNIS RESORT (800)874-9053, (904)324-3101

Mission Inn is traditionally ranked among the top courses in Florida. This beautifully conditioned layout is unusual on a number of counts. Originally

designed in 1926, it is positively ancient by Florida standards, and it sits over hilly terrain, which is rare in this part of the world. Although there is little rough,

MISSION INN GOLF AND TENNIS RESORT
ACCESS: Priority to hotel guests
SEASON: All year   HIGH: Jan.-May
GREEN FEES: $$$
REDUCED FEES: LS, PK
RESERVATIONS: Nonguests 1 week
WALKING: No   RANGE: Yes
• MISSION INN COURSE
18 holes   Par 72   6770/6224/5021 yds.
USGA: 70.9   SLOPE: 129
STYLE: Hills, tree-lined fairways, water
• LAS COLINAS COURSE
18 holes   Par 72

trouble is never more than a swing away due to the many trees that border the fairways, and a large collection of gaping bunkers. To top it off, there is water on thirteen holes. Most golfers remember the 544-yard fourth, nick-named "Devil's Delight," a slight, double dogleg through the woods, with the approach shot over water to an elevated green. Mission Inn is also opening a new eighteen-hole course.

MARRIOTT'S ORLANDO WORLD CENTER `16`

WORLD CENTER DR., ORLANDO, FL 32821 (407)239-5659 *(15 mi. SW of Orlando)*
ACCOMMODATIONS: MARRIOTT'S ORLANDO WORLD CENTER RESORT (407)239-4200

MARRIOTT'S ORLANDO WORLD CENTER
18 holes   Par 71   6265/5956/5048 yds.
USGA: 67.9   SLOPE: 117
STYLE: Lakes, bunkers, trees
ACCESS: Priority to hotel guests
SEASON: All year   HIGH: Jan.-Apr.
GREEN FEES: $$$$ (includes cart)
REDUCED FEES: LS, TW, PK
RESERVATIONS: Nonguests 5 days
WALKING: No   RANGE: Yes

Designed by Joe Lee, the Marriott's Orlando course reminds you of an immense, manicured tropical garden. Open since 1985, it features an attractive combination of blue lakes, palm trees, flowers, and eighty-five cloverleaf-shaped white sand bunkers. However, the most predominant attribute is the water which laces most of the fairways. The length is modest, but the water hazards and large greens present endless opportunities for skillfully crafted shots.

THE BAY HILL CLUB   `17`
9000 BAY HILL BLVD., ORLANDO, FL 32819 (407)876-2747 *(in SW Orlando)*
ACCOMMODATIONS: THE BAY HILL LODGE (407)876-2429

CHALLENGER AND CHAMPION COURSES
18 holes   Par 72   7114/6547/5214 yds.
USGA: 71.8   SLOPE: 127
STYLE: Tree-lined fairways, lakes
ACCESS: Hotel guests only
SEASON: All year   HIGH: Jan.-Apr.
GREEN FEES: $$$
REDUCED FEES: LS, PK
RESERVATIONS: At time of hotel booking
WALKING: At times   RANGE: Yes

THE FINISHING HOLE AT BAYHILL

When in Florida, Arnold Palmer can be found at The Bay Hill Club. The Challenger and Champion nines, which have Arnie's fingerprints all over the design, are like the man himself— tough, strong, dramatic, and fair. The course was actually an original Dick Wilson creation, but in 1989, the Arnold Palmer-Ed Seay design team reworked the 7,114-yard championship track. The layout is known for its length and many lakes, but it also features an abundance of trees and large bunkers. No. 18, with a narrow green fronted by water, is one of the sternest finishing holes on the PGA Tour. It received a lot of publicity when rookie tour pro Robert Gamez holed his 7-iron approach shot there, to win the 1990 Nestlé Invitational Tournament. Next to the tournament course, the nine-hole Charger Course offers another well-conditioned golfing challenge. Bay Hill is primarily a private club, but there are playing privileges for guests of The Bay Hill Lodge.

POINCIANA GOLF AND RACQUET RESORT   `18`
500 E. CYPRUS PKWY., KISSIMMEE, FL 34759 (407)933-5300 *(20 mi. SE of Disney World)*
ACCOMMODATIONS: POINCIANA GOLF AND RACQUET RESORT (800)331-7743

POINCIANA GOLF & RACQUET RESORT
18 holes   Par 72   6700/6030/4988 yds.
STYLE: Woods, lakes
ACCESS: Priority to hotel guests
SEASON: All year   HIGH: Feb.-Mar.
GREEN FEES: $$
REDUCED FEES: WD, LS, TW
RESERVATIONS: Nonguests 1 week
WALKING: No   RANGE: Yes

This Bruce Devlin-Robert von Hagge layout is carved through a thick forest of cypress, in such a way that even parallel holes are isolated from each other. In fact, the course is so well-hidden that some think it is one of Florida's best kept golf secrets. Water hazards—mostly lateral —lurk on twelve holes, sometimes in an intimidating fashion. The numerous bunkers are also large and craftily placed, and they catch a lot of balls. From the 6,700-yard back tees, the Poinciana course is a very serious affair.

GRAND CYPRESS GOLF CLUB

19

1 N. JACARANDA, ORLANDO, FL 32819 (407)239-4700 *(in Orlando city limits)*
ACCOMMODATIONS: HYATT REGENCY, GRAND CYPRESS VILLAS, (407)239-4700

> **GRAND CYPRESS GOLF CLUB**
> ACCESS: Hotel guests only
> SEASON: All year HIGH: Feb.-May
> GREEN FEES: $$$$$ (includes cart)
> REDUCED FEES: LS, TW, PK
> RESERVATIONS: 2 months
> WALKING: New Course only
> RANGE: Yes
> • **NEW COURSE**
>   18 holes Par 72 6773/6181/5314 yds.
>   USGA: 69.4 SLOPE: 117
>   STYLE: Scottish links
> • **NORTH, SOUTH, AND EAST COURSES**
>   27 holes 2912/2942/2878 yds.
>   STYLE: Scottish links, water hazards

Grand Cypress offers forty-five extraordinary holes of Jack Nicklaus-designed golf. The original Grand Cypress courses—the North, South, and East nines—opened for play in 1984 and have logged numerous awards for challenge, imagination, and aesthetics. Nicklaus created a multitude of grassy dunes, mounds, and hollows that, if not for the lush, vibrant green colors, could be mistaken for a lunar landscape. Finding the target greens on this "Scottish moon" will test your best shotmaking and orientation skills. In 1988, the New Course was inaugurated, confirming Grand Cypress's position on the golf map of "bests." Designed to emulate St. Andrews' venerable Old Course, the view from the first tee presents a deceptive panorama. It is set in the middle of "the links," and the slight elevation does not reveal the course's 145 bunkers, which range from twelve-foot-deep pot bunkers to a monstrous pit on No. 15, aptly named "Hell." Creeks —they call them "burns" in Scotland—meander throughout, and on the first hole a stone bridge was modeled after the famous one over St. Andrews' Swilcan Burn. No. 17 is similar to the "Road Hole," where the approach shot must stay clear of the pot bunker and the wall behind the green. On the last hole, a hollow reminiscent of the "Valley of Sin" must be avoided. In all, the New Course counts seven double greens, adding up to a square footage greater than the twenty-seven putting surfaces of the other Grand Cypress courses. The resort itself has been the recipient of numerous awards, and its golf academy is one of the most advanced in the country.

GRAND CYPRESS: HOLES NO. 11 & 7

THE NEW COURSE   THE SOUTH COURSE

GRENELEFE RESORT `20`

3200 STATE RD. 546, GRENELEFE, FL 33844 (813)422-7511, EXT. 5122 *(35 mi. W of Orlando)*
ACCOMMODATIONS: GRENELEFE RESORT AND CONFERENCE CENTER (813)422-7511

GRENELEFE RESORT
ACCESS: Restrictions on season
SEASON: All year   HIGH: Dec.-Apr.
GREEN FEES: $$$
REDUCED FEES: LS, PK
RESERVATIONS: 3 months
WALKING: No   RANGE: Yes
• **WEST COURSE**
18 holes   Par 72   7325/6199/5398 yds.
USGA: 73.1   SLOPE: 126
STYLE: Rolling hills, tree-lined fairways
• **EAST COURSE**
18 holes   Par 72   6802/6156/5114 yds.
USGA: 69.6   SLOPE: 117
STYLE: Rolling hills, trees, lakes
• **SOUTH COURSE**
18 holes   Par 71   6869/6333/5174 yds.
USGA: 70.3   SLOPE: 119
STYLE: Trees, lakes, waste areas.

Grenelefe Resort is situated on the shores of Lake Marion, one of central Florida's largest lakes. The property covers a thousand acres of secluded, wooded terrain, and for the golfer seeking a wide variety of golf in one location, it neatly fills the bill. The resort offers three eighteen-hole layouts with completely different characters. The West Course, a former entry in *Golf Digest*'s listing of the top one-hundred, was routed by Robert Trent Jones and completed by Dave Wallace. Site of several PGA Tour and U.S. Open qualifying events, it is a long and demanding layout that flows through thick stands of pine and oak. On the other hand, the Ed Seay-designed East Course is shorter, but it is noted for narrow fairways and small greens. Finally, there is the South Course, a Ron Garl creation that features lakes on six holes, numerous waste bunkers, and expansive, multi-tiered putting surfaces.

THE USGA SLOPE RATING SYSTEM

The Slope System is a formula designed by the USGA to let players adjust their handicap according to a golf course's difficulty. The standard rating for a course of average difficulty in the United States was arbitrarily set at 113. After receiving a Slope rating, a course posts a conversion chart showing the local equivalent of a player's USGA handicap. A different rating is assigned to each different set of tees on a same course. A higher number indicates a course more difficult than average, and a lower number a course easier than average. Here are examples of some of the highest Slope ratings in the USA taken from the championship tees:

• PGA WEST - STADIUM COURSE (CA): 151
• BLACKWOLF RUN - RIVER COURSE (WI): 151
• BRECKENRIDGE (CO): 146
• PRINCEVILLE - PRINCE COURSE (HI): 144
• KEMPER LAKES (IL): 143
• THE CONCORD MONSTER (NY): 142
• SPYGLASS HILL (CA): 141
• BARTON CREEK - FAZIO COURSE (TX): 140
• OYSTER BAY (NC): 137
• TPC AT SAWGRASS - STADIUM COURSE (FL): 135
• HARBOUR TOWN GOLF LINKS (SC): 134
• PINEHURST NO.2 (NC): 131

WALT DISNEY WORLD RESORT 21

LAKE BUENA VISTA, FL 32830 (407)824-2270 *(16 mi. SW of Orlando)*
ACCOMMODATIONS: WALT DISNEY WORLD (407)W-DISNEY

WALT DISNEY WORLD RESORT
ACCESS: No restrictions
SEASON: All year   HIGH: Jan.-Apr.
GREEN FEES: $$$$ (includes cart)
REDUCED FEES: TW, PK
RESERVATIONS: Nonguests 1 week
WALKING: No   RANGE: Yes
- **MAGNOLIA COURSE**
  18 holes   Par 72   7190/6642/5414 yds.
  USGA: 71.6   SLOPE: 128
  STYLE: Lakes, magnolia trees
- **PALM COURSE**
  18 holes   Par 72   6957/6461/5398 yds.
  USGA: 70.7   SLOPE: 129
  STYLE: Lakes, palm trees
- **LAKE BUENA VISTA COURSE**
  18 holes   Par 72   6655/6345/5359 yds.
  USGA: 70.0   SLOPE: 124
  STYLE: Lagoons, palm trees
- **TOM FAZIO COURSE**
  18 holes   Par 72   7015/6705/5305 yds.
  STYLE: Rolling hills, lakes
- **PETE DYE COURSE**
  18 holes   Par 72   6842/6224/5143 yds.
  STYLE: Tree-lined fairways, marshland

A round of golf with Sleeping Beauty's Castle towering over the tree line is something special. That, and a lot more, awaits you at the Walt Disney World Resort. The three Joe Lee-designed championship courses— Magnolia, Palm, and Lake Buena Vista—have just been complemented by two brand new layouts, one by Tom Fazio and the other by Pete Dye. While the jury is still out regarding the newcomers, the original trio has established quite a reputation over the years. The rolling and relatively open Magnolia Course challenges golfers with one hundred sandtraps, and lakes on ten holes—headache enough from the whites and, at almost 7,200 yards, a real migraine from the blues. Named one of the top twenty-five resort courses in the country by *Golf Digest,* the shorter and tighter Palm Course has just as many sandtraps and water hazards; its 454-yard, par-4 finishing hole is rated the fourth-toughest on the PGA Tour. After these two bruisers, golfers with battered egos will enjoy the Lake Buena Vista Course, a less rigorous track routed among scenic lagoons and lush, tropical vegetation. The Fazio and Dye courses add new dimension to Walt Disney golf. The Fazio Course features dramatic changes in elevation, with fairways that travel through remote areas of tropical wilderness. The Dye Course is flatter and shorter, with wetlands and thick groves of pine trees creating natural obstacles. Including a nine-hole executive course, there are now ninety-nine holes of golf to occupy your Disney World vacation!

SANDPIPER GOLF AND COUNTRY CLUB 22

6001 SANDPIPERS DR., LAKELAND, FL 33801 (813)859-5461 *(30 mi. E of Tampa)*

SANDPIPER GOLF AND COUNTRY CLUB
18 holes   Par 70   6442/5670/5024 yds.
USGA: 66.9   SLOPE: 113
STYLE: Links, waste areas
ACCESS: Restrictions on tee times
SEASON: All year   HIGH: Winter
GREEN FEES: $ (includes cart)
REDUCED FEES: WD, LS, TW
RESERVATIONS: 2 days
WALKING: No   RANGE: Yes

With water hazards coming into play on only four holes, and relatively few trees to obstruct any shots, you might be lulled into a false sense of optimism when contemplating Sandpiper's generous fairways. But don't think architect Steve Smyers was going to invite you to simply hit away with ease. Over one hundred treacherous sandtraps demand your attention and the severely contoured greens could very well shake your confidence on this Scottish-links layout—the only design of its kind in the area.

RIDGE RESORT AT SUN 'N LAKE 23

4101 SUN 'N LAKE BLVD., SEBRING, FL 33872 (813)385-4830 *(6 mi. N. of Sebring)*
ACCOMMODATIONS: RIDGE RESORT AT SUN 'N LAKE (800)237-2165, (813)385-2561

RIDGE RESORT AT SUN 'N LAKE
18 holes   Par 72   7024/6430/5760 yds.
USGA: 72.2   SLOPE: 131
STYLE: Tree-lined fairways, lakes
ACCESS: Priority to hotel guests
SEASON: All year   HIGH: Jan.-Mar.
GREEN FEES: $
REDUCED FEES: HG, LS, PK
RESERVATIONS: Anytime
WALKING: No   RANGE: Yes

Sun 'n Lake, designed by Don Dyer in 1975, follows an unusual, figure-eight layout. This championship course is located in a wooded setting, and most fairways are wide but attractively lined with trees. Players must contend with six lakes (including a large one on No. 8) and sixty sandtraps. Nos. 6 through 12 have been considered among the most challenging in the central Florida region, and No. 15 is a memorable and very picturesque, long dogleg hole.

SEVILLE GOLF AND COUNTRY CLUB 24

18200 SEVILLE CLUBHOUSE DR., BROOKSVILLE, FL 34614 (904)596-7888 *(40 mi. NW of Tampa)*
ACCOMMODATIONS: WEEKI WACHEE (904)596-2007

Located off the beaten path northwest of Tampa, and designed by Arthur Hills, Seville's new links-style course is easy on a golfer's soul. It winds and rolls through scenic areas planted with pine and palmetto, and no two holes run side by side. Hills elected to use the hard local sand in the many waste bunkers, and he took advantage of the natural obstacles presented by the rolling terrain. Maintained as though it were part of the landscape rather than imposed upon it, most golfers will find Seville a refreshing change of pace.

SEVILLE GOLF AND COUNTRY CLUB
18 holes   Par 72   7140/6163/5236 yds.
USGA: 70.5   SLOPE: 131
STYLE: Rolling hills, links, waste areas
ACCESS: No restrictions
SEASON: All year   HIGH: Jan.-Apr.
GREEN FEES: $ (includes cart)
REDUCED FEES: LS
RESERVATIONS: 1 week
WALKING: No   RANGE: Yes

SADDLEBROOK GOLF AND TENNIS RESORT 25

100 SADDLEBROOK WAY, WESLEY CHAPEL, FL 33543 (813)973-1111 *(15 mi. N of Tampa)*
ACCOMMODATIONS: SADDLEBROOK GOLF AND TENNIS RESORT (813)973-1111

**SADDLEBROOK GOLF
AND TENNIS RESORT**
ACCESS: Priority to hotel guests
SEASON: All year   HIGH: Jan.-Apr.
GREEN FEES: $$$$$ (includes cart)
REDUCED FEES: LS
RESERVATIONS: 1 week
WALKING: No   RANGE: Yes
• **SADDLEBROOK COURSE**
  18 holes   Par 70   6603/6144/5183 yds.
  USGA: 69.7   SLOPE: 122
  STYLE: Tree-lined fairways, lakes
• **PALMER COURSE**
  18 holes   Par 71   6469/6044/5212 yds.
  USGA: 69   SLOPE: 122
  STYLE: Rolling hills, trees, lakes

Arnold Palmer, with the help of Dean Refram, designed the Saddlebrook Course in 1979; then, in 1982, he teamed with Ed Seay to do the Palmer Course. The two tracks run through beautiful countryside, with tall pines, multiple blue lakes, and plenty of colorful flowers to highlight the landscape year round. The courses have character, too. The Saddlebrook layout may not be very long from the regular tees, but it keeps threatening, hole after hole. On No. 18, the player faces a tee shot with water on the right and woods on the left; the approach is played to an undulating green fronted by still more water. The Palmer Course is somewhat shorter but more hilly, and here again, there is water almost everywhere—on seventeen holes, to be precise.

INNISBROOK RESORT AND GOLF CLUB

26

P.O. DRAWER 1088, TARPON SPRINGS, FL 34688 (813)942-2000 *(20 mi. NW of Tampa)*
ACCOMMODATIONS: INNISBROOK RESORT AND GOLF CLUB (813)942-2000, (800)456-2000

Innisbrook's Copperhead Course was once a regular entry in *Golf Digest*'s top-hundred listing and has been rated Florida's number one course by *Golfweek* every year since 1986. It is currently the site of the annual J. C. Penney Mixed Team Classic on the PGA and LPGA Tours—and what a site it is! The course climbs and dips through some of the most rolling terrain in Florida, and in more than one instance, its avenues of tall pines are reminiscent of Pinehurst's No. 2. The greens, while ample, are contoured and bunkered enough to force exacting approaches. No. 14, the course's signature hole, is a long, uphill par 5 that travels through a narrow alley of pines to a heavily bunkered green. From the fairway, that green seems just a small, elusive target in the distance. The tee is surrounded by Innisbrook's trademark flowerbed. Architect Larry Packard also did the Island and Sandpiper Courses. Like the Copperhead, the Island is a long, demanding course, but it brings more water into play. The Sandpiper Course is now three nines, bringing the total number of holes to sixty-three at this outstanding golf resort.

INNISBROOK RESORT AND GOLF CLUB
ACCESS: Hotel guests only
SEASON: All year   HIGH: Feb.-Apr.
GREEN FEES: $$$$$ (includes cart)
REDUCED FEES: LS, PK
RESERVATIONS: As available
WALKING: No   RANGE: Yes
- **COPPERHEAD COURSE**
  18 holes   Par 71   7031/6440/5702 yds.
  USGA: 70.8   SLOPE: 129
  STYLE: Rolling hills, trees
- **ISLAND COURSE**
  18 holes   Par 72   6999/6570/5943 yds.
  USGA: 71.3   SLOPE: 129
  STYLE: Tree-lined fairways, lakes
- **SANDPIPER COURSE**
  27 holes   2793/2726/2999 yds.
  STYLE: Tree-lined fairways

INNISBROOK: HOLE NO. 14

BARDMOOR NORTH GOLF CLUB

7919 BARDMOOR BLVD., LARGO, FL 34647 (813)397-0483 *(18 mi. from Tampa)*

BARDMOOR NORTH GOLF CLUB
18 holes   Par 72   6960/6484/5569 yds.
USGA: 70.4   SLOPE: 122
STYLE: Trees, lakes
ACCESS: No restrictions
SEASON: All year   HIGH: Jan.-Apr.
GREEN FEES: $$$ (includes cart)
REDUCED FEES: LS, TW
RESERVATIONS: 4 days
WALKING: No   RANGE: Yes

While hosting the PGA and LPGA J. C. Penney Mixed Team Classic for thirteen years, the beautifully conditioned Bardmoor North course challenged some of the world's best golfers. Although the tournament has moved, Bardmoor remains a stern but fair test of a golfer's shot-making ability, with particular importance placed on approach shots to its small, elevated greens. It is also one of the few courses open to the public that provides every player with such amenities as a bag drop and club-cleaning service.

BLOOMINGDALE GOLFERS CLUB 28

1802 NATURES WAY BLVD., VALRICO, FL 33594 (813)685-4105 *(16 mi. E of downtown Tampa)*
ACCOMMODATIONS: CALL GOLF CLUB FOR INFORMATION

BLOOMINGDALE GOLFERS CLUB
18 holes   Par 72   7165/6651/5506 yds.
USGA: 71.6   SLOPE: 127
STYLE: Woods, lakes, marshland
ACCESS: Weekdays only
SEASON: All year   HIGH: Dec.-Mar.
GREEN FEES: $$$ (includes cart)
REDUCED FEES: LS, PK
RESERVATIONS: Recommended
WALKING: No   RANGE: Yes

This is a course for *golfers.* In fact, Bloomingdale boasts a membership that includes five PGA touring pros, eight LPGA pros, and two hundred single-digit handicappers. At the same time, it is a naturalist's dream, with its woodlands and forty acres of preserved wetlands serving as home to bobcats, otters, red foxes, sandhill cranes, and barred owls. And as a test of a golfer's skill, the Ron Garl-designed layout is no slouch either. *Golfweek* rated it number one in the Tampa area in 1990 and ninth best in the Sunshine State.

BLOOMINGDALE GOLFERS CLUB

THE RESORT AT LONGBOAT KEY CLUB **29**

301 GULF OF MEXICO DR., LONGBOAT KEY, FL 34228 (813)387-1630 *(4 mi. W of Sarasota)*
ACCOMMODATIONS: THE RESORT AT LONGBOAT KEY CLUB (800)237-8821, (813)383-8821

If you like the look of water on a golf course, Longboat Key is the place for you. The Billy Mitchell-designed Islandside Course has "wet stuff" on every hole. To make matters even more challenging, forty-two large bunkers and an abundance of tropical plants and palm trees dot the course—difficult to avoid when the Gulf winds are feeling mischievous...Greens are large and elevated and the fairways ample; even so, this remains one tough test. The backbreaker is No. 2, a five-hundred-yard par 5 to a green guarded by water to the left, right, and front. Longboat Key is also home to the private Harbourside Course.

ISLANDSIDE GOLF COURSE
18 holes   Par 72   6890/6158/5368 yds.
USGA: 70.7   SLOPE: 133
STYLE: Ponds, trees
ACCESS: Hotel guests only
SEASON: All year   HIGH: Feb.-Apr.
GREEN FEES: $$$$$ (includes cart)
REDUCED FEES: LS, PK
RESERVATIONS: 2 days
WALKING: No   RANGE: Yes

EASTWOOD GOLF COURSE **30**

4600 BRUCE HERD LA., FT. MYERS, FL 33905 (813)275-4848 *(5 mi. E of Ft. Myers)*

Owned and operated by the city of Fort Myers, Eastwood is situated in woody, park-like surroundings, and the nature center behind the course makes this as much of an attraction for exotic birds and wildlife as it is for golfers. On this Robert von Hagge-Bruce Devlin track, which opened in 1977, woods and water hazards are the main features. To score well, players must be able to keep the ball out of trouble—something there is plenty of! The 413-yard, par-4 No. 10 is a dogleg left; its tee shot is a two-hundred-yard carry over water. For the last eight years, *Golf Digest* has ranked Eastwood as one of the top fifty public courses in the United States.

EASTWOOD GOLF COURSE
18 holes   Par 72   6772/6234/5116 yds.
USGA: 70.7   SLOPE: 125
STYLE: Woods, water
ACCESS: No restrictions
SEASON: All year   HIGH: Nov.-Apr.
GREEN FEES: $$ (includes cart)
REDUCED FEES: LS
RESERVATIONS: 1 day
WALKING: No   RANGE: Yes

GATEWAY GOLF CLUB **31**

11360 CHAMPIONSHIP DR., FT. MYERS, FL 33913 (813)561-1010 *(3 mi. from Ft. Myers)*

All the Tom Fazio trademarks are in evidence at this scenic Fort Myers-area course, which opened in 1988. A Scottish-links-type layout, with an abundance of cypress heads, protected marshlands, and waste areas, Gateway challenges the average golfer without unfairly punishing him. Players inclined to let it rip may reconsider when they see the severe mounds and "Cape Cod" bunkers that define the fairways. According to staffers at Gateway, Fazio had seen these large, mounded traps in the Cape Cod area, and decided they would be complementary to the relatively flat grounds here. Lateral water hazards on nine holes and fast, contoured greens demand a sharp eye and steady nerves. The club has hosted the 1990 and 1991 Ben Hogan Gateway Open as well as the 1991 Southwest Florida Golf and Music Festival.

GATEWAY GOLF CLUB
18 holes   Par 72   6974/6606/5323 yds.
USGA: 71.9   SLOPE: 127
STYLE: Lakes, links, marshland
ACCESS: No restrictions
SEASON: All year   HIGH: Jan.-Mar.
GREEN FEES: $$$$
REDUCED FEES: LS, TW
RESERVATIONS: 2 days
WALKING: No   RANGE: Yes

SOUTHWEST FLORIDA

PORT LA BELLE INN AND COUNTRY CLUB `32`
1 OXBOW DR., PORT LA BELLE, FL 33935 (813)675-4411 *(30 mi. E of Ft. Myers)*
ACCOMMODATIONS: PORT LA BELLE INN AND COUNTRY CLUB (800)282-3375

Hundred-year-old mossy oaks border the course at Port La Belle, and superb views of the sparkling Caloosahatchee River add to the pleasure of golf here. Designed in 1974, this layout features a fairly open front, but the back nine begins to tighten up early as the woods seem to close in on you—and your scorecard! Water affects play on sixteen holes, two of which actually border the Caloosahatchee, and when the wind starts blowing in from the river, things get "interesting" fast. A hole that sticks to mind is No. 13, where a lone pine tree stands in the fairway 110 yards in front of the green, defiantly forcing players to hood the club-face and work the ball around his majesty.

PORT LA BELLE INN AND COUNTRY CLUB
18 holes   Par 72   6900/6400/5005 yds.
USGA: 70.3   SLOPE: 125
STYLE: Hills, woods, lakes
ACCESS: No restrictions
SEASON: All year   HIGH: Sept.-Mar.
GREEN FEES: $$ (includes cart)
REDUCED FEES: LS, PK
RESERVATIONS: 1 year
WALKING: No   RANGE: Yes

PELICAN'S NEST GOLF CLUB `33`
4450 BAY CREEK DR., BONITA SPRINGS, FL 33923 (813)947-4600, (800)952-6378 *(15 mi. N of Naples)*
ACCOMMODATIONS: RITZ-CARLTON NAPLES (813)598-3300; REGISTRY RESORT (813)597-3232

Located twenty miles south of Fort Myers in a natural setting of lush greenery and cobalt-blue lakes, "The Nest" has three Tom Fazio-designed nines—the Hurricane, the Gator, and the Seminole. These courses, which opened in 1985, are impeccably maintained and present the golfer with devilishly contoured fairways and greens, bunkers of every imaginable size and shape, and lateral water hazards on twenty of the twenty-seven holes. From the back tees it is a severe test, but four to five tee positions ensure that these layouts will be pleasurable for golfers of every level. The ninth on Hurricane is fairly typical: it is a 517-yard, par-5 dogleg right, with water on both sides of the peninsula fairway, two huge bunkers guarding the green, and no margin for error. Pelicans glide effortlessly over the scene, while lurking alligators remain indifferent to the golfers' prowess.

PELICAN'S NEST GOLF CLUB
27 holes   2962/3067/2916 yds.
STYLE: Lakes, marshland, waste areas
ACCESS: Priority to hotel guests
SEASON: All year   HIGH: Jan.-Apr.
GREEN FEES: $$$$ (includes cart)
REDUCED FEES: LS, TW, PK
RESERVATIONS: Nonguests 2 days
WALKING: No   RANGE: Yes

MARCO SHORES COUNTRY CLUB `34`
1450 MAINSAIL DR., NAPLES, FL 33961 (813)394-2581 *(20 mins. SE of Naples)*

Located near Marco Island, one of the ten thousand islands off Florida's southwest coast, the Marco Shores course is surrounded by the thick, tropical foliage and abundant, exotic wildlife characteristic of the Everglades. It is not the seven water hazards that create the most problems on Bruce Devlin's and Robert von Hagge's 1975 design, but the 120 bunkers, which may eventually sap your patience. Gene Sarazen, a longtime honorary chairman at the club, made many architectural improvements.

MARCO SHORES COUNTRY CLUB
18 holes   Par 72   6879/6368/5634 yds.
USGA: 70.7   SLOPE: 120
STYLE: Tree-lined fairways, bunkers
ACCESS: No restrictions
SEASON: All year   HIGH: Jan.-Apr.
GREEN FEES: $$$ (includes cart)
REDUCED FEES: LS
RESERVATIONS: 2 days
WALKING: No   RANGE: Yes

LELY FLAMINGO ISLAND CLUB

8002 LELY RESORT BLVD., NAPLES, FL 33962 (813)793-2223 *(40 mi. S of Ft. Myers)*

35

Open since 1990, the Lely Flamingo Island course is Robert Trent Jones's first design in southwest Florida. On what had been flat land, lush rolling fairways now travel through

> **LELY FLAMINGO ISLAND CLUB**
> 18 holes   Par 72   7171/6527/5377 yds.
> USGA: 70.9   SLOPE: 129
> STYLE: Hills, trees, water
> ACCESS: No restrictions
> SEASON: All year   HIGH: Jan.-Apr.
> GREEN FEES: $$$$ (includes cart)
> REDUCED FEES: LS, TW
> RESERVATIONS: 3 days
> WALKING: At times   RANGE: Yes

a multitude of lagoons, bunkers, and waste areas. Generally, the fairways are wide, but some have hourglass shapes that make for tight landing areas. Attractive tropical plants dot the rough, and elegant sable palms swing lazily in the wind. Water comes out of the picture and into actual play on ten holes. No. 14 is both extremely picturesque and challenging; the entire par-3 hole is built on an L-shaped island that players enter and depart via two different bridges. Getting to the green is only part of the story here. The putting surface has three levels, and hitting to the wrong one could transform a birdie opportunity into a nasty bogey hole. Overall, the layout is well-balanced, and no hole is too easy or too difficult. The attractive scenery only adds to the enjoyment.

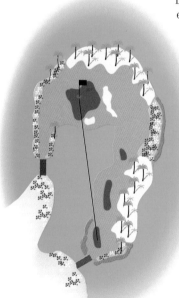

LELY FLAMINGO: HOLE NO. 14

From the 210-yards championship tees, the 14th "Island Hole" requires a hefty carry over water. It is a much more manageable test from the 159-yards regular or the 108-yards ladies markers.

LELY FLAMINGO ISLAND CLUB: HOLE NO. 14

PGA NATIONAL GOLF CLUB 36

1000 AVE. OF THE CHAMPIONS, PALM BEACH GARDENS, FL 33418 (407)627-1800
(15 mi. N of Palm Beach International Airport)
ACCOMMODATIONS: PGA NATIONAL RESORT (407)627-2000

Five championship courses make up the extraordinary PGA National Golf Club, a golfer's paradise offering an impressive range of golf experiences. The Champion Course, redesigned in 1990 by Jack Nicklaus, was made more playable by the "Golfer of the Century" and his design team. The course has considerable mounding, and water comes into play on a majority of holes. The new design also makes tournament viewing easier, and the Champion is home of the Senior PGA Championship. The Haig Course, by Tom and George Fazio, allows golfers the option of playing around all fifteen water hazards—a real advantage for high handicappers! Another design by the Fazio team is the Squire Course, open since 1981. Considered a "thinking man's course," this links-style layout is the shortest and narrowest. If you are ready to charge, the General Course is for you. The "army" will no doubt recognize that the course was designed by Mr. Arnold Palmer himself. The Scottish-style track has undulating fairways, many grass bunkers, and a big double green. A few miles away, the Estate Course delivers a masterful blend of eighty-six sand bunkers and seventeen water hazards set among a pleasant landscape of lakes, tropical vegetation, and Florida pines.

PGA NATIONAL GOLF CLUB
ACCESS: Hotel guests only
SEASON: All year HIGH: Dec.-Mar.
GREEN FEES: $$$$
REDUCED FEES: LS, PK, TW
RESERVATIONS: 1 year
WALKING: No RANGE: Yes
- **CHAMPION COURSE**
  18 holes Par 72 7022/6028/5377 yds.
  USGA: 69.4 SLOPE: 128
  STYLE: Scottish links, mounds, water
- **HAIG COURSE**
  18 holes Par 72 6806/6352/5645 yds.
  USGA: 70.6 SLOPE: 128
  STYLE: Tree-lined fairways, lakes
- **SQUIRE COURSE**
  18 holes Par 72 6478/6025/5114 yds.
  USGA: 69.1 SLOPE: 126
  STYLE: Links
- **GENERAL COURSE**
  18 holes Par 72 6768/6270/5324 yds.
  USGA: 70.8 SLOPE: 128
  STYLE: Links
- **ESTATE COURSE**
  18 holes Par 72 6784/6328/4955 yds.
  USGA: 70.4 SLOPE: 126
  STYLE: Trees, lakes

PALM BEACH POLO AND COUNTRY CLUB 37

13198 FOREST HILL BLVD., W. PALM BEACH, FL 33414 (407)798-7401 *(10 mi. W of W. Palm Beach)*
ACCOMMODATIONS: PALM BEACH POLO AND COUNTRY CLUB (407)798-7020

PALM BEACH POLO AND COUNTRY CLUB
ACCESS: Hotel guests only
SEASON: All year HIGH: Nov.-Apr.
GREEN FEES: $$$$ (includes cart)
REDUCED FEES: PK
RESERVATIONS: 2 days
WALKING: No RANGE: Yes
- **CYPRESS COURSE**
  18 holes Par 72 7116/6678/5172 yds.
  USGA: 72.1 SLOPE: 136
  STYLE: Lakes
- **DUNES COURSE**
  18 holes Par 72 7050/6620/5516 yds.
  USGA: 71.3 SLOPE: 126
  STYLE: Scottish links

Palm Beach Polo and Country Club's Cypress Course, which has hosted the PGA Tour's Chrysler Team Championship, was designed by the father/son team of Pete and P. B. Dye—and it shows. It has wide, undulating fairways and surprising changes in elevation. The greens range from the tiny to the enormous. No. 15, for example, covers 20,000 square feet! Water shows up on fourteen holes and, as one would expect from the Dyes, there are numerous pot bunkers and swales around the greens. The final four holes are a rigorous test—most notably the par-5 seventeenth, which plays into the prevailing wind to a small putting surface set against a bunkered hillside. The eighteen-hole Dunes Course, designed by Jerry Pate and Ron Garl, has a links feel, and there is also the nine-hole Olde Course, designed by George and Tom Fazio.

EMERALD DUNES GOLF COURSE

38

2100 EMERALD DUNES DR., W. PALM BEACH, FL 33411 (407)687-1700 *(1/2 mi. W of West Palm Beach)*
ACCOMMODATIONS: CALL GOLF COURSE FOR INFORMATION

The "Super Dune" is the focal point of this exciting Tom Fazio 1990 creation. Rising fifty-five feet above the fairway, the dune is Palm Beach's highest elevation. The rest of the terrain is fairly flat, but Fazio was able to blend mounds, grassy hollows, palm trees, rock outcroppings, freeform white sand bunkers, and waterfalls to create a unique design and visual treat. The entire course seems built over a vast lagoon system. Lakes surround the fairways, but water is here as much for aesthetics as it is for challenge. In fact, the course is quite playable, and many of the threatening obstacles enhance the course's beauty. Emerald Dunes is a spectacularly innovative creation that is sure to receive continuing attention in the years to come.

> **EMERALD DUNES GOLF COURSE**
> 18 holes   Par 72   7006/6120/4676 yds.
> USGA: 69.7   SLOPE: 125
> STYLE: Dunes, waste areas, lakes
> ACCESS: Restrictions on tee times
> SEASON: All year   HIGH: Jan.-May
> GREEN FEES: $$$$
> REDUCED FEES: PK
> RESERVATIONS: Nonguests 1 week
> WALKING: At times   RANGE: Yes

INVERRARY COUNTRY CLUB

39

3840 INVERRARY BLVD., LAUDERHILL, FL 33319 (305)733-7550 *(15 mi. from Ft. Lauderdale)*
ACCOMMODATIONS: INVERRARY COUNTRY CLUB (800)327-8661

> **INVERRARY COUNTRY CLUB**
> ACCESS: Hotel guests only
> SEASON: All year   HIGH: Nov.-Apr.
> GREEN FEES: $$$
> REDUCED FEES: WD, LS, TW, PK
> RESERVATIONS: 1 week
> WALKING: No   RANGE: Yes
> • **WEST COURSE**
>   18 holes   Par 71   6621/6331/5414 yds.
>   USGA: 71.5   SLOPE: 128
>   STYLE: Traditional
> • **EAST COURSE**
>   18 holes   Par 72   7124/6220/5668 yds.
>   USGA: 70.6   SLOPE: 126
>   STYLE: Traditional

Robert Trent Jones designed these courses, which have hosted events on both the PGA and LPGA Tours. The East Course is the championship track, producing winners such as Jack Nicklaus, Lee Trevino, Tom Weiskopf, and Johnny Miller. The traditional architecture features tree-lined fairways of comfortable width, and the rough is not especially threatening. The bunkering, however, is fairly intricate, and the greens are large enough to provide numerous pin placements. Water comes into play on twelve holes on the West Course and thirteen on the East. Both courses are very fair, without tricks or gimmicks. The best hole on the East is No. 16, a par 3 that plays over water and demands a sharp iron shot to the green. The West's best hole is the 440-yard, par-4 fifteenth—a tight driving hole to an extremely long, narrow green.

BOCA RATON RESORT AND CLUB  `40`

501 E. CAMINO REAL, BOCA RATON, FL 33431 (407)395-3000 *(22 mi. S of Palm Beach)*
ACCOMMODATIONS: BOCA RATON RESORT AND CLUB (407)395-3000

BOCA RATON RESORT AND CLUB
ACCESS: Hotel guests only
SEASON: All year   HIGH: Jan.-Apr.
GREEN FEES: $$$
REDUCED FEES: LS, PK
RESERVATIONS: At time of hotel booking
WALKING: No   RANGE: Yes
- **RESORT COURSE**
  18 holes   Par 71   6732/6154/5518 yds.
  USGA: 71.7   SLOPE: 123
  STYLE: Tropical, lakes
- **COUNTRY CLUB COURSE**
  18 holes   Par 72   6564/6175/5565 yds.
  USGA: 69.1   SLOPE: 123
  STYLE: Lakes

BOCA RATON RESORT

William Flynn designed Boca Raton's Resort Course in 1922, and following a $2.2 million renovation supervised by Joe Lee in 1988, the subtleties Flynn is noted for came back to life. The greens are magnificently contoured, four lakes affect play on five holes, and the bunkering is precise and artful. A tropical setting is created by a variety of palms, old banyan trees, and colorful plants and flowers. Most outstanding is the 598-yard, par-5 signature ninth, a dogleg left with a water hazard to the left, and a large, elevated bulkheaded green. A few miles from the resort, the Country Club Course is also available to resort guests. Its Florida-style layout is laced with connecting lakes, and water comes into play on fourteen holes. The course, considered very difficult, conveys a true private club atmosphere.

BONAVENTURE COUNTRY CLUB `41`

200 BONAVENTURE BLVD., FT. LAUDERDALE, FL 33326 (305)389-2100 *(25 mi. from Miami)*
ACCOMMODATIONS: BONAVENTURE RESORT AND SPA (305)389-3300

BONAVENTURE COUNTRY CLUB
ACCESS: No restrictions
SEASON: All year   HIGH: All year
GREEN FEES: $$$ (includes cart)
REDUCED FEES: HG, LS, PK
RESERVATIONS: Nonguests 3 days
WALKING: No   RANGE: Yes
- **EAST COURSE**
  18 holes   Par 72   7011/6557/5345 yds.
  USGA: 71   SLOPE: 126
  STYLE: Lakes, tree-lined fairways
- **WEST COURSE**
  18 holes   Par 70   6200/4900 yds.
  USGA: 68   SLOPE: 114
  STYLE: Lakes, tree-lined fairways

The Bonaventure Country Club offers golfers a choice of two distinct layouts. Most memorable is the Joe Lee-designed East Course, a regular inclusion in Florida's top ten. The well-trapped course winds through a lagoon system, and water is present on sixteen holes. The course is also generously endowed with mature deciduous trees and palms. Its famous, 160-yard No. 3 is an almost entire carry over water to a green fronted by a picturesque, man-made waterfall. The Charles Mahannah-designed West Course includes six par 3s and four par 5s. Its modest 6,200-yard length makes for an enjoyable change of pace.

TURNBERRY ISLE RESORT AND CLUB

19999 W. COUNTRY CLUB DR., AVENTURA, FL 33180 (305)932-6200, EXT. 3404 *(17 mi. from Miami)*
ACCOMMODATIONS: TURNBERRY ISLE RESORT AND CLUB (305)932-6200

Robert Trent Jones is the creator of both the South Course and the North Course at Turnberry Isle, and they are beauties. The South has hosted events on the LPGA and Senior PGA Tours, and the appeal of its lush landscaping is matched only by the challenge of its lakes, thick alleys of trees, and large, omnipresent bunkers. The dramatic, 545-yard, par-5 eighteenth sums it all up. A long lake borders the right side of the fairway. After a hefty drive, your second shot must be long and accurate to set up a mid-iron approach to a wide—and remote-looking—bunkered island green. The par-70 North Course, while shorter, is also a good test of nerves and skill at handling water and sand. When the wind begins to blow from the ocean at the edge of these two courses, they can show some real character.

TURNBERRY ISLE RESORT AND CLUB
ACCESS: Hotel guests only
SEASON: All year   HIGH: Nov.-Apr.
GREEN FEES: $$$
REDUCED FEES: PK, LS
RESERVATIONS: 2 days
WALKING: No   RANGE: Yes
- **SOUTH COURSE**
  18 holes   Par 72   7003/6458/5581 yds.
  USGA: 69.9   SLOPE: 118
  STYLE: Tree-lined fairways, lakes
- **NORTH COURSE**
  18 holes   Par 70   6323/5970/4991 yds.
  USGA: 67.8   SLOPE: 123
  STYLE: Tree-lined fairways, lakes

TURNBERRY ISLE RESORT AND CLUB

DORAL RESORT AND COUNTRY CLUB **43**

4400 NW 87 AVE., MIAMI, FL 33178 (305)592-2000 *(15 mins. from downtown Miami)*
ACCOMMODATIONS: DORAL RESORT AND COUNTRY CLUB (305)592-2000

DORAL RESORT AND COUNTRY CLUB
ACCESS: No restrictions
SEASON: All year   HIGH: Dec.-Apr.
GREEN FEES: $$$$$ (includes cart)
REDUCED FEES: HG, LS, PK
RESERVATIONS: Nonguests 1 day
WALKING: No   RANGE: Yes
• **BLUE COURSE**
  18 holes   Par 72   6939/6597/5786 yds.
  USGA: 70.4
  STYLE: Trees, lakes
• **SILVER COURSE**
  18 holes   Par 72   6801/6383/5064 yds.
  USGA: 70.17   SLOPE: 122
  STYLE: Lakes, links
• **GOLD COURSE**
  18 holes   Par 70   6279/5876/5422 yds.
  USGA: 68.7
  STYLE: Lakes
• **RED COURSE**
  18 holes   Par 71   6120/5681/5204 yds.
  USGA: 66.7
  STYLE: Lakes
• **WHITE COURSE**
  18 holes   Par 72   6208/5913/5286 yds.
  USGA: 67.6
  STYLE: Tree-lined fairways, lakes

The world-famous Doral Resort offers five eighteen-hole golf courses and a nine-hole short course. On top of the list is the Blue Course. Known as the "Blue Monster," it has hosted the PGA Tour's Miami tournament since 1962, producing such champions as Jack Nicklaus, Tom Weiskopf, Ben Crenshaw, Raymond Floyd, and Lee Trevino. The Monster is long and loaded with sand and water hazards. The signature hole is the 437-yard, par-4 eighteenth, a dogleg left that has disaster written all over it. The water is a threat off the tee and then again on the approach shot. There's room to bail out on the right, but not with a tournament—or match—on the line. It's a classic finish to one of America's finest courses, and it was designed by Dick Wilson. This doesn't mean that the Doral's other eighty-one holes, all designed by Robert von Hagge, are anything to sneeze at. The extremely difficult Silver and Gold Courses both have water on every hole! The former has severe, links-style mounding, and the latter's finishing hole has an island green completely surrounded by water. The Red Course, perhaps not as difficult, still brings a lot of challenge, with water on fifteen holes. But if you're easily intimidated, stick to the White Course. It has a pleasant, tree-lined layout that is playable for all skill levels.

GOLD COURSE: HOLE NO. 18

BLUE COURSE: HOLE NO. 3

BLUE COURSE: HOLE NO. 18

PGA TOUR GOLF CLUB OF MIAMI `44`

6801 MIAMI GARDENS DR., MIAMI, FL 33015 (305)826-4700 *(10 mi. from downtown Miami)*

PGA TOUR GOLF CLUB OF MIAMI
ACCESS: No restrictions
SEASON: All year   HIGH: Nov.-Mar.
GREEN FEES: $$
REDUCED FEES: WD, LS
RESERVATIONS: 3 days
WALKING: At times   RANGE: Yes
• **WEST COURSE**
  18 holes   Par 72   7017/6139/5298 yds.
  STYLE: Water, trees
• **EAST COURSE**
  18 holes   Par 70   6353/6110/5025 yds.
  STYLE: Water
• **SOUTH COURSE**
  18 holes   Par 62   5410/4370 yds.
  STYLE: Water

Arnold Palmer was the original club pro at the Golf Club of Miami. Jack Nicklaus played his first tour event on the West Course, and Lee Trevino won his first on the same layout. Designed by Robert Trent Jones, and redesigned by Bobby Weed in 1990, the West is gorgeously landscaped with trees and flowers, if relatively flat. All eighteen holes have some kind of water hazards, however, and the greens are large, contoured and kept tournament-fast. If that were not enough, sixty-eight sandtraps stand ready to bury any straying shots. The sixth hole, a monstrous par 4 that can stretch as much as 461 yards, is guarded by water on the right, while the left side is out-of-bounds. The East Course feels like a breeze, compared to the West, but even a slight lack of attention can get you into a lot of trouble. The shorter South Course completes this trio of exceptionally well-maintained county courses. The PGA Tour manages this facility, as the upkeep and amenities demonstrate. A state-of-the-art lighted driving range is available, use of which is recommended before tackling the West Course.

THE LINKS AT KEY BISCAYNE `45`

6700 CRANDON BLVD., KEY BISCAYNE, FL 33149 (305)361-9129 *(10 mi. from Miami)*

THE LINKS AT KEY BISCAYNE
18 holes   Par 72   7070/6389/5690 yds.
USGA: 71   SLOPE: 129
STYLE: Tree-lined fairways, lakes.
ACCESS: No restrictions
SEASON: All year   HIGH: Nov.-Mar.
GREEN FEES: $$
REDUCED FEES: LS, TW
RESERVATIONS: 1 day
WALKING: After 1:00 p.m.   RANGE: Yes

The site of the Royal Caribbean Classic on the Senior PGA Tour, this Bruce Devlin-Robert von Hagge course offers sensational views of both Biscayne Bay and the city of Miami. The track's exotic look, a result of the surrounding mangrove flats and the many coconut palms, is popular with both residents and visitors. Wide fairways welcome enthusiastic tee shots, but four large, scenic lakes, combined with difficult bunkering and wide, elevated greens, explain Key Biscayne's high slope rating.

OTHER EXCELLENT COURSES IN FLORIDA

CENTRAL FLORIDA

■ BELLEVIEW MIDO COUNTRY CLUB, Belleair (813)581-5498

▲ HUNTER'S GREEN COUNTRY CLUB, Tampa (813)973-1700

● PLANTATION INN AND GOLF RESORT, Crystal River (904)795-7211

▲ RAINBOW SPRINGS GOLF AND COUNTRY CLUB, Dunnellon (904)459-3566

● SANDRIDGE GOLF CLUB, Vero Beach (407)770-5000

THE GULF COAST

● THE MEADOWS COUNTRY CLUB, Sarasota (813)378-5153

● NAPLES BEACH HOTEL AND GOLF CLUB, Naples (813)261-2222

● TARA GOLF AND COUNTRY CLUB, Bradenton (813)758-7961

▲ TATUM RIDGE GOLF LINKS, Sarasota (813)484-6621

NORTHEAST FLORIDA

■ HAMMOCK DUNES LINKS, Palm Coast (904)446-6222

THE PANHANDLE

■ KILLEARN COUNTRY CLUB AND INN, Tallahassee (904)893-2144

● MARRIOTT'S BAY POINT RESORT, Panama City Beach (904)234-3307

▲ SANDESTIN, Destin (904)837-2121

SOUTHEAST FLORIDA

● CITY OF BOCA RATON MUNICIPAL GOLF COURSE, Boca Raton (407)483-6100

● COLONY WEST COUNTRY CLUB, Tamarac (305)726-8430

● KEY WEST RESORT GOLF COURSE, Key West (305)294-5232

● WEST PALM BEACH COUNTRY CLUB, West Palm Beach (407)582-2019

▲ RESTRICTIONS MAY APPLY   ■ HOTEL/RESORT GUESTS ONLY   ● OPEN WITHOUT RESTRICTIONS

The Sunshine State offers many more fine courses than our limited space allows us to feature. To assist you in planning a Florida golf vacation, here are some helpful numbers you can call:

◆ FLORIDA DIVISION OF TOURISM, VISITOR INQUIRY SECTION (904)487-1462

◆ PENSACOLA VISITORS AND CONVENTION BUREAU (800)343-4321

◆ JACKSONVILLE CONVENTION AND VISITORS BUREAU (904)353-9736

◆ ORLANDO/ORANGE COUNTY CONVENTION AND VISITORS BUREAU (407)363-5800

◆ TAMPA/HILLSBOROUGH CONVENTION AND VISITORS ASSOCIATION (800)826-8358

◆ SARASOTA COUNTY CHAMBER OF COMMERCE (813)955-8187

◆ GREATER FORT LAUDERDALE CONVENTION AND VISITORS BUREAU (800)356-1662

◆ PALM BEACH COUNTY CONVENTION AND VISITORS BUREAU (407)471-3995

CHAPTER TEN

BERMUDA & THE CARIBBEAN

There are many wonderful things to do while vacationing on a Caribbean island: sunning, shopping, scuba diving, and drinking mai tai's…Your clubs are safely stored in a closet back home, and the last thing on your mind is golf. You are just here to enjoy "the good life." After a few days of such indulgent behavior, however, chances are that you will ask the same question many others have asked before, "Is there a decent golf course on this island?" The good news is: yes! There *is* green after blue, and there *is* sand after the beach. In fact, there is even enough excellent golf out there to convince anyone to forego another afternoon of shell-picking!

Topography varies significantly from island to island. The tumultuous red-clay terrain of the U.S. Virgin Islands offers a dramatic setting for exciting courses such as Mahogany Run on St. Thomas, while the flat and sandy soil of the Bahamian courses is reminiscent of southern Florida. On Puerto Rico, preserving the rain forest still leaves a lot of land for golf, and several world-class golf resorts are being developed there to supplement well-known favorites such as Dorado Beach. Jamaica and the Dominican Republic offer still more championship courses in exotic tropical settings.

Yet, for a truly special golf experience, Bermuda is the place. At the same latitude as North Carolina, the island's climate is tempered by the warm waters of the Gulf Stream. The verdant rolling hills, blossoming with colorful flowers, blend effortlessly into shining aquamarine bays. Nurtured by three hundred years of impeccable British tradition, golf has found, on Bermuda, a natural place to flourish.